PROGRESS IN CLINICAL AND BIOLOGICAL RESEARCH

RECENT TITLES

Vol 48:   **Cloning of Human Tumor Stem Cells,** Sydney E. Salmon, *Editor*

Vol 49:   **Myelin: Chemistry and Biology,** George A. Hashim, *Editor*

Vol 50:   **Rights and Responsibilities in Modern Medicine: The Second Volume in a Series on Ethics, Humanism, and Medicine,** Marc D. Basson, *Editor*

Vol 51:   **The Function of Red Blood Cells: Erythrocyte Pathobiology,** Donald F. H. Wallach, *Editor*

Vol 52:   **Conduction Velocity Distributions: A Population Approach to Electrophysiology of Nerve,** Leslie J. Dorfman, Kenneth L. Cummins, and Larry J. Leifer, *Editors*

Vol 53:   **Cancer Among Black Populations,** Curtis Mettlin and Gerald P. Murphy, *Editors*

Vol 54:   **Connective Tissue Research: Chemistry, Biology, and Physiology,** Zdenek Deyl and Milan Adam, *Editors*

Vol 55:   **The Red Cell: Fifth Ann Arbor Conference,** George J. Brewer, *Editor*

Vol 56:   **Erythrocyte Membranes 2: Recent Clinical and Experimental Advances,** Walter C. Kruckeberg, John W. Eaton, and George J. Brewer, *Editors*

Vol 57:   **Progress in Cancer Control,** Curtis Mettlin and Gerald P. Murphy, *Editors*

Vol 58:   **The Lymphocyte,** Kenneth W. Sell and William V. Miller, *Editors*

Vol 59:   **Eleventh International Congress of Anatomy,** Enrique Acosta Vidrio, *Editor-in-Chief.* Published in 3 volumes:
Part A: **Glial and Neuronal Cell Biology,** Sergey Fedoroff, *Editor*
Part B: **Advances in the Morphology of Cells and Tissues,** Miguel A. Galina, *Editor*
Part C: **Biological Rhythms in Structure and Function,** Heinz von Mayersbach, Lawrence E. Scheving, and John E. Pauly, *Editors*

Vol 60:   **Advances in Hemoglobin Analysis,** Samir M. Hanash and George J. Brewer, *Editors*

Vol 61:   **Nutrition and Child Health: Perspectives for the 1980s,** Reginald C. Tsang and Buford Lee Nichols, Jr., *Editors*

Vol 62:   **Pathophysiological Effects of Endotoxins at the Cellular Level,** Jeannine A. Majde and Robert J. Person, *Editors*

Vol 63:   **Membrane Transport and Neuroreceptors,** Dale Oxender, Arthur Blume, Ivan Diamond, and C. Fred Fox, *Editors*

Vol 64:   **Bacteriophage Assembly,** Michael S. DuBow, *Editor*

Vol 65:   **Apheresis: Development, Applications, and Collection Procedures,** C. Harold Mielke, Jr., *Editor*

Vol 66:   **Control of Cellular Division and Development,** Dennis Cunningham, Eugene Goldwasser, James Watson, and C. Fred Fox, *Editors.* Published in 2 Volumes.

Vol 67:   **Nutrition in the 1980s: Constraints on Our Knowledge,** Nancy Selvey and Philip L. White, *Editors*

Vol 68:   **The Role of Peptides and Amino Acids as Neurotransmitters,** J. Barry Lombardini and Alexander D. Kenny, *Editors*

Vol 69: **Twin Research 3, Proceedings of the Third International Congress on Twin Studies,** Luigi Gedda, Paolo Parisi, and Walter F. Nance, *Editors*. Published in 3 volumes:
Part A: **Twin Biology and Multiple Pregnancy**
Part B: **Intelligence, Personality, and Development**
Part C: **Epidemiological and Clinical Studies**

Vol 70: **Reproductive Immunology,** Norbert Gleicher, *Editor*

Vol 71: **Psychopharmacology of Clonidine,** Harbans Lal and Stuart Fielding, *Editors*

Vol 72: **Hemophilia and Hemostasis,** Doris Ménaché, D. MacN. Surgenor, and Harlan D. Anderson, *Editors*

Vol 73: **Membrane Biophysics: Structure and Function in Epithelia,** Mumtaz A. Dinno and Arthur B. Callahan, *Editors*

Vol 74: **Physiopathology of Endocrine Diseases and Mechanisms of Hormone Action,** Roberto J. Soto, Alejandro De Nicola, and Jorge Blaquier, *Editors*

Vol 75: **The Prostatic Cell: Structure and Function,** Gerald P. Murphy, Avery A. Sandberg, and James P. Karr, *Editors*. Published in 2 volumes:
Part A: **Morphologic, Secretory, and Biochemical Aspects**
Part B: **Prolactin, Carcinogenesis, and Clinical Aspects**

Vol 76: **Troubling Problems in Medical Ethics: The Third Volume in a Series on Ethics, Humanism, and Medicine,** Marc D. Basson, Rachel E. Lipson, and Doreen L. Ganos, *Editors*

Vol 77: **Nutrition in Health and Disease and International Development: Symposia From the XII International Congress of Nutrition,** Alfred E. Harper and George K. Davis, *Editors*

Vol 78: **Female Incontinence,** Norman R. Zinner and Arthur M. Sterling, *Editors*

Vol 79: **Proteins in the Nervous System: Structure and Function,** Bernard Haber, Joe Dan Coulter, and Jose Regino Perez-Polo, *Editors*

Vol 80: **Mechanism and Control of Ciliary Movement,** Charles J. Brokaw and Pedro Verdugo, *Editors*

Vol 81: **Physiology and Biology of Horseshoe Crabs: Studies on Normal and Environmentally Stressed Animals,** Joseph Bonaventura, Celia Bonaventura, and Shirley Tesh, *Editors*

See pages following the index for previous titles in this series.

PHYSIOLOGY AND BIOLOGY OF HORSESHOE CRABS

STUDIES ON NORMAL AND ENVIRONMENTALLY STRESSED ANIMALS

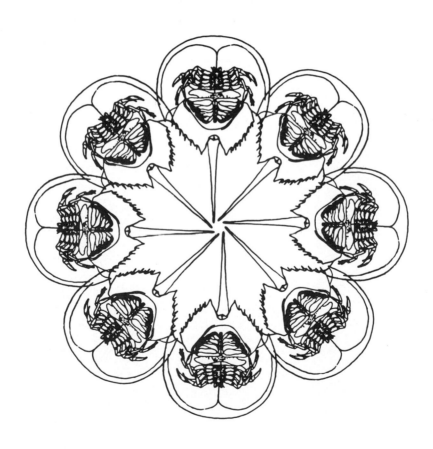

PHYSIOLOGY AND BIOLOGY OF HORSESHOE CRABS

STUDIES ON NORMAL AND ENVIRONMENTALLY STRESSED ANIMALS

Editors

JOSEPH BONAVENTURA
CELIA BONAVENTURA
SHIRLEY TESH

Marine Biomedical Center
Duke University Marine Laboratory
Beaufort, North Carolina

ALAN R. LISS, INC. • **NEW YORK**

Address all Inquiries to the Publisher
Alan R. Liss, Inc., 150 Fifth Avenue, New York, NY 10011

Copyright © 1982 Alan R. Liss, Inc.

Printed in the United States of America.

Library of Congress Cataloging in Publication Data
Main entry under title:

Physiology and biology of horseshoe crabs.

(Progress in clinical and biological research;
v. 81)
  Bibliography: p.
  Includes index.
  1. Xiphosura. I. Bonaventura, Joseph.
II. Bonaventura, Celia. III. Tesh, Shirley.
QL447.7.P48   595.3'92   82-188

ISBN 0-8451-0081-5   AACR2

39,816

This volume is dedicated to the memory of Doctor Frederik B. Bang.

The Duke University Marine Laboratory at Pivers Island, Beaufort, North Carolina.

Contents

Contributors xi

Preface
Joseph Bonaventura, Celia Bonaventura, and Shirley Tesh xv

Acknowledgments xvii

A Pictorial Review of the Natural History and Ecology of
the Horseshoe Crab Limulus polyphemus, With
Reference to Other Limulidae
Carl N. Shuster Jr. 1

Horseshoe Crab Developmental Studies I. Normal
Embryonic Development of Limulus polyphemus
Compared With Tachypleus tridentatus
Koichi Sekiguchi, Yoshio Yamamichi, and John D. Costlow 53

Horseshoe Crab Developmental Studies II. Physiological
Adaptation of Horseshoe Crab Embryos to the
Environment During Embryonic Development
Hiroaki Sugita and Koichi Sekiguchi 75

A Review of the Molting Physiology of the Trilobite Larva
of Limulus
Thomas C. Jegla 83

Temperature and Salinity Effects on Developmental and
Early Posthatch Stages of Limulus
Thomas C. Jegla and John D. Costlow 103

A Note on the Influence of Life-History Stage on
Metabolic Adaptation: The Responses of Limulus Eggs
and Larvae to Hypoxia
Stephen R. Palumbi and Bruce A. Johnson 115

Anaerobiosis in Limulus
Jeremy H. A. Fields 125

Circulatory Physiology of Limulus
James R. Redmond, Darwin D. Jorgensen, and
George B. Bourne 133

The Role of the Coxal Gland in Ionic, Osmotic, and pH
Regulation in the Horseshoe Crab Limulus polyphemus
David W. Towle, Charlotte P. Mangum, Bruce A. Johnson,
and Nicholas A. Mauro 147

The Relationship Between the Capacity for Oxygen Transport, Size, Shape, and Aggregation State of an Extracellular Oxygen Carrier
G. K. Snyder and Charlotte P. Mangum 173

The Nature of the Binuclear Copper Site in Limulus and Other Hemocyanins
E. I. Solomon, N. C. Eickman, R. S. Himmelwright,
Y. T. Hwang, S. E. Plon, and D. E. Wilcox 189

Chloride and pH Dependence of Cooperative Interactions in Limulus polyphemus Hemocyanin
Marius Brouwer, Celia Bonaventura, and Joseph Bonaventura 231

The Subunit Structure of Limulus Hemocyanin
Michael Brenowitz and Margaret Moore 257

Electron Microscopy of Limulus Hemocyanin
Martha M. C. Bijlholt, Wilma G. Schutter, Trijntje Wichertjes,
and Ernst F. J. van Bruggen 269

Limulus Lectins: Analogues of Vertebrate Immunoglobulins
Thomas G. Pistole 283

Pathologic Principles Revealed by Study of Natural Diseases of Invertebrates
Frederik B. Bang and Betsy G. Bang 289

Man's Influence as an Environmental Threat to Limulus
Anne Rudloe 297

Today Limulus, Tomorrow the World: The Roles and Responsibilities of Practicing Biologists in Contemporary American Society
Sidney R. Galler and Bernard J. Zahuranec 301

Index 307

Contributors

Betsy G. Bang [289]
Department of Pathobiology, The Johns Hopkins University, School of Hygiene and Public Health, Baltimore, Maryland 21205

Frederik B. Bang† [289]
Department of Pathobiology, The Johns Hopkins University, School of Hygiene and Public Health, Baltimore, Maryland 21205

Martha M.C. Bijlholt [269]
Biochemisch Laboratorium, Rijksuniversiteit Groningen, Nijenborgh 16, 9747 AG Groningen, The Netherlands

Celia Bonaventura [231]
Marine Biomedical Center, Duke University Marine Laboratory, Beaufort, North Carolina 28516

Joseph Bonaventura [231]
Marine Biomedical Center, Duke University Marine Laboratory, Beaufort, North Carolina 28516

George B. Bourne [133]
Department of Biology, University of Calgary, Calgary, Alberta T2N 1N4, Canada

Michael Brenowitz [257]
Department of Biochemistry, Duke University Marine Laboratory, Beaufort, North Carolina 28516

Marius Brouwer [231]
Marine Biomedical Center, Duke University Marine Laboratory, Beaufort, North Carolina 28516

Ernst F.J. van Bruggen [269]
Biochemisch Laboratorium, Rijksuniversiteit Groningen, Nijenborgh 16, 9747 AG Groningen, The Netherlands

John D. Costlow [53, 103]
Duke University Marine Laboratory, Beaufort, North Carolina 28516

N.C. Eickman [189]
Department of Chemistry, Massachusetts Institute of Technology, Cambridge, Massachusetts 02139

Jeremy H.A. Fields [125]
Department of Zoology, University of Washington, Seattle, Washington 98195

Sidney R. Galler [301]
6242 Woodcrest Avenue, Baltimore, Maryland 21209

R.S. Himmelwright [189]
Department of Chemistry, Massachusetts Institute of Technology, Cambridge, Massachusetts 02139

The number in brackets following each contributor's name indicates the opening page number of that author's paper.

†Deceased.

Y.T. Hwang [189]
Department of Chemistry, Massachusetts Institute of Technology, Cambridge, Massachusetts 02139

Thomas C. Jegla [83, 103]
Department of Biology, Kenyon College, Gambier, Ohio 43022

Bruce A. Johnson [115, 147]
Duke University Marine Laboratory, Beaufort, North Carolina 28516

Darwin D. Jorgensen [133]
Department of Zoology, Duke University, Durham, North Carolina 27706

Charlotte P. Mangum [147, 173]
Department of Biology, College of William and Mary, Williamsburg, Virginia 23185

Nicholas A. Mauro [147]
Department of Biology, College of William and Mary, Williamsburg, Virginia 23185

Margaret Moore [257]
Department of Zoology, University of Texas at Austin, Austin, Texas 78712

Stephen R. Palumbi [115]
Department of Zoology, University of Washington, Seattle, Washington 98195

Thomas G. Pistole [283]
Department of Microbiology, University of New Hampshire, Durham, New Hampshire 03824

S.E. Plon [189]
Department of Chemistry, Massachusetts Institute of Technology, Cambridge, Massachusetts 02139

James R. Redmond [133]
Department of Zoology, Iowa State University, Ames, Iowa 50011

Anne Rudloe [297]
Department of Biological Science, The Florida State University, Tallahassee, Florida 32306

Wilma G. Schutter [269]
Biochemisch Laboratorium, Rijksuniversiteit Groningen, Nijenborgh 16, 9747 AG Groningen, The Netherlands

Koichi Sekiguchi [53, 75]
Institute of Biological Sciences, The University of Tsukuba, Sakura-mura, Niihari-gun, Ibaraki 305, Japan

Carl N. Shuster Jr. [1]
Virginia Institute of Marine Science and School of Marine Science, The College of William and Mary, Gloucester Point, Virginia 23062

G.K. Snyder [173]
Department of Environmental, Population and Organismic Biology, University of Colorado, Boulder, Colorado 80309

E.I. Solomon [189]
Department of Chemistry, Massachusetts Institute of Technology, Cambridge, Massachusetts 02139

Hiroaki Sugita [75]
Institute of Biological Sciences, The University of Tsukuba, Sakura-mura, Niihari-gun, Ibaraki 305, Japan

David W. Towle [147]
Department of Biology, University of Richmond, Richmond, Virginia 23173

Trijntje Wichertjes [269]
Biochemisch Laboratorium, Rijksuniversiteit Groningen, Nijenborgh 16, 9747 AG Groningen, The Netherlands

D.E. Wilcox [189]
Department of Chemistry, Massachusetts Institute of Technology, Cambridge, Massachusetts 02139

Yoshio Yamamichi [53]
Department of Anatomy, Tokushima University School of Dentistry, Kuramoto-cho, Tokushima 770, Japan

Bernard J. Zahuranec [301]
Oceanic Biology Program, Ocean Science and Technology Detachment, Office of Naval Research, NSTL Station, Mississippi 39529

Preface

The Limulus Expedition was held at the Duke University Marine Laboratory in Beaufort, North Carolina, in the summer of 1980. This was a period of intense experimentation and discussion for researchers representing many disciplines and many countries. The Duke University Marine Biomedical Center hosted the one-month expedition. As Directors of the Center, we would like to take this opportunity to relate the background events and the philosophy which resulted in this collection of papers that represent the Limulus Expedition.

Until recently, few researchers realized the value of marine organisms in studying fundamental biomedical processes. In the past decade, however, increasing numbers of articles have appeared describing the utility of marine organisms in medical research. As a relevant example see Cohen (ed): "Biomedical Applications of the Horseshoe Crab (Limulidae)," New York: Alan R. Liss, Inc., 1979. Recognizing the need for more scientists to be trained simultaneously in the health sciences and in marine biology, the National Institute of Environmental Health Sciences (NIEHS) has funded a small number of Marine and Freshwater Biomedical Centers. As Directors of the Duke University Marine Biomedical Center (NIEHS Grant No. ESO 1908), we are charged with further encouraging marine-related health science research.

The Limulus Expedition proved to be a good example of how pioneering studies at marine laboratories can provide health scientists with useful tools for their own investigations. As other examples of this, we can refer to the new FDA-accepted and widely used tests for endotoxins and gram-negative bacteria which are based on a protein system isolated from amoebocytes of the horseshoe crab. Ameobocytes from crabs have also been noted to attack and kill certain types of human cancer cells. In addition, there are many useful pharmaceutical products derived from marine plants and animals. Marine toxins, like tetrodotoxin, saxitoxin and ciguateratoxin, have provided researchers and clinicians with important pharmacological probes of transport systems. These and other examples suggest that basic research in the marine sciences can have increasing importance in the biomedical realm.

The Limulus Expedition also proves the broader fact that the human species' spirit of adventure cuts across all lines of endeavor. This is certainly no less true in science than in any other field. The excitement of learning about the exotic and the unknown continues to drive scientists in their pursuit of knowledge. Some of this pursuit is done merely by thinking, sitting at a desk and exploring new ideas using only one's mind and a pencil and paper. In other cases, this pursuit is carried out by physically exploring previously unexplored areas of the earth. These sorts of studies, which we call expeditionary studies, are ones to which nearly all people can easily relate. Expeditionary studies, which have probably been carried out ever since the evolution of our species, have themselves undergone a sort of evolution — starting with natural history studies in relation to food gathering, proceeding to geographical research relevant to physical expansion of territory, then to more detailed geological and geophysical expeditions. Programs of outer-space exploration continue this tradition. A fairly modern type of expedition is one which deals with features of physiology and biochemistry of organisms in challenging and unexplored environments. The great extent of the oceans and rivers, covering roughly 70% of our planet, explains why expeditionary studies frequently involve the use of ships. The never-ceasing attraction of the sea makes ocean-related exploration particularly exciting.

From 1966 to 1978, the United States had a national facility devoted to marine and aquatic studies of physiology and biochemistry. This facility, the Research Vessel ALPHA HELIX, was used by hundreds of physiologists and biochemists to study interesting phenomena in a wide variety of areas. Expeditions were mounted in the Arctic, the Antarctic, the Amazon Basin, and the Great Barrier Reef, among others. Much was learned from these studies, and our scientific literature was enriched as a result of these expeditions. For a variety of reasons, the ALPHA HELIX was "denationalized" in 1978, and since that time there has been no facility exclusively devoted to expeditionary studies of the type that could be done by this ship.

Loss of the ALPHA HELIX should not put a stop to expeditionary studies of physiology and biochemistry. Expeditionary studies should continue in order to advance the state of knowledge of the flora, fauna, and geography of particular regions. When investigators gather together in an interesting location to focus their research activities on a common theme, the resulting synergistic interactions can have long-lasting and far-reaching effects. Additionally, it is not uncommon for a large amount of research to be conducted in a remarkably short period of time. These studies are also marked by conceptual breakthroughs which are, in part, brought about by the excitement of the expedition and by contributions from the varying perspectives of the participating scientists.

In the spirit of expeditionary studies, the Limulus Expedition was organized as a land-based study for the summer of 1980. Its overall theme was to learn how the physiology and biochemistry of the horseshoe crab, Limulus polyphemus, a fascinating evolutionary relic, allow it to adapt to its environment, which is subject to wide variations in temperature, salinity, oxygen availability, and human-induced stress. During the period of the expedition, the participants carried out experimental work in the field and in the laboratory and gave seminars on their individual specialties and on their results. In addition to the participants who stayed for the entire expedition, a number of short-term participants came for one to four days. These individuals also presented lectures and contributed papers and thereby added greatly to the scientific scope of the project.

Topics studied and discussed by the participants included the natural history of the organism, its circulation physiology, aspects of salt regulation, development, blood functions, metabolic pathways, and even detailed investigation of phenomena at the molecular and atomic levels. Articles on these topics have been drawn together in this volume. Although it is impossible to capture the spirit of an expedition merely with a collection of articles, nevertheless, we feel that this organized collection shows not only the importance of expeditionary studies but how such studies can lead to scientific advancements.

Joseph Bonaventura
Celia Bonaventura
Shirley Tesh

Acknowledgments

Organization and coordination of the Limulus Expedition was greatly helped by the inexhaustable enthusiasm of a number of people. Special thanks go to Belinda Beckwith, David Bickar, Mike Brenowitz, Teri Lynn Herbert, and Bruce Johnson. Without their help the Limulus Expedition would not have been possible. Specific acknowledgments from individual authors are given in each chapter. However, in a general sense, the National Institutes of Health and the National Science Foundation provided support through the facilities and equipment utilized by the participants. The Duke University Marine Biomedical Center hosted the expedition and provided partial support to participants through NIEHS Grant ESO-1908.

Physiology and Biology of Horseshoe Crabs: Studies on
Normal and Environmentally Stressed Animals, pages 1–52
© 1982 Alan R. Liss, Inc., 150 Fifth Avenue, New York, NY 10011

A Pictorial Review of the Natural History and Ecology of the Horseshoe Crab Limulus polyphemus, With Reference to Other Limulidae

Carl N. Shuster Jr.

INTRODUCTION

This review provides a base of information on the natural history and ecology of Limulidae. The review is organized around six series of illustrations: the species and their interrelationships, external appearance, life cycle, behavior and orientation, food and feeding, and symbiotic and other relationships.

While population dynamics are not addressed in this chapter, this topic will be of increasing importance if it becomes necessary to manage the species, particularly if more are harvested for scientific and commercial uses. So far, only a generalized account of Limuli populations can be portrayed. The account that follows is based upon several populations, not one of which has been intensively and adequately studied. The importance of this fact cannot be overemphasized. There are discrete populations of horseshoe crabs, and the behavioral patterns of the animals can differ. This presentation provides a background for further study of discrete populations and for comparative studies.

THE SPECIES AND THEIR INTERRELATIONSHIPS
Number and Distribution of Species

There are four extant species of horseshoe crabs (Limulidae), some of whose morphological and other characteristics are contrasted in Figures 1 and 2 and Table I. Limulus polyphemus is found along the eastern coast of North and Central America; and the three Indo-Pacific species, Tachypleus tridentatus, T. gigas, and Carcinoscorpius rotundicauda, occupy diverse habitats within different but overlapping geographic ranges (Fig. 3). The existence of a fifth species, T. hoveni, is so doubtful that it is no longer listed in recent taxonomic considerations

(Fig. 3) [158]. Each species has an extensive range, within which its distribution is intermittent. Their natural history/ecology [112, 157], morphology/morphometry [113, 114, 118, 127], and serology [130] are so similar that the four species could be grouped in a single genus [132]. Even so, genetic variation has been claimed between certain populations of L. polyphemus [117, 139].

Museum specimens have been studied [30, 31, 84]. It is apparent, that until 1953 [157] no one had ever observed living specimens of all extant Limulidae in the field or examined them, side by side, in the laboratory. This situation

TABLE I. Morphometric and Other Data on the Early Life Stages of Limulidae (Compiled From Several Sources—[69, 100, 112, 127]—and the Author's Data)

Species***	Number of eggs		Diameter of eggs		Prosomal width (in mm)	
	Per female per year	Per nest	(in mm)*	(mm)**	"Trilobite" larvae	"First-tailed" stage
T. tridentatus	20,000	200–500	3.0–3.3	5.1	5.3–5.7	7.9– 8.2
T. gigas	8,000	400	3.5–4.0	7.8	6.3–7.0	10.9–11.0
C. rotundicauda	10,000	80–150	2.0–2.2	4.2	4.0–4.2	6.0– 6.3
L. polyphemus	88,000	3,650	1.6–1.8	3.6	2.7–3.7	4.3– 5.5

*Newly laid and up to the time of rupture of the chorion.
**Just before hatching of the larvae.
***Indo-Pacific specimens courtesy of Dr. Koichi Sekiguchi (Institute of Biological Sciences, University of Tsukuba, Sakura-Mura, Japan); delivered to the author by Dr. Koichiro Nakamura in 1981.

Fig. 1. Topographical characteristics unique to adults of the Limulidae (modified from [112] and [127] and rechecked by observations on preserved specimens at the Smithsonian Institution Museum of Natural History). The opisthosomas of the females were all set to the same width to demonstrate proportionate differences between the species. Within each species, however, the relative dimensions of body parts are to scale. The males were drawn at about 80% of the female size. A) Outline of dorsal aspect of males: the variable body proportions and the lengths of the moveable, marginal spines of the opisthosomas are notable. B) Telson: Drawn separately to conserve space; the cross sections (b) were enlarged (only C. rotundicauda is subcircular in cross section; the other species triangulate, with ventral, concave grooves on the telsons of the two species of Tachypleus). The arrows at the anterior ends of the telsons indicate the midline of the telsons. C) Frontal aspect of prosoma of males, illustrating differences in prosomal heights and the extent of arching. D) The second (2) and third (3) prosomal appendages of males; the "claspers" are present in all species on the second pair of appendages, and also on the third pair of the Indo-Pacific species. E) Dorsal aspect of the opisthosoma of females: Note particularly the species differences in the six moveable, marginal spines. Further differences, seen in both sexes, are in the shape of the first entapophyseal pit (only L. polyphemus has a triangulate pit) and the number of spines on the dorsal yoke (only T. tridentatus has three fixed spines, one of which is the usual axial spine). F) Anterior faces of the operculi of both sexes (drawn to match the size of the female opithosomas); only L. polyphemus has endites (these are large and moveable; at arrow).

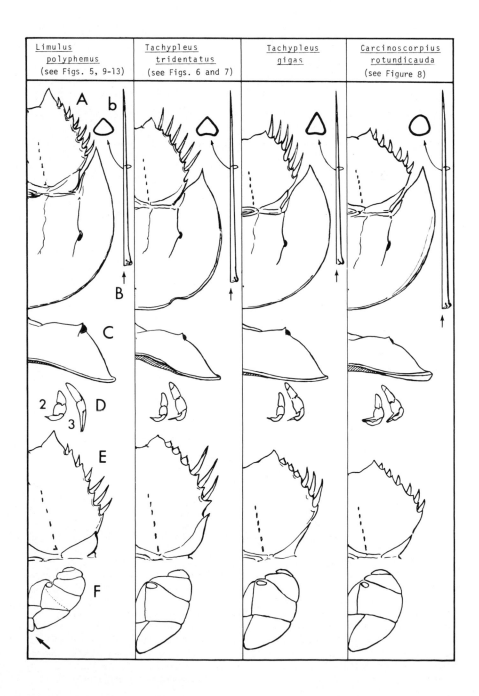

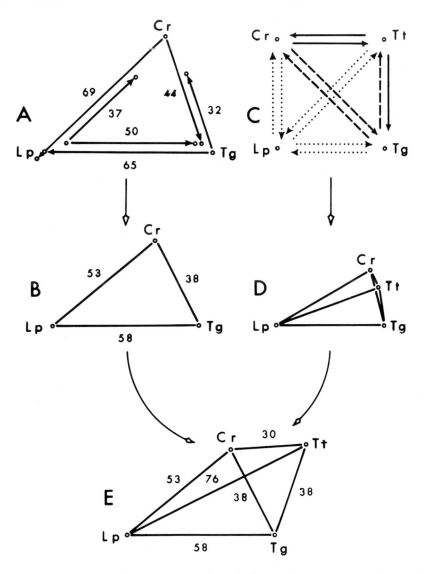

Fig.2. A summary of the serological and hybridization evidence of the systematic relationships among the Limulidae. A) The first stage in the construction of a "serological yardstick" diagram; reciprocal percents of homologous precipitin reactions indicate the serological "distance" between species [127, 130]. B) The second stage of the "serological yardstick," derived by averaging the reciprocal percents (from A). C) A hybridization matrix (modified after [116]); the arrows lead from the species providing the spermatozoa. The resulting development is indicated by the type of line: larvae = solid, blastulae = dashed, and infertility = dotted. D) A "hybridization yardstick," derived from averaging distances based on arbitrarily assigned values: larvae = 1, blastulae = 3, and infertility = 6. E) The hypothetical "systematic yardstick" suggested by Figure 2B and D.

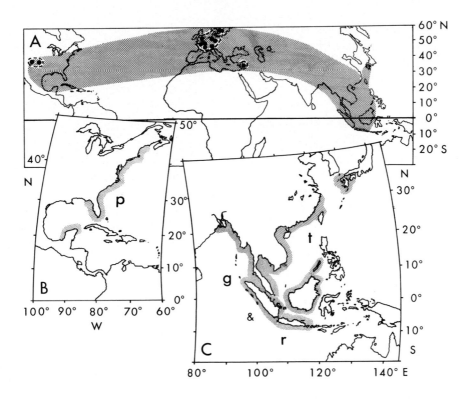

Fig. 3. Distribution of the Limulidae. A) Range of extinct and extent Limulid species. B) The shaded area shows the coastal region within which reproducing populations of L. polyphemus (p) have been found. Limuli have occasionally been reported well within the Gulf of Mexico, as at the Chadeleur Islands, Louisiana [15]. Adult Limuli have been collected from the eastern shore of the Yucatan Peninsula. C) The areas within which reproducing populations of the Indo-Pacific species occur. T. gigas (g) and C. rotundicauda (r) have essentially the same ranges, from the shores of the Bay of Bengal to the islands of Indonesia where they overlap the range of T. tridentatus (t) along the shores of Borneo. From there, T. tridentatus ranges from the westernmost portion of the Philippine Islands, along the coast of Vietnam and China to the southwestern part of Japan. Even where their ranges overlap, each species is esentially discrete and noncompetitive because they spawn in different habitats (Dr. Koichiro Nakamura, Tokyo, Japan; personal communication, 1981).

changed markedly in the 1970s, when a series of studies was undertaken at the Shimoda Marine Research Center of the University of Tsukuba [110–116].

Taxonomic Classification of Limulidae

Class: Merostomata Dana, 1852
Subclass: Xiphosura Latreille, 1802

Order: Xiphosurida Latreille, 1802
Suborder: Limulina Richter and Richter, 1929
Superfamily: Limulacea Zittle, 1885
Family: Limulidae Zittle, 1885 [22, 84, 112]

Taxonomic Affinities and Evolutionary Significance

Limulidae are believed to be the closest living relatives of trilobites [90, 142], with the Trilobita further from a protoarthropod than the Crustacea, although the two groups were not independently derived [108]. The first clear demonstration of arachnid similarity to L. polyphemus was in 1881 [55]. Neither L. polyphemus "nor its close relatives can be the progenitors of any known land arthropoda, living or fossil; its real importance is that, as the only aquatic survivor of the once very considerable merostome fauna, it provides information not available from the fossils" [150].

Both extinct and extant Limulidae have been found in the temperate and tropical zones of the Northern Hemisphere. The range of two extant species extends into the Southern Hemisphere and around the tropical islands of Indonesia as illustrated in Figure 3C: At least ten fossilized species have been found in two regions as listed below [41, 91, 141–143]: fossils of North America: Paleolimulus avitus (Permian; Kansas, U.S.A.), Limulus coffini (Cretaceous; Colorado, U.S.A.); fossils of Europe and Asia Minor: Psammonlimulus gottingensis (Lower Triassic; Germany), Limulitella bronni (Lower Triassic; France), Limulitella vicensis (Triassic; Keuper of Lorraine, France), Mesolimulus walchi (Jurassic; Solnhofen, Germany), Mesolimulus (?) nathorsti (Jurassic; Sweden), Mesolimulus (?) woodwardi (Jurassic; England), Mesolimulus syriacus (Cretaceous; Lebanon, Asia Minor), Tachypleus decheni (Miocene; Merseburg brown coal; Germany).

Although the range of each extant species is shown in Figure 3B and C [112, 132] as continuous, each species has an intermittent distribution within its own range. The ranges can be defined chiefly by the water temperatures, salinities, and depths at which Limulidae have been found. Temperature appears to be the limiting factor for the northern ranges of L. polyphemus and T. tridentatus. To the south, temperature seems less likely as the limiting factor, at least for T. gigas and C. rotundicauda. For them, the Java Trench and other deeps may have been the deterent to their movement southward to Australia—just as Cuba and the Caribbean Islands are isolated from L. polyphemus by deep water. Since neither L. polyphemus nor T. tridentatus extends as far southward as continental shelves would permit them, temperature may be a southward limiting factor, at least for L. polyphemus. T. tridentatus nearly reaches the Equator, where it overlaps the distribution of the other two Indo-Pacific species.

The present distribution of Limulidae suggests that they (or their progenitor species) migrated as shallow seas disappeared when the European land mass was formed. None of the species may have been derived from one of the others, but one or more of the species may have shared a common European ancestor [40]. Occasionally L. polyphemus, generally believed to have been released by fisherman returning from fishing off the coast of the United States, are found in European waters. They have not established a reproducing population there [162].

Artificial hybridization experiments among the four species have resulted in viable (ie, swimming) larvae from certain crosses between T. tridentatus and the other Indo-Pacific species but only to infertility when L. polyphemus gametes were used (Fig. 2) [116].

American Species of Limulidae, Subfamily Limulinae Zittle, 1885

Limulus polyphemus (L.) Müller, 1785 [49, 50, 59, 70, 76, 109]. This species ranges from the Yucatan Peninsula to northern Maine, from about 19°N to 42°N (Figure 3B). Distinct populations occur (Fig. 4). The size of adult L. polyphemus and the size of its populations show a distinct latitudinal gradient [97, 126, 127]. Larger animals and populations are in the middle portion of their distribution along the coast of the United States; smaller animals and populations are found north of Cape Cod, along the Florida coast of the Gulf of Mexico, and at the entrances to the gulf. Measurements have revealed the existence of discrete populations [97, 127]; physiological races may also exist [117, 131, 139]. The smallest adults were found in Plum Island Sound, Massachusetts, with a mean prosomal width for males of 118 mm; females, 156 mm. Largest adults collected [127] were from Bird Shoal, North Carolina: males PW = 232 mm mean, and females = 327 mm. Eye pigmentation [139] and color of carapace may also be characteristic of certain populations. Thus there may not be a fully "representative" L. polyphemus.

A recent multivariate analysis of morphometric data from discrete populations of Limuli demonstrated a great deal of morphological variation, both within and among populations [97]. Whereas the differentiation of populations was made on the basis of both "size" and "shape" variation, individuals from different populations could be distinquished from each other more by discriminant functions for "shape" than for "size." A linear combination, corresponding to "shape" variation, exhibited a monotonic north–south cline. The characters defining this cline were based upon the location of certain fixed spines and the length of the subfrontal area (PS).

The specimens illustrated in Figure 5 came from two distinct populations in the northern part of the midrange of the distribution of the species. This midrange, from Georgia to Cape Cod, is where the largest adults occur (Fig. 4). The two populations are found in adjoining bays, Chesapeake and Delaware, at virtually the same latitude. The difference in their adult sizes may be due to physiochemical differences in their respective habitats, especially in the salinity (lower in the area of the Miles River, Maryland, population, Fig. 4).

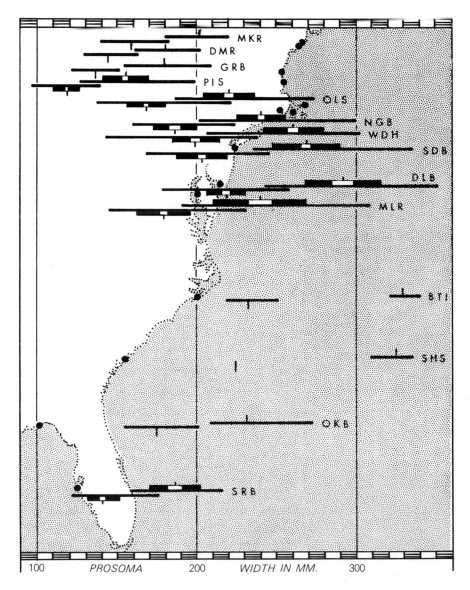

Fig. 4. The prosomal widths (PW) of 4,262 adult Limuli (2,200 males; 2,062 females) from fourteen populations are plotted in this figure, using a graphic technique that shows the range in prosomal widths (heavy horizontal lines) for each locality; the mean by a vertical spike. The open portion of each bar (white) comprises 2 standard errors of the mean on either side of the mean. One-half of the total length of the bar is 1 standard devitation on either side of the mean. Additional data not plotted on this figure are comparable: From specimens in the Smithsonian Institution/Museum of Natural History: at Tortugas, FL, four males with PW = 104–165 mm, average = 155 mm; and

Indo-Pacific Species of Limulidae, Subfamily Tachypleinae Pocock, 1902

Tachypleus tridentatus Leach, 1819 [29, 51, 71–73, 110, 111, 117–119]. This is the most studied of the three Indo-Pacific species. The drawings of Figure 6 have been reproduced because they are the most accurate ever prepared to show the macroscopic external anatomy of the carapace of a Limulidae. Unfortunately they are rarely referred to. Their presentation here corrects previous oversights and enables comparison with frontal and posterior views of the species (Fig. 7), as well as with L. polyphemus (Fig. 5) and C. rotundicauda (Fig. 8) (from Siebold, Fr de (1882) Fauna Japonica (Regis Auspiciis Edita), Amstelodami Apud J. Müller et Co.).

Tachypleus gigas (Müller) Leach, 1819 [69, 100, 113, 115, 135].

Carcinoscorpius rotundicauda (Latr.) [3, 69, 114, 115, 135]. Photographs of specimens from the coast of the Malay Peninsula are shown in Figure 8 (specimens courtesy of Dr. D. S. Johnson, University of Malaya, Singapore). Compare the relative appearance with L. polyphemus: the long, slender telsons, the flatter carapace, and the slender appendages.

EXTERNAL APPEARANCE
Morphology/Morphometry

Some of the unique characteristics of the extant species of Limulidae are illustrated in Figure 1. Morphometric studies on adult Limulidae demonstrate the following:

1) Certain characteristics are related to size. For example, the moveable, lateral spines of the opisthosoma, particularly the marginal spines of T. gigas [113], are more acutely angular in the smaller-sized adults of the species; and the angular dimensions of the posterior projections of the opisthosoma in L. polyphemus where the immature animals of a population, in which the adults are large-sized, have been found to be morphometrically alike, in most respects, to comparably-sized adults from a population in which the adults are small [127].

2) Morphometric measurements from specimens in small collections (as in museums) can be misleading because they may not be morphometrically rep-

---

from the northern shoreline of Espirita Santo Bay on the eastern side of Yucatan Peninsula, three males with PW = 123–130 mm, average = 127 mm, and four females with PW = 162–213 mm, average = 185 mm; at Thomas Point, Casco Bay, Maine, four males with PW range = 129–146 mm, five females = 172–208 mm; and at Barnstable Harbor, Cape Cod, Massachusetts, 32 males, PW range = 123–212 mm, mean = 166 mm, and 13 females = 175–238 mm with mean = 124 mm. The largest female seen by this author was taken at Kiptopeke Beach near Cape Charles, Virginia, in April 1953 by Mr. and Mrs. J. E. Snyder (Smithsonian Institution Museum of Natural History specimen: PW = 365 mm).

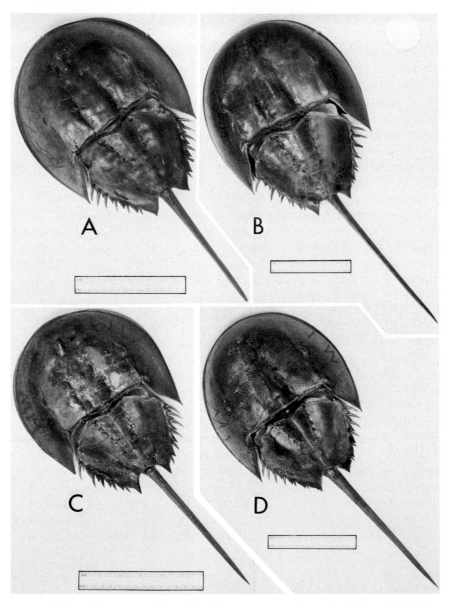

Fig. 5.   Representative adult Limulus polyphemus. A 6-inch (152 mm) rule is placed by each specimen for reference. From Delaware Bay, Cape May shore of New Jersey (population DLB in Figure 4): A) Male (prosomal width, 233 mm; body length, 272 mm). Compare slight indentation of the flange, subfrontal edge of prosoma, to that of the Indo-Pacific species, particularly T. tridentatus in Figure 7A and B. B) Female (prosomal width, 294 mm; body length, 387 mm). From the Miles River, Chesapeake Bay system, Maryland (population MLR in Fig. 4): C) Male (prosomal width, 191 mm; body length, 225 mm); D) female (prosomal width, 257 mm; body length, 316 mm). Note the relatively short, lateral, moveable spines of the opisthosoma, particularly the fifth and sixth spines. (See Figs. 9, 10, and 11 for nomenclature.)

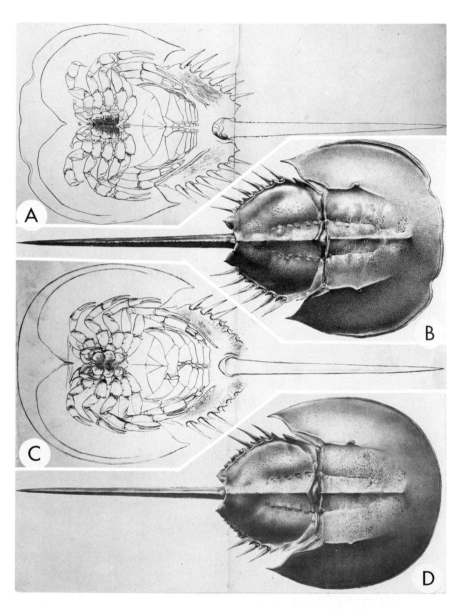

Fig. 6. Tachypleus tridentatus. A and B) Ventral and dorsal aspects, respectively, of an adult male. Note the character of the doublure (the ventral lining of the carapace), its indented anterior border, less angular (than in the female) subfrontal area, and broader lateral portions. The second and third prosomal appendages are monodactylid. C and D) Ventral and dorsal aspects, respectively, of an adult female. Note particularly, for comparison with L. polyphemus (see Figure 10A, B; 11), the characteristics of the ventral surface: the elongated mesial spine, relatively slender prosomal appendages, the operculum, the lateral ridges of the opisthosomal doublure, the deeply indented hemicircular margin of the terminal bay, and the lateral moveable spines.

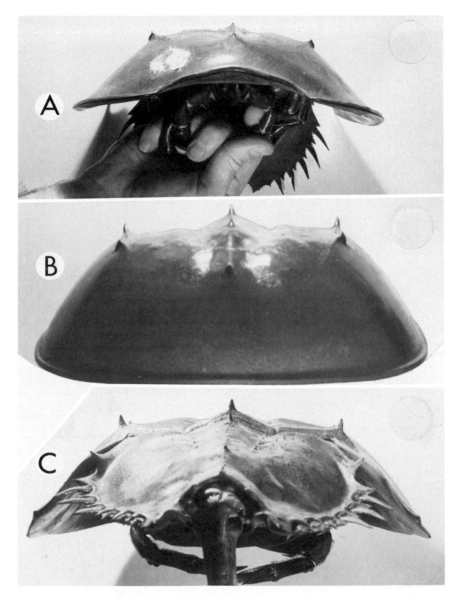

Fig. 7. Tachypleus tridentatus. Photographs of specimens preserved at the Smithsonian Institution National Museum of Natural History (USNM). A) Adult male (USNM 62300). Anterior view, showing the flattened appearance of the prosoma and the nature of the arch of the subfrontal area, as contrasted to the male of L. polyphemus (Figure 11A). B and C) Adult female (USNM 62299). Anterior and posterior views, respectively. Note the prominent spines, particularly along the posterior margin of the prosoma. The height of the flange or rim of the prosoma, greater frontally (PR1) than laterally (PR2), is characteristic of the females of all species, in contrast to the males where the reverse occurs (see Figures 11D and 12C for L. polyphemus and nomenclature; Figure 8E and F for the adult male and female, respectively, of C. rotundicauda).

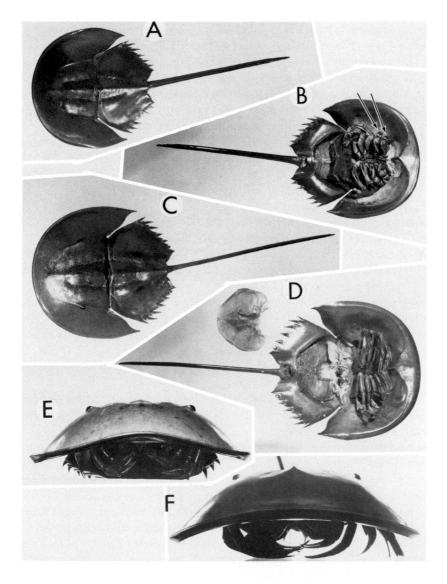

Fig. 8. Carcinoscorpius rotundicauda. A, B, and E) Dorsal, ventral, and frontal views, respectively, of an adult male (prosomal width, 11 cm). Note the two pairs of didactylid "claspers" (second and third pairs of prosomal appendages). C, D, and F) Dorsal, ventral, and frontal views, respectively, of an adult female (prosomal width, 13 cm). The operculum of this specimen was broken off in shipment; it is shown in the upper left portion of Figure 8D. This mishap, however, renders the five pairs of branchial appendages, with their book gills, visible.

resentative of either the population from which they were taken or of any other population.

3) Comparison of different populations may reveal interesting relationships, as in the "fist-and-thumb" claspers (second and third prosomal appendages) of male C. rotundicauda [114]. The difference in claspers in two populations appears to be an adaptation to the thickness of the lateral margin of the female opisthosoma: The population with the "swollen" opisthosomal margins had males with claspers that were more concavely curved in their "bite" and, seemingly, better adapted to grasping the double-convex margin of the adult females.

4) The Indo-Pacific Limulidae are all somewhat flatter (prosomal width to prosomal height ratio = about 1:0.3, while in L. polyphemus the PW/PH ratio = about 1:0.4) [data from 127] (see Fig. 1C).

Terminology of the external anatomy of L. polyphemus is given in Figures 9–11. In morphometric studies, several dimensions of the carapace are measured, particularly in studies of mated animals [86, 89] and of populations [97, 127]. Figure 12 illustrates linear and angular measurements frequently taken in studies of Limulidae [127]. If only one measurement is taken, the prosomal width (PW) is probably the easiest and most reliable. It can be accomplished by placing an animal on a measuring board [124].

Morphometric differences have been reported between populations of the same species from different geographical locations: L. polyphemus [97, 127] from the United States (see Figure 4) and T. gigas [113] and C. rotundicauda [114] from the Bay of Bengal and the Gulf of Siam.

Sexual Dimorphism

Certain sexual characteristics of adults have long been known. Males generally are smaller than females; pedipalps of males are monodactylus, didactylus in females; male genital pores are on the apex of a firm conical projection; female pores are broad slits in elliptical, soft, convex areas [29, 53, 89, 127]. In any one population, the mean prosomal width of adult males is 75–79% of the female mean prosomal widths [86, 89, 126] (see Fig. 4). The prosomal subfrontal arch of the male is higher than that of the females (see Figures 7A, B; 8E, F); the male prosomal length is shorter, and the flange of the male decreases in height as it proceeds anteriorly, whereas the female flange increases in height anteriorly [127]. Occasionally a hermaphroditic specimen is reported [7, 13, 127]. In the Indo-Pacific species, the dimorphism is usually more noticeable than in L. polyphemus, as in the indentations in the anterior portion of the rim of the adult male T. tridentatus (Figs. 5A, B; 6A, B); the much shortened, fourth-to-sixth, moveable opisthosomal spines of the female T. tridentatus (Fig. 6C, D) and T. gigas, compared to the female of L. polyphemus (Fig. 5B, D); and the two pairs of didactylid claspers of the male C. rotundicauda indicated by arrows on Fig. 8B).

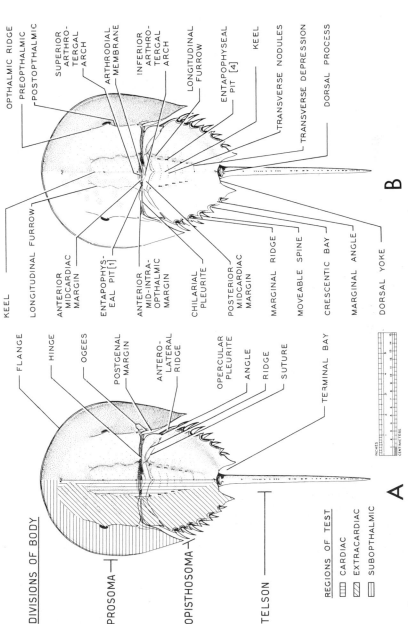

Fig. 9. Outline drawing of an adult male L. polyphemus [from 127], dorsal aspect. A) The three divisions of the body: prosoma, opisthosoma, and telson. The outline of the animal, particularly the body proportions, was based on a lantern slide made from a photograph of a specimen from the Miles River, Chesapeake Bay, Maryland (see Fig. 4C). The structural details were completed from a study of this specimen. The rule is 6 inches (152.5 mm) long. B) Several topographical characteristics. The right half of the drawing was stippled to show contour of the exoskeleton; stippling on the left half, the external markings indicative of the larger muscle attachments.

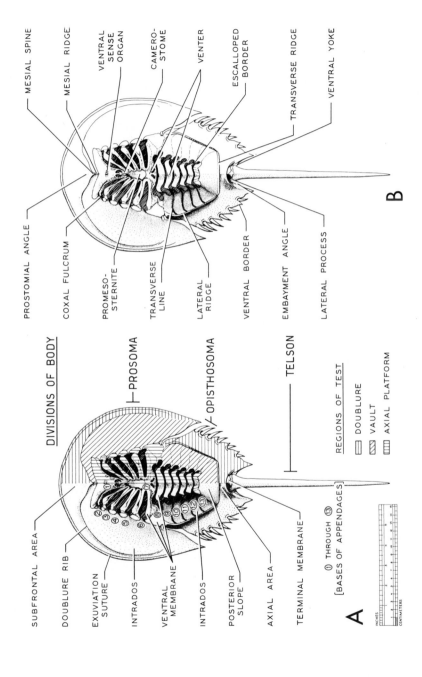

DIVISIONS OF BODY

PROSOMA

OPISTHOSOMA

TELSON

REGIONS OF TEST

DOUBLURE
VAULT
AXIAL PLATFORM

① THROUGH ⑬
[BASES OF APPENDAGES]

SUBFRONTAL AREA
DOUBLURE RIB
EXUVIATION SUTURE
INTRADOS
VENTRAL MEMBRANE
INTRADOS
POSTERIOR SLOPE
AXIAL AREA
TERMINAL MEMBRANE

A

MESIAL SPINE
MESIAL RIDGE
VENTRAL SENSE ORGAN
CAMERO-STOME
VENTER
ESCALLOPED BORDER
TRANSVERSE RIDGE
VENTRAL YOKE

PROSTOMIAL ANGLE
COXAL FULCRUM
PROMESO-STERNITE
TRANSVERSE LINE
LATERAL RIDGE
VENTRAL BORDER
EMBAYMENT ANGLE
LATERAL PROCESS

B

Some Variations in Exoskeleton

The spinous condition of the dorsal ridge of the telson of adults varies from individual to individual. The two views shown in Figure 13A contrast an entirely smooth telson of an animal from Narragansett Bay, Rhode Island (upper), with the serrate telson of a specimen from Barnstable Harbor, Massachusetts (lower). Spines are largest during the immature stages, gradually diminishing (proportionately) with the size of the animal (Fig. 13C, D). The drawing of the lateral aspect of an adult male shows the low, blunted dorsal spines characteristic of adult Limuli (Fig. 13B), in contrast to the exuviae of immature specimens. Female and male specimens (Fig. 13C, D, respectively), from Sandy Hook Bay, New Jersey, show the prominent dorsal spines that are so characteristic of young Limuli of this size.

The significance of the spines has been assumed 1) to enable young, small animals to gain a better purchase during burrowing (all fixed spines point slightly posteriorly [11], and 2) to render the young less likely prey because of the sharpness of the spines and the tendency to make the animals more ferocious [106]. And, for extinct species, eg, Euproops danae, experiments with models of the body conformation suggest that the array of spines effected a passive, nonoscillatory settling of the animal; this could have been a favorable escape reaction upon encounter with a potential predator [24].

Of all the parts of its external anatomy, the telson of L. polyphemus is subject to the greatest and most frequent anomalies. Yet the incidence of misshapen telsons is very low, suggesting that the deformations may have resulted from mechanical injury rather than from an inherited factor. It has been hypothesized [127] that the propensity for producing caudal spines may, after an injury, be concentrated at the site of a severe injury to the telson, thus producing an enlarged spine.

The series of photographs of L. polyphemus telsons in Figure 14 is arranged to show a gradation from an asymmetrical condition with an enlarged spine (F) to the symmetrical bifurcate (A–C) [from 127]. It is of interest to note that none of these telsons exhibited any other spines than the anomaly shown [see also 32, 33].

Fig. 10.   Outline drawing of an adult male L. polyphemus [from 127], ventral aspect. A) The three divisions of the body: prosoma, opisthosoma, and telson. The appendages have been omitted for clarity. The bases of the appendages have been identified by an encircled number placed just above or to the right of the base (indicated by heavy cross-hatched areas). These paired appendages are 1) chelicera; 2) pedipalps (first pair of legs); 3), 4), and 5) second, third, and fourth pairs of legs; 6) "pusher legs" the sixth pair of legs; 7) chilaria; 8) operculum (the "genital flap"); 9)–13) the brachial appendages that bear the book gills. B) Several topographic characteristics. The appendages have been removed to show other aspects of the ventrum. Bases of the appendages are indicated by the laterally hatched areas. The left-hand side of the drawing was stippled to suggest the contour of the exoskeleton.

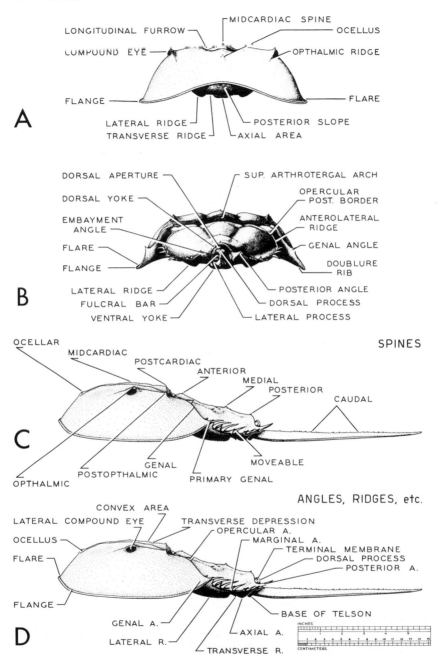

Fig. 11. Outline drawings of an adult male L. polyphemus; the appendages were omitted [from 127]: A) The trilobed character of the test (carapace); anterior view. B) Posterior view, showing the contour of the dorsal surface of the test. C) Axial spines (labeled from above) and lateral dorsal spines (labeled from beneath). D) Angles (A.), ridges (R.), and a few other characteristics of the test.

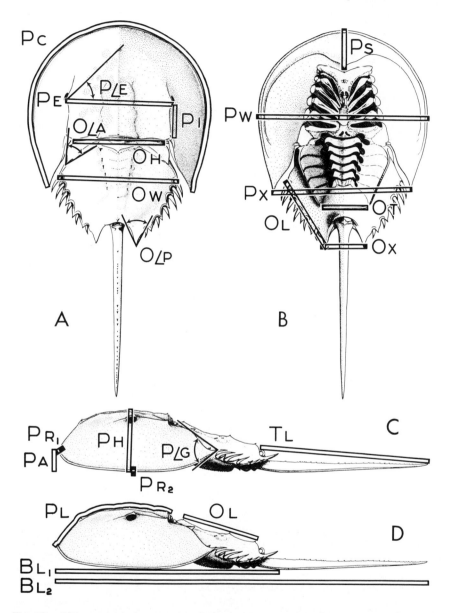

Fig. 12. Linear and angular measurements most frequently taken in morphometric studies of Limulidae [127]. A) Dorsal aspect: PC = prosomal circumference; PE = eye distance; PI = eye–spine distance; P/E = eye angle; OH = hinge length; OW = opisthosomal width; O/A = alar angle; O/P = posterior angle. B) Ventral aspect: PS = prosomal shelf; PW = prosomal width; PX = X distance (pros.); OL = lateral margin of opisthosoma; OT = length of transverse ridge; OX = X-distance of opisthosoma. C) Lateral aspect: PA = arch height; PH = prosomal height; PR_1 = rim (frontal); PR_2 = rim (lateral); P/G = genal angle; TL = telson length. D) Lateral aspect: PL = prosomal length; OL = opisthos. length; BL_1 = body length (without telson); BL_2 = body length (with telson).

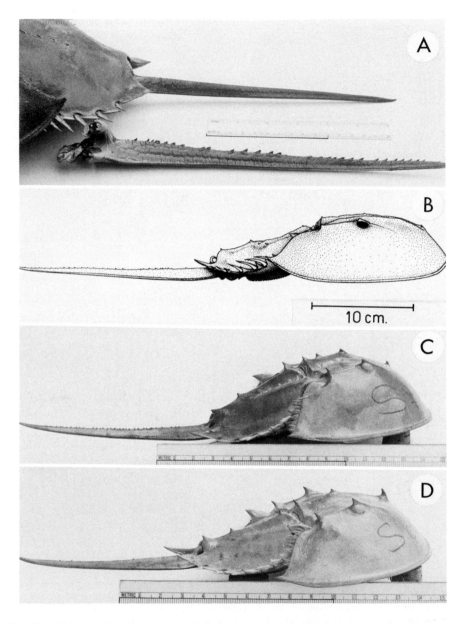

Fig. 13.   The normally occurring variations in the dorsal spines of the test of L. polyphemus [from 127]. See text.

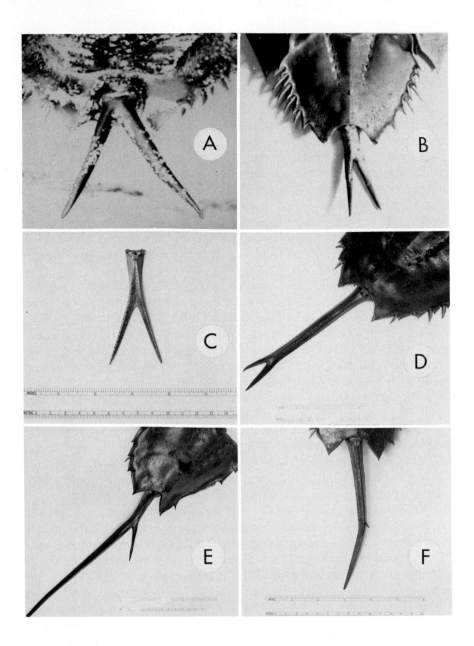

Fig. 14. A) "Forked-tail" animal found on the beach at Cape May, New Jersey. The white areas are grains of sand adhering to the exoskeleton (photograph courtesy Dr. Horace G. Richards, Academy of Natural Sciences, Philadelphia, 1949). B) A "forked-tail" specimen from Cape Henry, Virginia (U.S. National Museum 41532). C) A "forked-tail" found by Dr. Alden Stickney in 1949 in a marsh tide pool at Barnstable Harbor, Massachusetts. D) An adult female from Sandy Hook, New Jersey. E) Specimen with a greatly enlarged caudal spine (from the collection of Dr. Thurlow C. Nelson, Rutgers–State University of New Jersey; about 1950). Note the similarity in the right margin of the opisthosoma to that in the specimen in Figure 18 (A and C). F) Specimen with a bent telson and a laterally directed enlarged caudal spine. Locality not recorded; probably Barnstable Harbor, Massachusetts, about 1950.

LIFE CYCLE

Limulus polyphemus lays its eggs in "nests," in clusters in a beach (Figs. 15, 16). Early in embryonic development the first egg cover (chorion) splits, and a new membrane that has been secreted by the embryo enlarges slightly over double forming a transparent, spherical capsule. Larvae emerge from the egg capsule, which ruptures with age and larval (hatching) activity or by sand agitated by wave action. Upon liberation from the beach, they swim feebly, mostly at night. They have a short period, of about 6 days, when they may spend considerable time swimming. Then the larvae settle to the bottom and molt shortly thereafter. Despite the possibility for wide dispersion during their free-swimming period, many larvae settle in shallow water, often intertidal areas, near beaches where spawning occurred.

The young Limuli move, increasingly, away from the shoal water "nursery" areas into deeper water [127, 131]. By the time they have matured, Limuli may have moved several kilometers from the natal beaches before heading back to the beaches during the breeding season. Spawning time varies latitudinally, but generally it peaks in May and June. The adults seek beaches that are at least partially protected from surf, within bays and coves. The extent of migration appears to be limited to a few kilometers in the northern part of the Gulf coast of Florida, but the migration distance increases in the more northerly range along the Atlantic coast. Adults have been found up to 33.8 km from where they have been tagged in the Cape Cod Bay area and have been dredged off the mid-Atlantic portion of the continental shelf at depths up to 246 m (John W. Ropers, National Marine Fisheries Service, Woods Hole, Massachusetts; personal communication, 1980).

There is no evidence that the compound eyes aid Limuli in navigation, despite their polarized light sensitivity [156] and optimization of light concentration [58]. But, if the eyes can sense seasonal light patterns in deep water (up to 200 m), Limuli may have a sensory system that at least alerts them to the approach of another breeding season and starts them moving toward the beach [131].

The model presented in Figure 15B, a diagrammatic breakdown of the life cycle of L. polyphemus into component parts, is a start toward the development of a mathematical model. The molting and aging sequence in Atlantic coast populations of Limuli (Fig. 19A, for example) generally includes stages I–V in the first year, VI and VII the second year, VIII and IX the third year, and then a single molt a year from then on, with males reaching maturity at Stage XVI in the ninth year, whereas females have at least one more stage (XVII), reaching maturity one year later than males. They live as adults for several years [101].

Supportive information has come from other sources. Under aquacultural conditions in Israel [54], young Limuli grew from a PW of 2.4 to 15 mm (the equivalent of stages I–V) in 6 months. Tagged adults have been recovered up through 4 years after being released [101].

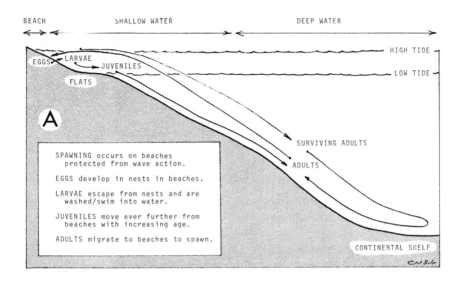

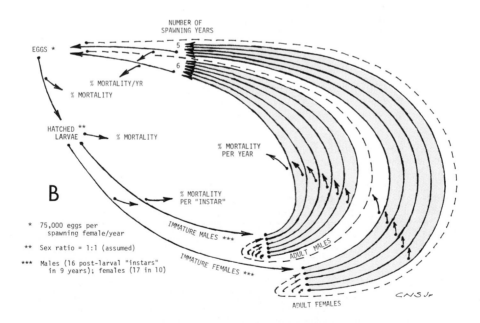

Fig. 15. The life cycle of L. polyphemus.

The main features of mate selection by L. polyphemus during the spawning season are shown in Figure 16A [133], and the distribution of egg nests on the shores of Delaware Bay, Cape May, New Jersey, in Figure 16D. When the Limuli head for the beach, the males patrol along the foot of the beach awaiting the females, which move directly to the beach [122]. Although there may be other means of identification, chemical attractants, and contact, the directional movement and the numbers of males involved (often several times the number of females) reduce the likelihood of a female reaching the beach unattended. One or more males may accompany a single female.

On Delaware Bay beaches, egg nests are found in a broad band starting about 3 meters from the low-water line to the spring high-tide water mark [133]. Embryonic development is, undoubtedly, mainly temperature-related and varies, therefore, according to the location of the nests in the beach. In 1974, at Lewes, Delaware, at the mouth of Delaware Bay there was barely any development by late June in nests low on the beach, whereas those eggs laid in the upper beach had developed and hatched [38].

Distribution of egg nests within a beach differs geographically. It appears to be dependent, at least in part, upon the amplitude of the tides (see Table II). The amplitude undoubtedly affects the microclimate of the nests and, therefore the contained, developmental stages of L. polyphemus. And the microclimate significant to the development of the eggs is probably a combination of temperature, moisture, and oxygen. Thus it may not be too far fetched to show the conditions in a beach at Woods Hole, Massachusetts (Fig. 16C redrawn from [85]), a beach that has a tidal amplitude similar to Delaware Bay, as being suggestive of what may be involved in relation to the observed distribution of nests on the beach at Cape May, New Jersey (Fig. 16D).

When the water is calm, many males may cluster around a nest-building female (Fig. 16B [from 122, 129]). This scene was possible during the late 1940s and early 1950s along the Cape May shore of Delaware Bay because the horse-

TABLE II. General Relationship Between Zone of Spawning on Beach and Tidal Amplitude

Amplitude (in meters)	Zone of spawning on beach	Representative location [Reference]
1	Narrow band near high tide level	Gulf coast, northern Florida [104]
2	Broad band (see Fig. 16c)	Delaware Bay, New Jersey [133]
3	Broad band, centered on midbeach but not near to either high-tide or low-tide levels	Barnstable Harbor, Massachusetts [121]

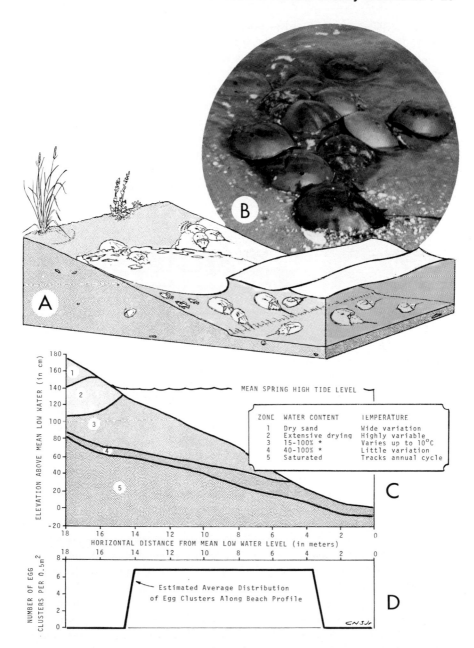

ZONE and environment table:

ZONE	WATER CONTENT	TEMPERATURE
1	Dry sand	Wide variation
2	Extensive drying	Highly variable
3	15-100% *	Varies up to 10°C
4	40-100% *	Little variation
5	Saturated	Tracks annual cycle

MEAN SPRING HIGH TIDE LEVEL

ELEVATION ABOVE MEAN LOW WATER (in cm)

HORIZONTAL DISTANCE FROM MEAN LOW WATER LEVEL (in meters)

NUMBER OF EGG CLUSTERS PER 0.5m²

Estimated Average Distribution of Egg Clusters Along Beach Profile

Fig. 16. L. polyphemus activity on spawning beaches. A) Mate selection. B) At least 12 males clustered around a nest-building female. C) The beach environment of egg clusters [after 93]. D) Distribution of egg nests on a shore of Delaware Bay, Cape May County, New Jersey [after 133].

shoe crab population was at a low point. In recent years, Limuli have been so plentiful in the same area that they virtually blanketed the beach for a great distance (up to 2 km) along the water's edge [133]. The reason for the large disparity in the relative numbers of the sexes in this photograph (by Dr. Thurlow C. Nelson, Rutgers–State University of New Jersey, May 7, 1949) is undoubtedly due to the early arrival of the males at the breeding area. By the time the first females arrive, they are greatly outnumbered.

While there are generally more males than females on spawning beaches [127], data from the continental shelf have shown a reverse trend (Dr. Paul A. Haefner, Jr., Virginia Institute of Marine Science, Gloucester Point, Virginia; personal communication, 1979). In the region off the north of Chesapeake Bay, Dr. Haefner encountered the following:

Season	Water depth (m)	Sex and number of Limuli
Early June 1973	17–39	no males
		53 females
Mid-November 1974	23–45	17 males
		96 females

The difference in the adult size of the sexes is well known and has been demonstrated in all populations that have been examined morphometrically (see Fig. 4). In more closely defined studies of mated pairs, the relationship also holds. A morphometric analysis, using 11 measurements, of 100 mated pairs from Slaughter Beach, Delaware, showed that the size of the female is greater than the male in each pair. This confirmed an earlier study, also on 100 mated pairs from Penzance Point, Massachusetts [86], and showed further that large males tended to mate with large females, medium-sized males with medium-sized females; but small males mated most often with medium-sized females [89].

The height of waves striking the beach has a significant effect upon the spawning activity of L. polyphemus [127]. Under various weather conditions on May 7, 1948, the spawning activity, recorded as the number of males that surrounded each female (spawning group), was observed. Large spawning groups (Fig. 16B) can assemble only during periods of calm or relatively calm water. Only those males, one to three and occasionally four, that can grasp the female and thus resist being washed away can remain in a spawning group when the waves increase in size and force. The rough water that accompanies a northwester in Delaware Bay will drive spawning animals off the beach or will prevent the animals from coming in to the beach at all. During a prolonged northwester the animals apparently move across Delaware Bay from the Cape May shore to the shores of the state of Delaware to spawn [125, 127, 129].

L. polyphemus casts its old shell many times. This has been described by a number of observers [14, 36, 57, 60, 74, 92]. There are four embryonic exuviae [25]. Then, after hatching, there may be 16 more molts (see Figs. 15B and 19A). The process of molting occurs seasonally during warm-water months and becomes more arduous and lengthy at each growth stage. Whereas the larvae shed their shells in a few minutes, the larger animals may require several hours. The two photographs in Figure 17 (by Claude Ronne, Woods Hole Oceanographic Institution, 1949) illustrate certain characteristics.

Prior to molting the animals at most of the larger stages burrow into areas that remain submerged at low tide [127]. Failure to do so can result in incomplete expansion (Fig. 18). Detailed studies have been made on the induction of molting by injection of steroids [42–46]. In the process of exuviation, the soft and pleated integument of the emerging animal unfolds and stretches taut as the osmotic pressure within the animal increases. Occasionally an animal has not expanded fully and hardens in a "wrinkled" condition. In such a case, molting presumably occurred during an ebbing tide; and the animal was at such a location that it was left stranded, out of water [127]. Figure 18 (from [127]) shows the most "wrinkled" specimen seen by the author. The animal, a female at an adult size, from Barnstable Harbor, Massachusetts, had a PW = 209 mm. The telson and the tips of the posterior angles of the opisthosoma were broken in storage. Note also the injury to the right opisthosomal lateral margin from which all but the last (sixth) moveable spine was eliminated. The results of injuries (or genetically caused anomalies) carry on in successive growth stages.

Measurement of incremental growth, the difference in dimensions between a postmolt animal and its exuvia, and the measurement of a large number of specimens have provided information on the increase of size at each molt (Fig. 19) and the number of life cycle stages. The best series of exuviae on record comes from the growth stages of a female horseshoe crab, obtained from the Woods Hole Marine Biological Laboratory and raised in an aquarium for 8 years. It was possible to study this excellent series of casts in 1950 through the courtesy of Mrs. Margaret Houck, Curator of Museum, Zoology Department, Wellesley College, Massachusetts.

Figure 19A features the size increases in the Wellesley specimen through eight stages (IX and XI–XVII) [from 127]. Data from the growth stages of other specimens have been added, from a study of other immature Limuli from the Cape Cod area, to complete the possible number of stages. The width (PW) and the length of the prosoma (PL) have been plotted against the circumference of the prosoma (PC) for each stage (see Fig. 12).

Except for the earliest stages (embryos through stage II), a straight-line relationship exists between the dimensions of the major external parts of the body [127]. The mathematical expression of this linear relationship between PL and PC is given in the equation $y = 3.25x^{0.61}$ (Figure 19B), where y = PL and x = PC. Throughout life, at least in the premolt phase, the ratio between the body

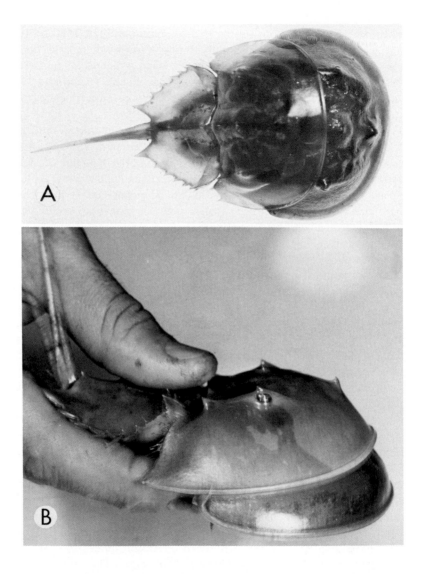

Fig. 17. A) A young animal emerging from its old exoskeleton (PW = 28.5 mm; it reached a new PW of 34 mm) has the consistency and feel of foam rubber [from 123, 129]. The exuvia is straw color and is nearly transparent. B) The molting animal is usually quiet, but it can be provoked into action, seen here as blurs around the rim of the exoskeleton and the upward-thrusting telson [from 128, 129]. Unlike Crustacea, which are virtually immobile when newly molted, Limuli are able to move about if disturbed, even when only partially emerged. The exuvia of this animal had a PW of 87 mm; the emerged animal, 108 mm.

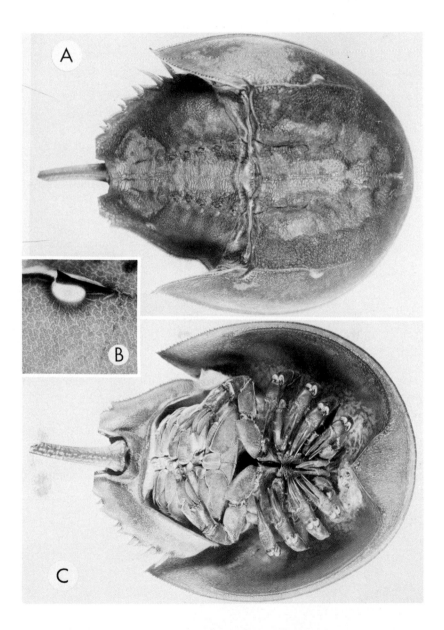

Fig. 18.   The dorsum (A) and ventrum (C) of a "wrinkled" adult female from Barnstable Harbor, Massachusetts (prosomal width = 209 mm). B) The lateral face of the prosoma, back-lit view of an exuvia, shows the pattern of folding in the previous, premolt integument. The light, zigzag lines were the creases; upon molting the new integument unfolds [123, 134].

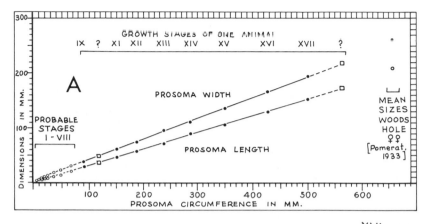

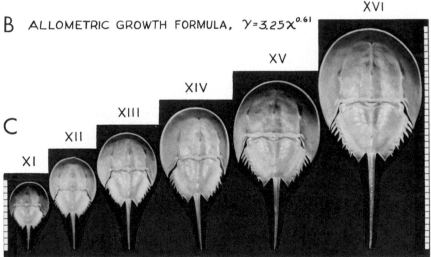

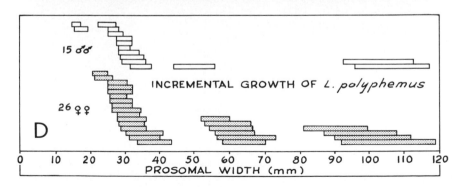

Fig. 19.   Growth stages of female horseshoe crabs (A–C: see text for details) and premolt/postmolt incremental data (D) from specimens collected in Barnstable Harbor, Cape Cod, Massachusetts, in 1949.

weight (in g) and the body volume (in ml) approximates 1. Composite estimates for a representative adult female from Delaware Bay [133] is PW = 28.0 cm; total weight = 3,000 g; total volume = 3,200 ml; blood volume (bled volume, hemolymph and amebocytes) = 300 ml; volume of mature eggs = 500 ml; and, the number of mature eggs = 88,000; and, there are about 1,550 gill lamellae with a total surface area of 11,600 sq cm.

Figure 19C shows six exuviae, stages XI–XVI, from the Wellesley series [123]. The vertical margins of this picture are ruled in 1-centimeter units. The amount of reduction of this picture renders a most interesting anomaly almost invisible. But there is an extra crescentic bay (cf Fig. 9B) in all of these casts, between the fifth and sixth moveable spines on the left side of the opisthosoma (see [92] for a study of another series of exuviae).

The most data thus far obtained on the growth stages within one population of L. polyphemus has come from an analysis of specimens collected in Pleasant Bay, with some specimens from neighboring bays, on Cape Cod, Massachusetts [127]. Exclusive of the incremental data (shown in Fig. 19D), a total of 1,246 immature and 403 adult Limuli were measured. The prosomal widths of the early stages (up to PW = 75 mm) and adults, when plotted on graphs, clearly showed size distribution for several growth stages. So few immature animals larger than PW = 75 mm were obtained (13 males and 22 females); however, that information on those growth stages could not be extracted. Of 617 unsexed juveniles (not sexed owing to their small size), 295 immature males, and 299 immature females, prominent peaks (of 18 or more specimens) in size occurred at the following widths: PW = 12, 16, 22, and 11 (unsexed), and at 53 for both immature males and females. This information was used to help derive Figure 19A.

The 115 adult females ranged in size (PW) from 186 to 272 mm, with a mean of 220 mm and a standard deviation of 16; two standard errors of the mean = 3.0. The 288 adult males ranged from 137 to 222 mm (PW), with a mean of 166 mm, SD of 12, and two SD mean = 1.4.

A comparison of three subsets of the adult males indicated that they did not molt after reaching maturity [127]:

"Age" of adult males	Number of specimens	Prosomal width (mm)	
		Range	Mean
"Virgin"*	22	148–184	166
"Middle-aged"*	195	137–222	167
"Old"**	71	137–213	169
All "Ages"	288	137–222	168

*Living specimens collected from the tidal flats just south of Hog Island, Pleasant Bay (July 10, 11, and 14, 1953) in shallow water during the early flood of the tide.
**Dead specimens collected from beach wrack on the western and southern shores of Hog Island.

BEHAVIOR AND ORIENTATION
Locomotor Activities

A review of the neuromuscular basis for locomotor movements [92–96] is found in references [52] and [163]: The animal's burrowing activities are described in [21, 23, 95, 154]. When the animal is on the sea bottom, water is pumped through the channel between the prosoma and opisthosoma and expelled from the terminal bay (ie, on either side of the telson, between the posterior projections of the opisthosoma; flabellum prevents back-flushing of water during expulsion; dorsal setae, distributed on the margins of the carapace, are mechanoreceptors that aid in keeping the animal buried [11].

In gill ventilation normal, metachronal respiratory movements are at a frequency of about 35 per minute in air-saturated water [159]. It varies proportionally to the ambient-oxygen content, ceasing in an anoxic environment, but responding immediately to the reintroduction of oxygen [75, 159, 160, 164]. In other cases ([47] and Dr. Charlotte P. Mangum, College of William and Mary, Williamsburg, Virginia; personal communication, 1981) L. polyphemus hyperventilates at low oxygen pressures.

Swimming, probably the most complex of the locomotor activities of Limuli, is described in [23, 49, 93, 154]; walking, a metachronal promotor-remotor swing, in [67] (esp. pp 49–51, 90–94, 140–143, and 461–465) and [94]; and righting movements are described in [95] and [154]. The position and density of mechanoreceptors, spines in pits, on sharp ridges and on the margin of the dorsal carapace suggest their role in directing locomotor activities and in sensing solid objects in the animal's path [48].

Temperature and light studies along the northern Gulf coast of Florida have revealed interesting behavioral patterns in Limuli, during retreat of adults released in the breeding season, and in the activity of the larvae in the nests and aquaria. Juveniles characteristically inhabit intertidal and shallow waters in areas associated with tidal marshes, and are usually near breeding beaches [127, 131]. Their activity patterns are diurnal and responsive to changes in water depth. Generally they are more active on an ebbing tide in the 2–3-hour period just before low tide [102]. Under experimental conditions, during 3-day trials in electric shuttle boxes, juveniles were four times as active at night as during the day [16]. They were also nocturnal in studies on locomotor activity and behavior [154]. Measurement of the final distribution of eight to ten Limuli after seven releases, four off the beach at Mashes Sands (Wakulla County, Florida) and three off St. James Beach (Franklin County, Florida), showed a close correlation to the direction of the wave surge [105]. Only on one release did the animals head away from the direction of the surge; all the rest, moving almost directly into the wave surge, headed for deeper water. In one release at Mashes Sands, even when each of the eyes of the animals had been painted over to block out the light, these animals also oriented into the wave surge [105]. In the absence of a wave surge, the Limuli displayed no preferred direction of movement [105]. Under surge-free conditions in a shallow cove near Woods Hole, Massachusetts, covering the eyes produced changes in orientation [39]: "Blindfolded" Limuli tended to travel parallel to the shoreline, remaining in the cove, whereas normal Limuli traveled out of the cove in approximately straight lines.

In nests where the larvae have hatched but have not yet been liberated from the beach, the small animals, reacting together apparently to a mutual urge, change their depth in the beach in relation to the time of high tides [104]. During nights of full moon the larvae ("nests") moved up to the surface of the beach by the peak of the high tide. There was less activity during nights of the new moon, and the movement of the nests to the surface did not occur. The mean depth of newly laid nests was 14.6 ± 1.9 cm [104]. The mean depth of larval nests at the hour of high tide was different at each lunar phase [103].

The swimming activity of larvae has been reported previously [26, 61, 77], but not quantitatively studied until recently [104]. It was markedly different during three separate combinations of temperature and light conditions in the laboratory [104]. In all three combinations the larvae were most active at night. Even in constant temperature and light the activity of 1,000 larvae steadily declined for 5 days, but swimming resumed immediately when the light was turned off for 5 minutes at 0100 hour. The percent swimming activity of 1,000 larvae under ambient conditions was much less than that of 500 larvae in constant darkness. Hourly observations were made of swimming larvae [104].

Salinity Studies

While Limuli are most often found in the more saline portions of estuaries (and on the continental shelf), they have euryhaline tendencies—a tendency that deserves more research attention. Small Limuli, some 60 mm in prosomal width, have survived an experimental period of 2–3 weeks in seawater diluted from 30 to 32 ppt down to about 8 ppt; lower salinities were lethal (26 hours in about 4 ppt and 2 hours in freshwater [78]). This tolerance to low salinities [78] is apparently normal in immature Limuli although slower growth has been demonstrated during the first four stages (stadia), after hatching of the larvae, at the lower salinities (Jegla and Costlow, in this book) as well as a decrease in the respiratory rate of the first-tailed stage [56]. The respiration rates of developing eggs and first three stadia of L. polyphemus decreased with decreasing salinity and temperature. When the animals were also exposed to No. 2 fuel oil, respiration rates were significantly higher at all salinity/temperature combinations than in control animals [56].

Except in certain populations (discussed further on), adult Limuli, at least under laboratory conditions [65], have not adapted and have succumbed to lowered salinities. The net result of the respiratory response to low salinity is a stability of aerobic metabolism [65]. The rate of oxygen consumption in L.

polyphemus is inversely related to body weight, regardless of salinity, with smaller animals having a greater oxygen consumption than larger ones [65]. When tested separately, each decrease in environmental variables (temperature, salinity, and oxygen tension) causes a decrease in heart rate (beats/minute) [18]. Oxygen-sensitive units have been demonstrated in the prosomal haemal nerve [149].

The most renowned low-salinity environment inhabited by L. polyphemus [12, 127], the Miles River area of the upper Chesapeake Bay, has had a salinity range from 10 to 18 ppt, with an average of about 13 ppt (Dr. Donald W. Pritchard, Chesapeake Bay Institute, Johns Hopkins University, Maryland; personal communication, 1953). In another habitat area, the upper portion of Plum Island Sound, Massachusetts, there are insufficient salinity data to describe the prevailing conditions adequately; but it appears that the salinity varies widely both seasonally and tidally, with salinities as low as 9 ppt and as high as 29 ppt [8]. Although it has not been demonstrated that the smaller-than-expected animals from these two regions (see MLR and PIS, respectively, on Fig. 4) are due to the lower salinities of their habitats, in comparison to neighboring populations, it is hard to avoid the speculation. Usually a bottom salinity from 18.4 to 30.6 ppt, as in the Ashepoo River and St. Helena Sound, South Carolina (G. Robert Lunz, Bears Bluff Laboratories, Wadmalaw Island, South Carolina; personal communication, 1953) is the expected range along the Atlantic coast.

The blood of L. polyphemus is isosmotic or slightly hypotonic at the higher salinities and hyperosmotic in low salinities [17, 65, 98]. Generally, the ability of adult Limuli to adapt to changes in salinity and to oxygen tension is due to counterbalancing reactions. The oxygen affinity of the hemocyanin is raised by the decrease of the chloride ion in low salinity [65]. A relatively low blood pH also contributes to a higher oxygen affinity as there is a reverse Bohr shift throughout the physiological pH range (6.5 to 8.0) [64]. Even when Limuli are exposed to air, there are balancing functions [66]; for hemocyanin transports less than half of the oxygen consumed in water but almost 90% in air. Half of this increase in hemocyanin function during exposure to air is due to the reverse Bohr effect.

These mechanisms and reactions enable L. polyphemus, in its normal activities, to survive environments and situations where oxygen tension may be low or ventiliation of the book gills hampered [66], as in intertidal and subtidal feeding or "resting" when partially buried (see Fig. 21A, B); spawning, where the mated pair is partially buried, particularly the female (see Fig. 16A, B); and, hypoxic waters on the continental shelf (see Fig. 15)A).

FOOD AND FEEDING

Histologically, the digestive tract of L. polyphemus does not complete differentiation until the premolt larval stage is reached (see Fig. 22A). Although the natural diet of the first-tailed stage (Fig. 22B) is not known, it has been fed a variety of organic matter and organisms in the laboratory; bits of Mytilus, Nereis, frozen brine shrimp, marine nematodes, small whole polychaetes, and the alga, Enteromorpha [25]. Of these, small living polychaetes are eaten most readily.

The diet of the larger immature Limuli and the adults includes several bivalve mollusks, such as Mya [63, 136, 138, 151], Macoma, Gemma, Spisul–a, Ensis, and Mytilus [121] (see Figs. 20A and B—BM; and 22—MO); and "worms"— Cerebratulus, Nereis, and Cistenides, [121] (see Fig. 22-WM). In one study, an immature L. polyphemus (PW = 78 mm) presumably ingested 99 Mya (average length of 12 mm) during a 72-hour period [151]. In its natural environment, it can locate this softshell clam [137] (see Fig. 21).

L. polyphemus digs after its food, grasping the prey with its pincer-tipped legs. The prey is moved to the gnathobases where crushing occurs between the gnathobase of the sixth pair of "pusher" legs and is then mauled and pushed forward toward and into the mouth. The bases of the five locomotor legs, covered with bristles and spines, are crowded together, resulting in the "slipping-sliding-chewing" motion that has two components. In a metachronal locomotor movement the second and fourth pairs of legs and the third and fifth move in unison, alternately, while a "biting" motion occurs at right angles. The chilaria (CM Fig. 20) push the food forward and the chelicera (CH, Fig. 20) push it backward. Endites on three pairs of legs point toward the mouth. Feeding has been described by several authors [67, 96, 163]. Contact chemoreceptors are located on the coxal gnathobases, or their spines, of the first four pairs of walking legs [9, 10].

Figure 22C shows a simplified food web for Delaware Bay and several predator-prey relationships involving the horseshoe crab. The arrows point to the consumers. The asterisk represents predation by birds and mammals (including scientific and commercial uses by man). Mollusks and worms are prevalent in the diet of Limuli; their eggs are eaten by shrimp, and the eggs, embryos, and larvae by a number of species of small fishes (and the young of larger species) and by shore birds.

SYMBIOTIC AND OTHER RELATIONSHIPS
Ectocommensals

The carapace of Limuli, particularly adults, is a suitable habitat for a number of species; so much so that L. polyphemus has been described as a "walking museum" [1]. Most of the organisms attached to Limuli attach to several other kinds of hard surfaces. There is also a sort of phoresis wherein certain gastropods (oyster drills, Urosalpinx cinerea and Eupleura caudata), as observed in New Haven Harbor on Long Island Sound [62], may be transported and in the example

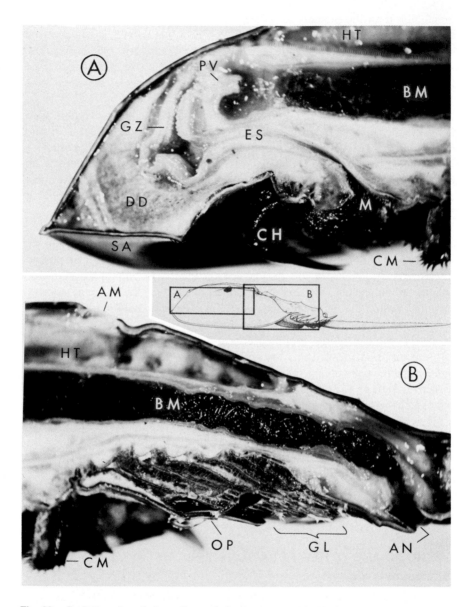

Fig. 20. Sagittal section of a horseshoe crab that has engorged itself on small blue mussels (BM), Mytilus edulis (5–7 mm to length). In the posterior portion of the tubular heart (HT) in B, note the five circular opening of the branchiocardia canals. Other abbreviations are AM, arthrodial membrane between prosoma and opisthosoma; AN, anus; CH, chelicerum; CM, chilarium; DD, digestive diverticulae ("liver"); ES, esophagus; GL, gill books (branchial appendages); GZ, gizzard (crop, proventriculus); M, mouth; OP, operculum (note that the distal portion is twisted over the branchiae); PV, pyloric (stomodaeal) valve; SA, subfrontal area. (See also Fig. 10A).

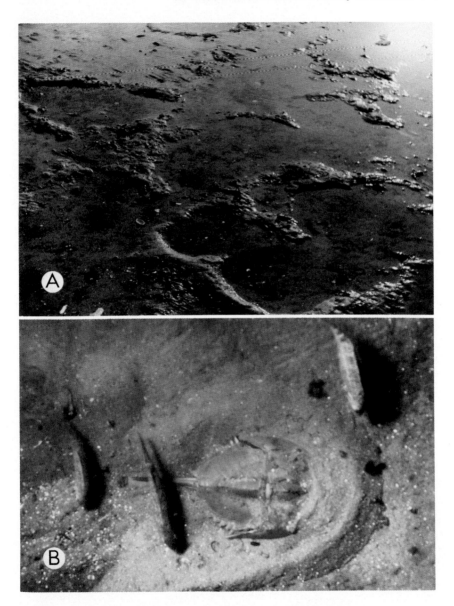

Fig. 21.   A) Typical excavations made by adult Limuli on an intertidal flat, as revealed during low tide and highlighted by a late afternoon sun; Barnstable Harbor, Massachusetts (photograph by author). These characteristic "puddles" are a telltale evidence of previous activity by horseshoe crabs, whether feeding or just digging in to wait out a low-tide period. B). Fish feeding on worms and sand shrimp dug up by a horseshoe crab (photograph by Bradford Luther Jr., Fairhaven, Massachusetts, taken with a flash camera at a 35-foot depth in Cape Cod Bay, Massachusetts; from collection of Col. Eugene S. Clark Jr., Sandwich, Massachusetts; personal communication, 1963).

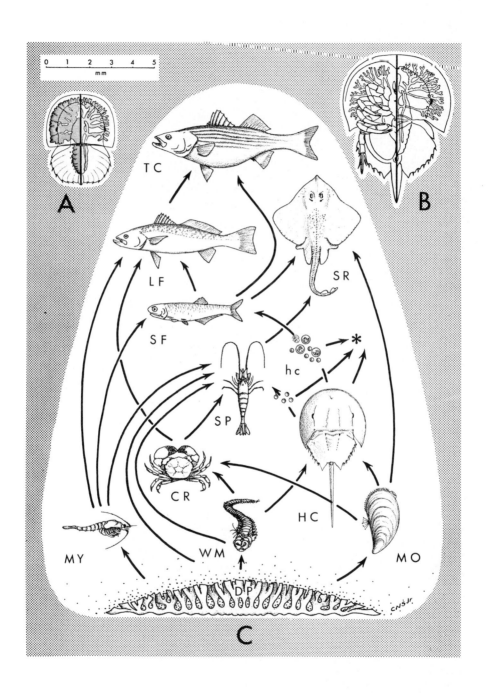

of an accidental clamping of a bivalve mollusk (Mercenaria mercenaria) on the claws (presumably when the horseshoe crab was moving over a hard clam bed or digging for food [127]).

The frequency of molting is probably a deterent to sustained attachment of ectocommensals. Thus attachment is most noticeable on Limuli larvae, because even small epiphytes are large in comparison, and is most prevalent on adult Limuli because they do not molt as frequently if at all (particularly the males [127]) permitting continued individual growth as well as population development of the attached organisms.

Several species of algae and protozoa attach to Limuli. Gorham [28] found larvae covered with the diatom, Rhabdonema adriaticum. Green algae are generally found in association with attached animals such as mussels; a colonial peritrich, Zoothamnium elegans (sp. ?) was found attached to the gnathobases (Professor Faure-Fermiet, visiting researcher at the Marine Biological Laboratory, Woods Hole, Massachusetts; personal communication, 1950); a folliculinid, Folliculina sp., was attached to the margin of egg capsules of the triclad turbellarian, Bdelloura sp., found on the lamellae (branchiae) of the branchial appendages [2].

Other organisms that develop commensal relationships with Limulus include the following: coelenterates [1], Hydractinia echinata, Podocoryne carnea, Obelia sp?, Metridium dianthus, and Sargartia luciae; triclad turbellarians [152, 153], Bdelloura candida [79, 80, 81], B. propinqua [1], Syncoelidium pellucidum [161] (see also Parasites following); bryozoans, Schizoporella sp? [1], S. unicornis [79], Membranipora sp? [1], M. crustulenta, Bugula turrita [1]; annelida [1, 79], Eupomatus dianthus; mollusks, Urosalpinx cinereus [62, 79], Eupleura caudata [62], Anomia ephippium [1], A. simplex [79], Modiolus modiolus, Mytilus edulis (see Fig. 23B), Acemea sp? [1], Crepidula plana [1, 79], C. fornicata [1, 79, 81], C. convexa [1], Crassostrea virginica [165]; barnacles [1],

---

Fig. 22. Representative levels in this simplified food web (C) are as follows: primary productivity, DP = organic detritus and plant life; consumers, MY = mysid shrimp, WM = detritus feeding worms, MO = mollusks, including the blue mussel (shown) and gem shells; carnivores, CR = crabs (mud crab shown), HC = horseshoe crab, its early developmental stages (hc = eggs, embryos, and larvae), SP = shrimp, including the sand shrimp (shown), SF = small fishes, including the anchovy (shown), LF = large fishes, including the weakfish (shown), SR = skates and rays, including the clearnose skate (shown), TC = top carnivores, including the striped bass (shown). [Modified from 87.] The marginal insets show the location and shape (shaded areas) of the digestive tract of early stages of L. polyphemus (the scale line is in millimeters; from [120]): A) Divided drawing of the larval stage, depicting changes in the lobed structure of the digestive tract during early (left half) and later (right) development. This is the "trilobite" larva, seen also in the food web (hc—the upper left specimen). B) The first-tailed stage, showing the ventral appendages, pushed sideways to show the position of the mouth (left half) and the digestive tract from the dorsal view (right).

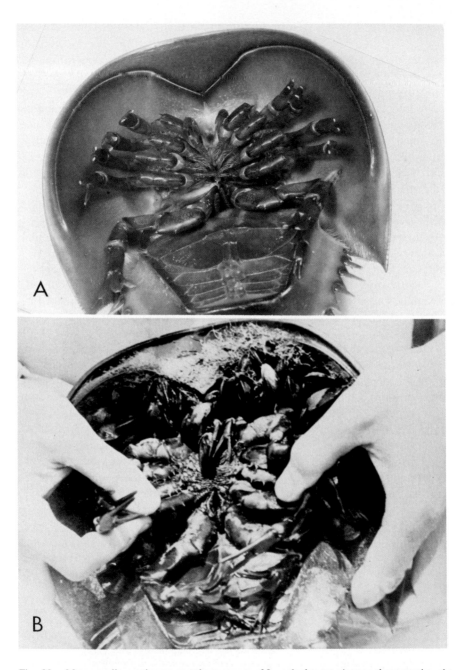

Fig. 23.   Many sessile species encrust the carapace of L. polyphemus. Among these species, the blue mussel, Mytilus edulis, may be very harmful if it attaches to the ventral surface. A) Immature animals shed their carapace at least annually and do not become encrusted, thus the "clean" ventrum (PW = 12 cm). B) Adult male from Delaware Bay, Cape May, New Jersey; PW = 21 cm. Movement of its locomotor, feeding, and respiratory appendages was severely hampered by the growth of some two dozen blue mussels (each about 30 mm in length). Byssal threads covered the subfrontal area, and bryozoa encrusted the bases of the legs; specimen collected in 1951.

Balanus balanoides [1], B. eburneus [1], B. amphitrite niveus [79], Chelonibia patula [79]; and tunicates [1], Amaroecium constellatum, Didemnum lutarium.

Community Associations

A differential in aggregation of meiofauna was associated with L. polyphemus nests on the beach at Roosevelt Inlet at Lewes, Delaware, during the summer of 1974 [38]. Populations of nematodes, gastrotrichs, oligochaetes, and rotifers increased in the proximity of the nests as the eggs developed.

Small egg clusters of striped killifish (Fundulus majalis) are occasionally found associated with Limuli nests [35]. Since this fish is also a predator on the eggs and larvae of Limuli [19, 68] this raises the question of whether it spawns and feeds during the same or different tides coincident with the spawning of Limuli.

L. polyphemus was a permanent influent in two communities at Cape Ann, Massachusetts: a subtidal bottom community (Laminaria-Cancer faciation) and a tidal sediment community (Mya-Nereis pelagica biome) [20].

Diseases

Occurrence and cause of disease in Limuli have not been fully studied. However, fairly recently, the susceptibility of L. polyphemus to disease was demonstrated [5]. Earlier, probably partly because of the generally observed lack of putrefaction of stored, unpreserved blood and the presumed bactericidal effect of the copper in the blood, little attention was given to the possibility of bacterial infections.

Laboratory-reared larvae and juveniles developed an unidentified filamentous growth on gill plates and legs. Treatment with malachite green was particularly effective in the presence of sand. The most effective cure for the infestation seems to have been molting in sand [25]. Algal growth on carapace and gills of larvae during an aquaculture experiment in Israel limited survival of the young Limuli [54].

Moribund and recently dead Limuli were found frequently with thick layers of bacteria on the surface of their gill leaflets, and in others the gill leaflets were dilated ("ballooned") [6]; dilated gill leaflets have been seen on numerous Limuli during mass mortalities at Slaughter Beach, Delaware in 1977 [133] (see Fig. 24B). Badly eroded branchial appendages and gill leaflets are often seen in association with ectocommensals that cover the ventral surfaces of Limuli (as by Mytilus, see Fig. 23B, and the triclad tubellarian, Bdelloura). Whether the ectocommensals cause the erosion or arrive afterwards, occupying the eroded area, is not known.

Entrance of pathogens through the carapace may be aided, in addition to physical erosion of the shell, by the activity of chitinoclastic marine bacteria (that attack the exuviae, at least, of L. polyphemus [37]) and the fungus, Ma-

Fig. 24. A) Limuli ready for the fertilizer factory (June 1924). B) Massive kill of Limuli, June 1979; cause is unknown. Both photographs are of Delaware beaches.

crocystis, that grows in the chitin of L. polyphemus [76]. There is also evidence of internal pathogenic growth of chitin [34].

Immunity/Defense Mechanisms

A glycoprotein exudate, produced by hypodermal glands and secreted through the carapace [76], serves as a mechanical barrier to pathogens owing to its viscosity and agglutinating properties [140]. Mucus secretion may aid also in the burrowing of juvenile Limuli (the early ontogenetic stages) [11].

Erosion of the carapace and other injuries expose the tissues to omnipresent gram-negative endotoxins. Reactions to endotoxin, tested by injections into the tissues [5], are a change in the shape of amebocytes, sticking of the blood cells to the sides of vascular channels, and finally the gelation of the blood [6]. Cultured blood cells of L. polyphemus phagocytose particles if bacterial endotoxins are absent; endotoxin immobilizes amebocytes and causes formation of extracellular gel that prevents cell-particle contact [4].

Parasites

The distinction between cases of parasitism and ectocommensalism has not always been made in studies on Limuli. Here the triclad, Bdelloura, has been included above with other ectocommensals; it has been categorized also as a parasite [107, 152].

In 1950, while studying the compound eye of L. polyphemus obtained from Pleasant Bay, Orleans, Massachusetts, Dr. Talbot H. Waterman discovered a previously undescribed internal parasite that produced intense and massive infections, with encysted metacercariae distributed throughout the body, even in interommatidial spaces [145]. The identity and life history of this, a digenetic trematode, Microphallus limuli, have been completely described [146, 147]. Sporocysts and cercaria were found in the snail Hydrobia minuta [144], and metacercaria were found in all stages of L. polyphemus (larvae to adults) [147]. Experimentally, the worms matured in the herring gull, Larus argentatus [146].

Predators

Unidentified species of nematodes (Cape May, New Jersey, 1951) and oligochaetes (Cape May, New Jersey, 1951, 1954), and maggots of flies (Cape May, New Jersey, 1951; and Miles River area, Maryland, 1953) abounded in "old" horseshoe crab nests, apparently feeding upon egg membranes as well as larval Limuli. The fly larvae were found only in the nests located in the upper reaches of the tide; the "worms" were not so limited in their distribution. Such nests contain greenish-yellow and brownish debris, giving an appearance and coloration entirely different from younger nests [127]. Predation may not be involved in the case of the "worms" [38].

As many as eight Melongena, mollusks, have been seen devouring one living horseshoe crab [83].

Several crustacean species prey upon L. polyphemus. Amphipods ate larvae during aquaculture experiments in Israel [54]. The sand shrimp, Crangon septemspinosa, in the shore zone of the Delaware Bay, feed upon horseshoe crab eggs [87, 88] (see Fig. 22—SP). In 1953, unidentified species of fiddler crabs that scurried over the the tidal flats at Beaufort, North Carolina, were feeding on the first- and second tailed stages of L. polyphemus [127]. In 1949 and 1950, at Barnstable Harbor, Massachusetts, the blue crab, Callinectes sapidus, the green crab, Carcinides maenus, and an unidentified species of spider crab, Libinia sp., were observed to attack immature Limuli, especially while the latter were molting [127].

In the tidal streams [19, 68] and shore zone [19] of the Delaware River estuary, horseshoe crab eggs are a preferred food item during May through August of striped bass, Morone saxatilis, and white perch, Morone americana. Eggs and larvae were also eaten by the American eel, Anguilla rostrata; striped killifish, Fundulus majalis; silver perch, Bairdiella chrysura; weakfish, Cynoscion regalis; northern kingfish, Menticirrhus saxatilis; Atlantic silverside, Menidia menidia; summer flounder, Paralichthys dentatus; and winter flounder, Pseudopleuronectes americanus [19] (see Fig. 22).

In southern Florida waters over a bushel of adult crabs was found in the stomach of a large leopard shark, Triakis semifasciata, caught some distance offshore (Kirk, personal communication, 1953).

Other aquatic animals that prey upon Limulus are listed below. Eels [155] worked their way along side spawning Limuli, apparently feeding on the eggs on the shore of the Kickemuit River, Rhode Island. In April, 1930, catfish [82], by the hundreds, surrounded Limuli spawning on a sandy flat near the mouth of the Caloosahatchee River, Florida, "voraciously and joyously" devouring the eggs as fast as they were laid. Puffers (Tetraodontidae), in an aquarium with several invertebrate species, attacked the undersides of half-grown L. polyphemus, biting off their legs [127]. Teale [148] records attacks by the devil ray, Mobula hypostoma, and swordfish (Xiphiidae). At Ochlockonee Point, Florida, large schools of an unidentified mullet (Mugilidae), and along the shores of Raritan and Delaware Bays, New Jersey, unidentified species of killifishes (Cyprinodontidae), were observed in 1953 feeding upon eggs and larvae of L. polyphemus washed from the beaches during high tide [127].

On Cape May shore of Delaware Bay, New Jersey, several species of bird were seen feeding upon Limulus eggs in the beach nests during the period of bird migrations in May, 1948 (Capt. Harold N. Gibbs, Barrington, Rhode Island; personal communication, 1953): semipalmated plover, Charadrius semipalmatus; black-bellied plover, Pluvialis squatarola; knot, Calidris sp?; pectoral sandpiper, Calidris melanotos; least sandpiper, Calidris minutilla; red back sandpiper; semipalmated sandpiper, Calidris pusilla; dowitcher, Limnodromus sp?; sanderling, Calidris alba; turnstone, Arenaria sp?; and laughing gull, Larus atricilla.

Boat-tailed grackles, Cassidix major, also have been observed eating the eggs of horseshoe crabs [99]. Sea gulls will attack overturned, adult Limuli on the beach or pull them from a tidal flat and tear at their soft undersides and rip them open [27].

Man may also be considered a predator of Limulus. Figure 24A shows stacks of Limuli near Bowers Beach, Delaware, June 1924, awaiting transport to a mill to be gound for fertilizer (photograph courtesy of the Delaware State Archives, Leon de Valinger Jr., State Archivist; 1958). Even larger quantitites of Limuli were taken on the Cape May side of the bay. For over 25 years horseshoe crab meal, "one of the finest nitrogenous organic materials available," was used in plant foods and soil conditioners (H. G. Sanders, President, Espoma Company, Millville, New Jersey; personal communications, 1958). In addition to the nitrogen content (10–11%), the horseshoe crab meal contains calcium, magnesium, iron, copper, manganese, boron, sulphur, molybdenum, zinc, and iodine.

The Delaware Bay population of horseshoe crabs has endured massive mortalities at different times at least during the past 100 years. In June 1979, an extensive windrow of dead and dying Limuli piled up along the shoreline on the upper portion of the beach, from just south of the Mispillion River inlet to Slaughters Beach, Delaware (Fig. 24B) (photo by author). The cause of death was not determined, but the immediate offshore area was covered deeply with a "soupy" mix of very fine sediment particles. It was firm enough to support shore birds and Limuli, but quicksand for a person. Many of the dead Limuli had the ballooned bookgill condition that has been associated with disease [6].

A key factor in the survival of Limulus may be the continued existence of extensive and unspoiled habitats where breeding and the development of the young occur with relatively little or no disturbance from man.

ACKNOWLEDGMENTS

Counsel and encouragement during my initial research on Limulidae by Drs. Thurlow C. Nelson and William C. Cole at Rutgers, The State University of New Jersey, Harry A. Charipper, New York University, and Alfred C. Redfield, Woods Hole Oceanographic Institution, have been gratefully acknowledged previously [127, 128, 130]. This chapter is a result not only of their interest but also of fellow workers on Limulidae with whom I have enjoyed rapport over the years. To do them justice would overwhelm this space as they are among the many references cited in this chapter. But one example of cooperation is so outstanding it must be stated. My understanding of the Indo-Pacific species would not have been possible without the information and specimens provided by Dr. Koichi Sekiguchi and his associates at the University of Tsubuka, Japan.

I am particularly indebted to Dr. William J. Hargis for establishing an academic outlet for my work:
Virginia Institute of Marine Science
and School of Marine Science,
The College of William and Mary,
Gloucester Point, Virginia 23062
Contribution No. 1019, Virginia Institute of Marine Science.

REFERENCES

1. Allee, WC: Studies in marine ecology. II. An annotated catalog of the distribution of common invertebrates of the Woods Hole littoral. In library, Marine Biological Laboratory, Woods Hole, Massachusetts.
2. Andrews EA, Nelson TC: A folliculinid carried by Limulus. Anat Rec 84:495, 1942.
3. Annandale N: The habits of Indian king crabs. Rec Indian Mus 3:294–295, 1909.
4. Armstrong PB, Levin J: In vitro phagocytosis by Limulus blood cells. J Invert Pathol 34:145–151, 1979.
5. Bang FB: A bacterial disease of Limulus polyphemus. Johns Hopkins Hosp 98:325–351, 1956.
6. Bang FB: Ontogeny and phylogeny of response to gram-negative endotoxins among the marine invertebrates. In Cohen E et al (eds): "Biomedical Applications of the Horseshoe Crab (Limulidae). Progress in Clinical and Biological Research," Vol 29. New York: Alan R. Liss, 1979, pp 109–123.
7. Baptist JP: Record of a hermaphrodite horseshoe crab. Limulus polyphemus L. Breviora 14, 4 pp, 1953.
8. Baptist JP, Smith OR, Ropes JW: Migrations of the horseshoe crab, Limulus polyphemus, in Plum Island Sound, Massachusetts. US Dept Interior, Spec Sci Rept Fisher 220, 15 pp, 1957.
9. Barber SB: Chemoreception and proprioception in Limulus. J Exp Zool 131:51–73, 1956.
10. Barber SB, Hayes WF: Properties of Limulus chemoreceptors. Proc XVI Int Cong Zool (Washington, D.C.) pp 76–78, 1963.
11. Barthel KW: Limulus: A living fossil. Horseshoe crabs aid interpretation of an Upper Jurassic environment (Solnhofen). Die Naturwissenschaften 61:428–533, 1974.
12. Beamont B, Mansueti R: Distribution of horseshoe crabs in Chesapeake Bay mystifies experts. MD Tidewater News 12:1; 3–4, 1955.
13. Bennett DC, Pezella PD, Herman WS: A sexual mosaic with internal embryogenesis in the dioecious horseshoe crab, Limulus polyphemus. Bijdragen tot de Dierkunde 42:192, 1972.
14. Bolau H: Moult of Limulus polyphemus (Lat.) described. Verh Ver naturw Unterh Hamburg 1879:22–23, 1879.
15. Cary LR: A contribution to the fauna of the coast of Louisiana. Gulf Biologic Station (Cameron, LA) Bull 6:50–59, 1906.
16. Casterlin ME, Reynolds WW: Diel locomotor activity pattern of juvenile Limulus polyphemus. Rev Can Biol 38:43–44, 1979.
17. Cole WH: The composition of fluids and sera of some marine animals and of the sea water in which they live. J Gen Physiol 23:575–584, 1940.
18. DeFur PL, Mangum CP: The effects of environmental variables on the heart rates of invertebrates. Comp Biochem Physiol 62A:283–294, 1979.
19. deSylva DP, Kalber FA Jr, Shuster CN Jr: Fishes and ecological conditions in the shore zone of the Delaware River estuary, with notes on other species collected in deeper water. Univ Del Marine Labs Info Ser Publ 5, 170 pp, 1962.
20. Dexter RW: The marine communities of a tidal inlet at Cape Ann, Massachusetts: A study in bio-ecology. Ecol Monogr 17:263–294, 1947.
21. Eldredge N: Observations on burrowing behavior in Limulus polyphemus (Chelicerata, Merostomata), with implications on the functional anatomy of trilobites. Am Mus Novitates 2436, 17 pp, 1970.
22. Eldridge N: Revision of the suborder Synziphosurina (Chelicerata, Merostomata), with remarks on merostome phylogeny. Am Mus Novitates 2543, 41 pp, 1974.
23. Fisher DC: Swimming and burrowing in Limulus and Mesolimulus. In Martinsson (ed): "Evolution and Morphology of the Trilobita, Trilobitoidea and Merostomata. Fossils and Strata No. 4." Oslo: Universitetsforlaget, 1975, pp 281–290.

24. Fisher DC: Functional significance of spines in the Pennsylvania horseshoe crab, Euproops danae. Paleobiol 3:175–195, 1977.
25. French KA: Laboratory culture of embryonic and juvenile Limulus. In Cohen E et al (eds): "Biomedical Application of the Horseshoe Crab (Limulidae)." New York: Alan R. Liss, 1979, pp 61–71.
26. French KA, Dolinger S: Photopositive behavior of young Limulus. Biol Bull 155:437–438, 1978.
27. Ganaros AE: The ecology of Mya arenaria L. and Venus mercenaria L. in Maquoit Bay and Falls Cove. MSc Thesis, Rutgers University, New Brunswick, New Jersey, 88 pp, 1954.
28. Gorham FP: Report of the special commission for the investigation of the lobster and soft-shell clam. III. The causes of death in artificially reared lobster fry. US Comm Fish Fisheries Rep Comm 1903:175–193, 1904.
29. Goto S, Seitaro, Hattori O: Notes on the spawning habits and growth stages of the Japanese king crab. Congres Int Xe Zool (Budapest) Pt 2 Sect IV Arthropodes: 1147–1155, 1927.
30. Gravier C: Sur les caracteres sexuels secondaires des Limules. Compt Rend Acad Sci 189:1–14, 1929.
31. Gravier C: Révision de la collection des Limules du Muséem National d'Histoire Naturell. Bull Mus Natl Hist Nat Ser 2, 1:313–331, 1929.
32. Gravier C: Sur les malformations d l'appendice caudel chez les Limules. Bull Mus Natl Hist Nat Ser 2, 2:89–91, 1930.
33. Gudger EW: Horseshoe crabs with forked tails. Bull NY Zool Soc 38:170–173, 1935.
34. Hanström B: Über einen Fall von pathologischer Chitinbildung im Inneren des Körpers von Limulus polyphemus. Zool Anzeiger 66:213–219, 1926.
35. Hardy JD Jr: "Development of Fishes of the Mid-Atlantic Bight. An Atlas of Egg, Larval and Juvenile Stages." Vol II. Washington, D.C.: US Fish and Wildlife Service (FWS/OBS-78/12), US Government Printing Office, 1978, pp 186–195.
36. Henriksen KL: The manner of moulting in Arthropoda. Notul ent Helsingfors 11:103–127, 1931.
37. Hock CW: Decomposition of chitin by marine bacteria. Biol Bull 79:199–206, 1940.
38. Hummon WD, Fleeger JW, Hummon MR: Meiofaunamacrofauna interactions. I. Sand beach meiofauna affected by maturing Limulus eggs. Ches Sci 17:297–299, 1976.
39. Ireland LC, Barlow RB Jr: Tracking normal and blindfolded Limulus in the ocean by means of acoustic telemetry. Biol Bull 155:445–446, 1978.
40. Ives JE: Crustacea from the northern coast of Yucatan, the harbor of Vera Cruz, the west coast of Florida and the Bermuda Islands. Proc Acad Nat Sci Phila 43:176–207, 1891.
41. Jackson RT: A new species of fossil Limulus from the Jurassic of Sweden. Arkiv f Zool 3(11):1–7, 1906.
42. Jegla TC: Development and molting physiology of horseshoe crab larvae. Am Zool 12:724, 1972.
43. Jegla TC, Costlow JD Jr: Induction of molting in horseshoe crab larvae by polyhydroxy steroids. Gen Comp Endocrinol 14:295–302, 1970.
44. Jegla TC, Costlow, JD: Ecdysteroids in Limulus larvae. Experientia 35:554–555, 1979.
45. Jegla TC, Costlow JD, Alspaugh J: Effects of ecdysones and some synthetic analogs on horseshoe crab larvae. Gen Comp Endocrinol 19:159–166, 1972.
46. Jegla TC, Costlow JD: The Limulus bioassay for ecdysteroids. Biol Bull 156:103–114, 1979.
47. Johansen K, Petersen JA: Respiratory adaptations in Limulus polyphemus (L). In Vernberg FJ (ed): "Physiological Ecology of Estuarine Organisms." Columbia: University of South Carolina Press, 1977, pp 129–145.
48. Kaplan E, Barlow RB Jr, Chamberlin SC, Stelzner DJ: Mechanoreceptors on the dorsal surface of Limulus. Brain Res 109:615–622, 1976.

49. Kingsley JS: The embryology of Limulus. J Morphol 7:35–66, 1892.
50. Kingsley JS: The embryology of Limulus, Pt 2. J Morphol 8.193–268, 1893.
51. Kishinouye E: On the development of Limulus longispina. J Coll Sci Imp Univ Jpn 5:53–100, 1892.
52. Knudsen EI: Muscular activity underlying ventilation and swimming in the horseshoe crab, Limulus polyphemus (Linnaeus). Biol Bull 144:355–367, 1973.
53. Koons BF: (1883). Sexual characters of Limulus. Amer Nat 17:1297–1299.
54. Kropach C: Observations on the potential of Limulus aquaculture in Israel. In Cohen E et al (eds): "Biomedical Applications of the Horseshoe Crab (Limulidae)." New York: Alan R. Liss, 1979, pp 103–106.
55. Lankester ER: Limulus an arachnid. Quart J Microsc Sci 21:504–548; 609–649, 1881.
56. Laughlin RB Jr, Neff JM: Interactive effects of temperature, salinity shock and chronic exposure to No. 2 fuel oil on survival, development rate and respiration of the horseshoe crab, Limulus polyphemus. In Wolfe DA (ed): "Fate and Effects of Petroleum Hydrocarbons in Marine Ecosystems and Organisms." New York: Pergamon Press, 1977, pp 182–191.
57. Laverock WS: On the casting of the shell in Limulus. Proc Trans Liverpool Biol Soc 41:13–16, 1927.
58. Levi-Seti R, Park DA, Winston R: The corneal cones of Limulus as optimized light concentrators. Nature 253:115–116, 1975.
59. Lockwood S: The horse foot crab. Am Nat 4:257–274, 1870.
60. Lockwood S: Moulting of Limulus. Am Nat 18:200–201, 1884.
61. Loeb J: Über künstliche umwandlung positiv heliotropischer Tiere in negativ heliotropishe und umgekehrt. Arch ges Physiol 54:81–107, 1893.
62. MacKenzie CL Jr: Transportation of oyster drill by horseshoe "crabs." Science 137:36–37, 1962.
63. MacKenzie CL Jr: Management for increasing clam abundance. Mar Fisher Rev Oct:10–22, 1979.
64. Mangum CP: Respiratory function of the hemocyanins. Am Zool 20:19–38, 1980.
65. Mangum CP, Booth CE, DeFur PL, Heckel NA, Henry RP, Oglesby LC, Polites C: The ionic environment of hemocyanin in Limulus polyphemus. Biol Bull 150:453–467, 1976.
66. Mangum CP, Freadman MA, Johansen K: The quantitative role of hemocyanin in aerobic respiration of Limulus polyphemus. J Exp Zool 19:279–285, 1975.
67. Manton SM: "The Arthropoda: Habits, Functional Morphology, and Evolution." Oxford: Clarendon Press, 1977, 527 pp.
68. Martin C: A biological, chemical, and physical survey of Delaware's tidal streams. Del Dept Nat Res Environ Control, Div Fish Wildl, Final Rept (Federal Aid in Fisher Restoration. F-22-R), 66 pp, 1974.
69. Meer Mohr JC van der: A note on two species of Malaysian king-crabs. Treubia 18:201–205, 1941.
70. Milne LJ, Milne MJ: Horseshoe crab—Is its luck running out? Fauna 9:66–72, 1947.
71. Nishii H (ed): "A Monograph on the Horseshoe Crab [in Japanese]." Published by Dr. Nishii (available from Educational Committee, Kasaoka City, Okayama Prefecture 714, Japan), 1975, 221 pp.
72. Oka H: Quelques observations dur le developpement de Limulus longispina. Proc Imp Acad Tokyo 11:450–452, 1935.
73. Okada A: On the chromosomes in the spermatogenesis of the king crab Tachypleus tridentata (Leach). J Sci Hirosima Univ, Ser B Div 1 (Zool) 6:37–52, 1938.
74. Packard AS Jr: Moulting of the shell in Limulus. Am Nat 17:1075–1076, 1883.
75. Page CH: Localization of Limulus polyphemus oxygen sensitivity. Biol Bull 144:383–390, 1973.
76. Patten W: "The Evolution of the Vertebrates and Their Kin." Philadelphia: P. Blakiston's Sons, 1912, 486 pp.

77. Pearl R: On the behavior and reactions of Limulus in early stages of its development. J Comp Neurol Psychol 14:138–164, 1904.
78. Pearse AS: On the ability of certain marine invertebrates to live in diluted sea water. Biol Bull 54:405–409, 1928.
79. Pearse AS: On the occurrence of ectoconsortes on marine animals at Beaufort, NC. J Parasitol 33:453–458, 1947.
80. Pearse AS: Observations on flatworms and nemerteans collected at Beaufort, NC. Proc US Natl Mus 100(3255):25–38, 1949.
81. Humm HJ, Wharton GW: Ecology of sand beaches at Beaufort, NC. Ecol Monogr 12:135–190, 1942.
82. Perry LM: Catfish feeding on the eggs of the horseshoe crab, Limulus polyphemus. Science 74:312, 1931.
83. Perry LM: Marine shells of the southwest coast of Florida. Bull Am Paleontol 26:1–260, 1940.
84. Pocock RI: The taxonomy of recent species of Limulus. Ann Mag Nat Hist 9:256–262, 1902.
85. Pollock LW, Hummon WD: Cyclic changes in interstitial water content, atmospheric exposure, and temperature in a marine beach. Limnol Oceanogr 16:522–535, 1971.
86. Pomerat CM: Mating in Limulus polyphemus. Biol Bull 64:243–252, 1933.
87. Price KS Jr: Sand shrimp, cross-link in an estuarine food web. Estuar Bull (Univ Del Mar Labs) 6(3/4):12–15, 1961.
88. Price KS Jr: Biology of the sand shrimp, Crangon septemspinosa, in the shore zone of the Delaware Bay region. Chesapeake Sci 3:244–255, 1962.
89. Purnell CH, Shevock RC, Shuster CN Jr: Biometric analysis of sexual dimorphism in Limulus polyphemus L., with particular reference to mated pairs. Univ Del Marine Labs, 1961.
90. Raw F: Origin of chelicerates. J Paleontol 31:139–192, 1957.
91. Reeside JB Jr, Harris DV: A cretaceous horseshoe crab from Colorado. J Wash Acad Sci 42:174–178, 1952.
92. Richter I-E: Beobachtungen bei der aufzucht von Limulus. Natur u Mus 95:1–7, 1965.
93. Richter I-E: Limulus polyphemus (Xiphosura) schwimmen. Encyclop Cinemat (Göttingen), Film E 1031/1966:237–240, 1968.
94. Richter I-E: Limulus polyphemus (Xiphosura) laufen. Encyclop Cinemat (Göttingen), Film E 1032/1966:241–247, 1968.
95. Richter I-E: Limulus polyphemus (Xiphosura) undrehen und eingraben. Encyclop Cinemat (Göttingen), Film E 1033/1966:249–254, 1968.
96. Richter I-E: Limulus polyphemus (Xiphosura) nahrungaufnahme. Encyclop Cinemat (Göttingen), Film E 1034/1966:255–258, 1968.
97. Riska B: Morphological variation in the horseshoe crab Limulus polyphemus. Evolution 35:647–658, 1981.
98. Robertson JD: Osmotic and ionic regulation in the horseshoe crab Limulus polyphemus (Linnaeus). Biol Bull 138:157–183, 1970.
99. Rood R: The crab that isn't. Audubon (May–June) 69:38-43, 1967.
100. Roonwal NL: Some observations on the breeding biology, and on the swelling, weight, water-content and embryonic movements in the developing eggs of the Moluccan king-crab, Tachypleus gigas (Müler), (Arthropoda, Xiphosura). Proc Ind Acad Sci Sec B, 20:115–129, 1944.
101. Ropes JW: Longevity of the horseshoe crab, Limulus polyphemus (L.). Trans Amer Fisher Soc 90:79–80, 1961.
102. Rudloe AE: Some ecologically significant aspects of the behavior of the horseshoe crab, Limulus polyphemus. PhD Diss., Florida State Univ, Tallahassee, 246 pp, 1978.
103. Rudloe AE: Limulus polyphemus: A review of the ecologically significant literature. In Cohen E et al (eds): "Biomedical Applications of the Horseshoe Crab (Limulidae)." New York: Alan R. Liss, 1979, pp 27–35.
104. Rudloe AE: Locomotor and sight responses of larvae of the horseshoe crab, Limulus polyphemus (L.). Biol Bull 157:494–505, 1979.

105. Rudloe AE, Herrnkind WF: Orientation of Limulus polyphemus in the vicinity of breeding beaches. Mar Behav Physiol 4:75–89, 1976.
106. Rudloe AE, Rudloe J: Horseshoe crabs, living fossils. Natl Geogr 159 (4):562–572, 1981.
107. Ryder JA: Observations on the species of planarians parasitic on Limulus. Am Nat 16:48–51, 1882.
108. Sanders HL: The cephalocarida and crustacean phylogeny. System Zool 6:112–128; 148, 1957.
109. Say T: An account of the crustacea of the United States. J Acad Sci Phil, II:423–458, 1818.
110. Sekiguchi K: On the embryonic moultings of the Japanese horse-shoe crab, Tachypleus tridentatus. Sci Rep Tokyo Kyoiku Daigaku, B, 14:121–128, 1970.
111. Sekiguchi K: A normal plate of the development of the Japanese horse-shoe crab, Tachypleus tridentatus. Sci Rep Tokyo Kyoiku Daigaku, B, 15:153–162, 1973.
112. Sekiguchi K, Nakamura K: Ecology of the extant horseshoe crabs. In Cohen E et al (eds): "Biomedical Applications of the Horseshoe Crab (Limulidae)." New York: Alan R. Liss, 1979, pp 37–45.
113. Sekiguchi K, Nakamura K, Sen TK, Sugita H: Morphological variation and distribution of a horseshoe crab, Tachypleus gigas, from the Bay of Bengal and the Gulf of Siam. Proc Jpn Soc System Zool 12:13–20, 1976.
114. Sekiguchi K, Nakamura K, Seshimo H: Morphological variation of a horseshoe crab, Carcinoscorpius rotundicauda, from the Bay of Bengal and the Gulf of Siam. Proc Jpn Soc System Zool 15:24–30, 1978.
115. Sekiguchi K, Nishiwaki S, Makioka T, Srithunya S, Machjajib S, Nakamura K, Yamasake T: A study of the egg-laying habits of the horseshoe crabs, Tachypleus gigas and Carcinoscorpius rotundicauda, in Chonburi area of Thailand. Proc Jpn Soc System Zool 13:39–45, 1977.
116. Sugita H: Systematics and hybridization in the four living species of horseshoe crabs. Evolution 34:712–718, 1980.
117. Selander RK, Yang SY, Lewontin RC, Johnson WE: Genetic variation in the horseshoe crab (Limulus polyphemus), a phylogenetic "relic." Evolution 24:402–414, 1970.
118. Shoji K: Morphological differences between the Japanese king crab, Limulus longispinus van der Hoeven, and its American ally, Limulus polyphemus Linnaeus. Dobutsugaku Zasshi 39:178–190, 1927.
119. Shoji K: Morphology and ecology of Japanese Limulus; and A historical review and the literature of the studies on Limulus (in Japanese). Fukuoka Hakub Zasshi 1:28–37; 38–52, 1932.
120. Shuster CN Jr: On the gross anatomy and histology of the alimentary tract in early developmental stages of Xiphosura (= Limulus) polyphemus Linn. MSc Thesis, Rutgers Univ, New Brunswick, New Jersey, 50 pp, 1948.
121. Shuster CN Jr: Observations on the natural history of the American horseshoe crab, Limulus polyphemus. Woods Hole Oceanogr Inst Contr 564:18–23, 1950.
122. Shuster CN Jr: Odyssey of the horseshoe "crab." Audubon 55:162–163; 167, 1953.
123. Shuster CN Jr: A horseshoe "crab" grows up. Ward's Nat Sci Bull 28:1–6, 1954.
124. Shuster CN Jr: A method for recording measurements of certain molluscs, arthropoda, and fishes. Prog Fish Culturist 16:39–40, 1954.
125. Shuster CN Jr: Horseshoe "crabs." Del Conserv 1:15, 1957.
126. Shuster CN Jr: Xiphosura (with especial reference to Limulus polyphemus). Geol Soc Am Mem 67, 1:1171–1174, 1957.
127. Shuster CN Jr: On morphometric and serological relationships within the Limulidae, with particular reference to Limulus polyphemus (L.). Diss Abst 18:371–372, 1958.
128. Shuster CN Jr: "Study these," the story of the horseshoe "crab." Staff Reporter (Wilmington Public Schools, DE) 10(8):2; 4–5, 1958.

129. Shuster CN Jr: Horseshoe "crabs"—In former years, during the month of May, these animals dominated Delaware Bay shores. Estuar Bull Univ Del Mar Labs 5(2):1–9, 1960.
130. Shuster CN Jr: Serological correspondence among horseshoe "crabs" (Limulidae). Zoologica 47:1–9, 1962.
131. Shuster CN Jr: Distribution of the American horseshoe "crab," Limulus polyphemus (L.) In Cohen E et al (eds): "Biomedical Application of the Horseshoe Crab (Limulidae)." New York: Alan R. Liss, 1979, pp 3–26.
132. Shuster CN Jr: Xiphosurida. In "Encyclopedia of Science and Technology", Vol 14. New York: McGraw Hill, pp 766–770, 1982.
133. Shuster CN Jr, Botton ML: An estimate of the 1977 spawning population of the horseshoe crab, Limulus polyphemus, in Delaware Bay. Submitted, 1979.
134. Shuster CN Jr, Horrell HC: Limulus exoskeleton as a teaching aid. Turtox News 44(1):40–41, 1966.
135. Smedley N: Malaysian king-crabs. Bull Raffles Mus (Singapore) 5:71–74, 1929.
136. Smith OR: Clam mortality in Massachusetts. Oyster Inst North Am 15:2, 1949.
137. Smith OR: Notes on the ability of the horseshoe crab, Limulus polyphemus, to locate soft-shell clams, Mya arenaria. Ecology 34:636–637, 1953.
138. Smith OR, Chin E: The effects of predation on soft clams, Mya arenaria. 1951 Conv Addresses, Natl Shellfisher Assoc, pp 37–44, 1953.
139. Sokoloff A: Observations on populations of the horseshoe crab Limulus (= Xiphosura) polyphemus. Res Population Ecol 19:222–236, 1978.
140. Stagner JI, Redmond JR: The immunological mechanisms of the horseshoe crab, Limulus polyphemus. Mar Fisher Rev 37(6/6):11–19, 1975.
141. Størmer L: On the relationships and phylogeny of fossil and recent Arachnomorpha. Skr Norske Vidensk Akad Oslo Matem-Naturvidenskap Kl, 1944(5), 158 pp, 1944.
142. Størmer L: Phylogeny and taxonomy of fossil horseshoe cabs. J Paleontol 26:630–640, 1952.
143. Størmer L: Merostomata. In Moore RC (ed): "Treatise on Invertebrate Paleontology" Pt. P Arthropoda. Univ Kansas Press 2, 1944, pp 4–41.
144. Stunkard HW: Microphallid metacercariae encysted in Limulus. Biol Bull 99: 347, 1950.
145. Stunkard HW: Observations on the morphology and life-history of Microphallus n. sp. (Trematoda: Microphallidae). Biol Bull 101:307–318, 1951.
146. Stunkard HW: Natural hosts of Microphallus limuli Stunkard. J Parasitol 39:225, 1953.
147. Stunkard HW: The asexual generations, life-cycle, and systematic relations of Microphallus limuli Stunkard, 1951 (Trematoda: Digenea). Biol Bull 134:332–343, 1968.
148. Teale EW: King crab—Modern creature of the past. Nat Hist 54:322–327, 1945.
149. Thompson C, Page CH: Nervous control of respiration: Oxygen-sensitive elements in the prosoma of Limulus polyphemus. J Exp Biol 62(3):545–554, 1975.
150. Tiegs OW, Manton SM: The evolution of the Arthropoda. Biol Rev 33:255–338, 1958.
151. Turner HJ Jr, Ayers JC, Wheeler CL: The horseshoe crab and boring snail as factors limiting the abundance of the soft-shell clam. Woods Hole Oceanogr Inst Contr 462:43–45, 1948.
152. Verrill AE: Marine planarians of New England. Trans CT Acad 8:459–520, 1893.
153. Verrill AE: Supplement to the marine nemerteans and planarians of New England. Trans CT Acad 9:141–152, 1895.
154. Vosatka ED: Observations on the swimming, righting, and burrowing movements of young horseshoe crabs, Limulus polyphemus. Ohio J Sci 70:276–283, 1970.
155. Warwell HC: Eels feeding on the eggs of Limulus. Am Nat 31:347–348, 1897.
156. Waterman TH: A light polarization analyzer in the compound eye of Limulus. Science 111:252–254, 1950.
157. Waterman TH: Xiphosura from Xuong-Ha. Am Sci 41:292–302, 1953.

158. Waterman TH: On the doubtful validity of Tachypleus hoeveni Pocock, an Indonesian horseshoe crab (Xiphosura). Postilla (Yale Peabody Mus) 36, 1958, 17 pp.
159. Waterman TH, Travis DF: Respiratory reflexes and the flabellum of Limulus. J Cell Comp Physiol 41:261–290, 1953.
160. Watson WH, Wyse GA: Coordination of the heart and gill rhythms in Limulus. J Comp Physiol 124:267–275, 1978.
161. Wheeler WM: Syncoelidium pellucidum, a new marine triclad. J Morphol 9:167–194, 1894.
162. Wolff T: The horseshoe crab (Limulus polyphemus) in North European waters. Vidensk Meddr dansk naturh Foren 140:39–52, 1977.
163. Wyse GA, Dwyer NK: The neuromuscular basis of coxal feeding and locomotory movements in Limulus. Biol Bull 144:567–579, 1973.
164. Wyse GA, Page CH: Sensory and central nervous control of gill ventilation in Limulus. Fed Proc 35:2007–2012, 1976.
165. Anonymous: Horseshoe crab. Bull NY Zool Soc 33:493, 1909.

Physiology and Biology of Horseshoe Crabs: Studies on
Normal and Environmentally Stressed Animals, pages 53–73
© 1982 Alan R. Liss, Inc., 150 Fifth Avenue, New York, NY 10011

Horseshoe Crab Developmental Studies I. Normal Embryonic Development of Limulus polyphemus Compared With Tachypleus tridentatus

Koichi Sekiguchi, Yoshio Yamamichi, and John D. Costlow

INTRODUCTION

Developmental studies on the American horseshoe crab have been done by many investigators [2, 3, 5, 6]. However, the opacity of the egg yolk made the study of some of the early stages very difficult. Oka's development of a vital staining method [4] was a major breakthrough in this area. Recently, Brown and Clapper [1] published a study of the normal developmental course observed on the living eggs of Limulus polyphemus. Sekiguchi [7] did a study of the development of the Japanese horseshoe crab, Tachypleus tridentatus.

Because the embryo of T. tridentatus hatches approximately 50 days after fertilization and the embryo of L. polyphemus hatches in about 2 weeks, the authors undertook this study to compare the developmental processes of the two crabs as seen under the same environmental conditions.

MATERIALS AND METHODS

T. tridentatus, collected from Imari, Saga Prefecture, were transported to Duke University Marine Laboratory in Beaufort, North Carolina, by K. Sekiguchi. L. polyphemus were collected in the vicinity of Beaufort and cultured in the laboratory. Both species were artificially inseminated at the laboratory in June and July, 1974 and 1975. The fertilized eggs were cultured in bowls containing 30‰ seawater at 30°C.

Limulus eggs that seemed to be newly laid were scooped from the shore near Beaufort and cultured under the same conditions.

Supplemental experiments were done in the summer of 1978, 1979, and 1980 at the Shimoda Marine Research Center, the University of Tsukuba, Shizuoka Prefecture, Japan, with 20 pairs of Limulus sent from the Marine Biological Laboratory, Woods Hole, Massachusetts. In this case, the fertilized eggs were kept in normal seawater (34–35‰) at 30°C.

In every case, seawater was changed twice a day. As the egg surface of L. polyphemus is less obscure than that of T. tridentatus, we were able to observe the living eggs without using vital staining. If necessary, Oka's vital staining method [4] was used. The method by which the granules surrounding the nuclei are stained is useful to affirm the locations of nuclei on the eggs from blastula to germ disk stages.

Microphotographs were taken with a Polaroid camera. Drawings were traced from these photographs. Immediately after fertilization the eggs were also filmed during the early developmental stages with a 16-mm cinemicrographic apparatus. The events seen in the films were analyzed in detail, and these data were added to the drawings.

DESCRIPTION OF STAGES

For convenience in comparing the two species, our description of the developmental stages of Tachypleus and Limulus follows closely those of Sekiguchi [7] on Tachypleus and Brown and Clapper [1] on Limulus. Distinctive characteristics of the developmental stages of L. polyphemus have been summarized in Figure 1 as a guide to the subsequent figures and discussion.

Most of the mature, unfertilized eggs taken out of the female Limulus immediately after dissection were depressed on one side (Fig. 2). The color was grayish green, sometimes tinged with pale blue or pale pink. Culturing various colored eggs showed no difference in the proportion fertilized. These colors seemed to change into rather deep gray during the development of eggs. They never became green as in naturally laid eggs. The diameter of the egg was normally 1.6–1.8 mm. The egg chorion was soft and sticky until about 15 h after insemination.

A rapid change of the yolk surface is the beginning of stage 1 (Fig. 2). About 5–10 min after fertilization, many depressions, called pits by Brown and Clapper [1], appeared on the egg surface inside the chorion (stage 1-1). Each of the pits increased in size and converged somewhat (stage 1-2), spreading to make folds (stage 1-3). Finally, the egg surface became smooth (stage 1-4) and remained

Fig. 1. Time line showing major stages and distinctive characteristics in the embryonic development of Limulus polyphemus.

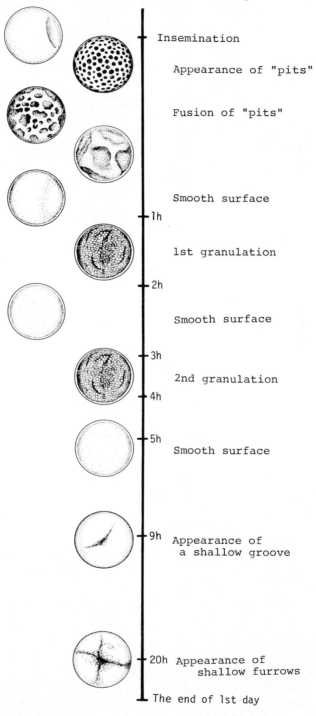

Insemination

Appearance of "pits"

Fusion of "pits"

Smooth surface

1h

1st granulation

2h

Smooth surface

3h

2nd granulation

4h

5h Smooth surface

9h Appearance of
a shallow groove

20h Appearance of
shallow furrows

The end of 1st day

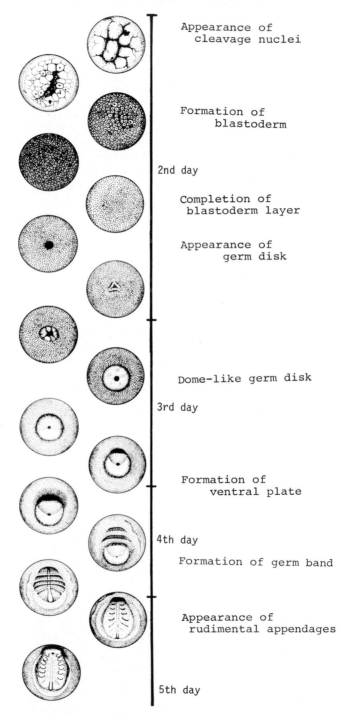

Appearance of
  cleavage nuclei

Formation of
  blastoderm

2nd day

Completion of
  blastoderm layer

Appearance of
  germ disk

Dome-like germ disk

3rd day

Formation of
  ventral plate

4th day

Formation of germ band

Appearance of
  rudimental appendages

5th day

Fig. 1. (continued)

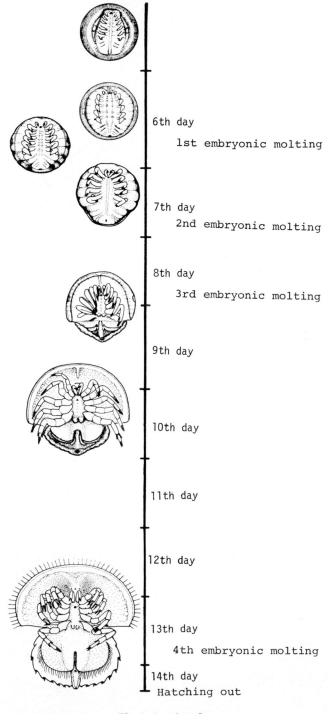

6th day

    1st embryonic molting

7th day

    2nd embryonic molting

8th day

    3rd embryonic molting

9th day

10th day

11th day

12th day

13th day

    4th embryonic molting

14th day

  Hatching out

Fig. 1. (continued)

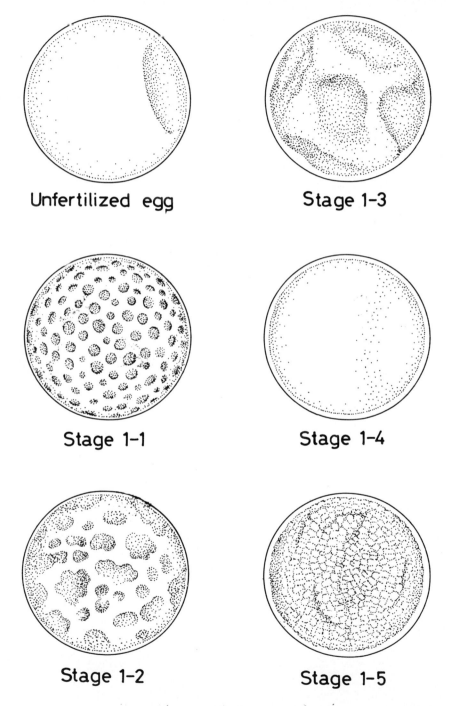

Fig. 2.

smooth for about 10 min. These changes on the egg surface occurred in 45–50 min after fertilization.

The next stage was the first granulation of the surface (stage 1-5, Fig. 2). It lasted about 1.5 h; then the surface became smooth again (stage 1-6, Fig. 3). The smooth surface continued for about 40 min. The second granulation cycle occurred about 3 h after fertilization and ended about 50–60 min later when the surface became smooth again for the third time.

After 3–4 h, a shallow groove appeared on the surface (stage 1-7,* Fig. 3). An analysis of the cinefilm showed that a remarkable flow and revolution of the egg substance were occurring in the chorion. It continued for about 10 h, during which time the granulation and the smoothness were repeated at least twice. The smoothness, however, was not as complete as in previous stages; and many fine granules remained on the surface. At the end of stage 1-7, about 20 h after fertilization, irregular, shallow furrows appeared on the upper surface of the egg (stage 1-8, Fig. 3).

It is worth noting that unfertilized eggs immersed in seawater underwent the same developmental process as the fertilized eggs at stage 1 except that the former took longer than the latter.

Stages 2 and 3 were the appearance and multiplication of nuclei cleavage. The furrows became deep and increased in number, and the egg surface was divided into blocks (called segmentation or yolk-block formation) at about 25 h after fertilization (Fig. 3). Before segmentation, we often observed some nuclei on the surface, as in stage 1-7 or stage 1-8; but they generally disappeared soon. At stage 2, some nuclei, which seemed to be in each small cell, were normally found on the surface. They were not distributed equally and were often observed at the edges of the yolk blocks or inside the furrows. In stage 3 the yolk blocks became smaller and increased in number until about 2–3 h later. The furrows became narrow and shallow on the whole egg, with some deep ones remaining. Although the number of nuclei increased, they were still various in size and restricted to a certain area. They often existed in pairs (stage 3, Fig. 3).

Stages 4 and 5 were the formation of the blastoderm layer and multiplication of the blastoderm cells. This change began about 2–3 h after stage 3. The yolk blocks of the surface, becoming still smaller, were changed into blastoderm cells, which were distributed over almost all of the egg surface. The furrows remained to some extent, and the sizes of the cells were unequal (stage 4, Fig. 3). About 35 h after fertilization, the egg surface became mostly smooth, although

*After this stage 1-7, the figures are drawn without the egg envelope.

Figs. 2–9. Drawings of Limulus embryonic development.

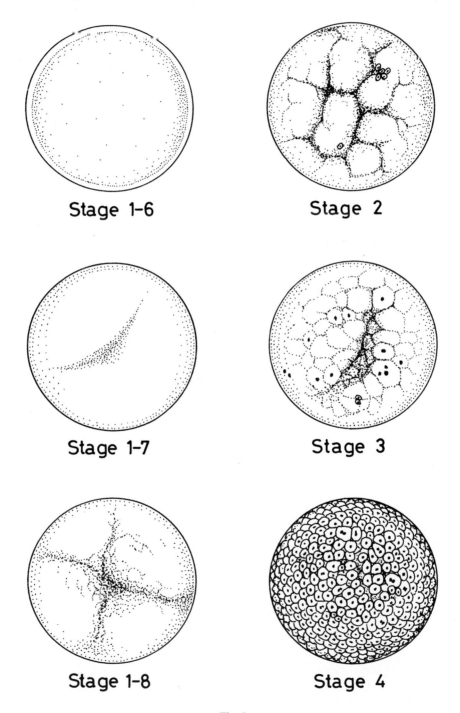

Stage 1-6

Stage 2

Stage 1-7

Stage 3

Stage 1-8

Stage 4

Fig. 3.

some blastoderm cells projected to the surface. The cells became smaller, and the variety in their size was less obvious. The nuclei of the cells often existed in pairs (stage 5, Fig. 4).

At stage 6, 3–5 h later, the surface of the egg became completely smooth, signaling the completion of the blastoderm layer. Cells were smaller and their outlines unclear. The nuclei became small and were distributed evenly over the egg surface. The figures of nuclear division were not easily observed (stage 6, Fig. 4). After this stage we observed changes of the egg surface using the vital staining method.

About 45 h after fertilization, a small aggregation of the nuclei, appearing on one side of the egg, was the beginning of the germ disk, a circular, depressed mass containing small nuclei (stage 7, Fig. 4). Three hours later the area of the germ disk spread, and irregular folds appeared in it (stage 8-1, Fig. 4). Then 2–3 h afterward, the germ disk became round and small, protruding from the egg surface. The center remained depressed (stage 8-2, Fig. 4). Stage 9 began about 55 h after fertilization. The germ disk spread further, and formed a circular and smooth swelling like a dome. On its surface the granules stained by neutral red were spread uniformly. At the center of it there was a small hollow, the blastopore, which was stained especially deeply. At this stage, the red spots on the surface of the germ disk became smaller than those of the extraembryonic area where the spots were still clearly visible.

About 60 h after fertilization, a semicircular part of the germ disk was pale in color, whereas the remainder of the circle was deep red (stage 10, Fig. 5). The blastopore was seen as a deeply stained hollow. The red spots on the extraembryonic area dispersed to fine granules.

Formation of the ventral plate began 70 h after fertilization. The deeply stained area of the germ disk changed from a semicircle to a sector with the blastopore remaining as the center of the germ disk. At the anterior margin of the fan-shaped area, the real embryonic area, a furrow that was also deeply stained was formed (stage 11-1, Fig. 5). About 5 h later, the deeply stained portion at the anterior margin of the fan-shaped embryonic area spread forward and outward. The furrow became especially depressed at the center; and the blastopore, migrating slightly to the posterior, became vague (stage 11-2, Fig. 5).

At stage 12, about 80 h after fertilization, a deeply stained band appeared at the anterior margin of the germ disk. In front of it, in the depressed area, two stained bands were seen. The blastopore became more indistinct. At this stage a noticeable constriction occurred in the egg, and wrinkles appeared at least on one side of the egg surface (Fig. 5, stage 12a, ventral view; 12b, lateral view). In the late stage of the germ band formation, about 90 h after fertilization, 5 germ bands, which were the first to the fifth segments of the prosoma, appeared (stage 13, Fig. 6). The sixth segment was not yet separated from the deeply stained posterior area. The telopore, which appeared near the posterior end of

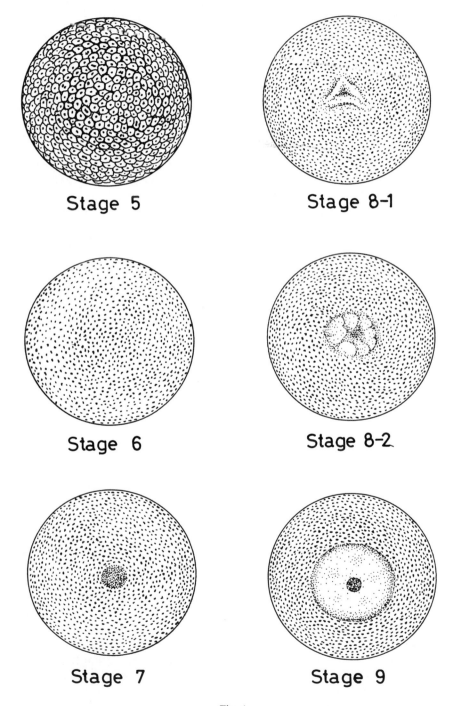

Fig. 4.

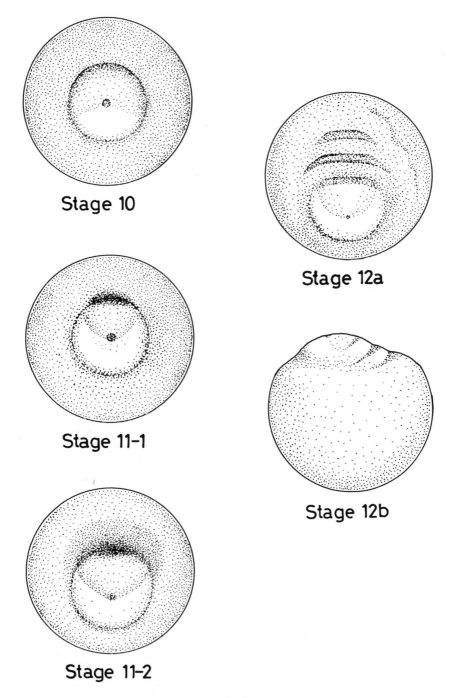

Stage 10

Stage 11-1

Stage 11-2

Stage 12a

Stage 12b

Fig. 5.

the germ disk as a pear-shaped white area, was the blastopore that had migrated from the middle of the germ disk. This conclusion was drawn from the continuous observation of the embryo. The wrinkles of the egg surface were also observed in this stage.

About 100 h after fertilization (fifth day), the rudiments of the appendages began to bulge in the prosomal segments (Fig. 6, stage 14); however, these rudiments did not develop simultaneously and differed in shape in each segment. The rudiment of the first appendage was stained deeply at both sides of the stomodaeum. The second and the third were the largest and were oval shaped. The fourth and fifth protruded a little, and the sixth segment was not yet distinctive from the other posterior portion. Stage 15 was identified by the rudiments of the first through the fifth appendages becoming round or button-like in shape, about 115 h (fifth day) after fertilization (Fig. 6). The first appendage was smallest, and the fourth was largest and most prominent. The sixth appendage was semi-circular, protruding posteriorly, and the stomodaeum was clearly visible in front of the first pair of the appendages. The area from which the stained granules had disappeared spread to some extent beyond the embryonic area.

Five days after fertilization, the first five appendages, especially the middle three, became elongated obliquely backward; the sixth appendages were small prominences (stage 16, Fig. 6). The stomodaeum was between the first appendages. The paired rudiments of the lateral organs faintly appeared as pinna-like protrusions on the marginal band, between the fourth and fifth appendages. The area from which the stained granules had disappeared spread further to a circular shape, and its margin separated widely from the embryonic area. Immediately before the first embryonic molt, during the fifth day, the appendages, especially three, four, and five, lengthened obliquely backward, and their tips sharpened somewhat (stage 17, Fig. 6, a, ventral view; b, lateral view). The area from which the stained granules had disappeared now reached near the equator of the egg and protruded noticeably from the egg surface. The cinefilms showed that the embryo at this stage did a remarkable expansion and contraction movement in the chorion.

Stage 18 is the first embryonic molt, occurring 6 days after fertilization (Fig. 7). All six appendages continued to lengthen and curve posteriorly. The tips, except for those of the first and sixth, were pointed. The lateral organs, now separated from the marginal band, became stainable to neutral red, and oval in shape. The area from which the stained granules had disappeared occupied most of the dorsolateral parts. Some segmentation and constrictions formed in this area. At the end of this stage the egg covered with chorion swelled to about 2.0 mm in diameter. The inner egg membrane, or deutovum, separated from the surface of the egg; and the embryo was able to rotate inside of the membrane. The exuviae of the first molt were difficult to find because they consisted of very fine membranes.

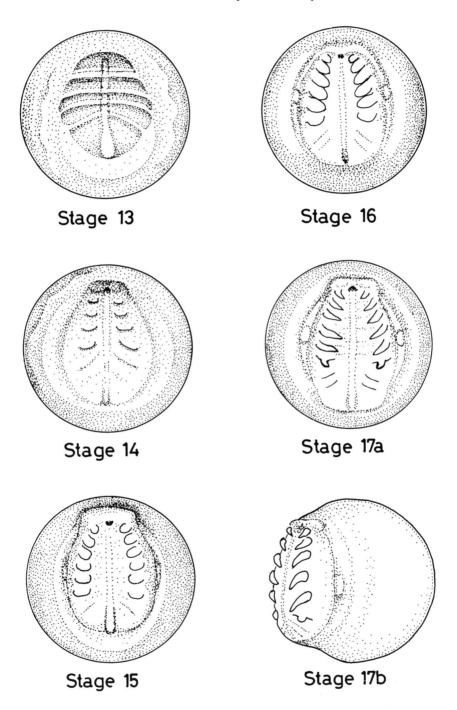

Fig. 6.

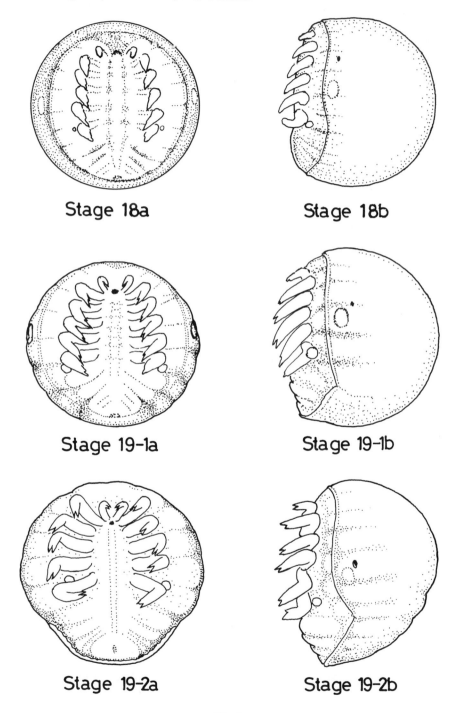

Stage 18a

Stage 18b

Stage 19-1a

Stage 19-1b

Stage 19-2a

Stage 19-2b

Fig. 7.

On the seventh day the second embryonic molt, stage 19, occurred (Fig. 7). The tips of the prosomal appendages became bifurcated as nippers. Those of the mesosoma were recognized as at least two pairs of lobe-shaped protuberances. The stomodaeum was situated between the first prosomal appendages, now called the chelicerae. The folds of the lateral lobe appeared at the lateral margin. The segmentation at the extraembryonic area further progressed, and constrictions became more clear. The lateral organs migrated further to the lateral side of the embryo and separated clearly from the marginal band. The exuviae of the second embryonic molt were attached to the dorsal side of the mesosoma even after the molt, as in the case of the Japanese horseshoe crab. The lateral eyes were formed at the dorsal side of each lateral organ, but they were often difficult to find except on fixed embryos. Immediately after the second molt, the diameter of the egg was similar to that of stage 18, and the embryo was almost round (stage 19-1). At the end of this stage, the egg swelled to reach about 2.2–2.4 mm in diameter. The mesosoma of the embryo protruded posteriorly, and the whole embryo was flattened dorsoventrally (stage 19-2, Fig. 7).* The rupture of the chorion occurred often at stage 19-2, especially in stained eggs. However, in most Limulus eggs it occurred after the third embryonic molt.

Stage 20, 8 days after fertilization, began with the third embryonic molt. The appendages of the prosoma lengthened conspicuously, and those of the mesosoma developed into two pairs of lobes (stage 20-1a, Fig. 8). The stomodaeum migrated to the level of the basal segments of the second prosomal appendages. The lateral organs, which were still stainable with neutral red, were situated on the dorsolateral side of the embryo. Although the lateral compound eyes become pale brownish spots on the dorsal side of the lateral organs, the central eye, which was situated at the anterior end of the prosoma, was only a small white spot. The lateral eyes migrated from the anterodorsal to the dorsal side of the lateral organs during this stage (stage 20-1b, Fig. 8). During this molt, the exuviae of the second embryonic molt, attached to the dorsal side of the mesosoma, were also cast off as if they were part of the exuviae of the third molt. These exuviae were contained in the inner egg membrane together with the embryo until hatching time. Immediately after the molt and the rupture of the chorion, the embryo filled the inner egg membrane, bending and rotating actively until the beginning of the fourth molt. The inner egg membrane swelled rapidly to reach 3.3 to 3.6 mm in diameter by the end of this stage. The width of the prosoma and the mesosoma increased remarkably (stage 20-2, Fig. 8).

Twelve to fourteen days after fertilization, the fourth, and final, embryonic molt occurred (stage 21, Fig. 9). Remarkable expansion of the embryo, especially of the mesosoma, occurred, and the embryo was not so active. The appendages

---

*This flattening is somewhat more obvious in fixed specimens.

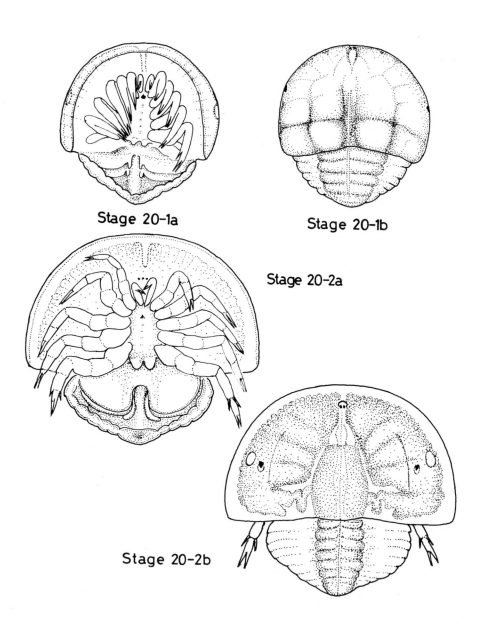

Stage 20-1a

Stage 20-1b

Stage 20-2a

Stage 20-2b

Fig. 8.

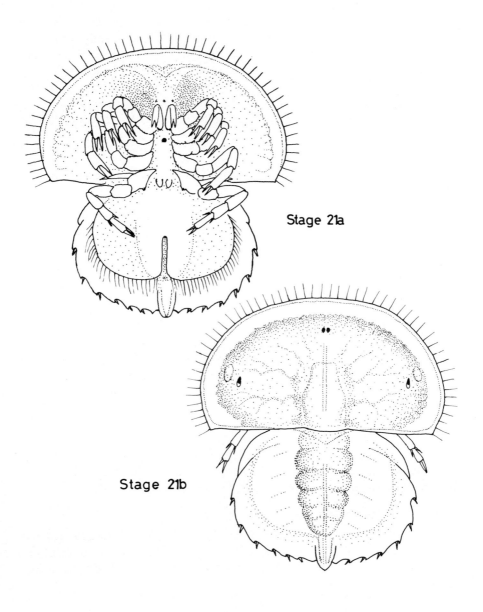

Stage 21a

Stage 21b

Fig. 9.

of the prosoma were further lengthened, and those of the mesosoma formed thin membranes. The stomodaeum migrated to the level of the basal segments of the third prosomal appendages. At the anterolateral margin of the prosoma short hairs grew at regular intervals, and at the posterior margin of the mesosomal appendages many long hairs grew. The central eye became clearly recognized as a semicircular brownish spot. The lateral eyes were situated on the dorso-posterior side of the prosoma. The lateral organs remained, but their stainability to neutral red disappeared as time passed. The diameter of the inner egg membrane was similar to that of the third embryonic molt.

The embryos hatched 1–3 days after the fourth molt, 13–15 days after fertilization.

COMPARISON OF THE DEVELOPMENT OF L. POLYPHEMUS AND T. TRIDENTATUS

In the developmental processes in both species, at least on superficial observation, we recognized few essential differences. However, we can describe some characteristics peculiar to each species.

Eggs

The eggs of Limulus, about 1–2 h after fertilization, were generally elliptical, 1.6 × 1.8 mm in diameter, and grayish green in color. The eggs of Tachypleus were generally spherical, 3.0 mm in diameter, and yellowish white in color. The differences of these colors depended mainly upon the yolk included in each egg. With continuing development, the color of the Limulus yolk changed to greenish yellow; there was no change in Tachypleus. After vital staining with neutral red, Tachypleus embryos showed more distinct red color than Limulus ones.

Appearance of Pits

Pits appeared on the egg surface of Limulus about 5–10 min after insemination. In Tachypleus eggs, Sekiguchi [7] overlooked these phenomena because the development of this species advanced too slowly. According to our recent observations, the pits appeared also on the eggs of T. tridentatus.

Germ Disk Formation

In Limulus, a small aggregation of nuclei on the surface of the egg appeared at first as a circle and later became hollow. In Tachypleus the germ disk, immediately after forming, was often irregular in shape and was not noticeably hollow.

Cumulus Posterior

Cumulus posterior is normally and easily found in Tachypleus eggs at stages 9 and 10. We could not find it in Limulus eggs in spite of repeated observations, although we often found something similar (Fig. 10). This may be the most important difference between the species. We cannot deny the existence of the cumulus posterior in Limulus eggs; we can say that our methods did not reveal it.

Segmentation of the Germ Band

This event was clearly observed in Limulus eggs. In Tachypleus the processes of the segmentation were very obscure, even in the stained eggs.

Protrusion of the Embryonic Area

From the stage of germ disk formation to that of the first embryonic molt, the embryonic area protruded noticeably on the egg surface in Limulus. This protrusion was not seen in Tachypleus.

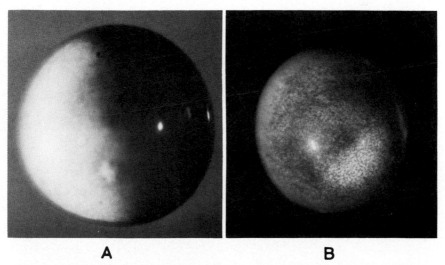

A   **B**

Fig. 10.   Photographs of Tachypleus tridentatus (A) and Limulus polyphemus (B) eggs at stage 10. In a typical Limulus egg at stage 10, cumulus posterior could not be found, whereas in a Tachypleus egg it was clearly formed on the egg surface.

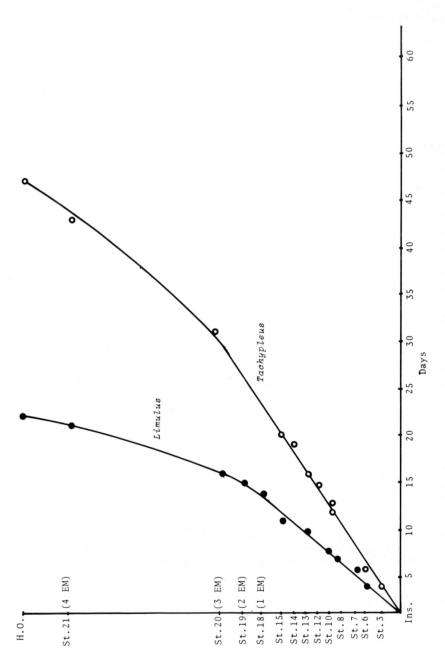

Fig. 11. The relations between developmental stages and days after insemination. Ins, Insemination; H.O., hatching out; 1 EM—4 EM, the first through the fourth embryonic molts.

Ratio of Embryonic Area to Egg Surface

Throughout the development, the ratio of the embryonic area occupying the hemisphere of the whole embryo was larger in Limulus than in Tachypleus.

Rupture of the Chorion

The rupture of the chorion in Limulus occurred generally at the time of the third embryonic molt, although sometimes it happened during the second molt or at a later part of the third molt. In Tachypleus, the rupture occurred normally at the moment of the second embryonic molt.

Speed of Development

It was very difficult to compare the speed of embryonic development in both species because the best environment seemed to be different for each. According to our first experiment, under the same conditions of temperature and salinity (30°C, 30‰), the fastest embryo of Limulus hatched 22 days after fertilization; that of Tachypleus hatched 47 days after fertilization, although the speed of development for the first 30 days was almost the same as that found by Sekiguchi [7] where conditions were 26–29°C and 35‰ seawater. The relation between some main stages and days after fertilization observed in the embryos of each species is shown in Figure 11.

Since completion of the experiments reported here, we have noticed that in a definite volume of culturing seawater the number of eggs has an important effect on the speed of development of the horseshoe crabs. We cultured about 50 Limulus eggs in 100 ml of seawater that was changed twice a day. The eggs hatched 13–15 days after fertilization. Tachypleus eggs did not hatch within 40 days even when only 20 eggs were cultured in the same volume of seawater. From these results it is clear that Limulus eggs develop about three times faster than Tachypleus eggs. Although the reason for the difference is not certain, it may partly depend on the volume of the egg.

REFERENCES

1. Brown GG, Clapper DL: Procedures for maintaining adults, collecting gametes, and culturing embryos and juveniles of the horseshoe crab, Limulus polyphemus. In Hinegardner RH, Atz JW, Fay RC, Fingerman M, Josephson RK, Meinkoth NA (eds): "Laboratory Animal Management, Marine Invertebrates." Washington: National Academy Press, 1981, pp 268–290.
2. Kingsley JS: The embryology of Limulus. J Morphol 7:35–68, 1892.
3. Kingsley JS: The embryology of Limulus. Part 2. J Morphol 8:195–268, 1893.
4. Oka H: Recherches sur l'embryologie causale du Limule. II. Sci Rep Tokyo Bunrika Daigaku, Sect B6:87–127, 1943.
5. Packard AS: On the embryology of Limulus polyphemus. III. Am Nat 19:722–727, 1885.
6. Patten W: "The Evolution of Vertebrates and Their Kin." Philadelphia: P. Blakiston's Son & Co., 1912, 486 pp.
7. Sekiguchi K: A normal plate of the development of the Japanese horse-shoe crab, Tachypleus tridentatus. Sci Rep Tokyo Kyoiku Daigaku Sect B15:153–162, 1973.

Physiology and Biology of Horseshoe Crabs: Studies on
Normal and Environmentally Stressed Animals, pages 75–82

Horseshoe Crab Developmental Studies II. Physiological Adaptation of Horseshoe Crab Embryos to the Environment During Embryonic Development

Hiroaki Sugita and Koichi Sekiguchi

Horseshoe crabs lay their eggs in the sand just below the high-tide level at new moon or full moon. This area is exposed to rain and sunlight; that is, the eggs might be washed with rain or left above the seawater level under hard sunlight for some time. To adapt themselves to this harsh environment during embryonic development, the eggs form the inner egg membrane, an embryonic envelope, under the chorion after the blastula stage [3]. The inner egg membrane is expanded by influx of water into the inside of the membrane followed by the chorion puncture. Afterwards, subsequent swelling of the inner egg membrane provides the developing embryo an adequate space to repeat embryonic molting four times [4] and change its shape from a spherical one to an arched one. Such an increase in volume of the embryo is considered to be a phenomenon favorable for the development of the horseshoe crabs. How can they keep water around their embryonic bodies in a harsh outer environment in which the salinity may change with the tide or the climate?

The Japanese horseshoe crab, Tachypleus tridentatus, contains four kinds of proteins in the perivitelline fluid which is kept inside the inner egg membrane [6]. According to our results, most of these were found in the perivitelline fluid at all stages of development, but the B-2 protein was found in the fluid only after the fourth embryonic molt. Hemocyanin was synthesized by the Tachypleus embryo after the first embryonic molt and was secreted into the perivitelline fluid before the third embryonic molt. To compare Tachypleus perivitelline fluid to Limulus perivitelline fluid, we examined the protein components in the fluid of the Limulus embryo. The mechanism of keeping water in an expanded space around the embryonic body is also discussed.

MATERIALS AND METHODS

The American horseshoe crab, Limulus polyphemus, was collected from the vicinity of Beaufort, North Carolina. The eggs were artificially inseminated and kept in a 30°C incubator at Duke University Marine Laboratory. The Japanese horseshoe crab, Tachypleus tridentatus, was obtained from Kasoka, Japan, and the eggs were inseminated and reared at the Shimoda Marine Research Center, the University of Tsukuba. The developmental stage of the embryo was determined by comparing it to the description of the Japanese horseshoe crab given by Sekiguchi [5].

Preparation of embryo extract and perivitelline fluid, electrophoretic and immunological analyses, and identification of hemocyanin were carried out as described in a previous paper [6]. The concentration of Na^+ ion in the perivitelline fluid was measured according to the method of Komatsu [2], and Cl^- ion concentration was calculated from the data obtained by titration with 0.1 N $AgNO_3$ in the presence of a few drops of 0.1% K_2CrO_4 as an indicator.

RESULTS

The protein components in Limulus embryo extracts (Fig. 1A) and perivitelline fluids (Fig. 2) were studied using polyacrylamide gel electrophoresis according to the method of Davis [1]. The electrophoretic pattern of the embryo extract showed many heavy protein bands derived from the embryonic body (Fig. 1A). When the extract of embryos after the second embryonic molt (2EM) or the third embryonic molt (3EM) was used, it showed, in addition to the heavy bands, a group of protein bands that looked like those of larval hemocyanin (Fig. 1B).

The electrophoretic patterns of the perivitelline fluid from Limulus embryos showed many kinds of protein bands, and the two main proteins in the fluid after the fourth embryonic molting (4EM) were named the B-1 protein and B-2-like protein conforming to a previous paper (Fig. 2) [6]. Limulus B-1 protein was found at all stages where perivitelline fluid could be collected, and it seemed that the B-2-like protein existed even in the perivitelline fluid of the embryo at stage 20 (after 3EM) (Fig. 2).

In order to obtain more information about the characteristics of the components in Limulus embryo extract and perivitelline fluid, we compared their antigenicities with those of the components in Tachypleus perivitelline fluid using antiserum to Tachypleus tridentatus perivitelline fluid. Reacting with T. tridentatus perivitelline fluid antiserum, Limulus B-1 protein, which was cut from acrylamide gel, formed a precipitin line that was identical with one of the two precipitin lines of Limulus extract prepared from eggs after 3EM. This precipitin line was similar to that of Tachypleus B-1 protein (Fig. 3A). Tachypleus B-1 protein was found in the extract of unfertilized eggs, but in this experiment Limulus B-1 protein could not be detected in unfertilized egg extract (Fig. 3B). A precipitin line, other than that of B-1 protein, was formed by Limulus embryonic hemocyanin reacting with T. tridentatus perivitelline fluid antiserum. This line could not be formed by Limulus egg extracts before 1EM and Limulus perivitelline fluid.

Protein components in the perivitelline fluid must act as osmo-active substances to swell the inner egg membrane. We know that NaCl is a main osmo-active substance in seawater; therefore, it was necessary to examine permeability

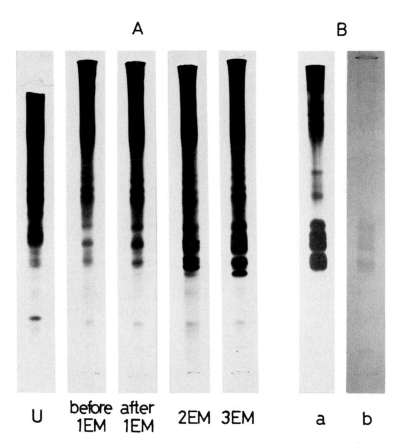

Fig. 1. Electrophoretic patterns of Limulus embryo extracts (A) and the detection of hemocyanin (B). A) Gels were stained by Coomassie Brilliant Blue R to detect protein. U, Unfertilized egg extract; before 1EM and after 1EM, extracts of the embryos before and after the first embryonic molt; 2EM, extract of the embryos after the second embryonic molt; 3EM, extract of the embryos after the third embryonic molt. B) Gels were stained to detect protein (a) and copper (b) using the extract of the first-instar larvae.

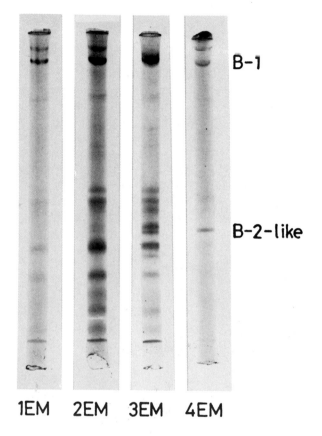

Fig. 2. Electrophoretic patterns of Limulus perivitelline fluids. The two main protein components in the perivitelline fluid after the fourth embryonic molt were named B-1 and B-2-like. 1EM, 2EM, 3EM, and 4EM represent the perivitelline fluid of the embryos after the first, second, third, and fourth embryonic molt, respectively.

of the inner egg membrane to NaCl. Twenty Tachypleus embryos in the middle of stage 20 (after 3EM) were immersed in about 500 ml seawater of higher or lower than normal salinity. The former was prepared by adding solid NaCl and $CaCl_2$ to seawater at final additional concentrations of 0.4 M NaCl and 0.01 M $CaCl_2$. The latter was made by diluting seawater with an equal volume of distilled water. After a specified bathing time as shown in Figure 4, the embryos were taken out of the seawater, and the external water drops were wiped off on filter paper. The measurement of ion concentration was carried out by using the perivitelline fluid collected from these bathed embryos after the fluid was diluted with nine volumes of distilled water. The change in Na^+ and Cl^- ion concen-

A   B

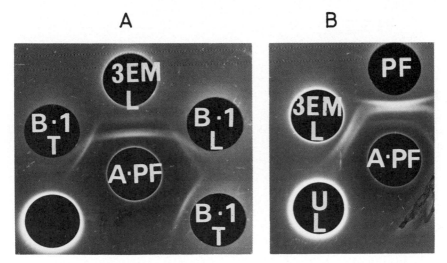

Fig. 3. Immunological comparison between the protein components in the perivitelline fluid of T. tridentatus and L. polyphemus. PF, Tachypleus perivitelline fluid from the 7-day-old embryos after the third embryonic molt; A-PF, antiserum against PF; UL, Limulus unfertilized egg extract; 3EM L, extract of Limulus embryos after the third embryonic molt; B-1 T and B-1 L, extracts of Tachypleus and Limulus B-1 protein, respectively.

tration inside the inner egg membrane is shown in Figure 4. In the experiments with a high salinity seawater, the concentration of both Na^+ and Cl^- ions changed rapidly to 160% of the initial within 10 min and gradually to 200% in the next 70 min. Such a rapid change of ion concentration was also observed in the experiments with the low salinity seawater.

DISCUSSION

Quantitative change of four protein components in the perivitelline fluid of Tachypleus embryos was shown, and their possible role was discussed in a previous paper [6]. From the results obtained it was considered that the B-1 protein of the four components might be one of the potent contributors to continual swelling of the inner egg membrane since it was contained in the perivitelline fluid at all stages and its content increased slowly but constantly during the development.

In order to summarize the results obtained thus far, the quantitative change of the B-1 protein and all proteins in Tachypleus perivitelline fluid is shown in Figure 5 with illustrations of egg size and embryo shape. When the Tachypleus eggs that did not secrete hemocyanin into the perivitelline fluid [7] were used,

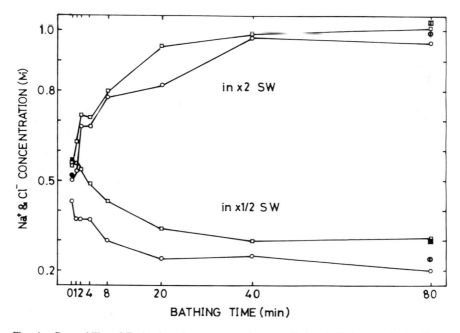

Fig. 4. Permeability of Tachypleus inner egg membrane to Na^+ and Cl^- ions. A high salinity seawater ($\times 2$ SW) was prepared by adding NaCl and $CaCl_2$ to seawater, and a low salinity ($\times \frac{1}{2}$ SW) by diluting seawater with an equal volume of distilled water. After the specified bathing time, Na^+ ion (open circles) and Cl^- ion (open squares) concentrations inside the inner egg membrane were measured. Solid circle represents Na^+ ion concentration of normal seawater; solid square, Cl^- ion concentration of normal seawater; circles with line, Na^+ ion concentration in prepared seawater; and squares with line, Cl^- ion concentration in prepared seawater.

the B-1 protein clearly increased during the development. This result supports the supposed role of the B-1 protein.

We note that hemocyanin could not be detected in the Limulus perivitelline fluid, although it was synthesized by the Limulus embryo after 2EM. Limulus B-1 protein, contained in the perivitelline fluid at all stages examined, was immunologically similar to Tachypleus B-1 protein. It therefore seems that Limulus B-1 protein may play the same role as Tachypleus B-1 protein during the development.

How can the horseshoe crab embryo keep a given volume of water around its body in such an environment of variable salinity? The answer is shown in Figure 4; that is, the inner egg membrane lets inorganic ions pass through freely and rapidly. Such a rapid change of inorganic ion concentration inside the inner egg membrane can also be explained in another way. The concentration is changed by efflux of water from the embryo at high salinity and by influx at low salinity without any substantial transfer of the ions. If this is the case with the

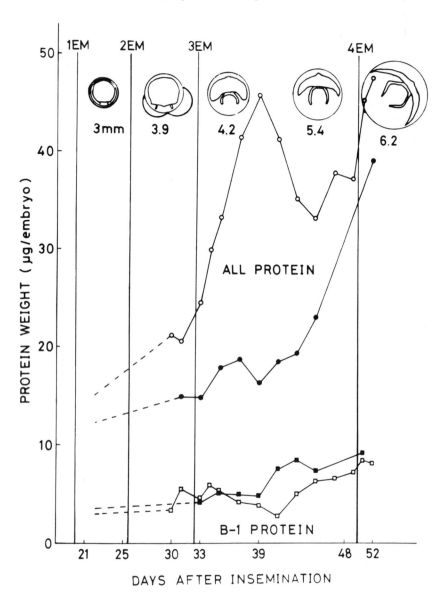

Fig. 5. Quantitative changes of the B-1 protein and all proteins in the perivitelline fluid during Tachypleus development. The results obtained by using the perivitelline fluid from eggs inseminated in July and in October are plotted by open symbols and solid symbols, respectively. In the former, the amount of hemocyanin increased between the 33rd and 45th days (the second day and the seventh day after the third embryonic molt) [6]. In the latter, hemocyanin could not be found at any stage [7]. 1EM, 2EM, 3EM, and 4EM represent the first, second, third, and fourth embryonic molts.

embryos, its volume would be changed within the experimental period. However, the volume decrease of embryos was less than 8% at high salinity and the increase was less than 5% at low salinity [7]. At any rate, such volume changes as this cannot account for the change of the ion concentration that is shown in Figure 4.

For a horseshoe crab embryo that develops in the sand just below the high tide level, the physiological character of this inner egg membrane is very favorable. The inorganic ions in the perivitelline fluid get out of the membrane in order to prevent the membrane from puncturing when the embryo is washed with rain, and the ions in seawater come into the perivitelline fluid to keep the water inside the inner egg membrane when the embryo is washed with seawater after the rain.

REFERENCES

1. Davis BJ: Disc electrophoresis. II. Method and application to human serum proteins. Ann NY Acad Sci 121:404–427, 1964.
2. Komatsu S: Sodium in serum and urine (micro quantitative analysis). In Sekine T, Sasagawa Y, Morita S, Kimura T, Kuratomi K (eds): "The Electrophotometrical Method in Biochemical Field." Tokyo and Kyoto: Nanko-do, [in Japanese], 1963, pp 8–13.
3. Sekiguchi K: On the inner egg membrane of the horseshoe crab. Zool Mag 79:115–118 [in Japanese], 1970a.
4. Sekiguchi K: On the embryonic moultings of the Japanese horse-shoe crab, Tachypleus tridentatus. Sci Rep Tokyo Kyoiku Daigaku Sect B14:121–128, 1970b.
5. Sekiguchi K: A normal plate of the development of the Japanese horse-shoe crab, Tachypleus tridentatus. Sci Rep Tokyo Kyoiku Daigaku Sect B15:153–162, 1973.
6. Sugita H, Sekiguchi K: Protein components in the perivitelline fluid of the embryo of the horseshoe crab, Tachypleus tridentatus. Dev Biol 73:183–192, 1979.
7. Sugita H, Sekiguchi K: Swelling mechanism of the embryo of the Japanese horseshoe crab, Tachypleus tridentatus. Zool Mag 90:271–282, 1981.

Physiology and Biology of Horseshoe Crabs: Studies on
Normal and Environmentally Stressed Animals, pages 83–101
© 1982 Alan R. Liss, Inc., 150 Fifth Avenue, New York, NY 10011

A Review of the Molting Physiology of the Trilobite Larva of Limulus

Thomas C. Jegla

Extensive experimentation on the molting physiology and biochemistry of the first posthatch larva of the horseshoe crab, Limulus polyphemus, a chelicerate arthropod, is reviewed and discussed, particularly in reference to the control of molting and development in insects and crustaceans, representatives of the mandibulate arthropods. The Limulus trilobite larva is a hardy marine organism that carries its own yolk supply and develops in a preprogrammed sequence of events. The program can be stopped at the beginning of premolt, and the animals can be stored at 13–15°C for 6–8 months. A return to an environment of 20°C restarts the program. The larvae, which can be easily manipulated and handled in large numbers with small effort, may serve as an important test organism for pollution studies and quality of the marine environment.

The molt cycle has been staged, using the system now well established for crustaceans. It is diecdysic in Limulus larvae since the premolt period occupies over 50% of the cycle. Although a number of experiments have been performed, the neuroendocrine control of molting remains unknown. The larvae do, however, synthesize the molting hormone 20-hydroxyecdysone and have many of the basic mechanisms for handling ecdysteroid compounds that occur in insects and crustaceans. There is a large (600–900-fold) increase in sensitivity to injected ecdysteroids during the molt cycle; and sharp, large changes at three points in the cycle are correlated with the morphology and physiology of the epidermal cells. Insufficient supply of ecdysteroids at the beginning of premolt appears to be the cause of the developmental arrest. Compounds that have juvenile hormone effects on development in insects have no morphogenetic effects on eggs, embryos or, trilobite larvae of Limulus. Ecdysone alone appears to be the major hormonal force for regulation of molting and development in the posthatch larvae and, by deduction, perhaps also in embryos. Regeneration of ambulatory appendages can occur in the trilobite larva, but is dependent on the stage of the cycle when amputation occurs and the amount of time between amputation and molting. The most favorable conditions for extensive limb regeneration seem to include low concentrations or even absence of ecdysteroids during the early stages but then higher levels during or for the differentiation and growth phases.

INTRODUCTION

The trilobite larva, the first posthatch instar in horseshoe crabs, has been a curiosity figure in zoology for over a century. Its name is derived from its superficial resemblance to trilobites [2]. The trilobite larva has been used only sparingly in research outside of my laboratory, but we have used it for 12 years in a variety of studies, most of them having some aspect of its molting physiology as their principal or at least partial goal. In addition to my personal investigations, nine undergraduate projects have been performed, five culminating with an Honor's thesis. Since much of this work is unpublished, the present work is an attempt to synthesize many of our isolated experiments and results into a unified theme, hopefully presenting some understanding of the physiology of Limulus as the larva progresses in time from hatching to the molt to the second instar. I am indebted to my students, Jon Alspaugh, Vicki Dapper Alspaugh, Eugene DePasquale, Francis Glasser, Sandra Lane, Timothy Rich, Vickery Trinkaus-Randall, Patti Hoak Sampson, and Robert Tomsick, whose hard work and perseverence make the present synthesis and interpretation possible.

THE TRILOBITE LARVA AS AN EXPERIMENTAL ORGANISM

The trilobite larva of Limulus is a self-contained biological unit. It does not feed, carries a sufficient supply of yolk, and develops in programmed sequence. The trilobite larva is a very hardy animal that tolerates a wide range of environmental temperatures and salinities (see Jegla and Costlow, chapter 5, this volume) and has proved to be an excellent experimental organism in studies where improper nutrition may have a significant bearing on the results. The materials packaged in the egg by an adult female have proved to be an excellent nutritional source for the trilobite, which completes its development in about 20 days at a temperature of 25°C and a salinity of 30‰. Developmental time is influenced in the expected way by temperatures above 20°C and is slowed by salinity extremes. If subjected to a temperature below about 20°C before or a few days after hatching, the larva goes into a developmental arrest and can be kept in good physiological condition for at least 8 months at 13–15°C. Development continues normally upon transfer to a suitable environment above 20°C. Based on physiological evidence, the arrest begins when the animal is in the intermolt phase of its molt cycle (stage C) and is complete at the beginning of premolt. Larvae maintained for several months at low temperature are characterized by their physiological synchronization. They are all at the same point in the molt cycle according to Lane [28], namely early D_0. Aiken [1] reported a similar phenomenon in the lobster, Homarus americanus. His animals did not proceed beyond the initial state of epidermal retraction at low temperature, a condition that corresponds exactly to what we find in Limulus larvae. The larvae do show signs of "aging" if kept too long in a low temperature environment; much of the yolk is expended in routine maintenance, and the larva loses the capacity to develop normally and molt to the second instar. Larvae that hatch buried in sand, a regular occurrence in the natural beach habitat, also undergo developmental arrest, but will resume normal development after transfer to ambient seawater [18, 19].

The trilobite instar of Limulus is large for a marine arthropod larva, averaging about 3 mm in prosomal width, 4 mm total length, and 5 mg mass. It can be easily obtained and cultured in large numbers. In suitable beach habitats eggs or developing embryos can be obtained in enormous numbers and easily held in large numbers, about 2,000 per 8-inch glass bowl. Shuster (chapter 1, this volume) estimates 75,000 eggs laid per spawning female each year, and I have observed one large female lay 50,000 eggs during one visit to a spawning beach. Therefore, collection of thousands of eggs or embryos for experimental purposes will probably have no effect whatever on most local populations. Collections during the spawning season and maintenance at low temperature in the laboratory can provide experimental material for 6–8 months. In addition, fairly large numbers of larvae can be obtained by artificial fertilization of the oocyte mass in a mature female during winter months, using the techniques developed by Brown [7].

Although the larva is relatively small, it can easily be injected with experimental materials. In my laboratory we have injected about 25,000 larvae with various ecdysteroids, sterols, plant and animal extracts, and substances with insect juvenile hormone activity. The larva is too small for most surgical manipulations, but laser-beam irradiation can be used for extirpation of parts. Because of its size and its hardiness and the fact that it requires no feeding, it may serve as an increasingly important test organism for pollution studies and quality of the marine environment.

MOLTING AND STAGING OF THE MOLT CYCLE

Molting, the actual process of shedding the exoskeleton, occurs in larvae in the same manner as described for adults by Laverock [30]. The exuvium splits on the perimeter of the prosoma, immediately below the dorsal margin. The split begins in the midline, and the animal begins to protrude through the split. This process continues along the lateral margins. Finally, the larva extracts its legs and abdomen from the old cuticle. The propelling force for this molting process is the rapid uptake of water, causing the animal to swell. The second stage instar that emerges is 50% larger in prosomal width. Swelling is visible with the unaided eye at least several hours before the prosomal renting occurs; after this event exuviation may be completed within 15 minutes.

The physiological and biochemical control of molting in arthropods is best understood in crustaceans [24] and insects [36]. At the biochemical level, ecdysone induces molting in chelicerate arthropods (Limulus [13, 19, 21]; ticks [52]; spiders[4, 5, 25]), as well as in insects and crustaceans; but in general not much information is available on the control system of molting in chelicerates. Insects and crustaceans use a neurohormone to regulate a molting gland that releases ecdysone. In insects the neurohormone is stimulatory; in crustaceans it is inhibitory. In the latter group it is released from neurosecretory cells of the fourth optic ganglion. Waterman and Enami [46] discovered large axons in the optic nerve of Limulus and traced them to large cells, that appeared to be neurosecretory, in the lateral rudimentary eye. This structure is infiltrated with guanine pigment and located medially adjacent to the lateral eye. Because of the high pigment content it is readily visible through the cuticle and absorbs energy from laser irradiation, which heats and cauterizes the large cells.

I tested the hypothesis that these rudimentary eye cells, because of their proximity to retinal nerve tissue, might be an analogue of the inhibitory system of molting gland control in crustaceans and might inhibit molting in Limulus. The lateral rudimentary eyes were ablated by laser irradiation in a systematic manner throughout the molt cycle of the trilobite instar, but there was no significant effect on length of the cycle (Table I). Similar cells occur in the median rudimentary eye, located behind the dorsal ocelli. Ablation of these alone or in combination with lateral rudimentary eyes also had no effect on molting. In some tests sham operations were conducted on tissues lateral to the compound eyes to control for injury effects. None were apparent, except for the short delay in larvae irradiated in late premolt (day 12).

In insects the brain and prothoracic gland were shown to control molting. Williams demonstrated this in cecropia moth larvae by ligating and thus separating specific sections of the body [49]. We tried this technique in Limulus larvae, but with no apparent success. Ties were made between thorax and abdomen, proximal to the lateral eyes, proximal to the frontal eyes, and in various combinations. The trilobite larva, so unlike a caterpillar, is not conducive to ligation techniques. Mortality was high, and in survivors injury effects were severe. Separating and cauterizing sections of the larva gave the same results, all of which were neither consistent nor interpretable. Therefore, at this point we do not know whether horseshoe crabs have a control system for molting that includes a neurohormone and a molting gland, let alone whether there may be an inhibitory control as in crustaceans or a stimulatory one as in insects.

TABLE I. Mean Time (days) From Hatching to Molting ± 2 SEM for Limulus Larvae After Ablation of Both Lateral Rudimentary Eyes by Laser Irradiation

Age at time of ablation (days)					Control
1	2	6	8	12	(No irradiation)
15.1 ± 0.31	16.4 ± 0.38	15.7 ± 0.30	14.9 ± 0.32	17.5 ± 0.25	15.5 ± 0.20
(10)	(9)	(11)	(11)	(13)	(18)

Temperature 30°C, salinity 30‰. Numbers of animals indicated in parentheses.

Identification of specific times or events in the molt cycle in the living animal is extremely important and indeed necessary for many physiological and biochemical studies on molting in arthropods, since events occur in cyclical fashion from one molt to the next and since the time of each event is relative, depending on a number of environmental parameters. Basically, in crustaceans the major subdivisions are postmolt, intermolt, premolt and ecdysis (molting). These major divisions have been further divided or refined in several species, based on specific physiological or morphological characters, the latter identified in the living animal with the aid of a microscope [see for example 10, 41]. This technique has been successfully used for staging the first instar of Limulus [28, 29], the first time for a chelicerate arthropod.

Lane's technique consisted of mounting the larva, ventral side up, immersed in a few drops of seawater on a glass slide, applying a glass coverslip (22 sq mm) with enough pressure to flatten the animal. She observed the animals for formation of new spines and changes in the epidermis, cuticle and setae of the operculum, and telson and lateral edge of the prosoma with transmitted light of a compound microscope at magnifications of 20, 100, or 200. The major subdivisions and stages used for crustaceans are applicable to Limulus (Table II), and the staging is significant in terms of identifying the times of important physiological events in the molt cycle. For example, initiation of premolt, stage D_0, when ecdysone titers begin to rise in crayfish [23], can be readily discerned in Limulus. Stage D_1, a time of increased DNA synthesis in crayfish [42], is also discernable in Limulus, and the later D stages are particularly easy to distinguish. After some practice the larvae can be rapidly staged.

Features of an adult crustacean molt cycle are clearly present in Limulus larvae, but obvious differences in the trilobite larva from an adult crab or crayfish are the relatively short intermolt and long premolt periods. The molt cycle is therefore diecdysic in Limulus larvae, the premolt occupying over 50% of the cycle. In the eighth nymphal stage of the spider, Pisaura mirabilis (a chelicerate),

TABLE II. Some Criteria Used to Distinguish Specific Portions or Stages of the Molt Cycle of Trilobite Larvae of Limulus When Viewing a Live Individual With Transmitted Light of a Compound Microscope

Major subdivision	Stage	Duration %	Approximate distinguishing features
Postmolt	A	4	No distinct boundaries between cuticle, epidermis, and underlying tissues; animal very soft.
	B	8	Cuticle doubles in thickness and shows two major layers; epidermis and basement membrane begin to differentiate.
Intermolt	C	32	Basement membrane is distinct and reflects circulating blood cells; cuticle relatively harder and thicker.
Premolt	D_0	20	From the first signs of apolysis to development of a space parallel to old cuticle; proximal boundary of epidermis becomes indistinct; retraction of setae from old sheaths begins.
	D_1	12	Primordia of new setae and spines become apparent on telson and prosoma, respectively; retracting setae on operculum form parallel lines in apolytic space.
	D_2	12	New setae clearly visible; opercular epidermis distinct and dense; extensive retraction of opercular setae and scalloping of opercular epidermis where setae attach.
	D_3	8	Maximal setal retraction; extensive folding of epidermis; animal soft.
	D_4	4	Opercular surface and apolytic space distinctly yellow; surface extensively cracked.
Ecdysis	E	—	Renting of old cuticle and exuviation.

Modified from Lane [28].

Bonaric [5] found that premolt occupies less than 20% of the molt cycle, although the cycle is of the same duration as for the Limulus larvae used in our studies.

THE MOLT CYCLE FROM HISTOLOGICAL ANALYSES

Usually in our work we have counted the age of the trilobite larvae from the time of hatching, a most convenient marker. The last embryonic molt (of four) to the trilobite instar occurs 1 or more days before hatching, in Lane's system 7% of the instar time, hatching occurring during stage B. Vicki Dapper Alspaugh has done extensive work on deciphering changes in the epidermis and cuticle during the molt cycle, and Patti Hoak Sampson performed an elegant study on changes after an injection of ecdysone. Larvae in both studies were on a 20-day hatch–molt cycle, about 21.5 day's duration of the trilobite instar. In the first study larvae were preserved in alcoholic Bouin's solution each day throughout the cycle, imbedded in paraffin, sectioned at 10 μm, and stained by Mallory's triple stain [15]. In the second, larvae aged 10 days after hatching were injected with ecdysone (20 ng = 4 μg/g) and fixed in Bouin's solution at the time of injection and every 24 h thereafter. Treatments for microscopic observation were as described above, except for sectioning at 8 μm. In addition, larvae were dissected every day to observe the appearance of a new cuticle, the method used to score a positive or negative effect of an ecdysteroid injection when using larvae as a bioassay tool [19]. Descriptions of changes in the cuticle and epidermal cells in these studies were made in the dorsal prosoma at the level of the lateral eyes, an area analogous to the "gastric region" of the cephalothorax in crustaceans, a region that Aiken [1] has urged investigators to use for comparative purposes.

The epidermal cells synthesize the new cuticle in arthropods, and in Limulus larvae they undergo cyclical changes in some ways similar to those observed in the insect Rhodnius [48] and in the crustacean Gecarcinus [38]. The cells change shape and size (Fig. 1). Cell volume increases about 2-fold after hatching, reaching a peak near the end of stage C, intermolt. An increase in cell height to form a columnar shape is responsible for the volume change. The volume decreases by a factor of 4 as the cells become activated for premolt and as the various premolt events of apolysis, new cuticle synthesis, and resorption of old cuticle progress. But the small amount of cytoplasm, changing shape, and indistinct cell boundaries made an accurate determination of size during much of the last half of premolt impossible. During intermolt the nuclei were clearly discernible in a grainy matrix that stained with aniline blue. Granules were very abundant after hatching, and their decrease and eventual disappearance during premolt were closely correlated with release of molting fluid and dissociation of the old endocuticle. After ecdysone injection the cells went from a very granular to agranular condition in about 5 days, half of the time compared to the normal cycle. At the time of ecdysis, epithelial cell membranes are discernible in some areas. The cells are larger and more uniformly spaced compared to the preceding few days, and the cytoplasm stains more densely again.

The cuticle is 5–6 μm thick at hatching and continuously thickens until reaching a short plateau in late intermolt—early premolt, then increases to a peak in stage D_1 of premolt. The first increase occurs as the endocutical layer is formed; the second is probably due to dissociation and swelling of the endocuticle as premolt proceeds. This was clearly evident after telescoping of premolt by exogenous ecdysone when the old cuticle swelled to twice its preinjection size. The cuticle is transformed from a solid-looking compact state to one that is diffuse and transparent-looking under light microscopy. In the normal, uninjected larva the new epicuticle appears 12–13 days after hatching; resorption of the endocuticle begins and proceeds rapidly, thinning the cuticle to about 4 μm at the time of exuviation. After injection of a strong dose of ecdysteroid, such as was used in these experiments, there is often not enough time for complete endocuticle absorption, and the exuvium is often thicker than normal. This

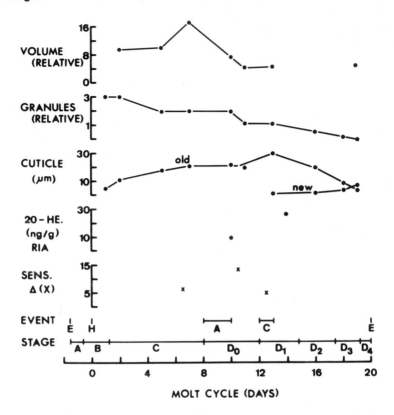

Fig. 1. Correlation of 1) changes in the epidermis and cuticle of the Limulus trilobite larva, 2) its sensitivity to injected 20-hydroxyecdysone during the course of the molt cycle, 3) some discrete events in the molting physiology and, 4) 20-hydroxyecdysone concentrations with the staging system given in Table I. Relative cell volume, number of granules in epidermal cells, and thickness of old and new cuticles are plotted on the graphs. Sens. $\triangle$(X) shows the increasing sensitivity to exogenous molting hormones and 20-HE indicates levels of 20-hydroxyecdysone measured by an RIA; E, ecdysis; H, hatching; A, apolysis; C, appearance of new cuticle. From data compiled by Vicki Dapper Alspaugh, Patti Hoak Sampson and Jegla and Costlow (1979a). All data are normalized to a 20-day hatch–molt period.

phenomenon was also observed in crayfish [25]. Apolysis, withdrawal of the epidermal cells from the old cuticle, occurs soon after peak cell volume is reached (Table I) and is used to determine the onset of premolt in both the living and preserved larvae. It does not begin uniformly throughout but progresses over the entire epithelial surface during a several day course. The first appearance of new cuticle was observed only in histological sections and occurred about 4 days after initiation of apolysis. The new cuticle consists of epicuticle only for several days. During this time the apolytic space widens and is filled with molting fluid, and resorption of the old cuticle begins, as evidenced by its thinning. During the time of D_2, judged by Lane's criteria, the new cuticle increases in size as exocuticle is added to the epicuticle. In the injected animals there appeared to be a trace of new endocuticle at the time of ecdysis. The new cuticle reached a thickness of 7–8 μm at molting in both the normal and ecdysone-injected larvae.

The apolytic space became very wide (20–30 μm) in injected larvae and was filled with a correspondingly large amount of granular fluid. Large numbers of hemocytes appeared in the fluid during stage D_3, a phenomenon also observed in a spider [5]. Finally, the molting fluid disappeared, the old cuticle was relatively thin, and the epidermal cells were larger and denser in stained preparations. This then, is evidence for the resorption of molting fluid and digested cuticular products across the new cuticle and into the epithelial cells.

Exogenous ecdysone telescoped premolt by about 50%, resulting in a significantly shorter hatch–molt time period. The normal larva showed a more general, gradual, and complete decrease in the old cuticle compared to ecdysone-treated larvae. Therefore, exposure to high levels of ecdysone must accelerate the synthetic and absorptive activities of the Limulus epidermal cell. Dissection of injected larvae produced positive scores for a new cuticle only when the new cuticle was uniformly present and 1–2 days after molting fluid had been secreted in copious quantities.

THE MOLT CYCLE FROM PHYSIOLOGICAL ANALYSES

Juvenile horseshoe crabs clearly respond to single injections of 20-hydrox-yecdysone [25] and ecdysone analogs [13] by undergoing at least apolysis. Doses administered, however, were very high compared to levels occurring in arthropod hemolymph. Such information allows one to know only that the system is receptive to a particular exogenous substance. Experiments my colleagues and I have performed over several years have provided information on specific sensitivities of the system during a molt cycle and on insights into the physiology and biochemistry of the Limulus system [for example, see 17]. Systematic tests from hatching showed three abrupt changes in sensitivity to exogenous ecdysteroids (Fig. 2). The larvae are not very sensitive until the latter half of stage C when the first sensitivity increase (about 7-fold) occurs. Based on histological studies this event coincides with the peak in epidermal cell size and is probably the time when the epidermal cells are "activated" for the soon-to-occur event of apolysis. Another change in sensitivity (about 13-fold) occurs during D_0. At this time the cell volume is near a relative low, granules in the cells are decreasing in number, and the cells are most probably in the initial stages of new cuticle synthesis. The third shift (about 5-fold) occurs at the beginning of stage D_1,

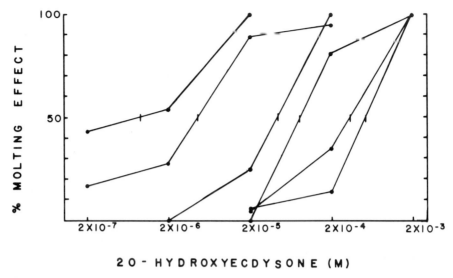

Fig. 2. Response of Limulus larvae to 20-hydroxyecdysone injected at different times (2, 4, 6, 8, 10, 12 days-lines from right to left, respectively) during a hatch–molt cycle of 20 days. Each point represents 18–20 animals; small vertical lines indicate the 50% effect level, which changed three orders of magnitude in this experiment. Injected concentrations of hormone (in molarity = 20 pg to 200 ng/larva) are shown on the abscissa; initial concentrations in the hemolymph after injection are about 6 times lower.

which, from histological data, coincides with the onset of new cuticle deposition. The total change in sensitivity to ecdysone and 20-hydroxyecdysone during the molt cycle of the trilobite instar is in the 600–900-fold range, the maximum sensitivity occurring during D_1 when old cuticle is being digested and new cuticle deposited.

There is definitely a programmed sequence of events in the molting physiology of the Limulus trilobite larva. Exogenous ecdysteroid injected early in the cycle, or anytime at high doses (20 ng or 4 µg/g), causes abnormal development similar in some ways to that described for the cecropia moth [50]. The larvae may deposit cuticle and swell somewhat, but they are unable to extract themselves from the old cuticle and eventually die. Larvae injected after about midstage C with doses in the low picogram to 20 ng range respond with an accelerated, apparently normal molt. They take on water at the proper time, undergo and deposit cuticle over the entire body region, and exhibit the proper behaviors that lead to normal ecdysis. The resultant second stage larvae are also the normal size. In the normal condition cuticle is first deposited on the dorsal surface, then the ventral surface, and finally the appendages. In the accelerated but abnormal larvae there are usually an apparent interference with the mechanism of water uptake and an imbalance between water uptake and cuticle deposition over the entire body surface. The products are 1) larvae that do not swell properly and are unable to emerge from the old cuticle and, 2) larvae that emerge from the prosomal and opisthosomal portions but are unable to extract the appendages because of the upset in relative timing of apolysis and cuticle deposition in the diverse body parts.

The developmental program may be stopped by exposure to below room temperature (20°C), but injections of proper doses of ecdysteroids will, nonetheless, induce the larvae to synthesize a new cuticle and ecdyse normally. It appears, then, that the low temperature blockage of development of the trilobite larva is ultimately due to insufficient supply or level of molting hormone. Most likely the block is on the neuroendocrine system, preventing the onset of premolt. In crustaceans, neuroendocrine organs in the eyestalk prevent secretion of ecdysteroids from the Y-organ in the cephalothorax [24]. Removal of eyestalks at appropriate times results in initiation of premolt and rapid limb regeneration. Low temperatures, however, inhibit the initiation of limb regeneration and premolt in the crustaceans Uca pugilator [47] and Sesarma reticulatum [33], which had eyestalks removed; but Weis found that once premolt and limb regeneration are initiated in Uca, low temperature exposure will slow but not inhibit these processes, and eyestalkless Uca eventually molt. The interpretations of the data for Limulus larvae and for the crabs Uca and Sesarma would be the same. Low temperature prevented the levels of ecdysone from reaching points sufficient to trigger the onset of premolt but, once premolt activities had progressed or were initiated under ecdysteroid stimulation, low temperature slowed but did not inhibit the processes that culminated with ecdysis.

Injections of Limulus larvae, maintained at 19.7°C, showed during a course of 20 days after hatching that the first sensitivity change to ecdysteroids described above occurs at temperatures that block molting. The larvae change only slightly thereafter and reach a sensitivity to exogenous ecdysteroids that approximates larvae at the beginning of premolt at 25°C. These data correlate with observations from Lane's study on staging of the larvae, that low temperature stops the molt cycle program at about stage D_0, the time when premolt activities become obvious under light microscopy.

An interesting problem that arises here is how the embryonic molts of Limulus are controlled physiologically. Limulus embryos molt four times during development (see Sekiguchi et al and Sugita and Sekiguchi, chapters 2 and 3, this volume) becoming the trilobite larva after the fourth embryonic molt. Complete embryonic development, including the embryonic molts, occurs at temperatures as low as 12–13°C. Are these molts under a different system of control than the trilobite larva, or are they not ecdysteroid mediated? Although no data are available to answer these questions, an interpretation can be made based on work on crustaceans and insects. Ecdysteroids are clearly present in the ovary and eggs of the crab, Carcinus maenas [27]. Embryonic molts in the insect Locusta migratoria are clearly mediated by ecdysteroids in the embryonic yolk, put there by the female during synthesis of the egg [14]. These were apparently mobilized from the yolk at the proper time for control of the embryonic molts. My current hypothesis is that Limulus yolk also contains ecdysteroids that regulate the embryonic molts before development of the neuroendocrine system is completed, and that this supply is only sufficient to prime the system of the trilobite larva, hence the initiation of D_0 and premolt. But low temperature blocks the operation of the newly developed neuroendocrine system, and the larva is thus unable to complete premolt and ecdysis. Addition of exogenous ecdysteroid allows these processes to be completed.

Another type of physiological analysis we performed was the injection of an antiserum to 20-hydroxyecdysone in various concentrations at different times during the molt cycle in an attempt to elucidate the onset of peak periods of ecdysteroid accumulation in the hemolymph, based on occurrence of such peaks in crustaceans [23] and insects [36]. Single injections had no effect, but multiple, alternate-day injections, begun from the latter half of stage C to the onset of stage D_0 and continued into the latter half of D_0, delayed molting from 1 to 2 days (4–9% of the molt cycle). The longest delay (2–2½ days or 10–12% of the intermolt period) occurred when injections were given first at about the time of apolysis and continued until about the time of new cuticle formation in stage D_1. Actually, when one considers that the injections were begun halfway through the period, the delay, in relation to time available for delay, is more on the order of 20%. There was no delay in molting when injections were begun in the latter half of D_0. These results indicate an ecdysteroid-sensitive period from a few days before to shortly after apolysis—onset of D_0 in our system of staging. Since we did not continue injections of antiserum beyond D_0 or the first half of D_1, we do not know whether ecdysis could be delayed indefinitely by this method.

ECDYSTEROIDS AND STRUCTURE-FUNCTION STUDIES

Winget and Herman [51] reported the occurrence of 20-hydroxyecdysone in juvenile Limulus. We have extracted free ecdysteroids from the trilobite larva at two specific times in the molt cycle, using the purification techniques of thin-layer (TLC) and high pressure liquid chromatography (HPLC), and have analyzed them by a radioimmuno assay (RIA) and the Limulus bioassay [16, 20]. Large-batch extractions were used, and the average larva was in D_0 or D_1 stages. These are referred to as intermolt and premolt respectively, in the second paper [20]. We believe that a predominant, free ecdysteroid is 20-hydroxyecdysone, although a large amount of a less polar, unknown compound, that was not very active in the RIA test, was detected by the bioassay. The 20-hydroxyecdysone levels were in the 10 ng/g wet weight range during the D_0 and 30 ng/g range in D_1, levels comparable to some crustaceans [see 40]. Actual levels are probably higher, as one can expect a fair amount of loss through the large number of steps involved in large-batch extraction and purification. The trilobite larva's small size makes direct sampling of the hemolymph a very difficult procedure, one that we have not yet perfected.

Based on our evidence, 20-hydroxyecdysone appears to be the molting hormone in Limulus, as it is now thought to be in insects and crustaceans. The ^{3}H-ecdysone that was injected into Limulus larvae during late premolt was converted to [3]H-20-hydroxyecdysone. Dr. David King, who performed the extractions and radio-TLC analyses, found about a 66% conversion during the 8–14-hour incubation period in the larvae. He eluted the 20-hydroxyecdysone from the TLC plates, reacted it in an acetic acid-pyridine system, and chromatographed the reaction products, obtaining the familiar fingerprint of the four 20-hydroxyecdysone acetates. Again, these data are in agreement with what has been found in insects and crustaceans. We have tested 14 ecdysteroids and synthetic analogues, one possible degradation product, and two sterols in Limulus larvae, most of these at least three doses and throughout an entire molt cycle. The data, much of which are presented in Jegla et al [21] and Jegla and Costlow [19], provide some insights into the biochemical pathways for ecdysteroids in this species. Synthetic analogues without any side-chain hydroxyl groups are ineffective 1) if they contain a methyl group at the 24-carbon position, 2) if the 5-carbon position has an α-function in place of the normal β-OH, and 3) if they lack an α-function at the 14-carbon position, physiological properties that Limulus larvae have in common with the housefly, Musca [37]. The so-called "triol" or synthetic analogue with the ecdysone nucleus and cholesterol side chain is a very effective molt stimulator. In the insects Manduca [22] and Calliphora [43, 11] this compound generates ecdysone and 20-hydroxyecdysone; similar processing could explain its effectiveness in Limulus larvae, at least in the premolt stages. Other ecdysteroids—cyasterone, ponasterone A, and makisterone A—are also very effective molt stimulators in Limulus; however, interconversion of these to or reaction with natural and/or endogenous ecdysteroids is probably not the reason for their potency. Cyasterone and the "triol" are very effective stimulators during early stage C when the levels of endogenous ecdysteroids are quite likely very low and when ecdysone and 20-hydroxyecdysone themselves are at least 40 times less effective. Bergamasco and Horn [3] suggest that the greater effectiveness of compounds, such as the "triol" in Calliphora stygia, may be due to their action as a partial agonist and their lower water solubility, resulting in a greater-than-expected, intrinsic binding constant (K) to the ecdysteroid receptor. This explanation for the potency of certain analogues in Limulus larvae is a more acceptable and plausible one than interconversion, based on our data. Slow inactivation of compounds, such as cyasterone, may also play a role in their potency. Ohtaki and Williams [32] postulated such a phenomenon for the

2-fold greater effectiveness of cyasterone compared to ecdysone in the fly Sarcophaga peregrina, based on its "half-life" after injection.

As there are similarities in the interaction of certain ecdysone analogues with the Limulus larva and specific insect physiological systems, there are also specific differences. These are dealt with in a recent paper [19]. Of general interest is the low sensitivity of Limulus larvae to inokosterone, a natural ecdysteroid in the crustacean Callinectes sapidus and 2-deoxy-20-hydroxyecdysone, from another crustacean Jasus lalandei. The latter compound is also highly active in the blowfly, Calliphora stygia; Thomson et al [44] suggest that it is efficiently converted to the molting hormone, 20-hydroxyecdysone. Not enough information is available to determine whether this conversion occurs in Limulus larvae.

STUDIES WITH JUVENILE HORMONE

The occurrence and some effects of compounds with juvenilizing action in insects are well known. Various effects have been catalogued for some of these compounds in crustaceans [for example, see 8], but a juvenilizing effect is not among them. In the chelicerate arthropods only a small amount of information is available. Pound and Oliver [34] successfully used juvenile hormone III to negate the effects of the insect antiallatotropin precocene II and to reestablish oogenesis in the soft tick Ornithodoros parkeri. The roles of juvenile hormone in regulation of reproductive functions in ticks are at least similar to those in insects. But whether this hormone is used to regulate morphogenesis in ticks is another matter and remains unknown.

In my laboratory Robert Tomsick tested some compounds for juvenilizing effects on Limulus eggs, embryos, and trilobite larvae. He used the terpene farnesol; "cecropia oil," a crude, viscous extract from male cecropia moth abdomens; synthetic cecropia juvenile hormone; and an aromatic terpenoid ether, a homologue of a methylenedioxyphenyl ether of 6,7 epoxygeraniol. The latter two compounds were generously provided by Dr. William S. Bowers. The three techniques of injection, topical application, and immersion in a test solution were performed. Injection was possible only in larvae; compounds were topically applied to eggs and larvae. Immersion, after removal of embryonic membranes, an operation that in no detectable way retarded or altered development, was the only technique feasible for embryos. Doses were based on a compound's effectiveness in the pupae of the insect Tenebrio as assayed in our laboratory or calculated from the results of Bowers [6]. In 6-day-old trilobite larvae (stage C) injected doses of "cecropia oil" at levels highly effective in Tenebrio were without any apparent effects, but farnesol was toxic. The synthetic juvenile hormone and analogue were also toxic; however, the concentrations were much higher than those effective in Tenebrio pupae. Topical application of farnesol in a variety of penetrating agents at levels effective for Tenebrio, and immersion in the juvenile hormone analogue at 10 and 100 μg/l did not prevent normal molting or inhibit normal structural features.

Further work was performed on eggs by topical application of farnesol (9 μg/egg) or juvenile hormone (5 μg/egg). Embryos removed from their membranes were immersed in juvenile hormone or analogue (10 and 100 μg/l) at two stages in development: 1) at or before the first embryonic molt, and 2) after the second embryonic molt. The experiments extended through the molt to the second larva. No juvenilizing effects were observed in any of the experiments. In embryos subjected to 100 μg/l juvenile hormone after the second embryonic molt, abnormal development of the dorsal organ (a structure that disappears after the trilobite stage) occurred in 65% of the animals. Other than this, the animals were normal [45]. Based on these experiments it seems appropriate to conclude that juvenile hormones do not have a role in the morphogenesis of Limulus, unlike that in the insects.

REGENERATION DURING THE MOLT CYCLE

Regeneration of limbs is a general phenomenon in arthropods and is particularly highly developed in crustaceans, where a preformed breakage plane is built into the appendages. Limulus also regenerates limbs, but no special reflex for breaking off an appendage (autotomy) at a predetermined area occurs. In crustaceans, after autotomy, the healing of the wound is followed by the development of a regenerating bud. After initial growth in brachyuran crustaceans, the limb bud remains on a growth plateau until the premolt period when ecdysone-dependent growth occurs; a functional limb unfolds from its protective cuticular sac after the molt. Autotomy of two or more limbs during the intermolt period in the crab Uca pugilator [9] or five or more in Gecarcinus lateralis [39] accelerates limb regeneration and ecdysis, but in the cockroach Blattella germanica molting events are delayed when limb regeneration is induced by autotomy of only 1 limb [26].

An extensive study of limb regeneration in Limulus larvae has been performed in my laboratory by Francis Glasser. Limulus has seven pairs of prosomal appendages, five of which are walking legs, consisting of six segments. The latter two segments form the pincers of the four anterior appendages. Glasser cut off the fifth or fifth and sixth limbs on the right side just above the basal segment (coxa), at five different points in an average molting cycle of about 24 days (stage B, early C, late C, D_0, D_1), at 17°C and 25°C. In separate experiments he repeated the procedures at 25°C and, in addition, injected 20-hydroxyecdysone at 2 or 20 ng doses in larvae during the middle of stage C or at the beginning of D_0. He found that limb regeneration does occur in Limulus larvae, but the time of the molt cycle when amputation takes place is critical in determining what will actually regenerate [12]. Several phases in the process are apparent and resemble the regeneration process in brachyuran crustaceans. After amputation, wound healing and formation of a blastema were observed; then there was a period of no apparent change. This in turn was followed by a premolt growth phase, characterized by a partial clearing of the cuticular sac that surrounds the regenerant, and rapid growth and differentiation of the regenerant within the sac. Finally, after the molt to the second stage, the partially regenerated limb was released from its protective sac. Such a regenerant had a normal prefemur, the segment of amputation; the next two (femur and tibia) were smaller than normal, and the distal two segments that form the pincers of the fifth appendage or leaf-like flaps of the sixth were missing. A functional replica of the original limb appeared after the molt to the third stage. This is an example of an extensively regenerated limb. Many regenerants did not exhibit such capacity to reform and consisted only of a mass of unsegmented tissue. In general, the longer the period of the molt cycle, the greater the chance for extensive regeneration.

Glasser also found a definite correlation between the stage of the molt cycle when a limb was amputated and the amount of limb regeneration. Nearly half of the limbs removed before the middle of stage C showed extensive regeneration, whereas about 90% of those removed during D_0 and D_1 exhibited little regenerative capacity. Surely some of the difference may be due to time available for regeneration before ecdysis. But low concentration or absence of ecdysteroids during the early stages of regeneration, followed by the higher concentrations of premolt, appears to be most favorable for extensive regeneration. Limb regeneration did not proceed past the initial stages in larvae at 17°C, a condition where the animals lack sufficient amounts of ecdysteroids to sustain premolt (see section on "The molt cycle from physiological analyses"). This type of growth resembles the ecdysteroid-independent growth in brachyuran crustaceans [see 31]. Like the situation in Uca, a brachyuran crustacean, where exogenous ecdysteroid blocks initiation of limb regeneration [35], regeneration is inhibited by such treatment in Limulus. Regenerants, after ecdysteroid injections, were similar to regenerants in normal larvae that had limbs removed during later stages of the molt cycle. Only a mass of unsegmented tissue was regenerated in both cases. Although exogenous ecdysteroid accelerated the average molt cycle, insufficient time to complete the various stages of regeneration cannot be totally responsible for the inhibitory effect of 20-hydroxyecdysone. In animals where controls and experimentals required the same amount of time to a molt, regenerants of the nontreated larvae were significantly larger. Initial wound healing can occur in the presence of premolt levels of ecdysteroids, but the tissue differentiation process seems to be inhibited.

We do not know whether multiple limb autotomy influences the molt cycle as it does in Uca and Gecarcinus. Limulus larvae did not survive amputation of six legs, but amputation of one or two limbs at various times in the molt cycle had no effect on timing of the ensuing ecdysis.

ACKNOWLEDGMENTS

This research was supported in part by grants GB-16874 and GB-40620 from the National Science Foundation.

REFERENCES

1. Aiken DE: Proecdysis, setal development, and molt prediction in the american lobster (Homarus americanus). J Fish Res Board Can 30:1337–1344, 1973.
2. Barnes RD: "Invertebrate Zoology," 4th Ed. Philadelphia: Saunders, 1980.
3. Bergamasco R, Horn DHS: The biological activities of ecdysteroids and ecdysteroid analogs. In Hoffmann JA (ed): "Progress in Ecdysone Research." New York: Elsevier/North-Holland Biomedical Press, 1980, pp 299–324.
4. Bonari JC: Effects of ecdysterone on the molting mechanisms and duration of the intermolt period in Pisaura mirabilis C1. Gen Comp Endocrinol 30:267–272, 1976.
5. Bonari JC: Contribution à l'étude de la biologie du développement chez l'Araignée Pisaura mirabilis (Clerck, 1758). Approche physiologique des phénomènes de mue et de diapause hivernale. Thèse Doctorat d'Etat, Montpellier (F), 1980.
6. Bowers WS: Juvenile hormone: Activity of aromatic terpenoid ethers. Science 164:323–325, 1969.
7. Brown GG, Clapper DL: Cortical reaction in inseminated eggs of the horseshoe crab, Limulus polyphemus. Dev Biol 76:410–417, 1980.
8. Christiansen ME, Costlow JD Jr, Monroe RJ: Effects of the insect growth regulator Dimilin (TH 6040) on larval development of two estuarine crabs. Marine Biol 50:29–36, 1978.
9. Fingerman M, Fingerman S: The effects of limb removal on the rates of ecdysis of eyed and eyestalkless fiddler crabs, Uca pugilator. Zool Jb Physiol 78:301–309, 1974.
10. Freeman JA, Bartell CK: Characterization of the molt cycle and its hormonal control in Palaemonetes pugio (Decapoda, Caridea). Gen Comp Endocrinol 25:517–528, 1975.
11. Galbraith MN, Horn DHS, Middleton EJ, Thomson JA, Wilkie JS: Metabolism of 3β, 14α-dihydroxy-5β-(3α-³H)-cholest-7-en-6-one in Calliphora stygia. J. Insect Physiol 21:23–32, 1975.
12. Glasser FR: A study of limb regeneration in horseshoe crab larvae, Limulus polyphemus. Honors Thesis, Kenyon College, 1978.
13. Herman WS: Molt induction in response to phytoecdysones and low doses of animal ecdysones in the chelicerate arthropod, Limulus polyphemus. Gen Comp Endocrinol 18:301–305, 1972.
14. Hoffmann J, Lagueux M, Hetru C, Charlet M, Goltzene F: Ecdysone in reproductively competent female adults and in embryos of insects. In Hoffmann JA (ed): "Progress in Ecdysone Research." New York: Elsevier/North-Holland Biomedical Press, 1980, pp 431–465.
15. Humason GL: "Animal Tissue Techniques," 4th Ed. San Francisco: WH Freeman, 1979.
16. Jegla TC: Ecdysone activity in Limulus polyphemus. Am Zool 14:1288, 1974.
17. Jegla TC, Costlow JD Jr: Induction of molting in horseshoe crab larvae by polyhydroxy steroids. Gen Comp Endocrinol 14:295–302, 1970.
18. Jegla TC, Costlow JD Jr: The Limulus bioassay for ecdysones. Gen Comp Endocrinol 29:297, 1976.
19. Jegla TC, Costlow JD Jr: The Limulus bioassay for ecdysteroids. Biol Bull 156:103–114, 1979.

20. Jegla TC, Costlow JD Jr: Ecdysteroids in Limulus larvae. Experientia 35:554–555, 1979.
21. Jegla TC, Costlow JD Jr, Alspaugh J: Effects of ecdysones and some synthetic analogs on horseshoe crab larvae. Gen Comp Endocrinol 19:159–166, 1972.
22. Kaplanis JN, Robbins WE, Thompson MJ, Baumhover AH: Ecdysone analog: Conversion to alpha ecdysone and 20-hydroxyecdysone by an insect. Science 166:1540–1541, 1969.
23. Keller R, Schmid E: In vitro secretion of ecdysteroids by Y-organs and lack of secretion by mandibular organs of the crayfish following molt induction. J Comp Physiol 130:347–353, 1979.
24. Kleinholz LH, Keller R: Endocrine regulation in Crustacea. In Barrington EJW (ed): "Hormones and Evolution." New York: Academic Press, 1979, pp 160–213.
25. Krishnakumaran A, Schneiderman HA: Control of molting in mandibulate and chelicerate arthropods by ecdysones. Biol Bull 139:520–538, 1970.
26. Kunkel JG: Cockroach molting. I. Temporal organization of events during the molting cycle of Blattella germanica (L). Biol Bull 148:259–273, 1975.
27. Lachaise F, Hoffmann J: Ecdysone et développement ovarien chez un Décapode, Carcinus maenas. Compt Rend Acad Sci Paris Series D 285:701–704, 1977.
28. Lane SE: Staging of the molt cycle in horseshoe crab larvae, Limulus polyphemus. Honors Thesis, Kenyon College, 1979.
29. Lane SE, Jegla TC: Staging of the molt cycle in Limulus polyphemus larvae. Gen Comp Endocrinol 40:359, 1980.
30. Laverock WS: On the casting of the shell in Limulus. Proc Trans Liverpool Biol Soc 41:13–16, 1927.
31. McCarthy JF, Skinner DM: Proecdysial changes in serum ecdysone titers, gastrolith formation and limb regeneration following molt induction by limb autotomy and/or eyestalk removal in the land crab, Gecarcinus lateralis. Gen Comp Endocrinol 33:278–292, 1977.
32. Ohtaki T, Williams CM: Inactivation of α-ecdysone and cyasterone by larvae of the fleshfly, Sarcophaga peregrina and pupae of the silkworm, Samia cynthia. Biol Bull 138:326–333, 1970.
33. Passano LM, Jyssum S: The role of the Y-organ in crab procedysis and limb regeneration. Comp Biochem Physiol 9:195–213, 1963.
34. Pound JM, Oliver JH: Juvenile hormone: Evidence of its role in the reproduction of ticks. Science 206:355–357, 1979.
35. Rao KR: Effects of ecdysterone, inokosterone and eyestalk ablation on limb regeneration in the fiddler crab, Uca pugilator. J Exp Zool 203:257–269, 1978.
36. Riddiford LM, Truman JW: Biochemistry of insect hormones and insect growth regulators. In Rockstein M (ed) "Biochemistry of Insects." New York: Academic Press, 1978, pp 307–357.
37. Robbins WE, Kaplanis JN, Thompson MJ, Shortino TJ, Joyner SC: Ecdysones and synthetic analogs: Molting hormone activity and inhibitive effects on insect growth, metamorphosis and reproduction. Steroids 16:105–125, 1970.
38. Skinner DM: The structure and metabolism of a crustacean integumentary tissue during a molt cycle. Biol Bull 123:635–647, 1962.
39. Skinner DM, Graham DE: Molting in land crabs: Stimulation by leg removal. Science 169:383–385, 1970.
40. Spindler KD, Keller R, O'Connor JD: The role of ecdysteroids in the crustacean molting cycle. In Hoffman J (ed): "Progress in Ecdysone Research." New York: Elsevier/North-Holland Biomedical Press, 1980, pp 247–280.
41. Stevenson JR: Metecdysial molt staging and changes in the cuticle in the crayfish Orconectes sanborni (Faxon). Crustaceana 14:169–177, 1968.
42. Stevenson JR: Changing activities of the crustacean epidermis during the molting cycle. Am Zool 12:373–380, 1972.

43. Thomson JA, Hafferl W, Galbraith MN, Horn DHS, Middleton EJ: Possible biosynthetic precursors of β-ecdysone in Calliphora stygia. Chem Commun 1023–1024, 1971.
44. Thomson JA, Horn DHS, Galbraith MN, Middleton EJ: Some aspects of the biosynthesis of the molting hormones in Calliphora. In Burdette WJ (ed): "Invertebrate Endocrinology and Hormonal Heterophylly." New York, Berlin, Heidelberg: Springer-Verlag, 1974, pp 153–160.
45. Tomsick RS: On the developmental and molting physiology of the horseshoe crab, Limulus polyphemus: Studies with molt inhibiting hormones. Honors Thesis, Kenyon College, 1971.
46. Waterman TH, Enami M: Neurosecretion in the lateral rudimentary eye of Tachypleus, a xiphosuran. Publ Stat Nap Suppl 81–82, 1954.
47. Weis JS: Effects of environmental factors on regeneration and molting in fiddler crabs. Biol Bull 150:152–162, 1976.
48. Wigglesworth VB: "The Control of Growth and Form: A Study of the Epidermal Cell in an Insect." Ithaca, New York: Cornell University Press, 1959.
49. Williams CM: Physiology of insect diapause. IV. The brain and prothoracic glands as an endocrine system in the cecropia silkworm. Biol Bull 103:120–138, 1952.
50. Williams CM: Ecdysone and ecdysone-analogues: Their assay and action on diapausing pupae of the cynthia silkworm. Biol Bull 134:344–355, 1968.
51. Winget RR, Herman WS: Occurrence of ecdysone in the blood of the chelicerate arthropod, Limulus polyphemus. Experientia 32:1345–1346, 1976.
52. Wright JE: Hormonal termination of larval diapause in Dermacentor albipictus. Science 163:390–391, 1969.

Physiology and Biology of Horseshoe Crabs: Studies on
Normal and Environmentally Stressed Animals, pages 103–113
© 1982 Alan R. Liss, Inc., 150 Fifth Avenue, New York, NY 10011

Temperature and Salinity Effects on Developmental and Early Posthatch Stages of Limulus

Thomas C. Jegla and John D. Costlow

Eggs and freshly hatched larvae of the American horseshoe crab Limulus polyphemus were reared in various combinations of temperature and salinity (25°C constant, daily cycles of 20–25, 25–30, and 30–35°C at 10, 20, 30, 34, and 40‰). The embryonic events of chorion shedding, final prehatch molt, and hatching, particularly the latter two, were delayed in time by salinities of 10 and 40‰ compared to 20 and 30‰. These events occurred at the same time or earlier in the 20–25°C cyclical tests compared to a constant 25°C. They occurred earlier yet at 25–30°C and the shortest times were in the 30–35°C regimen. Embryonic mortality was negligible in all the combinations of temperature and salinity.

In one experiment freshly hatched larvae were reared through seven stages at 25°C. The intermolt period of the first three instars and the total time from hatching through four molts was significantly longer at 10 and 40‰ compared to 20 and 30‰. Increased intermolt periods and inevitable individual variation masked any effects in later instars. There was significant mortality in this long-term experiment, and it tended to be highest at 10‰ and lowest at 40‰. Increased temperature shortened the duration of early instar intermolt periods in the sequence of 20 to 25 = 25 > 25 to 30 > 30 to 35°C. Finally, when a portion or all of embryonic development occurred in the laboratory, particularly when a period of acclimation to low temperature was included, the intermolt length of the first posthatch stage was progressively increased.

INTRODUCTION

Limulus polyphemus lays its eggs on the sand beaches or tidal flats of bays and estuaries. In the region of Beaufort, North Carolina, the estuarine waters vary in temperature and salinity during the course of a summer day where the horseshoe crab eggs, embryos, and early posthatch stages live. Horseshoe crab embryology is well understood through the works of Kingsley [11, 12] and Iwanoff [7]; their embryonic molting periods have been clarified by Sekiguchi [17, 18] (unpublished observations); and growth of the posthatch stages has been estimated by Shuster [19, 20]. In addition, the molting physiology and biochemistry of the first stage larva has been studied extensively [8–10]. Most of the laboratory work from these varied studies apparently was performed in reasonably controlled environments at a temperature of about 25°C and a salinity of about 30‰. Temperature and salinity do have effects on the physiology and growth of Limulus. The upper lethal limit for animals from Massachusetts is about 6°C lower than for those from Florida [15]. Maximum size of the adults is reached in the "temperate" regions of its range, with the smallest average adult of a local population occurring in the warm tropical waters of Yucatan and cold waters north of Cape Cod, Massachusetts [20]. Shuster also found significantly smaller adults in populations living in salinities below 18‰.

We have a continuing interest in the developmental and molting physiology of embryonic and early posthatch stages of horseshoe crabs, and in this paper we will describe some effects of varying temperatures and salinities on early stages of the life cycle of Limulus polyphemus. The Limulus larva appears to be an excellent test organism for environmental pollutants, and the work presented here is important for such studies in that it defines optimal temperature and salinity conditions for laboratory experiments on Limulus. It may also provide an explanation for the occurrence of unusually small adult size in populations living in low salinity water. The data can be useful to comparative physiologists interested in assessing rates (Q_{10}) of biological processes (in this case development and intermolt periods) at different temperatures and salinities. It is clear that the embryonic and early posthatch stages are hardy and that they readily tolerate and grow in a wide range of temperatures and salinities; therefore, they may be good objects for testing the effects of pollutants and environmental stresses on estuarine organisms.

MATERIALS AND METHODS

Freshly laid eggs were collected on Shackleford Banks near Beaufort, North Carolina, brought to the Duke Marine Laboratory and stored at 10–15°C in filtered seawater of 30‰ salinity until used in the experiments. Very little development occurred at 10°C. Two separate experiments were performed using these eggs. In the first, eggs were tested at four temperatures (25 constant, 20–25, 25–30, and 30–35°C cyclical daily) and three salinities (20, 30, and 34‰). The cyclical temperatures were of equal periodicity (COEP) and controlled by a Honeywell temperature programmer unit, which was set to produce 6-h periods of maximum, minimum, increase, and decrease in temperature during each 24-h period. The maximum temperature in each cycle occurred from 10:00

to 16:00 h. Developing embryos were cultured in glass bowls until limb bud formation, which is before the first embryonic molt. Then each embryo was transferred to an individual compartment (34 × 34 × 30 mm deep, holding about 20 ml of water) of a transparent polystyrene box with a hinged lid. They were maintained through the first posthatch molt. Water was changed on alternate days, and the embryos and larvae were checked once or twice a day. Events noted were 1) ejection of the chorion, which occurs after the 60% point from fertilization to molting; 2) the last (fourth) prehatch molt; 3) hatching; and 4) the first larval molt. The second experiment was similar to the first but was started 3 weeks later, and the embryos were still in early development. The same temperatures were used in combination with a wider range of salinities; namely, 10, 20, 30, and 40‰. Eggs at 30–35°C were observed through the first posthatch molt, the others only through hatching.

For other experiments embryos were collected in advanced development and held in large glass bowls in the laboratory at 25°C and 30‰ salinity. In one experiment, started a few hours after hatching, each larva was transferred to the compartment of the plastic boxes and observed through two posthatch molts. The four temperatures and three salinities of the first experiment on eggs were used. The water was changed on alternate days and, for second stage larvae, this was followed by a feeding of recently hatched Artemia nauplii. In a second experiment larvae that hatched the day of collection were tested at 25°C and a salinity of 10, 20, 30, or 40‰. However, in this experiment, each larva was cultured separately in a glass bowl (3½" diameter). The water was changed daily, and after the first molt the animals were fed daily with an excess of Artemia nauplii and Arbacia embryos. The experiment was terminated after all of the animals had either died or progressed through seven posthatch molts.

All embryos, larvae, and postlarvae were treated with a 13/11 light/dark regimen during their entire laboratory experience.

RESULTS
Influence of Salinity

Salinities in the range of 10–40‰ had a significant effect on the various developmental events, including hatching (Fig. 1). The trend is evident already at the time of chorion ejection, an event that occurred about two-thirds through embryonic development, and is particularly clear at the time of hatching. Total developmental time is prolonged at 40‰, taking 11–14% longer to occur than at 20 or 30‰ over the range of experimental temperatures. It also tends to be longer at 10‰, which produces a U- or J-shaped function at the experimental salinities. The overall trend for time of embryonic development is 20‰ ≤ 30‰ ≤ 10‰ ≤ 40‰. In a different experiment, a salinity of 34‰ significantly prolonged development, especially in comparison to that at 20‰, and tended

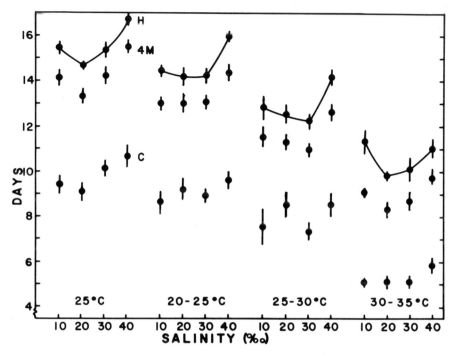

Fig. 1. Some developmental events of Limulus at 16 combinations of temperature and salinity. Time to chorion shedding (C), fourth embryonic molt (4M), and hatching (H) are plotted for each combination. Mean times of 15–20 embryos and 95% confidence limits are given.

to prolong it when compared to 30‰. Therefore, based on our experiments, the optimal salinities for the shortest time from fertilization to hatching are in the range of 20–30‰. There were no other significant effects observed during development. No morphological abnormalities or increased mortality were observed at the salinity extremes tested. Mortality in the embryonic stages is very low, as only an occasional embryo that began development failed to complete it.

The experimental salinities also had significant effects on the posthatch stages. Increased duration of the intermolt periods at 10 and 40‰ compared to 20 or 30‰ occurred during the first three periods (Fig. 2) when they were relatively short and variability relatively small. The intermolt periods were shortest at 30‰, longest at 10‰. The trend for effects of salinity on intermolt length is 30‰ ≤ 20‰ ≤ 40‰ ≤ 10‰. Later periods became relatively long, and variability tended to obscure significant differences. There were, however, significant differences in the time after hatching taken to reach the fifth instar (Fig. 2). The total time was equal at 20 and 30‰, longer at 10 (about 26%) and 40‰.

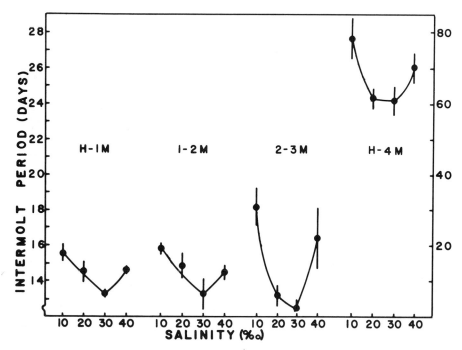

Fig. 2. Length of the first three posthatch intermolt periods and total time to the fifth instar (H-4M) of Limulus as a function of salinity at 25°C. Mean times of 12–20 animals and 95% confidence limits are plotted.

The animals in this experiment were reared through seven posthatch molts. Mortality was low through the first three instars and relatively low throughout at 40‰ (Table I). Survival was lowest at 10‰. The trend for effect of salinity on survival in the posthatch stages of Limulus was 40‰ > 30‰ > 20‰ > 10‰.

Influence of Temperature

Temperature, in addition to salinity, had a significant effect on developmental events (Fig. 1). Interestingly, there is a trend for these events to occur at the same time or earlier in time at the 20–25°C regimen than at 25°C in any specific salinity tested. The phenomenon is particularly clear at the times of the fourth prehatch molt and hatching in the experiment shown in Figure 1. Time to occurrence of these events is clearly different at each cyclical temperature for a given salinity. Times of the last embryonic molt and hatching became progressively shorter at each higher step of 5°C cyclical. Q_{10} values for the time of

TABLE I. Effects of Salinity on Survival of the Early Instars of Limulus polyphemus

Instar No.	Salinity ‰			
	10	20	30	40
1	100	100	100	100
2	86	79	100	100
3	86	79	100	100
4	57	67	95	100
5	29	58	75	85
6	14	32	40	75
7	10	10	30	65

Values listed are percent survival to the end of each instar. The initial number of animals from lowest to highest salinity was 21, 24, 20, and 20.

complete embryonic development at the average temperatures of 22.5 vs 32.5°C were 3.58, 4.24, 4.08, and 4.24 at a salinity of 10, 20, 30, and 40‰, respectively.

Temperature also had an effect on length of the intermolt cycle in early posthatch stages. In two sets of experiments, one shown in Figure 3, the length of the first stage was the same at 25°C and 20–25°C COEP, in two optimal salinities of seawater (20 and 30‰). It was significantly shorter at 25–30°C COEP, which in turn was significantly longer than the period at 30–35°C COEP. After two instars the periods separated into two significantly different groups, one at the 25 and 20–25°C regimens, the other at the 25–30 and 30–35°C tests. The periods within each group were essentially the same and were nearly identical in the two experimental salinities. Q_{10} values for the time from hatching to the third instar at the average temperatures of 22.5 vs 32.5°C were 4.88 and 4.03 at a salinity of 20 and 30‰, respectively.

In our experiments on embryos mortality was negligible at the four temperatures and five salinities used. In one experiment on posthatch stages there was significant (25–37%) mortality only at the highest temperature used.

Influence of Prehatch Environment

We have observed for many years that the first instar of Limulus is much shorter in duration at a specific laboratory temperature and salinity when complete embryonic development occurs in the natural environment. Embryonic development in laboratory conditions that approximate the natural environment significantly lengthens the duration of the first instar, especially after a period of acclimation to low temperature. This effect is shown in Table II. Larvae hatched immediately after collection have an average intermolt period of 13–15 days and, complete two posthatch molts in the same time required to complete one molt by larvae reared in the laboratory from the time of fertilization. We have

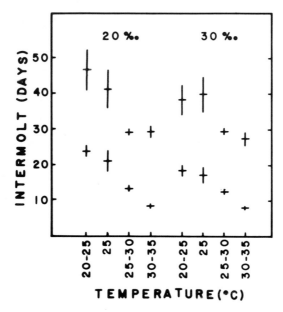

Fig. 3. Intermolt length of the first posthatch instar (lower set of plots) and time from hatching to the third instar (upper set) in Limulus as a function of temperature at two optimal salinities. Mean times of 12–20 animals and 95% confidence limits are plotted.

TABLE II. Effects of Embryonic Environment on Posthatch Intermolt Periods of Limulus polyphemus at 25°C

	Salinity ‰	
Condition	20	30
Complete embryonic development in beach habitat	14.5 ± 0.60	13.3 ± 0.21
About half of the embryonic development in laboratory, <20°C 1 week, then 25°C, 30‰	21.0 ± 3.04	17.2 ± 2.13
Complete embryonic development in laboratory, <20°C 4 weeks, then 25°C, 30‰	31.1 ± 5.16	29.2 ± 4.09

Values listed are mean time and 2 SEM from hatching to the molt to the second instar.

observed this phenomenon during many separate experiments over a period of 10 years, particularly where the developing embryos were subjected to a temperature below 20°C, for several months before experimentation at 25°C. The exposure to a lower temperature not only slows embryonic development but shuts down the developmental "program" of the first instar [9].

DISCUSSION

Limulus is an ancient genus of animal, showing little change from the genus Paleolimulus that lived about 200 million years ago [5]. L. polyphemus is also a very hardy species, inhabiting the estuaries from the cold waters of Maine to the tropical waters of Yucatan in a variety of salinities [20]. Temperature and salinity do affect the rates of embryonic development and duration of the post-hatch intermolt stages as shown in the experiments reported in this paper. Both the embryos and posthatch stages develop and molt in the shortest times when exposed to salinities in the range of about 20–30‰. Although Limulus survives in salinities as low as 10‰ and as high as 40‰, growth rates are slowed significantly. A similar trend was observed by Costlow et al [2] in the Xanthid crab, Rhithropanopeus harrisii. Perhaps the lower Q_{10} value for developmental time of Limulus in a salinity of 10‰ vs the other experimental salinities indicates that salinities at this level may be stressful ones.

Effects of salinity on embryonic development are clearer after the chorion is jettisoned and the embryo is enclosed only by the thin second embryonic membrane (inner egg membrane of Sekiguchi [17]). This latter membrane must be rather freely permeable to water and salts, and the fluid surrounding the embryo most likely equilibrates with the salinity of the experimental solution in order for it to have the effects observed, since no conspicuous swelling at 10‰ or shrinking at 40‰ was observed. (Normal development in horseshoe crab embryos occurs in laboratory conditions without the two embryonic membranes according to Tomsick [21] and Yamamichi and Sekiguchi [22].) A similar conclusion was drawn by Crisp and Costlow [4] in their study of salinity effects on barnacle embryos. This hypothesis was confirmed by the recent studies of Laughlin [14]. Flux rates of $^{22}Na^+$ and $^{36}Cl^-$ were not salinity-dependent, and half-times were short, 8 and 17 min, respectively. Half-times for ^3H_2O were also in the low-minute range.

Shuster [20] reported the occurrence of adult populations of Limulus that had significantly smaller animals at maturity than other populations at a similar geographical locality. He speculated that salinity may be a critical factor in limiting adult size since at least one of these "abnormal" populations lived in low salinity water (average of about 13‰). Based on growth rate data presented by Shuster, these smaller adults appear as if they matured 1 or 2 molts early. The lower developmental rates of the embryos and early posthatch stages that we observed could result in a smaller adult animal, if 1) the slower rate of molting continued at least throughout the first and perhaps second year of an individual's life, 2) it did not show proportionately greater increases in size at each molt, and 3) the rate of attainment of sexual maturity was not altered by the low salinity. Limulus molts about six times during the first year and several additional times during the second. In our experiments on posthatch stages individuals in a salinity of 10‰ were one-half to one instar behind those at 20 or 30‰ after four molts. According to Hartnoll [6], parameters of early growth can apparently be used to predict the final size of a species, but, unfortunately, we do not have growth data for the early posthatch growth of Limulus. At the very least, since salinity extremes may have adverse effects on developmental rates and survival, this environmental factor may be an important one in limiting the distribution within estuaries throughout the rather large latitudinal range. Salinity appears to have this role in a number of crustacean species, eg, R. harrisii [3].

A constant temperature of 25°C is a common one used in laboratory experiments, and we have used it extensively in physiological studies [8–10]. But as Costlow and Bookhout [1] have pointed out, environmental parameters in estuaries are largely variable. In their studies cyclical temperatures of 5°C COEP had significant effects on larval development of R. harrisii. Duration of the larval stages in a cyclical temperature regimen was essentially the same as duration at a constant temperature equal to the highest in the cycle, but much shorter than at a constant temperature equal to the lowest. For example, duration of larval stages averaged 20.8 days at 20–25°C COEP, 18.7 at 25°C, and 32.9 at 20°C constant. The same phenomenon apparently occurred in our experiments on Limulus posthatch instars (Fig. 3). An interesting question is why cyclical temperatures averaging several degrees lower than a constant temperature might have the same effect on time to a specified number of posthatch instars in both of these species. An extension of this phenomenon is an acceleration of embryonic events at the average lower temperature that we observed in Limulus. Perhaps the cyclical temperature acts as the dominant "Zeitgeber" for the organisms' circadian rhythms, which, if running at a period of 24 hours (the period of our temperature cycles), is more conducive to faster development than what occurs under a constant temperature condition, where the rhythms might actually drift from 24 hours to a longer period.

Delayed responses to salinity and temperature acclimation in the embryonic period were observed in the crab Rhithropanopeus harrisii by Rosenberg and Costlow [16]. For example, acclimation of embryos in a salinity of 30‰ resulted in normal zoea larvae but abnormal megalopa, and the longer the period of acclimation, the higher the number of abnormal megalopa. In our experiments acclimation to constant laboratory conditions of temperature and salinity, particularly 10°C or 15°C, which block development of the first larval stage but not embryonic development, is translated into significantly slower growth and molting in the posthatch instars at 25°C and a salinity of 20 or 30‰. We also found that the longer the period of acclimation of the embryos, the greater the subsequent effect. This appears to be an example of the so-called nongenetic adaptation of Kinne [13] and Rosenberg and Costlow [16], and is the first report of its occurrence in horseshoe crab development. If exposure to low temperature is responsible for part of the effect, an ecological implication of some importance arises. It could be a factor responsible for the somewhat smaller-sized adult populations found in northern climates, particularly if the rate of attainment of sexual maturity remains unchanged.

The shutdown of the developmental "program" of the first instar is most probably an adaptation in the sense of conferring survival value on Limulus larvae, particularly in northern climates. If the embryos are exposed to temperatures below 20°C, the developmental program stops in the first posthatch stage, and the larva can survive for at least 6 months on its complement of yolk, and then continue development to the second stage after the temperature increases and natural environment is suitable for food finding, growth, and molting to subsequent instars.

ACKNOWLEDGMENTS

This research was supported in part by grant GB-40620 from the National Science Foundation and by grant DE-AS05-76EV04377 from the Department of Energy.

We wish to thank Mrs. Berta Willis and Patti Hoak Sampson for technical assistance. The first author would like to especially thank Ms. Mamre Wilson for all the courtesies and help during his visits to the Duke Marine Laboratory.

REFERENCES

1. Costlow JD Jr, Bookhout CG: The effect of cyclic temperatures on larval development in the mud-crab Rhithropanopeus harrisii. In Crisp DJ (ed): "Fourth European Marine Biology Symposium." Cambridge, England: Cambridge University Press, 1971, pp 211–220.
2. Costlow JD Jr, Bookhout CG, Monroe RJ: Salinity-temperature effects on the larval development of the crab, Panopeus herbstii Milne-Edwards, reared in the laboratory. Physiol Zool 35:79–93, 1962.
3. Costlow JD Jr, Bookhout CG, Monroe RJ: Studies on the larval development of the crab. Rhithropanopeus harrisii (Gould). I. The effect of salinity and temperature on larval development. Physiol Zool 39:81–100, 1966.
4. Crisp DJ, Costlow JD Jr: The tolerance of developing cirripede embryos to salinity and temperature. Oikos 14:22–34, 1963.
5. Dunbar CO: Kansas Permian insects. Part 2. Paleolimulus, a new genus of Paleozoic Xiphosura with notes on other genera. Am J Sci. Ser 5, 5:443–454, 1923.
6. Hartnoll RG: The effect of salinity and temperature on the post-larval growth of the crab Rhithropanopeus harrisii. In McLusky DS, Berry AJ (eds): "Physiology and Behavior of Marine Organisms." New York: Pergamon Press, 1978, pp 349–358.
7. Iwanoff PP: Die embryonale Entwicklung von Limulus moluccanus. Zool Jahrb Abt Anat Ont 56:163–348, 1933.

8. Jegla TC, Costlow JD Jr: Induction of molting in horseshoe crab larvae by polyhydroxy steroids. Gen Comp Endocrinol 14:295–302, 1970.

9. Jegla TC, Costlow JD Jr: The Limulus bioassay for ecdysteroids. Biol Bull 156:103–114, 1979.

10. Jegla TC, Costlow JD Jr, Alspaugh J: Effects of ecdysones and some synthetic analogs on horseshoe crab larvae. Gen Comp Endocrinol 19:159–66, 1972.

11. Kingsley JS: Notes on the embryology of Limulus. Quart J Microscop Sci 25:521–576, 1885.

12. Kingsley JS: The embryology of Limulus. J Morphol 7:35–68, 1892.

13. Kinne O: Non-genetic adaptation to temperature and salinity. Helgol Wiss Meeresunters 9:433–458, 1964.

14. Laughlin R: Water, sodium and chloride fluxes in the early developmental stages of the horseshoe crab, Limulus polyphemus. Am Zool *19*(3):958, 1979.

15. Mayer AG: I. The effects of temperature upon tropical marine animals. Papers Tortugas Lab, Carnegie Inst, Washington, Publ 183, 6:1–24, 1914.

16. Rosenberg R, Costlow JD Jr: Delayed response to irreversible non-genetic adaptation of the brachyuran crab Rhithropanopeus harrisii, and some notes on adaptation to temperature. Ophelia 18:97–112, 1979.

17. Sekiguchi K: On the embryonic moultings of the Japanese horse-shoe crab, Tachypleus tridentatus. Sci Rep Tokyo Kyoiku Daigaku, Sect B 14:121–128, 1970.

18. Sekiguchi K: A normal plate of the development of the Japanese horse-shoe crab, Tachypleus tridentatus. Sci Rep Tokyo Kyoiku Daigaku, Sect B 15:153–162, 1973.

19. Shuster CN Jr: Observations on the natural history of the American horseshoe crab, Limulus polyphemus. Woods Hole Oceanogr Inst, Contract No. 564, 1950, pp 18–23.

20. Schuster CN Jr: On morphometric and serological relationships within the Limulidae, with particular reference to Limulus polyphemus (L.) PhD Dissertation, New York University, 1955.

21. Tomsick RS: On the developmental and molting physiology of the horseshoe crab, Limulus polyphemus: Studies with molt inhibiting hormones. Honors Thesis, Kenyon College, 1971.

22. Yamamichi Y, Sekiguchi K: Embryo and organ cultures of the horseshoe crab, Tachypleus tridentatus. Dev Growth Diff 16:295–304, 1974.

Physiology and Biology of Horseshoe Crabs: Studies on
Normal and Environmentally Stressed Animals, pages 115-124
© 1982 Alan R. Liss, Inc., 150 Fifth Avenue, New York, NY 10011

A Note on the Influence of Life-History Stage on Metabolic Adaptation:
The Responses of Limulus Eggs and Larvae to Hypoxia

Stephen R. Palumbi and Bruce A. Johnson

INTRODUCTION

The evolutionary adaptation to a particular environmental stress is often associated by investigators with the probability that a given species will experience that stress. Augenfeld [2] associated the size of glycogen reserves (and by implication, the capacity for anaerobiosis) in intertidal worms with the risk of exposure of these annelids to anoxia. In addition, molecular and physiolgoical characteristics of other intertidal and infaunal invertebrates are related to the variability and physical harshness of their environment [5, 6, 15, 19, 20, 22, 23, 31, 34, 36].

Some organisms, however, by undergoing transitions from one morphology to another, exhibit discrete life history stages. These physical transformations are often accompanied by changes in habitat, which lead to differences in the environmental stress experienced by each developmental form. Invertebrates, in particular, display a variety of life cycles that expose each individual to a spectrum of environmental regimes. Intertidal bivalves and crustaceans, and infaunal polychaetes, for example, possess planktonic larval forms that probably experience different environments from their later benthic stages [1, 36, 37].

Little is known of the mechanisms of physiological adaptation of a single organism as it proceeds through a complex series of life-history stages. Is the capacity of such an organism to deal with environmental stress during a particular life-history stage strictly related to the probability that the organism will experience that stress in that stage, or are such physiological capacities carried over from one developmental stage to another?

The horseshoe crab, Limulus polyphemus (L.), buries its eggs intertidally, and has a free-swimming "trilobite" larva [9, 30]. The oxygen content of sandy, intertidal sediments is often low [7, 27, 28]; thus Limulus eggs may be subjected to at least periodic hypoxia. Limulus larvae, by contrast, are probably not normally subjected to such conditions.

The "Limulus Expedition" afforded us the opportunity to conduct a preliminary investigation into the responses of Limulus eggs and larvae to hypoxia. We observed development time of eggs and larvae under normoxic and hypoxic conditions in order to assess the relative ability of these two forms to respond metabolically to low oxygen conditions. Furthermore, as a preliminary investigation into the mechanism of response to hypoxia, oxygen consumption rates of larvae that had been cultured in hypoxic vs normoxic media were measured. We also monitored lactate dehydrogenase and electron transport chain activities, which are both important in energy-producing pathways.

METHODS
Enzymology

Extracts of trilobite larvae were prepared by homogenizing 25 mg of tissue (wet weight of five larvae) in 0.5 ml of 50 mM phosphate buffer, pH 8.2, by five passes in a glass homogenizer. Homogenates were centrifuged at 1,000g for 5 min to remove large debris, and supernatants were decanted. These crude extracts were maintained at 4°C and were used within an hour of their preparation.

Lactate dehydrogenase was measured in 100 mM imidazole buffer, pH 7.0. Substrate concentrations were 0.30 mM pyruvate and 0.2 mM NADH [18]. Assays were initiated by the addition of crude extract, and the change in the absorbance at 340 nm was monitored in a Cary 14 recording spectrophotometer.

Assays of electron transport system (ETS) activity, as measured by the method of Packard [25] and subsequent workers [21, 24], were performed by monitoring the transfer of reduction potential from NADH or NADPH through the electron transport chain to a tetrazolium dye acceptor, 2-(p-iodophenyl)-3-(p-nitrophenyl)-5-phenyl tetrazolium chloride (INT). Reduced INT absorbs strongly at 490 nm, whereas oxidized INT does not [25]. Assays were monitored by recording the increase in absorbance at 490 nm in a Cary 14 spectrophotometer. Substrate concentrations were 0.2mM INT (oxidized), 0.27 mM NADH, and 0.04 mM NADPH. Triton X-100 was also added to the reaction mixture to a final concentration of 0.2% [24].

LDH and ETS activities are reported in terms of units per wet weight of larvae. Each unit represents one micromole of product formed (NAD or reduced INT) per minute in the reaction mixture. The millimolar extinction coefficient of reduced INT used for these calculations was 15.9 [24]. All enzyme assays were repeated five times.

Development

Thirty trilobite larvae were placed in each of ten small (100 ml) culture vessels. Half of these jars were placed under a nitrogen atmosphere and were continuously bubbled with nitrogen gas; the other five served as normoxic controls. These cultures were monitored daily for larval activity and the number of individuals that had molted to the first juvenile stage, a benthic form which resembles the adult in morphology [9]. Another ten jars each contained 30 Limulus embryos that had reached the third embryonic molt, the molt before the final embryonic stage and hatching [9, 33]. Half of these cultures were subjected to hypoxia as above. Cultures were monitored daily for activity (embryos are visible through the transparent egg membrane [33]), the incidence of molting to the final embryonic stage, and the number of hatched eggs.

On both days 5 and 8, one culture jar containing trilobite larvae was aerated, and the larvae were subsequently allowed to develop under normoxic conditions. On each of days 4, 9, and 12, one culture jar containing embryos was aerated. The water in all cultures was changed daily; hypoxic cultures were refilled with deoxygenated seawater. Oxygen levels were monitored with a Yellow Springs Instruments oxygen meter, and were never higher than 0.75 ppm O_2 in hypoxic cultures.

Oxygen Consumption

A small, plastic, mesh cage was fabricated and placed in a 1.5 ml glass electrode vessel from a Gilson Oxygraph. This effectively protected the larvae from a stirring bar in the vessel, yet allowed water circulation past the larvae and the electrode. The partial pressure of oxygen was continuously monitored with a Clark-type oxygen probe (Yellow Springs Instruments, model 5331) connected to a Transidyne General Chemical Microsensor. Temperature was regulated at 20°C with a Lauda K2-R thermostated circulator.

Five larvae were placed in the electrode vessel for each measurement. They were allowed to consume oxygen until essentially none remained. To prevent bacterial contamination, both the plastic cage and the electrode vessel were cleaned between experiments; and Millipore-filtered seawater was used. Control experiments without larvae indicated a neglible rate of oxygen consumption by bacteria. After each experiment, the larvae were removed from the electrode vessel, blotted dry, and weighed. Larval activity fell with decreasing oxygen tensions, but all larvae resumed activity after return to normoxic conditions.

We noted that oxygen consumption rates were generally lower during the day than at night. To avoid this interesting complication, all experiments reported here were conducted during the afternoon.

RESULTS

ETS activities, as measured by the Packard method, and LDH activities did not change with the incubation of trilobite larvae under hypoxic conditions (Table I). Comparisons made between larvae under hypoxic conditions and control groups were not different as determined by the Mann-Whitney U-test ($P > 0.05$).

A few trilobite larvae became inactive after 5 days of hypoxia; yet if subsequently exposed to normoxic conditions, these larvae developed normally and exhibited no lag in the time required to molt to the juvenile stage, as compared to control groups (Fig. 1C). Approximately 50% of the larvae released from hypoxia after 9 days survived (Fig. 1D). No larvae incubated strictly under nitrogen molted to the juvenile stage (Fig. 1B).

Third stage embryos quickly became inactive when exposed to hypoxic conditions (Fig. 2B), but if released from hypoxia even after 9 days (Fig. 2C) they were capable of regaining activity, molting, and hatching. Embryos released from hypoxia after 12 days showed increased activity and molting on days 13 and 14, but experiments were terminated before hatching was observed in this group (Fig. 2D). Regardless of the duration of hypoxic incubation, molting followed approximately 1 day after activity was regained, and hatching followed approximately 1 day later (Fig. 2). Thus, development appeared simply to have stopped at the onset of hypoxia and resumed when normoxic conditions were restored.

Limulus trilobite larvae exhibited substantial oxygen-regulatory ability at moderate oxygen tensions. Figure 3 shows that above a critical P_{O_2} of approximately 40 mm Hg, the rate of oxygen consumption was independant of ambient P_{O_2}. Below this critical P_{O_2}, oxygen consumption sharply decreased. Preexposure of larvae to hypoxic conditions did not result in a measurable difference in the critical P_{O_2} or in the oxygen consumption rate in the plateau region above the critical P_{O_2}.

DISCUSSION

Descriptive investigations of the embryology of Limulus have been greatly facilitated by the tolerance of Limulus eggs and larvae to poor conditions [13, 14, 16, 17, 26]. Figure 1 shows that the LD_{50} for duration of hypoxia (that point at which 50% of the experimental animals have died) for larvae is approximately 9 days. By contrast, planktonic larvae of other marine arthropods succumb to hypoxia after a period of hours [35].

TABLE I. Activities of Lactate Dehydrogenase (LDH) and the Electron Transport System (ETS) in Limulus Larvae Cultured Under Normoxic and Hypoxic Conditions

	Days in culture							
	3		5		7		11	
Culture conditions	Normoxic	Hypoxic	Normoxic	Hypoxic	Normoxic	Hypoxic	Normoxic	Hypoxic
LDH*	9.9	11.0	10.0 ± 0.8	8.0 ± 0.4			11.3 ± 0.6	9.5 ± 0.3
ETS*	1.13 ± 0.05	1.15 ± 0.22	0.81 ± 0.06	0.71 ± 0.05	1.27 ± 0.08	1.13 ± 0.05	1.27 ± 0.06	1.13 ± 0.17

*Activities are presented as units activity/gram wet weight larva (Means of 3–5 replicates ± SD).

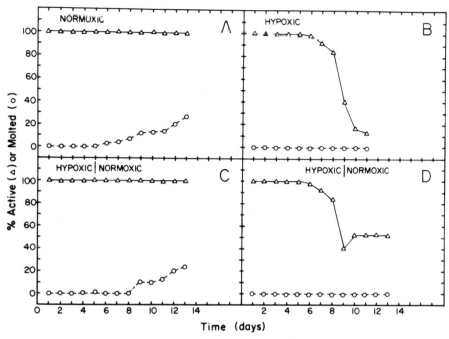

Fig. 1. The response of Limulus larvae to hypoxia. Triangles (△) denote the percent of larvae active; circles (○), the percent of larvae that molted to the first juvenile stage. A) Aerated controls. B) Larvae cultured under hypoxic conditions; activity falls precipitously, and molting does not occur. C) Hypoxic larvae aerated on day 5; the normal molting schedule resumes. D) Hypoxic larvae aerated on day 9; 50% of the larvae so treated remained active.

Limulus embryos show slightly greater tolerance to hypoxia than do Limulus larvae. Embryos released from hypoxia after 9 days were capable of regaining activity, molting to the final embryonic stage, then hatching (Fig. 2). The final embryonic molt occurs 1–2 days later (Fig. 2). Our data indicate no change in the length of these refractory periods with increased exposure to hypoxia. Thus, development appears to halt at the inception of hypoxia, resuming when normoxic conditions are reestablished. Such developmental plasticity has also been observed in Limulus subjected to variations in temperature (Jegla, this volume), and in barnacle nauplii subjected to anoxia [1].

Limulus larvae and embryos, then, can be characterized by extreme tolerance to hypoxic conditions. This capacity in embryos correlates well with the physical environment of Limulus nest sites [27, 28, 30]. Once the trilobite larvae hatch and are freed from the buried nests, however, they are free-swimming. Larvae in such environments probably do not experience severe hypoxia [35].

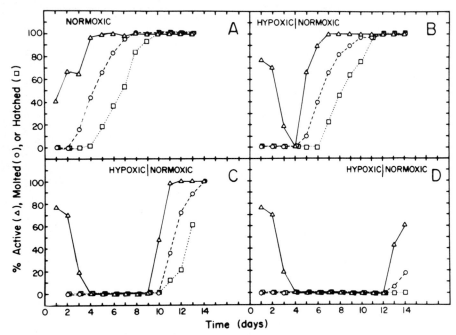

Fig. 2. The response of Limulus embryos to hypoxia. Triangles (△) denote the percent of embryos active; circles (○), the percent of embryos that molted from the third to the fourth embryonic molt; squares (□), the percent that hatched. A) Aerated controls. B) Embryos cultured under hypoxia and aerated on day 4; activity, molting and hatching resumed. C) Embryos aerated on day 9; activity, molting and hatching resumed. D) Embryos aerated on day 12; activity and molting resumed.

Do Limulus larvae develop the ability to survive hypoxia as a short-term metabolic adaptation to local conditions, or do they retain this capacity from earlier stages? Our data on LDH activity, electron transport system activity, and oxygen consumption reveal no differences between larvae cultured under hypoxia for as long as 11 days and the control groups, suggesting that survival during hypoxia is a latent ability of Limulus larvae, carried over from embryonic stages.

The kinetic properties and titers of lactate dehydrogenases are important in the anaerobic metabolism of a diverse array of organisms [2, 8, 10, 32]. In Limulus, LDH catalyzes the terminal reaction in glycolysis and is important in redox regulation (Fields, this volume). Our data, however, indicate that levels of LDH are independent of exposure to hypoxia (Table I). Similarly, although measurement of electron transport system (ETS) activity is an excellent indicator of the capacity of a planktonic organism to utilize oxygen [11, 12], and has been shown to be affected by changes in environmental conditions [4], ETS activity

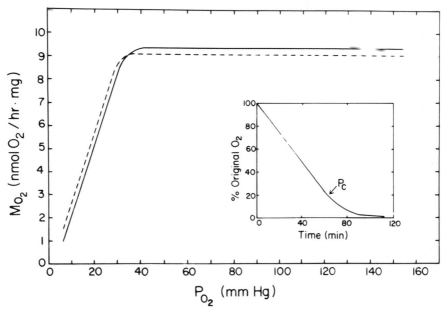

Fig. 3.   Metabolic rate (nmol O_2 consumed/h wet weight larva) vs ambient O_2 tension (mm Hg) for Limulus larvae cultured under normoxic conditions (solid line) and hypoxic conditions (dashed line). These curves were calculated from plots of O_2 tension vs time (see inset for example). The critical oxygen tension (P_c sensu Prosser [29]) is the oxygen tension below which metabolic rate decreases with decreasing P_{O_2}.

does not change in Limulus larvae cultured under hypoxic conditions (Table I).

The oxygen consumption of larvae in conditions of declining ambient oxygen tension is also independent of culture conditions (Fig. 3). The "critical pressure," (P_c), that partial pressure of oxygen below which an oxygen regulator becomes an oxygen conformer [29], is negatively correlated in some animals with tolerance to hypoxia [6, 31]. P_c is identical for larvae cultured under normoxia or hypoxia. Thus, by this criterion, there is no increase in the ability of larvae cultured under hypoxic conditions to tolerate low O_2 levels.

In summary, Limulus embryos and larvae are remarkably tolerant of hypoxic conditions and are indistinguishable in several physiological and molecular characteristics that may be associated with metabolic adaptations to conditions of oxygen stress. The ability of larvae to tolerate hypoxic conditions does not appear to stem from short-term changes in the characteristics we have examined, and seems to be a holdover from earlier embryonic stages, although significant changes in other characteristics are possible. In this preliminary report, we have presented some observations on the tolerance of Limulus eggs and larvae to hypoxia, and hope to encourage further study of metabolic adaptations through metamorphic life cycles.

ACKNOWLEDGMENTS

We thank Dr. J. H. A. Fields for comments on the manuscript and Drs. Joseph and Celia Bonaventura for providing laboratory space. This work was supported in part by NSF graduate fellowships to S.R.P. and B.A.J.

REFERENCES

1. Achituv Y, Blackstock J, Barnes M, Barnes H: Some biochemical constituents of stage I and stage II nauplii of Balanus balanoides (L.) and the effect of anoxia on stage I. J Exp Mar Biol Ecol 42:1–12, 1980.
2. Augenfeld JM: Lactic dehydrogenase activities in invertebrates in relation to environment and mode of gas exchange. Comp Biochem Physiol 18:983–985, 1966.
3. Augenfeld JM: Relation of habitat to glycogen concentration and glycogen synthetase in polychaetes. Mar Biol 48:57–62, 1978.
4. Båmstedt U: ETS activity as an estimator of respiratory rate of zooplankton populations. The signficance of variations in environmental factors. J Exp Mar Biol Ecol 42:267–283, 1980.
5. Barnes H, Finlayson DM, Piatigorsky J: The effect of desiccation and anaerobic conditions on the behaviour, survival and general metabolism of three common cirripedes. J Anim Ecol 32:233–252, 1963.
6. Bayne BL: The responses of three species of bivalve mollusc to declining oxygen tension at reduced salinity. Comp Biochem Physiol 45A:793–806, 1973.
7. Brafield AE: The oxygen content of interstitial water in sandy shores. J Anim Ecol 33:97–116, 1964.
8. Cripps RA, Reish DJ: The effect of environmental stress on the activity of malate dehydrogenase and lactate dehydrogenase in Neanthes arenaceodentata (Annelida: Polychaeta). Comp Biochem Physiol 46B:123–133, 1973.
9. French KA: Laboratory culture of embryonic and juvenile Limulus. In Cohen E (ed): "Biomedical Applications of the Horseshoe Crab (Limulidae)." New York: Alan R Liss, 1979, pp 61–72.
10. Hochachka PW, Somero GN: "Strategies of Biochemical Adaptation." Philadelphia: W. B. Saunders Co., 1973, 358 pp.
11. Kenner RA, Ahmed SI: Measurements of electron transport activities in marine phytoplankton. Mar Biol 33:119–127, 1975.
12. King FD, Packard TT: Respiration and the activity of the respiratory electron transport system in marine zooplankton. Limnol Oceanogr 20:849–854, 1975.
13. Kingsley JS: The Embryology of Limulus. J Morphol 7:36–66, 1892.
14. Kingsley JS: The Embryology of Limulus. J Morphol 8:195–268, 1893.
15. Lent CM: Adaptations of the ribbed mussel, Modiolus demissus (Dillwyn), to the intertidal habitat. Am Zool 9:283–292, 1969.
16. Lockheed JH: Xiphosura polyphemus. In Brown FA (ed): "Selected Invertebrate Types." New York: John Wiley and Sons, 1950, pp 360–382.
17. Lockwood S: The horsefoot crab. Am Nat 4:257–273, 1870.
18. Long GL, Kaplan NO: Diphosphopyridine nucleotide-linked D-lactate dehydrogenases from the horseshoe crab, Limulus polyphemus, and the seaworm, Nereis virens. I. Physical and chemical properties. Arch Biochem Biophys 154:696–710, 1973.

19 Lockwood S: Diphosphopyridine linked D-lactate dehydrogenases from the horseshoe crab, Limulus polyphemus, and the seaworm Nereis virens. II. Catalytic properties. Arch Biochem Biophys 154:711–725, 1973.

20. Mangum CP: Activity patterns in metabolism and ecology of polychaetes. Comp Biochem Physiol 11:239–256, 1964.

21. Mangum CP, Towle DW: Physiological adaptation to unstable environments. Am Sci 65:67–75, 1977.

22. McEdward LR: Respiratory electron transport activity during development of Lytechinus variegatus Lamark (Echinodermata: Echinoidea). MA thesis, University of South Florida, Tampa, 1979.

23. Newell RC: Effect of fluctuations in temperature on the metabolism of intertidal invertebrates. Am Zool 9:293–307, 1969.

24. Newell RC: Factors affecting the respiration of intertidal invertebrates. Am Zool 13:513–528, 1973.

25. Owens TG, King FD: The measurement of respiratory electron-transport-systems activity in marine zooplankton. Mar Biol 30:27–36, 1975.

26. Packard TT: The measurement of respiratory electron-transport activity in marine phytoplankton. J Mar Res 29:235–244, 1971.

27. Patten W: Variations in the development of Limulus polyphemus. J Morphol 12:21–149, 1896.

28. Pearse AS, Humm HJ, Warton GW: Ecology of sand beaches at Beaufort, N.C. Ecol Monogr 12:135–190, 1942.

29. Pollock LW, Hummon WD: Cyclic changes in interstitial water content, atmospheric exposure and temperature in a marine beach. Limnol Oceanogr 16:522–535, 1971.

30. Prosser CL: "Comparative Animal Physiology," Ed 3. Philadelphia: W.B. Saunders Co., 1973, 966 pp.

31. Rudloe A: Locomotor and light responses of larvae of the horseshoe crab, Limulus polyphemus (L.). Biol Bull 157:494–505, 1979.

32. Sassaman C, Mangum CP: Adaptations to environmental oxygen levels in infaunal and epifaunal sea anemones. Biol Bull 143:657–678, 1972.

33. Sastry AN, Ellington WR: Lactate dehydrogenase during the larval development of Cancer irroratus: Effect of constant and cyclic thermal regimes. Experientia 34:308–309, 1978.

34. Sekiguchi K: A normal plate of the development of the Japanese horseshoe crab Tachypleus tridentatus. Sc Rep TKD Sect B 15:153–162, 1973.

35. Thompson RK, Pritchard AW: Respiratory adaptations of two burrowing crustaceans, Callianassa californiensis and Upogebia pugettensis (Decapoda, Thalassinidea). Biol Bull 136:274–287, 1969.

36. Vargo SL, Sastry AN: Acute temperature and low dissolved oxygen tolerances of brachyuran crab (Cancer irroratus) larvae. Mar Biol 40:165–171, 1977.

37. Vernberg FJ: Acclimation of intertidal crabs. Am Zool 9:333–341, 1969.

38. Vernberg FJ, Vernberg WB: Adaptation to extreme environments. In Vernberg FJ (ed): "Physiological Ecology of Estuarine Organisms." Columbia: University of South Carolina Press, 1975, pp 165–180.

Physiology and Biology of Horseshoe Crabs: Studies on
Normal and Environmentally Stressed Animals, pages 125–131
© 1982 Alan R. Liss, Inc., 150 Fifth Avenue, New York, NY 10011

Anaerobiosis in Limulus

Jeremy H. A. Fields

INTRODUCTION

The horseshoe crab, Limulus polyphemus, is a living representative of a group of animals extant since the Jurassic. It is sometimes considered to be a member of the phylum Arthropoda, and sometimes it is placed in a separate phylum. As such, it might be a useful organism for elucidating the evolution of the patterns of metabolism found in invertebrates. Our knowledge of the metabolism of the Arthropods, particularly that of the insects, is expanding, and one wonders about the biochemical relationships of this very large group of animals. When compared with the research done on insects and crustaceans, very little has been done on the closely related horseshoe crabs.

The Arthropods utilize glycogen as well as fats as fuel [7, 11, 13, 22], and Limulus may use the same fuel. For although glycogen content of the tissues is uncertain, the overall lipid content is high [14], the eggs accounting for the largest fraction and the digestive gland having a substantial amount. In its lipid content and composition, Limulus resembles copepods rather than the larger crustaceans [14]. Limulus also has a high carnitine content [6], and since this compound is required for fat catabolism [15] it is possible that fats play a large role in the overall energy metabolism. The activity of hexokinase in the muscle is similar to that of other crustaceans and insects [33], suggesting that the ability to use glucose is similar.

Studies on the kinetic properties of lactate dehydrogenase [17, 18], pyruvate kinase [33], arginine kinase [2], glyceraldehyde 3-phosphate dehydrogenase [30], aldolase [31], and phosphoenolpyruvate carboxykinase (PEPCK) [5] have been performed recently. The lactate dehydrogenase of Limulus is unique in being D-specific [16–18]. It is a dimeric enzyme [17, 21, 26], unlike the lactate dehydrogenase of vertebrates, which is tetrameric [25]. There are several iso-zymes present in the tissues, but Long and Kaplan [17] have shown that one group predominates in the muscle and the others occur in other tissues. They have also shown that the muscle isozymes are kinetically different from the others, exhibiting a larger Michaelis constant for pyruvate and being relatively insensitive to inhibition by pyruvate, whereas the isozymes from the heart were inhibited by concentrations of pyruvate greater than 0.2 mM. Falkowski [5] has shown that the activity of PEPCK increases in the muscle and hepatopancreas of Limulus when the animal is exposed to anoxia over a period of days. The Michaelis constants determined for the substrates of PEPCK from Limulus are similar to those of other invertebrates studied [23, 33, 34]. The presence of substantial activities of PEPCK in the muscle of Limulus is unusual. Another unusual feature is that pyruvate kinase is inhibited by alanine and activated by fructose 1,6-bisphosphate [33]. These facts led to the suggestion that the anaerobic metabolism of Limulus is similar to that of bivalves and that succinate might be formed as a result of glucose catabolism [5, 33]. The kinetic properties of glyceraldehyde 3-phosphate dehydrogenase and aldolase are similar to those of other species studied [30, 31]. The arginine kinase is a monomer of molecular weight 38,000, similar to that of the enzyme from crustacea and other arthropods [2]. There are two isozymes present in the muscle of Limulus, but their kinetic properties are not significantly different [1]. The Michaelis constants are similar to the values reported for arginine kinase from other Arthropoda [1, 2].

Hammen and Osborn [10] showed that tissues of many marine invertebrates, including the digestive gland of Limulus, have the ability to fix carbon dioxide into organic compounds, particularly succinic, fumaric, and malic acids. This is an interesting observation in that many intertidal bivalves that produce succinic acid under anoxic stress also incorporate carbon dioxide into succinic acid [20, 27–29]. Those invertebrates that are more tolerant to anoxia and produce succinic acid show a higher fumarate reductase/succinate dehydrogenase ratio [9]. The values obtained for the digestive gland, heart, and muscle of Limulus were intermediate between the groups [8], suggesting some ability to form succinic acid under anoxic stress. Those invertebrates that produce succinate have altered metabolic pathways that produce more ATP during anoxia than if lactate were produced [12, 35, 36]. This increase in the yield of ATP may in part assist them in surviving prolonged anoxia. The heart of Limulus is quite tolerant of anoxia or hypoxia [4, 5], and it is possible that it has the ability to produce substantial amounts of succinate during anoxia.

To test this theory the degradation of (^{14}C)glucose by the heart of Limulus was monitored under aerobic and anaerobic conditions to determine whether lactic acid or succinic acid was the predominant product. This tissue was chosen because I found it had a greater activity of hexokinase than did the muscle, and the properties of the lactate dehydrogenase suggested that it might not accumulate large amounts of lactate during anoxia. The incorporation of radioactivity into the amino acids was also followed to see if there was any similarity to bivalves.

These studies showed that the heart produces lactic acid predominantly, with a small amount of succinate and alanine.

MATERIALS AND METHODS

All biochemical reagents were obtained from Sigma Chemical; other chemicals were reagent grade. The (U-^{14}C)glucose was purchased from New England Nuclear. The succinate dehydrogenase was a gift from Dr. W. A. Bridger, Department of Biochemistry, University of Alberta; D-lactate dehydrogenase was purified from Limulus muscle by the procedure described by Long and Kaplan [17].

Incubation With Radioactive Glucose

The heart was dissected from a freshly killed Limulus, cut longitudinally, and then transversely into small segments. These were weighed and placed in small vials containing 1 ml of seawater that had been passed through a Millipore filter. The vials were then either gassed with air or with nitrogen for 30 min at room temperature (26–30°C). At the end of this period 1 mCi of (U-^{14}C)glucose was injected into each vial, which was then placed on a shaker; the incubation continued for 1 h. The incubation was stopped by the injection of 1 ml of 2 M hydrochloric acid. The tissue was removed and homogenized in 1 ml of 70% ethanol. The homogenate was centrifuged at 5,000g for 10 min, and the supernatant was removed and the pellet was discarded. The amino acid and acidic fractions were separated by a modification of the ion exchange method of [29]. The supernatant was applied to a small column (bed volume of 2 ml) of Bio-Rad AG-50W ion exchange resin. The filtrate was collected, the column washed with 5 ml distilled water, and the filtrates combined. This fraction contained the acidic and neutral compounds. The amino acids were then eluted from the column with 5 ml of 2M ammonium hydroxide. Both fractions were freeze-dried prior to the separation of their components by thin layer chromatography.

Thin Layer Chromatography

The fractions were prepared for chromatography by dissolving them in 0.4 ml of methanol with 0.05 ml of 1 N HCl added. Silica gel plates, 5 × 20 cm (EM Reagents), were used and each plate was divided into half. To each half 0.2 ml of a sample was applied. The solvent systems used were 1) for the amino acids—ethanol/34% ammonium hydroxide 7/3, and butanol/acetic acid/water 3/1/1; and 2) for carboxylic acids and neutral compounds—ethanol/water/25% ammonium hydroxide 100/12/6, and chloroform/formic acid/methanol 80/1/1 [37]. Standards were also subjected to chromatography in the same chamber, but on separate plates. Amino acids were detected on the standard plates by spraying with 0.2% ninhydrin in butanol and heating at 100°C for 5 min. Carboxylic acids were detected by spraying with 0.1% 2,6-dichlorophenolindophenol in ethanol and heating at 60°C for 20 min.

The radioactive plates were dried in air at room temperature, then marked in 1 cm units from the origin, and each 1 cm strip was scraped off and placed in a 5 ml plastic sintillation vial to which 3.5 ml of Aquasol-2 was added. The vial and contents were shaken vigorously for 1 min, and then counted in a Beckman LS8000 scintillation counter. A plot of the distribution of radioactivity on the plate was made, and the peaks were identified by reference to the standards.

After the initial experiments had been performed, the conditions were altered to see if the pattern of incorporation would be altered. In the first case incubations were prolonged up to 6 h; in the second the preincubation under nitrogen was extended to 5 h and then the isotope was added; and in the third case 100 mM alanine was added to the incubation medium. All tissues were treated as described previously, and the incorporation of isotope into alanine, lactate, and succinate was determined as desribed.

Production of Lactate and Succinate

The hearts were removed from three freshly killed animals, and each was divided into three pieces of about the same size. The portions were quickly weighed; one was immediately placed in cold 7% perchloric acid, the second was placed in 1 ml seawater and aerated, and the third was placed in a vial with 1 ml seawater and gassed with nitrogen for 1 h. Then both the aerobic and anaerobic tissues were placed in 1 ml of 7% perchloric acid. The tissues were homogenized with a Teflon glass homogenizer, and the solution was centrifuged at 5,000g for 10 min. The supernatants were neutralized with 3 M potassium carbonate and then assayed for lactate and succinate by standard enzymatic methods [19, 32].

RESULTS

The patterns of incorporation of radioactivity into the acidic and neutral compounds, and the amino acids are shown in Table I. In all of the anaerobic incubations, most of the radioactivity was found in lactate, with a small amount present in succinate and malate. Alanine was the only amino acid that was significantly labeled.

The concentrations of lactate, succinate, aspartate, and alanine before and after in vitro incubation are shown in Table II. The changes in these metabolites are very slight and insignificant.

DISCUSSION

These preliminary results indicate that the heart of Limulus degrades glucose primarily to lactate under hypoxic conditions in vitro. It would therefore appear

TABLE I. Anaerobic Metabolism of (U-^{14}C)Glucose by the Heart of Limulus polyphemus

	1 h air	1 h N_2	5 h air	5 h N_2	1 h air, + 50 mM alanine	1 h N_2, + 50 mM alanine
% Total ^{14} in tissue extract*	6.5	8.5	25.0	6.6	9.3	8.0
% Metabolized glucose in:						
Succinate	9	12	13	9	5	5
Lactate	62	57	18	45	61	53
Alanine	17	21	46	35	17	31

*The data represent the averages of two experiments.

TABLE II. Concentrations of Selected Metabolites in the Heart of Limulus polyphemus Under Aerobic and Anaerobic Conditions (the data are expressed as μmole/g wet wt)

	Preparation*	Lactate	Succinate	Alanine	Aspartate
Freshly isolated	1	2.5	1.7	1.6	3.2
	2	3.6	2.1	1.4	5.2
	3	3.0	2.4	1.0	6.4
Air, 1 h	1	2.3	1.6	1.7	3.2
	2	3.0	1.5	1.0	3.0
	3	2.7	3.6	1.7	5.7
N_2, 1 h	1	3.6	2.4	1.1	3.8
	2	3.6	1.7	0.9	4.0
	3	2.6	2.6	0.9	4.7

*Individual hearts were divided into three portions for the experiment.

that the unusual regulatory properties of pyruvate kinase in the muscle of this animal seem unrelated to the production of succinate during anoxia. A small amount of glucose is converted to succinate, but this does not necessarily involve PEPCK, since the Krebs' cycle might still function at a much reduced level during anoxia. It is possible that the conditions in vivo are different from those in vitro, and that more succinate would be produced in vivo. Robertson [24], however, has shown that the concentration of lactate in Limulus muscle can be quite high, which provides additional support for the notion that lactate is the predominant anaerobic product.

It is notable that there was little or no change in the concentrations of the alanine, succinate and lactate when these were measured in an in vitro system. Possibly the tissues were damaged in the dissection, and the metabolites leaked into the medium during the experiment, or the metabolic rate of the tissue was very low. In thinking about anaerobic metabolism in Limulus, it is important to note that the concentrations of free amino acids in the tissues of this animal arc lower than those found in marine crustacea [3, 24]. On this basis it seems unlikely that Limulus would produce amino acids during anaerobiosis in a pattern similar to bivalves [35, 36]. Further work will be required to obtain a viable, in vitro system in which it will be possible to measure the heart rate during anoxia simultaneously with the rates of lactate production and succinate production.

REFERENCES

1. Blethen SL: Kinetic properties of the arginine kinase isoenzymes of Limulus polyphemus. Arch Biochem Biophys 149:244–251, 1972.
2. Blethen SL, Kaplan NO: Characteristics of Arthropod arginine kinases. Biochemistry 7:2123–2135, 1968.
3. Bricteux-Grégoire S, Duchâteau-Bosson G, Jeuniaux C, Florkin M: Les constituants osmotiquement actifs des muscles et leur contribution à la regulation isosmotique intracellulaire chez Limulus polyphemus. Comp Biochem Physiol 19:729–736, 1966.
4. De Fur PL, Mangum CP: The effects of environmental variables on the heart rates of invertebrates. Comp Biochem Physiol 62A:283–294, 1979.
5. Falkowski PG: Facultative anaerobiosis in Limulus polyphemus: Phosphoenolpyruvate carboxykinase and heart activities. Comp Biochem Physiol 49B:749–759, 1974.
6. Fraenkel G: The distribution of vitamin B1 (carnitine) throughout the animal kingdom. Arch Biochem Biophys 50:486–495, 1954.
7. Friedman SG: Metabolism of carbohydrates in insects. In Florkin M, Scheer BT (eds): "Chemical Zoology," Vol 5. New York: Academic Press, 1970, pp 167–197.
8. Hammen CS: Lactate and succinate oxidoreductase in marine invertebrates. Mar Biol 4:233–238, 1969.
9. Hammen CS, Lum SC: Carbon dioxide fixation in marine invertebrates. Quantitative relations (Bdelloura candida, Limulus polyphemus, Heterakis gallinae). Nature (Lond) 201:416–417, 1964.
10. Hammen CS, Osborn PJ: Carbon dioxide fixation in marine invertebrates: A survey of major phyla. Science 130:1409–1410, 1959.
11. Hansford RG, Sacktor B: Oxidative metabolism of Insecta. In Florkin M, Scheer BT (eds): "Chemical Zoology," Vol 6. New York: Academic Press, 1971, pp 213–247.
12. Hochachka PW, Fields J, Mustafa T: Animal life without oxygen: Basic biochemical mechanisms. Am Zool 13:543–556, 1973.
13. Hohnke L, Sheer BT: Carbohydrate metabolism in crustaceans. In Florkin M, Scheer BT (eds): "Chemical Zoology," Vol 5. New York: Academic Press, 1970, pp 147–165.
14. Horst DJ van der, Oudejans RCHM, Plug AG, Sluis I van der: Fatty acids of the female horseshoe crab Xiphosura (Limulus polyphemus). Mar Biol 20:291–296, 1973.
15. Lehninger AI: "Biochemistry," Ed 2. New York: Worth, 1975, 1104 pp.
16. Long GL, Kaplan NO: D-lactate specific pyridine nucleotide lactate dehydrogenase in animals. Science 162:685–686, 1968.
17. Long GL, Kaplan NO: Diphosphopyridine nucleotide-linked D-lactate dehydrogenase from the horseshoe crab, Limulus polyphemus and the seaworm, Nereis virens. I. Physical and chemical properties. Arch Biochem Biophys 154:696–710, 1973.
18. Long GL, Kaplan NO: Diphosphopyridine nucleotide-linked D-lactate dehydrogenase from the horseshoe crab, Limulus polyphemus and the seaworm, Nereis virens. II. Catalytic properties. Arch Biochem Biophys 154:711–725, 1973.

19. Lowry OH, Passonneau JV: "A Flexible System of Enzymatic Analysis." New York: Academic Press, 1972.
20. Loxton J, Chaplin AE: The metabolism of Mytilus edulis L. during facultative anaerobiosis. Biochem Soc Symp 1:419–421, 1973.
21. Massaro EJ: Horseshoe crab lactate dehydrogenase: Tissue distribution and molecular weight. Science 167:994–996, 1970.
22. Munday KA, Poat PC: Respiratory and energy metabolism in Crustacea. In Florkin M, Scheer BT (eds): "Chemical Zoology," Vol 6. New York: Academic Press, 1971, pp 191–211.
23. Mustafa T, Hochachka PW: Enzymes in facultative anaerobiosis of molluscs. II. Basic catalytic properties of phosphoenolpyruvate carboxykinase in oyster adductor muscle. Comp Biochem Physiol 45B:639–656, 1973.
24. Robertson JD: Osmotic and ionic regulation in the horseshoe crab Limulus polyphemus (Linnaeus). Biol Bull 138:157–183, 1970.
25. Rossman MG, Liljas A, Branden CI, Banaszak LJ: Evolutionary and structural relationships among dehydrogenases. In Boyer PD (ed): "Enzymes," ED 3. New York: Academic Press, 1975, pp 61–102.
26. Selander RK, Yang SY: Horseshoe crab lactate dehydrogenases: Evidence for a dimeric structure. Science 169:179–181, 1970.
27. Simpson JW, Awapara J: Phosphoenol pyruvate carboxykinase activity in invertebrates. Comp Biochem Physiol 12:457–464, 1964.
28. Simpson JW, Awapara J: The pathway of glucose degradation in some invertebrates. Comp Biochem Physiol 18:537–548, 1966.
29. Stokes TM, Awapara J: Alanine and succinate as end-products of glucose degradation in the clam Rangia cuneata. Comp Biochem Physiol 25:883–892, 1968.
30. Suzuki K, Watanabe M, Imahori K: Glyceraldehyde 3-phosphate dehydrogenase of horseshoe crab (Tachypleus tridentatus). J Biochem 77:269–279, 1975.
31. Suzuki K, Shiho O, and Imahori K: Fructose-diphosphate aldolase of horseshoe crab (Tachypleus tridentatus). J Biochem 77:281–289, 1975.
32. Williamson JR, Corkey BE: Assays of intermediates of the citric acid cycle and related compounds by fluorometric enzyme methods. In Lowenstein J (ed): "Methods in Enzymology," Vol 13. New York: Academic Press, 1969, pp 434–513.
33. Zammit VA, Newsholme EA: Properties of pyruvate kinase and phosphoenolpyruvate carboxykinase in relation to the direction and regulation of phosphoenolpyruvate metabolism in muscles of the frog and marine invertebrates. Biochem J 174:979–987, 1978.
34. Zwaan A de, Bont A de: Phosphenolypyruvate carboxykinase from adductor muscle tissue of the sea mussel Mytilus edulis L. J Comp Physiol 96:85–94, 1975.
35. Zwaan A de, Kluytmans JHFM, Zandee DI: Facultative anaerobiosis in molluscs. Biochem Soc Symp 41:133–168, 1976.
36. Zwaan A de, Wijsman TCM: Anaerobic metabolism in Bivalvia (Mollusca): Characteristics of anaerobic metabolism. Comp Biochem Physiol 54B:313–324, 1976.
37. Zweig G, Sherma J: "Handbook of Chromatography," Vol I. Cleveland: CRC Press, 1972.

Physiology and Biology of Horseshoe Crabs: Studies on
Normal and Environmentally Stressed Animals, pages 133–146
© 1982 Alan R. Liss, Inc., 150 Fifth Avenue, New York, NY 10011

Circulatory Physiology of Limulus

James R. Redmond, Darwin D. Jorgensen, and George B. Bourne

INTRODUCTION

Like other arthropods, the circulatory system of Limulus is open. The general
body cavity is part of the circulatory space and is filled with blood. The anatomy
of the circulatory system has been well described by Milne-Edwards [12] and
Patton and Redenbaugh [13]. These early studies found the circulatory system
to be unusually well developed, with a large muscular heart and a surprisingly
extensive system of blood vessels. This degree of development so impressed
Milne-Edwards that he stated

> L'appareil circulatoire des Limules est plus parfait, plus compliqué que chez aucun
> animal articulé. Le sang veineux, au lieu d'être répandu dans des lacunes inter-
> organiques comme chez les Crustacés, est, dans une portion considérable de son
> parcours, renfermé dans des vaisseaux particuliers, à parois parfaitement distinctes
> des organes adjacents, naissant souvent par des ramifications d'une délicatesse
> remarquable et se redant dans des réservoirs bien circonscrits pour le plupart.

In addition to this extensive vessel system, the arterial system is remarkable in
that the central nervous system (brain and ventral nerve cords) and peripheral
nerves lie within the lumen of the arteries.

In the rest of this chapter we briefly review the literature covering various
aspects of Limulus circulatory anatomy and physiology. Next we describe and
discuss a series of experiments in which we measured the blood pressure levels
existing in different parts of the Limulus circulatory system under well-described
conditions. Blood pressure measurements are given for the pericardium, ventricle, aortae, and prebranchial venous circulation under normoxia and during aerial
exposure.

CIRCULATORY ANATOMY

Following is a brief description of the major aspects of the circulatory system. For a detailed account see Milne-Edwards [12] or Patten and Redenbaugh [13]. More recently, Shuster [17] has also described general aspects of the circulatory system and blood.

The heart is a long, muscular, middorsal tube that extends from just anterior of the level of the compound eyes posteriorly through the prosoma and back about halfway through the opisthosoma (Fig. 1). It is largest near its midpoint and tapers toward either end. The dorsal surface bears eight pairs of ostia, which open to the dorsal pericardium. A vestigial ninth pair of ostia, which do not penetrate the heart wall, is located at the extreme anterior end of the heart between the aortic valve and the origin of the paired anterior aortae. The aortic valve is interesting in that it is located in the heart lumen about 1 cm prior to the origin of the aortae. This placement of the aortic valve appears to be characteristic also of the arachnids occurring in spiders and scorpions [14]. The heart is suspended in the pericardium by nine pairs of ligaments, and like other arthropods, blood flows from the pericardium through the ostia into the lumen of the heart.

Blood leaves the heart from a series of vessels all located in the prosoma. At the anterior end of the heart, a pair of large aortae pass anteriorly and sharply ventrally. A much smaller frontal artery may be found passing anteriorly. The latter may arise from the anterior tip of the heart between the two aortae or may originate from either of the aortae near their bases. Four pairs of lateral arteries each with a pair of semilunar valves, leave the heart at the levels of the four anterior pairs of ostia. These terminate quickly in two collateral arteries that course parallel to the heart just outside the pericardium. Anteriorly, the collateral arteries give off several small branches. Posteriorly, at the tip of the heart, the two collateral arteries join in the midline and continue posteriorly as the superior abdominal artery. In the region of the second lateral artery, each collateral artery gives off a major branch that passes posteriolaterally. Near the hinge of the prosoma-opisthosoma, this vessel branches into an hepatic artery going anteriorly, an anterior marginal artery following the edge of the prosoma, and a posterior marginal artery passing posteriorly along the edge of the opisthosoma. Both anterior marginal arteries meet at the anterior border of the prosoma where they anastomose with the frontal artery. Similarly, both posterior marginal arteries meet near the base of the telson and anastomose with the superior abdominal artery. Along the length of the collateral arteries, there is a series of smaller arteries that pass laterally into the tissues, and a group that pass ventrally to the gut.

Ventrally, the two anterior aortae curve down alongside the proventriculus and esophagus toward the mouth. Above the mouth, the two aortae join to form the vascular ring encircling the mouth. In the lumen of this circular vessel lies the nerve ring (brain). Numerous arteries pass peripherally from the vascular ring, each containing a nerve attached to the ring of nervous tissue. These vessels and nerves terminate in such structures as the legs, chelicerae, lateral and median eyes, and operculum. Medially, a ventral artery passes posteriorly. The ventral nerve cord lies in its interior. The ventral artery supplies the abdominal muscles, beneath the intestine, the gills, and the caudal spine (telson). Near the base of

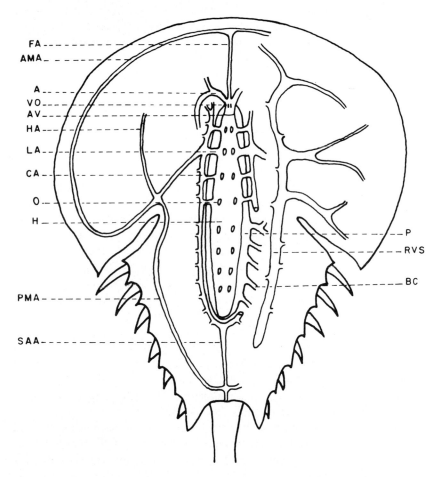

Fig. 1. Diagram of the heart, major dorsal arteries, and major ventral venous return channel. A, aorta; AMA, anterior marginal artery; AV, aortic valve; BC, branchiocardiac canal; CA, collateral artery; FA, frontal artery; H, heart; HA, hepatic artery; LA, lateral artery; O, ostium; P, pericardium; PMA, posterior marginal artery; RVS, right ventral sinus; SAA, superior abdominal artery; VO, vestigial ostia.

the caudal spine, branches of the ventral artery pass upward and anastomose with the superior abdominal artery The arterial system is very extensive, with repeated branchings, terminating in very fine vessels (Fig. 2).

The venous system, like the arterial, also appears more highly organized in Limulus than in other arthropods. Particularly in the prosoma there is an extensive branching system of channels through which blood is returned from the tissues to the book gills. Like the venous sinuses of other open systems, these channels do not have membranous walls but appear to be passageways between the cells of various tissues. These channels eventually drain into right and left ventral sinuses. These large vessel-like sinuses (sometimes called cardinal veins) convey the blood to the five pairs of book gills. After passing through the book gills, the blood is conducted to the pericardium through five pairs of branchiocardiac canals. Blood from the operculum drains into the first pair of branchiocardiac canals.

CIRCULATORY PHYSIOLOGY

Early studies on circulatory physiology in Limulus were concerned mainly with the origin of the heart beat. Carlson [3] had hoped to establish the Limulus heart as one of several invertebrate models with which to support his thesis that the mammalian heart is neurogenic. Although subsequent experimentation proved Carlson to be incorrect about the origin of the mammalian heart beat, the Limulus heart became firmly established as a useful experimental preparation for neurobiologists.

Since much of the older literature on Limulus heart control has been summarized elsewhere [1, 17], only two of the more recent findings on Limulus heart control will be mentioned here. Unlike the neurogenic adult Limulus heart, the embryonic Limulus heart was long assumed to be myogenic [4, 5, 15]. However, evidence gathered by electron microscopy and intracellular recordings has produced no indication that the embryonic Limulus heart has an initial myogenic phase [8]. Watson and Wyse [20] were able to demonstrate that Limulus coordinates gill and heart rhythms during normal activity and under conditions of hypoxia, and that such coordination is probably important in maintaining efficient circulatory-respiratory interactions.

Unlike the large body of literature on heart control and pacemaker ganglion function, the literature covering other aspects of Limulus circulatory physiology is sparse. The only studies dealing with aspects of hemodynamics are those of

---

Fig. 2. Ventral view of a cast of the circulatory system of a small Limulus (5 cm wide), prepared with Batson's No. 10 corrosion compound. The extensive branching of the arterial vessels is clearly evident. Specimen prepared by Dr. John I. Stagner.

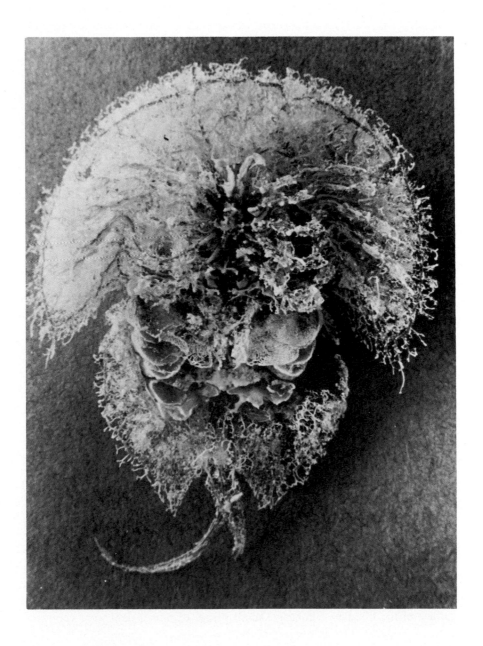

Sumwalt and McLane [19] and Abbott et al [1]. By measuring blood pressure in the frontal artery with a mercury manometer, Sumwalt and McLane [19] found that in 19 adult males blood pressure averaged 16 cm H_2O, with a range between 6 and 32 cm H_2O. Abbott et al [1] presented a single blood pressure record taken from the heart of an adult Limulus. These authors remarked that their needle catheter probably damaged the myocardium which in turn led to below normal results. They also studied the mechanical properties of rings cut from the Limulus heart muscle, demonstrating that although the Limulus heart is activated by nerves it exhibits length-tension properties characteristic of cardiac muscle. Furthermore, they showed that the force–velocity behavior is a good approximation to the Hill characteristic equation for the contractile component.

Several of the older studies were concerned with the effect of temperature on heart rate [5, 7], but more recently deFur and Mangum [6] examined the effects of environmental variables such as temperature, salinity, and low oxygen tension on the heart rate of Limulus. DeFur and Mangum found that heart rate declined by 25% with a change in salinity from 30–20%; however, after a 3-day acclimation, the rates stabilized. The temperature coefficient (Q_{10}) of the Limulus heart rate was within the physiological range. With exposure to acute hypoxia Limulus showed bradycardia, a feature that appears common to other invertebrates. These authors noted that the Limulus responses to low salinity were predictable from Fick calculations of cardiac output, and that these responses play a role in enhancing the respiratory function of hemocyanin in the altered ionic environment.

BLOOD PRESSURE MEASUREMENTS

A series of measurements were made to establish normal blood pressures in the pericardium, ventricle, aortae, and prebranchial circulation. Pressures were measured with Statham p23Db and p23V pressure transducers using 70 cm PE 160 (1.14 mm ID) polyethylene tubing catheters tipped with No. 18 hypodermic needle barrels. PE 205 (1.57 mm ID) tubing and No. 16 needles were used for venous pressures. Signals were amplified by Gould Biophysical Brush preamplifiers and recorded on a Gould model 260 Brush two-channel recorder. Snug holes were drilled through the carapace of the prosoma over the heart for the ventricular and pericardial catheters. Aortic pressures were measured through a similar hole over the base of the aortae, anterior to the aortic valve. Prebranchial venous pressures were measured ventrally, lateral to the midline, at the level of the last pair of legs. The latter opening was prepared by inserting a short length of PE 205 tubing into the left ventral sinus. This tubing passed through, and was anchored in place by, dental rubber dam material cemented to the ventral surface of the Limulus. Similarly, small pieces of rubber dam were cemented over all holes drilled for catheters. These sealed the holes to prevent bleeding and helped hold the catheter needles in place.

The Limulus was allowed to rest for several hours or overnight before measurements were taken. The animal was placed in a 30 × 36 × 16 cm plastic chamber. A rapid flow of seawater kept the chamber well aerated. A layer of sand was placed in the bottom of the chamber, and the chamber was covered with a shade to shield the experimental specimen from visual disturbance. Blood tended to clot in the catheter needles, reducing both the amplitude and frequency response of the recording system. Consequently only recordings showing good frequency response and consistent amplitude and shape of pressure pulses were used for measurements. Successful measurements were obtained from 16 specimens, 10 female and 6 male. Weights ranged from 738 to 2,078 grams, with a mean of $1,523 \pm 359$ grams.

Pressure measurements are summarized in Table I. Recordings of pericardial, ventricular, aortic, and venous pressure pulses may be seen in Figure 3. The pressures varied considerably from one specimen to the next, but the mean values seem representative of the pressure gradients in the system during resting conditions or mild activity. As would be expected, increased physical activity tended to be reflected in higher pressures in all parts of the circulatory system.

Figure 4 summarizes the events of the Limulus cardiac cycle. As the ventricle contracts, there is an initial rapid rise of pressure, probably isovolumetric, until the aortic valve opens. Then pressure continues to rise as blood is forced into the aortae and frontal artery. It seems likely that the valves to the eight lateral arteries open at the same time as the aortic valve, since the lateral arteries and the frontal artery are continuous by way of the anterior marginal artery and pressures in all should be similar. As the ventricle begins to relax, pressures fall in it and the aorta, and the aortic valve closes. Ventricular pressure drops rapidly whereas that in the aorta drops slowly. The nine pairs of elastic ligaments expand the ventricle, and blood enters from the pericardium. The ventricular–aortic pressure relationships are very much like those of a vertebrate heart.

TABLE I. Blood Pressures and Heart Rates in Limulus polyphemus

	Ventricle (23)[a]		Aorta (14)		Pericardium (9)		Ventral sinus (6)		Heart rate (30)
	Systole[b]	Diastole	Systole	Diastole	Systole	Diastole	Systole	Diastole	Beats min⁻¹
Maximum	53	9	48	34	12	7.2	20	16	51
Minimum	12	−1	10.4	5.6	0	−2.4	0	0	12
Mean	25.6	2.7	21.0	12.7	5.3	3.4	6.8	4.3	34.2
SD	11.2	2.5	10.2	7.8	2.7	3.2	1.8	2.3	10.6

[a]Number of measurements in parentheses.
[b]All pressures in cm H_2O.
Temperature 23–24°C.

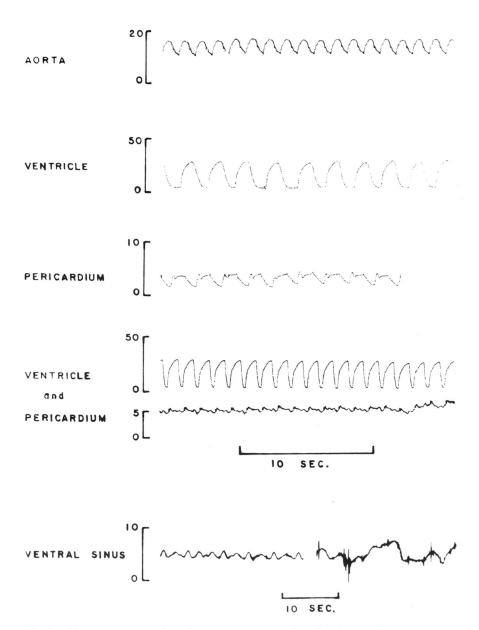

Fig. 3. Blood pressure recordings from various regions of the Limulus circulatory system. All pressures are in cm H₂O. The two examples of ventral sinus pressures represent (left) a very quiescent specimen, and (right) a typical recording from a slightly active specimen.

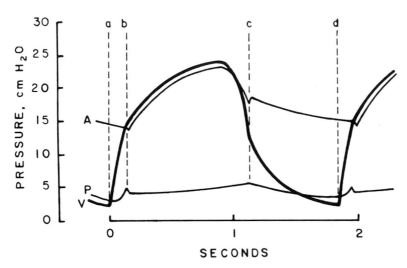

Fig. 4. The cardiac cycle in Limulus based on average blood pressures. Individual specimens varied considerably. a) Beginning of systole. a–b) Rapid tension development (isovolumetric?). b) Opening of aortic valve. b–c) Flow of blood into aortae, frontal artery, and, presumably, the lateral arteries. c) Closure of aortic valve. c–d) Relaxation and filling of ventricle. The exact point at which ventricular and pericardial pressures cross is uncertain.

Pressure fluctuations in the pericardium are much less in amplitude and tend to follow the direction of ventricular pressure pulses. The opening and closing of the aortic valves can be seen as small peaks. It is somewhat surprising that pericardial pressure rises as ventricular contraction occurs, but this may be the result of the attachment of the ventricular suspensory ligaments to the pericardial walls. In animals with a closed pericardium, pericardial pressure changes are reciprocal to those of the ventricle. In eight specimens where pericardial and ventricular pressures were measured simultaneously, the difference between minimal pericardial and minimal ventricular pressure was 2.64 ± 2.44 cm H_2O.

Limulus moves onto muddy beaches to lay eggs and thus experiences exposure to air. To examine the effect of air exposure on heart rate and blood pressure, we drained water from the experimental chamber while monitoring heart rate and ventricular or aortic blood pressure. Six animals were tested in this fashion. In all cases a prompt bradycardia occurred with air exposure (Figs. 5 and 6). The reduction in heart rate varied from 17% to 55% with a mean of 37.6%. As water was readmitted to the chamber, the heart rate returned to normal levels very rapidly.

Changes in blood pressures followed changes in heart rate fairly closely (Fig. 6). Although heart rate and blood pressure dropped during air exposure, blood

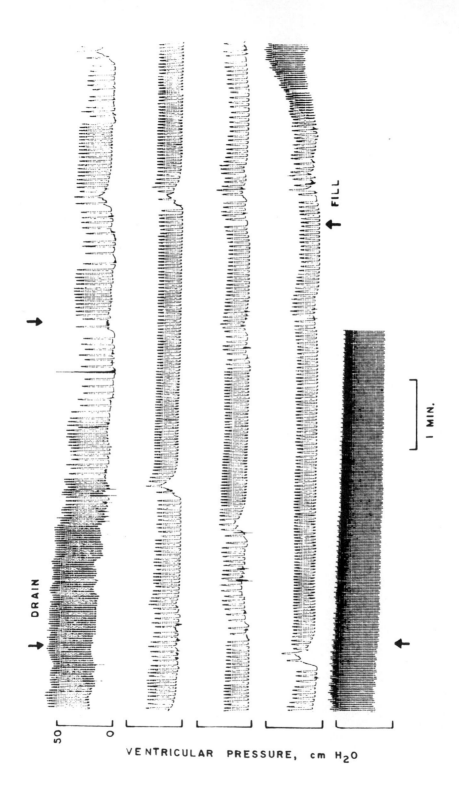

DRAIN

FILL

1 MIN.

VENTRICULAR PRESSURE, cm H₂O

50

0

continued to be pumped, and a rapid recovery occurred upon reimmersion. Occassionally, during air exposure, the heart rate would oscillate between slower and faster rates. Figure 5 illustrates this phenomenon. In all but one of the air-exposed specimens another behavior appeared. A pressure pulse lasting over several heart beats would appear periodically (Fig. 5). This pressure pulse was found simultaneously in the venous, pericardial, ventricular, and arterial blood. Its origin was a physical movement, an arching of the opisthosoma, possibly to increase the surface exposure of the gills. The magnitude of this body movement

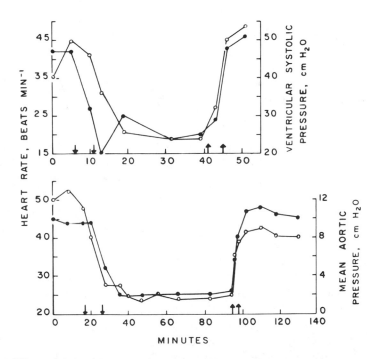

Fig. 6. Effects of air exposure on the heart rate and blood pressure of two specimens of Limulus. Downward-pointing arrows indicate draining of chamber; upward arrows indicate filling interval. Heart rate ●; Blood pressure ○.

Fig. 5. Changes in heart rate and ventricular blood pressure of a Limulus exposed to air and reimmersed. The interval between the first pair of arrows indicates water draining from the tank; the second pair indicate the filling period. Note the decrease in heart rate and pressure during air exposure and the rapid recovery upon reimmersion. The tachycardia shown in this record following reimmersion did not occur in all specimens. The periodic slow triangular pressure pulses coincided with movements of the opisthosoma during air exposure.

pulse was either equal wherever measured, or was slightly higher in the ventral venous circulation.

CONCLUSIONS

The results of the present study support Milne-Edwards' contention that the circulatory system of Limulus is well developed and, anatomically, among the most extensive of the arthropods. Circulatory casts (Fig. 2) demonstrate not only the very extensive branching of the arterial system, but also the apparent absence of the very large venous sinuses that characterize many "open" circulatory systems.

The large muscular heart is capable of generating appreciable pressures. The range of blood pressures recorded was great. To what extent this represents individual variation, physical condition, or activity levels was not determined. Certainly the activity of the individual specimens differed; however, values were not taken from specimens showing more than moderate activity. Perhaps some of the variation is an expression of the discrete levels of activity that Limulus has been reported to exhibit [6]. We did not measure blood flow, but estimates based on Fick measurements by Mangum et al [9, 10] indicate cardiac outputs of 78 and 105 ml·kg $^{-1}$·min^{-1} at 15° and 20°C respectively. These rates are similar to values reported for decapod crustaceans [6], and are greater than the cardiac outputs reported for many poikilothermic vertebrates [16].

During air exposure, heart rate and blood pressure decrease together. It should be pointed out that the pressure measurements presented here do not take into account the pressure change resulting from the drop in water level in the chamber as the water was drained out. This change in level amounted to 10 cm of water. In the case of animals with low blood pressure, such as the specimen represented in the lower half of Figure 6, the drop in pressure as the water was lowered, if it was transmitted entirely to the circulatory system, could account for most or all of the observed blood pressure changes. However, since the blood pressure drop was usually greater than 10 cm of water and was present in all animals tested, it is believed to be a normal physiological response to air exposure. Regardless of the magnitude of the decrease in heart rate and blood pressure, the heart continued to beat and pump blood during air exposure. The significance of these changes is difficult to assess without knowledge of simultaneous changes in the chemistry of the blood. It is known that many invertebrates, including Limulus, respond to hypoxia with a bradycardia [6]. Although it seems likely that some degree of hypoxia does develop in the blood of Limulus exposed to air, the magnitude of the hypoxia is unknown.

The rapid recovery of heart rate and blood pressure as water was readmitted to the chamber was striking. Whether this recovery was triggered by changing blood conditions or by a more superficial reflex, such as wetting of the gills, has not been established. It is tempting to interpret this rapid recovery as an aspect of adaptation to periodic aerial exposure whereby Limulus can immediately assume normal activity levels upon reentrance into the water.

Like other invertebrates, the circulatory physiology of Limulus is poorly known. It is perhaps surprising to find that one of the most primitive of the arthropods possesses such a complex, extensive, and apparently effective circulatory system. Yet, this fits the pattern emerging from studies on decapod crustaceans [2, 6, 11, 18], indicating that these forms also possess circulatory systems with high cardiac outputs, rapid flow, and often moderately high pressures. Obviously many questions remain to be answered before the real capabilities of these "open" systems can be properly assessed.

REFERENCES

1. Abbott BC, Lange F, Parnas I, Parmley W, and Sonnenblick E: Physiological and pharmacological properties of Limulus heart. In McCann FV (ed): "Experientia Supplementum 15, Comparative Physiology of the Heart: Current Trends." Stuttgart: Birkhauser Verlag, 1969, pp 232–243.
2. Belman BW: Some aspects of the circulatory physiology of the spiny lobster, Panulirus interruptus. Mar Biol 29:295–305, 1975.
3. Carlson AJ: The nervous origin of the heart beat in Limulus, and the nervous nature of coordination or conduction in the heart. Am J Physiol 12:67–74, 1904.
4. Carlson AJ, Meek WJ: On the mechanism of the embryonic heart rhythm in Limulus. Am J Physiol 21:1–10, 1908.
5. Crozier WJ, Stier TJB: Temperature and frequency of cardiac contractions in embryos of Limulus. J Gen Physiol 10:501–518, 1927.
6. deFur PL, Mangum CP: The effects of environmental variables on the heart rates of invertebrates. Comp Biochem Physiol 62A:283–294, 1979.
7. Garrey WJ: Dynamics of nerve cells. I. The temperature coefficient of the neurogenic rhythm of the heart of Limulus polyphemus. J Gen Physiol 3:41–48, 1920.
8. Gibson D, Lang F: Is embryonic Limulus heart really myogenic? Am Zool 19:39–51, 1979.
9. Mangum CP, Booth CE, deFur PL, Heckel NA, Henry RP, Oglesby LC, Polites G: The ionic environment of hemocyanin in Limulus polyphemus. Biol Bull 150:453–467, 1976.
10. Mangum CP, Freadman MA, Johansen K: The quantitative role of hemocyanin in aerobic respiration of Limulus polyphemus. J Exp Zool 191:279–285, 1975.
11. McMahan BR, Wilkins JL: Periodic respiratory and circulatory performance in the red rock crab Cancer productus. J Exp Biol 202:363–374, 1977.
12. Milne-Edwards A: Recherches sur l'anatomie des Limules. Ann Sci Nat 17, 4:1–67, 1872.
13. Patten W, Redenbaugh WA: Studies on Limulus. II. The nervous system of Limulus polyphemus with observations upon the general anatomy. J Morphol 16:91–200, 1899/1900.
14. Petrunkevitch A: The circulatory system and segmentation of Arachnida. J Morphol 36:157–189, 1922.
15. Prosser CL: An analysis of the action of acetylcholine on hearts, particularly in arthropods. Biol Bull 83:145–164, 1942.
16. Prosser CL: "Comparative Animal Physiology." Philadelphia: W.B. Saunders Co., 1973, pp 1–966.
17. Shuster CN Jr: The circulatory system and blood of the horseshoe crab. U.S. Department of Energy, Federal Energy Regulatory Commission, 0014. 1978.

18. Spaargaren DH: On stroke volume of the heart and cardiac output in aquatic animals. Neth J Sea Res 10:131–139, 1976.
19. Sumwalt HM, McLane K: The blood pressure of Limulus. Biol Bull 65:372, 1933.
20. Watson WH III, Wyse GA: Coordiantion of heart and gill rhythms in Limulus. J Comp Physiol 124:267–275, 1978.

Physiology and Biology of Horseshoe Crabs: Studies on
Normal and Environmentally Stressed Animals, pages 147–172
© 1982 Alan R. Liss, Inc., 150 Fifth Avenue, New York, NY 10011

The Role of the Coxal Gland in Ionic, Osmotic, and pH Regulation in the Horseshoe Crab Limulus polyphemus

David W. Towle, Charlotte P. Mangum, Bruce A. Johnson, and Nicholas A. Mauro

Following reduction of environmental salinity, blood levels of total osmolality, Na^+, Cl^-, Ca^{+2}, and Mg^{+2} reached steady-state levels within 12–24 hours after the salinity change. The increasingly hyperosmotic nature of the blood at the lower salinities was accompanied by reduced urine/blood ratios of Na^+ and Cl^-, both of which appeared to be maintained out of electrochemical equilibrium in those salinities. Of several tissues examined, only coxal gland contained substantial levels of the Na^+-transporting enzyme, $Na^+ + K^+$-dependent ATPase. Most notable was the low $Na^+ + K^+$-ATPase activity in the gills, chitinous envelopes that lack the complex transporting epithelium found in gills of other aquatic arthropods. Ultrastructural studies of the coxal gland substantiated our conclusion that, in contrast to the excretory organs of crustaceans, the coxal gland of Limulus polyphemus is associated with regulation of the major blood ions, Na^+ and Cl^-.

INTRODUCTION

The horseshoe crab Limulus polyphemus is a euryhaline chelicerate whose capacity for extracellular anisosmotic osmoregulation was reported as long ago as 1905 [19]. The blood of L. polyphemus remains essentially isosmotic to the medium in salinities above 35‰, but becomes increasingly hyperosmotic as the salinity is decreased [12, 47]. The lower limit of tolerance appears to be a function of maturity or size, with the smaller specimens showing greater adaptability to low salinities [34].

Although the concentrations of Na^+ and Cl^-, the major ions in the blood, are isoionic to the medium in small (< 118 g) L. polyphemus acclimated to high salinities (> 32‰) [47], the blood of large horseshoe crabs (> 824 g) is slightly but significantly hypoionic to the medium in high salinity [34]. In both large and small animals, however, the blood becomes increasingly hyperionic to the medium as the salinity is decreased. At 8.8–9.4‰, for example, the blood/ medium ratios of Na^+ and Cl^- were reported to be 2.17 and 1.53, respectively [34].

Whether these differences in ionic concentrations are the result of active transport or diffusive permeability changes is not known, because no measurements of transepithelial potentials in L. polyphemus have been reported. Water permeability was shown to decline substantially in very small L. polyphemus subjected to salinity reduction [24]. The site of permeability changes was not investigated, however. Although the gills of other aquatic arthropods are well recognized as important sites of ion and water flux, both active and passive [3, 36], no quantitative estimate of the significance of the gills in ionic regulation by horseshoe crabs is available.

The excretory organ of euryhaline arthropods has been regarded generally as a major route of salt loss that imposes an additional load on the osmoregulatory activities at the gills, although freshwater species are able to produce a somewhat dilute urine [44]. Earlier observations on L. polyphemus indicated that both Na^+ and Cl^- are conserved during urine formation in low salinities, resulting in a reduction of urine osmolality [34].

Embryologically related to the crustacean antennal glands, the interconnected coxal glands at the bases of the second through fifth appendages of L. polyphemus expel urine through nephropores on the posterior surface of the fifth appendage [2]. Although several biochemical and ultrastructural studies of mandibulate antennal glands and coxal glands have appeared [14, 42, 43, 49, 55], few similar studies of chelicerate coxal glands have been reported [46], and little information is available on their capacity for ion excretion and reabsorption.

A biochemical marker of tissues that transport large amounts of Na^+ is the enzyme $Na^+ + K^+$-dependent adenosine triphosphatase ($Na^+ + K^+$-ATPase) [5, 62]. This membrane-bound enzyme moves Na^+ across the plasma membrane out of animal cells in exchange for K^+ or NH_4^+, using energy released from the hydrolysis of ATP [48]. The enzyme is localized in interdigitating lateral membranes and in invaginations of basal membranes of ion-transporting cells, usually adjacent to abundant mitochondria, and therefore pumps Na^+ into intercellular spaces [62].

Several investigators have suggested that the regulation of blood Na^+ and pH are coupled at a physiological level [eg, 15]. However, even the site of acid-base regulation in aquatic arthropods is poorly known. Whereas L. polyphemus excretes urine that is highly acidic to the blood at high salinity and alkaline to the blood at low salinity [34], the antennal gland in freshwater-adapted Callinectes sapidus produces a urine that has essentially the same pH as the blood under normoxic conditions, and lacks a compensatory response to hypercapnic conditions [11].

In this contribution we report data that provide further support for the greater importance of the coxal gland in L. polyphemus than the antennal gland in crustaceans, in both osmotic and respiratory regulation.

MATERIALS AND METHODS

Animals and General Experimental Procedures

Adult specimens of Limulus polyphemus weighing 0.80–3.39 kg (19–32 cm prosomal width) were maintained unfed for up to 2 weeks in outdoor, shaded tanks of rapidly running seawater (34–35‰, 23–25°C). Acclimation to different salinities was accomplished in closed, shallow tanks of aerated seawater diluted with tap water. These experimental media were replaced every 1 or 2 days. Exposure to hypoxic water was accomplished in the same tanks, after lowering the PO_2 with N_2. Animals were exposed to air in large plastic bags that had been moistened to create a high humidity. Nephropores of some experimental animals were plugged with sealed polyethylene tubing held in place with cyanoacrylate adhesive.

In the experiments designed to describe the time course of adaptation to low salinity or low oxygen, the data were taken and analyzed as paired observations on the same individuals, according to Student's t-test. The data for the composition of the blood and urine were also taken from the same individuals, and analyzed as the urine/blood ratio, the null hypothesis being that it equals unity.

Blood Ionic and Respiratory Properties

Blood samples were taken for ionic analyses by puncturing the membrane at the base of the telson with a hypodermic needle. After centrifuging the samples in a Beckman Microfuge for 5 min, the supernatant was analyzed. Urine was taken by catheterization as described earlier [34]. Osmolality was measured with a Wescor vapor pressure osmometer (model 3130A), free Na^+, Ca^{+2}, and Mg^{+2} with ion-selective electrodes (described in detail by Mangum et al [35]), total Na^+ by flame photometry (Coleman model 21), total Cl^- by coulometric titration (Buchler Chloridometer model 4-2500), and ammonia by the phenol hypochlorite method [21, 60].

For the determination of respiratory and metabolic properties, blood was taken anaerobically into hypodermic syringes from the base of the telson (prebranchial) and the junction of the pro- and opisthosomae (postbranchial). Blood PCO_2 and pH were analyzed with a Radiometer BMS1 apparatus, using the pH module as the readout for both electrodes. The PCO_2 electrode was calibrated with seawater equilibrated with precision gas mixtures in the range 0.50–3.03% CO_2 (Matheson and Radiometer). Urine was collected in large volumes (1.5 ml) with the tip of the catheter several cm below the air interface, and the bottom cm used.

Because the enzyme responsible for lactate production in Limulus yields the D stereoisomer [33], total blood lactate was measured according to the modification of the Barker and Summerson procedure described by LePage in Umbreit et al [66]. Samples of 0.5 ml were used, and the calibration curve was constructed with zinc lactate.

Transepithelial Potential Measurements

Transepithelial potentials were measured according to the procedure described by Kirschner [32]. Individual animals were placed in an acrylic bath partially filled with water from the acclimation tank so that a large portion of the dorsal prosoma was exposed to air; the ventral portion of the body including the gills was completely immersed. A bridge electrode fabricated from PE-90 tubing filled with 3% agar and balanced salt solution was inserted into a 1.6-mm hole through the air-exposed carapace in the region of the digestive gland. A small leakage of blood prior to insertion indicated that the bridge was in contact with hemolymph. A second bridge, consisting of PE-240 tubing containing 2% agar and 3 M KCl was placed in the bath. Both bridges were connected via calomel electrodes in 3 M KCl to a Keithley 600-B electrometer. Asymmetry potentials of bridges and electrodes were less than 2 mV, and junction potentials at the tip of the bath bridge were assumed to be negligible. After correcting for asymmetry, the measured potentials were allowed to stabilize for at least 20 min before recording the measurement. Equilibrium potentials for Na^+ and Cl^- were calculated from the Nernst equation, using values of free Na^+ in the blood and total ion concentrations elsewhere, at a temperature of 22°C.

Measurements of $Na^+ + K^+$-ATPase Activities

Dissected tissues were placed in ice-cold homogenizing medium (0.25 M sucrose, 6 mM disodium ethylenediamine tetraacetic acid, 20 mM imidazole, pH 6.8 with acetic acid), briefly blotted, weighed, and homogenized in 20 volumes of fresh homogenizing medium containing 0.1% sodium deoxycholate [26, 64]. Homogenates were filtered through two layers of cheesecloth and were assayed immediately for enzymatic activity.

$Na^+ + K^+$-dependent ATPase activity was measured at 30°C by a coupled assay system in a medium containing up to 0.1 ml of filtered homogenate plus 20 mM imidazole (pH 7.8), 90 mM NaCl, 10 mM KCl, 5 mM $MgCl_2$, 5 mM disodium ATP, 0.1 mM nicotinamide adenine dinucleotide (reduced), 2.5 mM phosphoenol pyruvate, and 20 µl pyruvate kinase/lactate dehydrogenase mixture (Sigma 40-7) in a final volume of 2.0 ml [53, 56]. Control assays contained 1

TABLE I. Osmotic and Ionic Composition of the Medium and of Blood and Urine of Limulus polyphemus Acclimated to High (35‰) and Low (8‰) Salinity

	Osmolality (mOsm)	Na^+ (mM)	Ca^{+2} (mM)	Mg^{+2} (mM)	Cl^- (mM)
High salinity					
Medium	1,043–1,059	465–473	8.89–9.13	46.0–48.1	554–565
Blood	1,053 ± 2 (12)	428 ± 5 (6)	7.73 ± 0.11 (6)	41.6 ± 0.1 (6)	532 ± 9 (6)
Urine	1,040 (2)	463 ± 5 (6)	8.14 ± 0.13 (6)	47.3 ± 0.8 (6)	557 ± 10 (6)
Low salinity					
Medium	240	93–113	2.83	12.3–16.9	119–142
Blood	542 ± 33 (5)	239 ± 16 (5)	3.81 ± 0.25 (5)	16.2 ± 2.0 (5)	277 ± 21 (5)
Urine	487 ± 20 (5)	212 ± 18 (5)	2.43 ± 0.25 (5)	13.8 ± 0.6 (5)	237 ± 23 (5)

Data are expressed as mean ± SE of osmolalities, Na^+, Ca^{+2}, and Mg^{+2} activities, and Cl^- concentrations. Number of animals is in parentheses.

mM ouabain in addition to the above ingredients. The $Na^+ + K^+$-dependent portion of total ATPase activity was calculated as the difference between catalytic rates measured at 340 nm with and without ouabain, and is expressed as nanomoles P_i released from ATP per min per mg protein. The spectrophotometer (Bausch and Lomb 700 equipped with multisample cell changer and recorder) was standardized with known additions of ADP. Protein concentrations of homogenates were measured by a Coomassie blue dye-binding assay, using bovine serum albumin as standard [7].

Light and Electron Microscopy

Gills were dissected and fixed in Bouin's solution, dehydrated with ethyl alcohol, embedded in paraffin, sectioned, and stained with hematoxylin and eosin. The lobes of the coxal glands were dissected and fixed for 2 h in 4% glutaraldehyde in 0.1 M phosphate buffer (pH 7.3) plus 0.47 M sucrose at room temperature. They were then postfixed for 2 h in 1% OsO_4 in the same buffer, and dehydrated in acetone. The material was embedded in Epon 812 and examined with a Zeiss EM 9S electron microscope.

RESULTS

Composition of Blood and Urine and Transepithelial Potentials Under Steady-state Conditions

At 35‰, the urine of Limulus polyphemus was found to be isosmotic and hyperionic to the blood (Table I). At 8‰, the urine became hypoosmotic to the blood and, with the exception of free Mg^{+2}, hypoionic (P < 0.05). The activities of free monovalent cations in the blood were found to compare favorably with previously reported values for total concentration [34, 47]. Free Ca^{+2}, however, was several mM lower at both salinities, and free Mg^{+2} was lower than total Mg^{+2} at high salinity.

In an effort to determine if either of the major blood ions (Na^+ or Cl^-) was maintained out of electrochemical equilibrium, transepithelial potentials were measured in animals acclimated to each of four different salinities. Negligible transepithelial potential was developed in animals acclimated to 35‰, whereas small negative potentials were developed in animals acclimated to 24, 15, and 8‰ (Table II). The calculated Nernst potentials for both Na^+ and Cl^- were significantly different from the measured potentials in animals acclimated to 15 and 8‰, and, in addition, the Nernst potential for Cl^- was significantly different from the measured potential at 24‰.

Acclimation to Reduced Salinity

When animals were transferred from high salinity (35‰) to lower salinities (24, 15, and 8‰) in a stepwise manner with 24 h between each salinity change, blood osmolality stabilized within 24 h (Fig. 1A), an observation previously reported for smaller animals [38]. New steady-state levels of Na^+ activity and Cl^- concentration were also reached in the same time period (Fig. 1B and C). The isosmotic relationship between the blood and the medium at 35‰ was replaced by increasing hyperosmoticity at lower salinities. With regard to free Na^+ the blood was hypoionic to the medium at 35‰, essentially isoionic at 24‰, and substantially hyperionic at 15 and 8‰. With regard to Cl^- concentration, the blood was slightly hypoionic at 35‰, but became increasingly hyperionic to the medium at the lower salinities.

Free Ca^{+2} levels in the blood remained essentially isoionic to the medium in 35, 24, and 15‰, reaching steady-state values within 12–24 h after each transfer (Fig. 1D). However, at the lowest salinity, free Ca^{+2} appeared to become slightly hyperionic 36 and 48 h after the transfer. Free Mg^{+2} levels in the blood were hypoionic to the medium in all but the lowest salinity (Fig. 1E), where the blood-medium difference either became insignificant or, at 36 h following the transfer from 15 to 8‰, slightly positive ($P < 0.05$, $N = 6$). The values appeared to be declining even 36 h after the transfer from 35 to 24‰, but reached steady-state levels within 24 h after transfer to 15 and 8‰. Blood ammonia levels never showed a clear increase during acclimation to low salinity and, as reported earlier [34], became significantly lower ($P < 0.001$) after reaching steady state at low salinity (Fig. 1F).

Effects of Plugging the Nephropores

Plugging the nephropores of six animals acclimated to 35‰ resulted in no mortality and no significant change in blood osmolality, Na^+, Ca^{+2}, Mg^{+2}, or

TABLE II. Calculated Equilibrium Potentials for Na$^+$ and Cl$^-$ and Measured Transepithelial Potentials in Limulus polyphemus Acclimated to Four Different Salinities

Salinity (‰)	N	Sodium			Chloride			Measured Transepithelial potential (mV)
		Blood activity (mM)	Medium Concentration (mM)	Equilibrium potential (mV)	Concentration Blood (mM)	Medium (mM)	Equilibrium potential (mV)	
35	2	465	481	+0.9	555	571	−0.7	−0.2
24	4	359 ± 11	339 ± 3	−1.4 ± 0.7	418 ± 9	399 ± 2	+1.1 ± 0.7*	−2.0 ± 0.5
15	5	278 ± 3	192 ± 5	−9.4 ± 0.5*	308 ± 6	232 ± 4	+7.2 ± 0.5*	−4.4 ± 0.5
8	4	239 ± 6	103	−21.3 ± 0.6*	251 ± 7	129	+16.8 ± 0.7*	−5.8 ± 0.7

Signs of potentials are inside relative to outside. Data are given as mean ± SE. Number of animals = N.
*Difference between equilibrium and measured transepithelial potentials is statistically significant, $P < 0.01$.

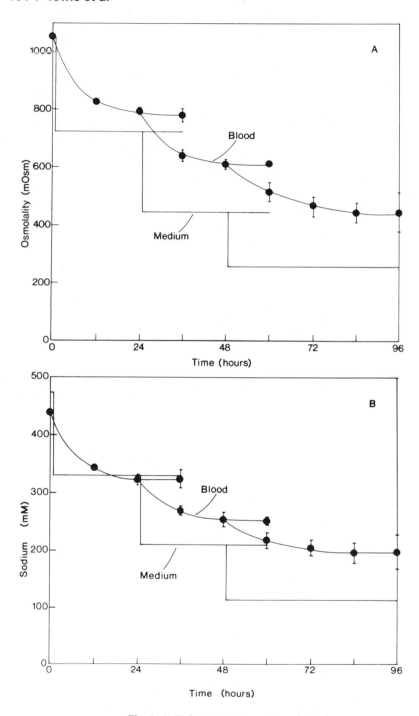

Fig. 1. A–F. See page 157 for figure legend.

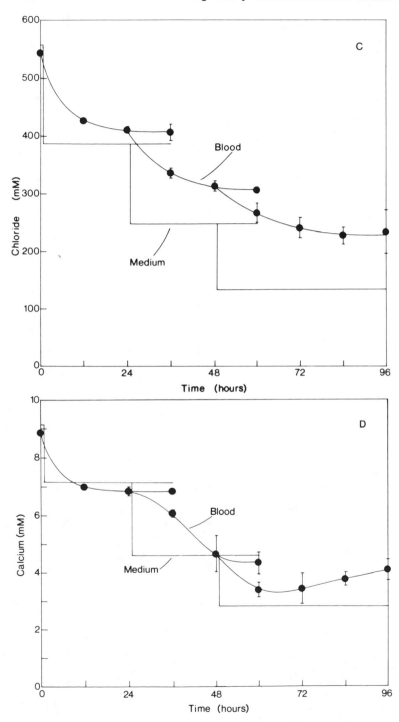

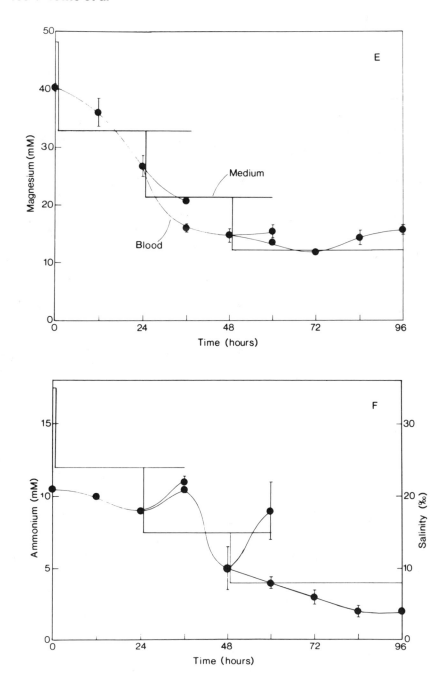

Fig. 1. (continued)

Cl^- during the 20-h experimental period ($P < 0.05$). Plugging the nephropores of five animals acclimated to 8‰ resulted in no mortality during the 18-h experimental period, but two animals were conspicuously weak and failed to survive an additional 18 h when the plugs were pulled. The average weight gain in the plugged animals was 16% (14% in the three survivors). In the three healthy animals, blood osmolality decreased by 35–45 mOsm, free Na^+ by 15–19 mM, and Mg^{+2} by 0.9–1.0 mM; blood Ca^{+2} showed no clear trend, and Cl^- was not measured. Much larger changes were found in the two moribund animals. Immediately after the plugs were pulled, a jet of fluid emerged from the nephropore, often reaching 0.5 m in height. Eighteen hours later, the three survivors had lost 12% of their body weight, and blood osmotic and ionic concentrations had risen. An unfortunate increase in the salinity of the medium, which was renewed shortly after pulling the plugs, renders the latter results of dubious meaning.

$Na^+ + K^+$-dependent ATPase Activity

A quantitative estimate of the level of Na^+ pumping in tissues of L. polyphemus was obtained by measuring specific activities of the transporting enzyme, $Na^+ + K^+$-ATPase. Homogenates of book gills, opercular integument, and intestine (midportion) contained activities of 8–26 nanomoles P_i min^{-1} mg protein^{-1} (Table III). Other soft tissues in the region of the gills, such as the fleshy regions of the exopodites and the branchial warts, contained similar or lower levels of $Na^+ + K^+$-ATPase activity. The coxal gland, on the other hand, contained 180–316 nanomoles P_i min^{-1} mg protein^{-1} of $Na^+ + K^+$-ATPase activity, much higher than any other tissue examined. $Na^+ + K^+$-ATPase activity in coxal gland homogenates was lowest in animals acclimated to 35‰, and was activated 65‰ upon transfer to 24 and 15‰ seawater, a slight additional activation occurring at 8‰.

A study of the characteristics of coxal gland $Na^+ + K^+$-ATPase indicated a linear relationship between the amount of homogenate and the measured $Na^+ + K^+$-ATPase activity (Fig. 2A). The Michaelis constant (K_m) for Na^+, determined by Lineweaver-Burke inversion and regression analysis, was 15.3 mM

Fig. 1. Response of blood osmotic and ionic composition following transfer of Limulus polyphemus to reduced salinities. Measurements were performed using the same individuals throughout. Twelve animals were transferred from 35 to 24‰ at the beginning of the experiment. Twenty-four h later, nine of these animals were transferred to 15‰, leaving three animals at 24‰. And 24 h later, six of the nine animals were transferred to 8‰, leaving three at 15‰. Blood values are given by solid circles, representing mean ± SE of osmolality (A), free Na^+ (B), total Cl^- (C), free Ca^{+2} (D), free Mg^{+2} (E), and NH_4^+ (F). Values for the medium are presented as solid lines without symbols, with the exception of Figure 1F, where the solid line represents salinity in ‰ (parts per thousand). Ammonium levels in the medium were barely detectable. Error bars were obscured by symbols at data points lacking them.

TABLE III. Na$^+$ + K$^+$-dependent ATPase Activity in Homogenates of Tissues Taken From Limulus polyphemus Acclimated for a Minimum of 36 Hours to Different Salinities

	Na$^+$ + K$^+$-ATPase Specific Activity (nanomoles P$_i$ min^{-1} mg protein^{-1})			
	Salinity: 35‰	24‰	15‰	8‰
Book gill		18 ± 2 (3)	17 ± 1 (3)	18 ± 2 (6)
Opercular integument	8 (1)	12 ± 4 (3)		12 (1)
Intestine			26 ± 1 (3)	24 ± 2 (6)
Coxal gland	180 ± 24 (6)*	298 ± 13 (3)	291 (2)	316 ± 25 (6)

Animals acclimated to the lower salinities were allowed 24 h in each intermediate salinity. The animals were the same individuals used in the experiment described in Figure 1. Data are presented as mean ± SE with the number of animals in parentheses.
*Significantly different from remaining values for coxal gland, P < 0.01.

(Fig. 2B). The K$_m$ for ATP, determined in the same way, was 3.9 × 10^{-5} M (Fig. 2C). The concentration of ouabain producing 50% inhibition of Na$^+$ + K$^+$-ATPase activity was 1.5 × 10^{-6} M (Fig. 2D). The pH optimum of the coxal gland Na$^+$ + K$^+$-ATPase was pH 7.2–7.4 (Fig. 2E). An Arrhenius plot of the effect of temperature on coxal gland Na$^+$ + K$^+$-ATPase activity showed a transition point of 25°C (Fig. 2F).

Response to Hypoxia and the Respiratory Role of the Coxal Gland

Unlike crustaceans, blood pH in L. polyphemus increased very little at low salinity, whereas urine pH shifted from strongly acid to somewhat alkaline (Table IV) [34]. Urinary HCO$_3^-$ levels increased by a factor of 6 upon transfer to low salinity, where Cl$^-$ was apparently being reabsorbed.

Exposure of L. polyphemus to hypoxic seawater resulted in significant reductions in blood pH, by as much as 0.31 pH units following 12 h at PiO$_2$ = 50 mm Hg (Table IV). Although exposure to PiO$_2$ = 109 mm Hg produced no significant changes in blood PCO$_2$ or HCO$_3^-$ concentrations, subjecting the animals to PiO$_2$ = 50 mm Hg for 2.5 h resulted in more than doubling of these two blood constituents. The 12-h exposure to seawater of PiO$_2$ = 50 mm Hg produced an 8-fold increase in blood lactate. Despite the compensatory hyperventilation inferred by Johansen and Petersen [31], there was no sign in Limulus of the blood alkalosis that develops in crustaceans exposed to moderately hypoxic water [9, 37].

Shortly after the animals emerged into air, prebranchial blood PCO$_2$ rose from 3–4 mm Hg to 6–12 mm Hg; prolonged air exposure up to 48 h was reported to result in further increases of PCO$_2$ to 11–14 mm Hg [31]. The present study showed that air exposure produced concomitant reduction in blood pH (by 0.51

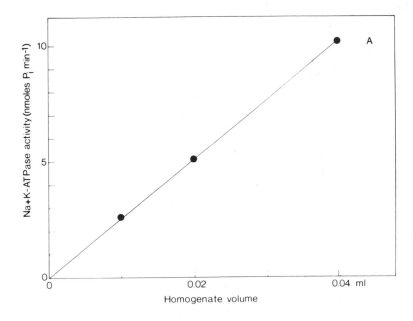

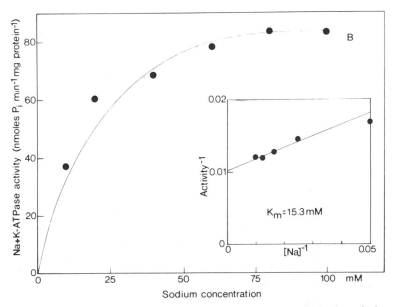

Fig. 2. Properties of $Na^+ + K^+$-dependent ATPase in homogenates of Limulus polyphemus coxal gland. The relationship between volume of homogenate and measured enzyme activity is given in A. The effects of varying concentrations of Na^+ and ATP on enzyme activity are presented in B and C, respectively. Inhibition by ouabain and the effects of pH variation are shown in D and E. An Arrhenius plot of the effect of temperature on $Na^+ + K^-$-ATPase activity (nanomoles P_i min^{-1} mg protein^{-1}) is given in F.

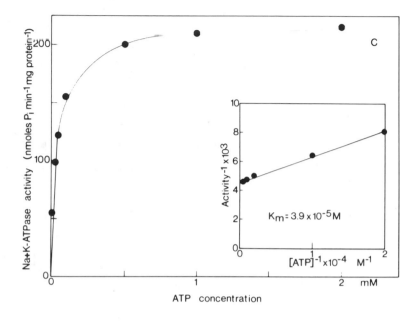

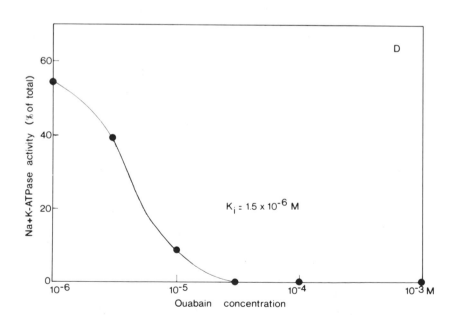

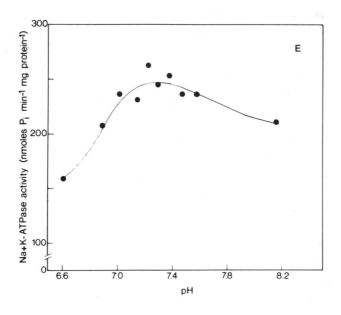

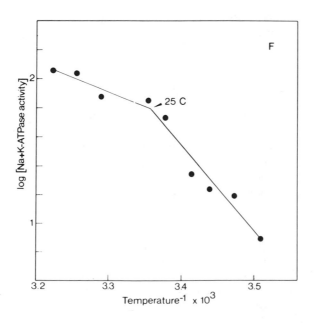

Fig. 2. (continued)

TABLE IV. Acid-Base Status of the Blood and Urine in Limulus polyphemus at 25°C.

	pH	PCO$_2$ (mm Hg)	HCO$_3^-$ (mM)	Lactate (mM)
Salinity = 35‰, PiO$_2$ = 155 mm Hg				
Blood	7.42 ± 0.02 (13)	3.8 ± 0.6 (9)	2.58 ± 0.52 (9)	0.8 ± 0.1 (6)
Urine	6.77 ± 0.04 (6)	3.4 ± 0.6 (6)	0.62 ± 0.13 (5)	
Salinity = 8‰, PiO$_2$ = 140 mm Hg				
Blood	7.47 ± 0.05 (5)	5.2 ± 0.6 (5)	3.91 ± 0.62 (5)	
Urine	7.58 ± 0.09 (5)	8.5 ± 2.4 (5)	4.06 ± 0.61 (5)	
Salinity = 35‰, 2.5 h at PiO$_2$ = 109 mm Hg				
Blood	7.39 ± 0.03 (9)	3.4 ± 0.7 (10)	2.09 ± 0.46 (9)	1.4 ± 0.3 (5)
Salinity = 35‰, 2.5 h at PiO$_2$ = 50 mm Hg				
Blood	7.30 ± 0.03 (11)	11.6 ± 0.6 (12)	7.03 ± 0.48 (11)	2.0 ± 0.7 (6)
Salinity = 35‰, 12 h at PiO$_2$ = 50 mm Hg				
Blood	7.11 ± 0.02 (9)			6.5 ± 1.0 (6)
Air-exposed, 12–26 h				
Blood	6.91 ± 0.07 (10)	11–14*	1.8–2.3	5.2 ± 1.6 (6)
Urine	6.61 ± 0.05 (3)	2.9 ± 0.4 (3)	0.37 ± 0.05 (3)	

Bicarbonate concentrations were calculated according to the Henderson-Hasselbalch equation from solubility and dissociation constants given by Horne [30]. Data are presented as mean ± SE, with the number of animals in parentheses.
*Johansen and Petersen [31].

pH units) and elevation in blood lactate (4-fold) (Table IV). Blood HCO$_3^-$ was not affected by air exposure. The coxal gland appeared to respond to air exposure by acidifying the urine more strongly, although the blood-urine difference in pH was diminished.

Structure of the Gill and Coxal Gland

Light micrographs of the gill leaflet of L. polyphemus revealed a thin layer of cells within the chitinous envelope (Fig. 3A). Traversing the blood space were pillar-like arrangements of cells and connective tissue elements.

Light microscopy of the lobed coxal gland demonstrated a labyrinth of tortuous channels throughout the gland (Fig. 3B). The channels were lined with cells joined by extensive junctional complexes composed of adhering junctions, and septate junctions extending deeply between adjacent cells (Fig. 3C). These cells possessed interdigitating basal and lateral plasma membranes, which were in close proximity to abundant mitochondria.

The ultrastructure of the coxal gland of L. polyphemus is similar to that of coxal glands in other arthropods; the glands of scorpions, centipedes, and dipluran insects possess similar deep infoldings of plasma membranes [14, 46, 49]. The epithelial cells lining the labyrinth in antennal glands of decapod crustaceans also possess basolateral membranes with extensive infoldings [42, 55, 57]. Especially notable is the similarity in the nature of the junctional complexes to those seen in the crayfish antennal gland [57].

DISCUSSION

The horseshoe crab Limulus polyphemus is an example of a weak hyperosmoregulator. As salinities decrease below that of full-strength seawater, blood becomes increasingly hyperosmotic to the medium, in agreement with earlier findings [34, 47, 67]. In comparison to euryhaline crustaceans, however, the degree of regulation is less marked (Fig. 4), and homeostatic conditions are clearly not maintained. Nevertheless, regulation of blood osmolytes is readily apparent in L. polyphemus.

If the excretory organ is the site of regulation of a particular osmolyte, a negative value for the blood-medium difference should be accompanied by a urine/blood ratio appreciably less than 1, and a positive value for the blood-medium difference by a urine/blood ratio greater than 1. The osmotic role of the coxal gland in L. polyphemus becomes quite clear when this relationship is compared with data available for crustaceans. In making the comparison, we have chosen subtidal, marine, or euryhaline species where possible, but a few intertidal and freshwater crustaceans have been included owing to scarcity of information. With respect to Mg^{+2}, the regulatory role of the excretory organ in both crustaceans and L. polyphemus is very clear (Table V). There is even a correlation between the size of the blood-medium difference and the size of the urine/blood ratio, although it is not perfect because the rate of urine flow increases so much at low salinity [22]. Volume regulation is also an important function of the excretory organ in both groups; indeed, mortality in L. polyphemus at low salinity appears to be due in part to the failure of extracellular volume regulation, as indicated by ballooning of the gills in animals with blocked nephropores.

Our data indicate that, unlike euryhaline crustaceans, the excretory organ in Limulus plays an important part in the regulation of total osmolality, NaCl, Ca^{+2}, and blood pH. The comparison of Ca^{+2} regulation is limited by the apparent absence of a general trend in the data for crustaceans (Table V), and also by the fundamental distinction between our data for free ions and the earlier data for total Ca^{+2}. Nonetheless, the regulation of Ca^{+2} at the coxal gland is clear. The only other data for Na^+ that show a hypoionic blood and a concentrated urine at high salinity, and a hyperionic blood and a concentrated urine at low salinity, are those for the crabs Potamon and Callinectes in freshwater where the excretory organ is regarded as more important in osmoregulation [44], and in Hemigrapsus and Cancer at high salinity, where the blood-medium differences are regarded as the result of passive processes.

TABLE V. The Relationship Between the Osmotic and Ionic Composition of the Medium, the Blood, and the Urine in Euryhaline Arthropods (B-M = blood-medium difference, U/B = urine : blood ratio)

	Mg^{+2} (mM)		Ca^{+2} (mM)		Na^+ (mM)		Cl^- (mM)		Osmolality (mOsm)		Source
	B-M	U/B	B-M	U/B	B-M	U/B	B-M	U/B	B-M	U/B	
Limulus polyphemus	−6.5	1.14*	−1.40	1.05	−45	1.08	−33	1.05	3*	1.00*	Present data
	3.9	0.89	0.98	0.64	126	0.89	135	0.86			Gifford [20]
Callinectes sapidus		1.05	3.5	0.94	−14	1.03	−29	1.03	77	1.06 "nearly isotonic"	Cameron [10]
					299	0.95	293	1.11			
Cancer antennarius	−20.4	1.74	13.7	0.99	28	0.98					Gross [22]
C. magister	−31	3.9									Holliday [27]
	−27	2.6									
Crangon vulgaris	−7.5	4.67	~8	~0.6			13	1.29		1.00	Hagerman [23]
Hemigrapsus nudus	−32	1.62	3.6	1.00	44	1.00	166	1.38			Dehnel [13]
	−3.3	2.25	8.6	0.91	287	1.00					
H. oregonensis	−28.5	4.96	4.8	1.14	22	0.84			−31	1.02	Gross [22]
Homarus americanus	−8.8	2.43	10.4	1.31	99	1.14	−33	1.08	157	1.09	Burger [8]
	−44	1.68	~6	0.81	32	1.00			19	1.00	
Palaemonid shrimp (4 species)							116–301	1.08–1.11	390	1.00	Parry [40]; Born [6]
Potamon edulis					~290	0.85					Harris [25]

*Not significant (P < 0.05).

Not even freshwater crabs or shrimp are able to conserve Cl⁻ from the urine (Table V), and the antennal gland is always an avenue of loss. But in L. polyphemus the inverse correlation between the blood-medium difference and the urine/blood ratio remains clear. Only in L. polyphemus is a hyperosmotic blood accompanied by a hypoosmotic urine, and only in L. polyphemus is an isosmotic relationship between blood and medium accompanied by an isosmotic condition of blood and urine.

Coxal glands of other chelicerates have been reported to produce urine that is different from blood in ionic composition. The urine of argasid ticks may be either hypertonic (Argas sp.) or hypotonic (Ornithodoros sp.) to the blood, perhaps reflecting the volume of water excreted following a blood meal [1]. The labyrinth in coxal glands of freshwater species of oribatid mites is elongated in comparison to that of brackish water and littoral species, suggesting that the reabsorptive function of labyrinth cells may serve in maintaining blood that is hyperosmotic to the medium [69]. Coxal glands of argasid ticks also reabsorb amino acids from the primary urine, most likely via a Na^+-dependent process [4].

That an active process is central to the regulation of blood Na^+ and Cl^- in Limulus acclimated to lower salinities is supported by our measurements of transepithelial potentials, which were significantly different from equilibrium potentials for both Na^+ and Cl^- at 8 and 15‰ and for Cl^- at 24‰. The transepithelial potential can be a diffusion potential generated by ionic gradients across an epithelium whose permeability to anions and cations is not equal, or it can result from electrogenic transport processes. In eggs, globe stages, and trilobites of L. polyphemus, permeability to Na^+ was found to be substantially higher than permeability to Cl^- (R. B. Laughlin, personal communication). Although parallel data do not exist for adult horseshoe crabs, a similar relationship of differential permeability of the integument to Na^+ and Cl^- could give rise to the inside negative potentials we observed. As the salinity was decreased, the blood became increasingly electronegative with respect to the medium. Such electronegativity would force Cl^- out into the medium and would reduce the total electrochemical gradient for Na^+ in hyperionically regulating horseshoe crabs. Assuming that the animals were in steady state, the discrepancies between equilibrium potentials and measured potentials would indicate that the maintenance of the concentration gradients of Na^+ and Cl^- was the result of an active process. Both Na^+ and Cl^- appear to be actively transported at the lower salinities, a finding consistent with data on other hyperionic regulators [16].

Animal tissues that carry on high rates of Na^+ transport usually exhibit high specific activities of the Na^+-transporting enzyme, $Na^+ + K^+$-ATPase. In our survey of potential ion-transporting tissues of L. polyphemus, only the coxal gland showed substantial $Na^+ + K^+$-ATPase activity. The lack of high activity in the gill was especially notable, because of the well-described role of the gills

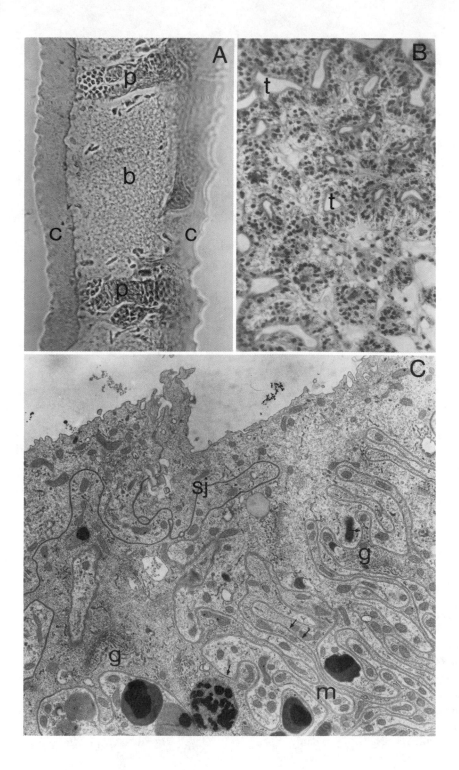

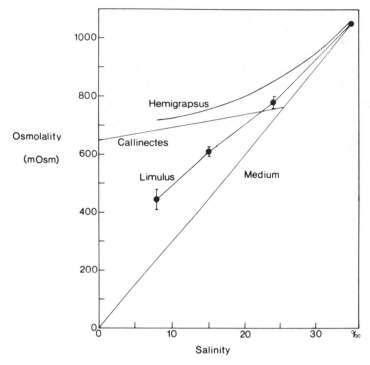

Fig. 4. Osmoregulation in the intertidal crustacean Hemigrapsus oregonensis, the subtidal crustacean Callinectes sapidus, and the subtidal chelicerate Limulus polyphemus. Data from Gross [22], Weiland and Mangum [68], and present data (mean ± SE).

in ionic regulation by other aquatic arthropods [36, 62, 64]. A chitinous envelope lined with only a thin layer of cells, the gill of L. polyphemus also appeared to lack the typical structure of a transporting epithelium.

The coxal gland, on the other hand, is composed of a labyrinth of interconnected channels lined with epithelial cells ultrastructurally similar to "chloride

Fig. 3. Light micrographs of gill (A) and the lobe of the coxal gland (B) of Limulus polyphemus; electron micrograph of epithelial cells lining the coxal gland labyrinth (C). The gill is composed of parallel layers of chitin (c) enclosing a blood space (b). Pillar-like arrangements of cells (p) partially subdivide the blood space. The coxal gland is composed of a labyrinth of tubules (t). The epithelial cells lining the tubule are joined apically by extensive septate junctions (sj), which extend deeply between adjacent cells. In the basal region, numerous adhering junctions (arrows) join the interdigitating plasma membranes. Golgi complexes (g) are abundant, as are mitochondria (m), in both basal and apical regions. Dense granules are observable in both light and electron micrographs of coxal gland epithelium. Magnification: A and B, 218×; C, 10,000×.

TABLE VI. Kinetic Properties of Arthropod Na$^+$ + K$^+$-ATPases

Species	Tissue	K$_m$:Na$^+$ (mM)	K$_m$:ATP (mM)	K$_i$:ouabain (µM)	pH optimum	Transition temperature	Source
Horseshoe crab, Limulus polyphemus	Coxal gland	15	0.039	1.5	7.2–7.4	25°C	Present data
Tick, Amlyomma hebraeum	Salivary gland	21		0.25	7.0		Rutti et al [51]
Cockroach, Periplanata americana	Rectum	20		5.0	7.0		Tolman and Steele [61]
Locust, Locusta migratoria	Rectum			1.0			Peacock [41]
Moth, Manduca sexta	Nerve cord			10	7.5		Rubin et al [50]
Midge, Chironomus thummi	Salivary gland	3.5	0.5	0.12	7.5–7.6		Schin and Kroeger [54]
Brine shrimp, Artemia salina	Larval salt gland	10	0.8	8.0	7.5		Ewing et al [17]
Crayfish, Procambarus clarki	Gill		0.71	250		27°C	Horiuchi [28]
	Antennal gland		0.9	79	8.4		Horiuchi [29]
Land crab, Cardisoma guanhumi	Gill		1.4	100			Quinn and Lane [45]
Shore crab, Carcinus maenas	Nerve	6		130	7.2		Skou [58,59]
Blue crab, Callinectes sapidus	Gill		0.19	150		23°C	Neufeld et al [39]

cells" of many invertebrate and vertebrate transporting tissues. Despite the apparent differences in function, the coxal gland showed many ultrastructural similarities to the antennal gland of crustaceans. Biochemical similarities also became apparent. The antennal gland of the freshwater crustacean Procambarus was reported to contain 181–270 nanomoles P_i min^{-1} mg protein^{-1} of $Na^+ + K^+$-ATPase activity, similar in magnitude to the levels reported here [43]. Antennal glands of three terrestrial decapods also contained high levels of $Na^+ + K^+$-ATPase activity (55–161 nanomoles P_i min^{-1} mg protein^{-1}) [63].

Comparison of the properties of Limulus coxal gland $Na^+ + K^+$-ATPase with those of other arthropod tissues indicates a greater similarity to insect $Na^+ + K^+$-ATPases than to crustacean $Na^+ + K^+$-ATPases (Table VI). The K_m for Na^+ and the pH optimum are similar for all arthropod tissues examined. However, crustacean $Na^+ + K^+$-ATPases, with the exception of the enzyme from Artemia, exhibit a much lower sensitivity to ouabain inhibition, as indicated by the 100-fold greater concentrations of ouabain required to produce 50% inhibition ($= K_i$). The K_i for ouabain of the two merostomate $Na^+ + K^+$-ATPases is quite similar to values for the insect $Na^+ + K^+$-ATPases. Although the physiological significance of these differences is unclear, a biochemical divergence between crustacean and chelicerate $Na^+ + K^+$-ATPases is apparent. The low K_m for ATP noted for Limulus coxal gland may allow the enzyme to function effectively at lower in vivo ATP concentrations than the remaining arthropod enzymes. Transition temperatures derived from Arrhenius plots are similar for the three $Na^+ + K^+$-ATPases for which data are available, perhaps indicating a similar lipid environment within the plasma membrane.

The high $Na^+ + K^+$-ATPase activity noted in coxal glands of L. polyphemus acclimated to 35‰, where active transepithelial transport of Na^+ did not appear to occur, may be related to the generation of transmembrane Na^+ gradients used to drive transepithelial movements of other ions. The Mg^{+2}-excreting ability of the antennal gland of the crustacean Cancer magister, for example, is inhibited by ouabain, the specific inhibitor of the $Na^+ + K^+$-ATPase [27]. Sodium-coupled Cl^- transport systems have been recognized in many animal tissues [18]; such a system may be responsible for the active Cl^- movements indicated by our data.

The activation of coxal gland $Na^+ + K^+$-ATPase upon transfer of horseshoe crabs from 35‰ to lower salinities is consistent with increasing requirements for NaCl retention by the gland. Stabilization of blood osmotic and monovalent ionic parameters within 24 h after such salinity reduction indicated that the biochemical modifications required for hyperionic regulation were induced within that time period. Rapid modulation of $Na^+ + K^+$-ATPase activity in response to salinity change has been observed in several invertebrates as well as teleosts [52, 53, 64, 65]. Although the role of the coxal gland in ion retention seems clear, the pathway of salt uptake from the medium remains to be elucidated.

ACKNOWLEDGMENTS

The research reported here was supported in part by a National Science Foundation grant to C.P.M. and a University of Richmond faculty research grant to D.W.T.

REFERENCES

1. Araman SF, Said A: Biochemical and physiological studies of certain ticks (Ixodoidea). The ionic regulatory role of the coxal organs of Argas (Persicargas) persicus (Oken) and A. (P.) arboreus Kaiser, Hoogstraal, and Kohls (Argasidae). J Parasitol 58:348–353, 1972.
2. Beklemishev WN: "Principles of Comparative Anatomy of Invertebrates," Vol 2. Chicago: University of Chicago Press, 1969.
3. Berridge MJ, Oschman JL: "Transporting Epithelia." New York: Academic Press, 1972.
4. Boctor FN, Araman SF: Biochemical and physiological studies of certain ticks (Ixodoidea). Total free amino acids in gut, hemolymph, and coxal fluids of Argas (Persicargas) persicus (Oken) and A. (P.) arboreus Kaiser, Hoogstraal and Kohls (Argasidae). J Med Entomol 8:525–528, 1971.
5. Bonting SL: Sodium-potassium activated adenosinetriphosphatase and cation transport. In Bittar EE (ed): "Membranes and Ion Transport," Vol 1. London: John Wiley and Sons, 1970, pp. 257–363.
6. Born JW: Osmoregulatory capacities of two caridean shrimps, Syncaris pacifica (Atyidae) and Palaemon macrodactylus. Biol Bull 134:235–244, 1968.
7. Bradford MM: A rapid and sensitive method for the quantitation of microgram quantities of protein utilizing the principle of protein-dye binding. Anal Biochem 72:248–254, 1976.
8. Burger JW: The general form of excretion in the lobster, Homarus. Biol Bull 113:207–223, 1957.
9. Burnett LE: The effects of environmental oxygen levels on the respiratory function of hemocyanin in the crabs, Libinia emarginata and Ocypode quadrata. J Exp Zool 210:289–300, 1979.
10. Cameron JN: Effects of hypercapnia on blood acid-base status, NaCl fluxes, and trans-gill potential in freshwater blue crabs, Callinectes sapidus. J Comp Physiol 123:137–141, 1978.
11. Cameron JN, Batterton CV: Antennal gland function in the freshwater blue crab, Callinectes sapidus: Water, electrolyte, acid-base and ammonia excretion. J Comp Physiol 123:143–148, 1978.
12. Cole WH: The composition of fluids and sera of some marine animals and of the sea water in which they live. J Gen Physiol 23:575–584, 1940.
13. Dehnel PA: Chloride regulation in the crab Hemigrapsus nudus. Physiol Zool 34:259–265, 1966.
14. Eisenbeis G: Fine structure and histochemistry of the transport-epithelium of abdominal coxal vesicles in the dipluran species Campodea staphylinus (Diplura: Campodeidae). Entomol Germ 3:185–201, 1976.
15. Evans DH: Ion exchange mechanisms in fish gills. Comp Biochem Physiol 51A:491–496, 1975.
16. Evans DH: Salt transport mechanisms in branchial epithelia. In Gilles R (ed): "Animals and Environmental Fitness." New York: Pergamon Press, 1980, pp 61–78.
17. Ewing RD, Peterson GL, Conte FP: Larval salt gland of Artemia salina nauplii. Localization and characterization of the sodium + potassium-activated adenosine triphosphatase. J Comp Physiol 88:217–234, 1974.
18. Frizzell RA, Field M, Schultz SG: Sodium-coupled chloride transport by epithelial tissues. Am J Physiol 236:F1–F8, 1979.
19. Garrey WE: The osmotic pressure of sea water and of the blood of marine animals. Biol Bull 8:257–270, 1905.

20. Gifford CA: Some aspects of osmotic and ionic regulation in the blue crab, Callinectes sapidus, and the ghost crab, Ocypode albicans. Publ Tex Inst Mar Sci 8:97–125, 1962.

21. Gravitz N, Gleye L: A photochemical side reaction that interferes with the phenol hypochlorite assay for ammonia. Limnol Oceanogr 20:1015–1017, 1975.

22. Gross WJ: Trends in water and salt regulation among aquatic and amphibious crabs. Biol Bull 127:447–466, 1964.

23. Hagerman L: The regulation of calcium and magnesium in the urine during the moulting cycle of Crangon vulgaris (Fabr.). J Exp Mar Biol Ecol 46:51–58, 1980.

24. Hannan JV, Evans DH: Water permeability in some euryhaline decapods and Limulus polyphemus. Comp Biochem Physiol 44A:1199–1213, 1973.

25. Harris RR: Urine production and urinary sodium loss in the freshwater crab Potamon edulis. J Comp Physiol 96:143–153, 1975.

26. Hendler ED, Torretti J, Kupor L, Epstein FH: Effects of adrenalectomy and hormone replacement on Na-K-ATPase in renal tissue. Am J Physiol 222:754–760, 1972.

27. Holliday CW: Magnesium transport by the urinary bladder of the crab, Cancer magister. J Exp Biol 85:187–201, 1980.

28. Horiuchi S: Characterization of gill Na,K-ATPase in the freshwater crayfish, Procambarus clarki (Girard). Comp Biochem Physiol 56B:135–138, 1977.

29. Horiuchi S: Characterization of antennary gland Na,K-ATPase in the freshwater crayfish, Procambarus clarki Girard. Comp Biochem Physiol 65B:391–394, 1980.

30. Horne RA: "Marine Chemistry." New York: Wiley Interscience, 1969.

31. Johansen K, Petersen JA: Respiratory adaptations in Limulus polyphemus (L.) In Vernberg FJ (ed): "Physiological Ecology of Estuarine Organisms." Columbia: University of South Carolina Press, 1975, pp 129–146.

32. Kirschner LB: The study of NaCl transport in aquatic animals. Am Zool 10:365–376, 1970.

33. Long GO, Kaplan NO: Diphosphopyridine nucleotide linked D-lactate dehydrogenase from the horseshoe crab Limulus polyphemus and the seaworm Nereis virens. Arch Biochem Biophys 154:696–725, 1973.

34. Mangum CP, Booth DE, deFur PL, Heckel NA, Henry RP, Oglesby LC, Polites G: The ionic environment of hemocyanin in Limulus polyphemus. Biol Bull 150:453–467, 1976.

35. Mangum CP, Haswell MS, Johansen K, Towle DW: Inorganic ions and pH in the body fluids of Amazon animals. Can J Zool 56:907–916, 1978.

36. Mantel LH: Asymmetry potentials, metabolism and sodium fluxes in gills of the blue crab, Callinectes sapidus. Comp Biochem Physiol 20:743–753, 1967.

37. McMahon BR, Butler PJ, Taylor EW: Acid-base changes during recovery from disturbance and during longterm hypoxic exposure in the lobster Homarus vulgaris. J Exp Zool 205:361–370, 1978.

38. McManus JJ: Osmotic relations in the horseshoe crab, Limulus polyphemus. Am Midl Nat 81:569–573, 1969.

39. Neufeld GJ, Holliday CW, Pritchard JB: Salinity adaption of gill Na,K-ATPase in the blue crab, Callinectes sapidus. J Exp Zool 211:215–224, 1980.

40. Parry G: Osmoregulation in some freshwater prawns. J Exp Biol 34:417–423, 1957.

41. Peacock AJ: Further studies of the properties of locust rectal Na^+-K^+-ATPase, with particular reference to the ouabain sensitivity of the enzyme. Comp Biochem Physiol 68C:29–34, 1981.

42. Peterson DR, Loizzi RF: Ultrastructure of the crayfish kidney—Coelomosac, labyrinth, nephridial canal. J Morphol 142:241–264, 1974.

43. Peterson DR, Loizzi RF: Biochemical and cytochemical investigations of $(Na^+$-$K^+)$-ATPase in the crayfish kidney. Comp Biochem Physiol 49A:763–773, 1974.

44. Prosser CL: "Comparative Animal Physiology." Philadelphia: W.D. Saunders Co, 1973.

45. Quinn DJ, Lane CE: Ionic regulation and Na^+-K^+-stimulated ATPase activity in the land crab, Cardisoma guanhumi. Comp Biochem Physiol 19:533–543, 1966.

46. Rasmont R, Vandermeersche G, Castiaux P: Ultra-structure of the coxal glands of the scorpion. Nature 182:328–329, 1958.

47. Robertson JD: Osmotic and ionic regulation in the horseshoe crab Limulus polyphemus (Linnaeus). Biol Bull 138:157–183, 1970.

48. Robinson JD, Flashner MS: The (Na$^+$ + K$^+$)-activated ATPase: Enzymatic and transport properties. Biochim Biophys Acta 549:145–176, 1979.

49. Rosenberg J, Seifert G: The coxal glands of geophilomorpha (Chilopoda): Organs of osmoregulation. Cell Tissue Res 182:247–252, 1977.

50. Rubin AL, Clark AF, Stahl WL: Sodium, potassium stimulated adenosine triphosphatase in the nerve cord of the hawk moth, Manduca sexta. Comp Biochem Physiol 67B:271–275, 1980.

51. Rutti B, Schlunegger B, Kaufman W, Aeschlimann A: Properties of Na,K-ATPase from the salivary glands of the ixodid tick Amblyomma hebraeum. Can J Zool 58:1052–1059, 1980.

52. Sabourin TD, Saintsing DG: Transport ATPases in the osmoregulating hermit crab Clibanarius vittatus. Physiologist 23:175, 1980.

53. Saintsing DG, Towle DW: Na$^+$ + K$^+$-ATPase in the osmoregulating clam Rangia cuneata. J Exp Zool 206:435–442, 1978.

54. Schin K, Kroeger H: (Na$^+$ + K$^+$)-ATPase activity in the salivary gland of a dipteran insect, Chironomus thummi. Insect Biochem 10:113–117, 1980.

55. Schmidt-Nielsen B, Gertz KH, Davis LE: Excretion and ultrastructure of the antennal gland of the fiddler crab Uca mordax. J Morphol 125:473–496, 1968.

56. Schwartz A, Allen JC, Harigaya S: Possible involvement of cardiac Na$^+$,K$^+$-adenosine triphosphatase in the mechanism of action of cardiac glycosides. J Pharmacol Exp Ther 168:31–41, 1969.

57. Shivers RR, Chauvin WJ: Intercellular junctions of antennal gland epithelial cells in the crayfish, Orconectes virilis. Cell Tissue Res 175:425–438, 1977.

58. Skou JC: The influence of some cations on an adenosine triphosphatase from peripheral nerves. Biochim Biophys Acta 23:394–401, 1957.

59. Skou JC: Further investigations on a Mg^{++} + Na$^+$-activated adenosintriphosphatase, possibly related to the active, linked transport of Na$^+$ and K$^+$ across the nerve membrane. Biochim Biophys Acta 42:6–23, 1960.

60. Solórzano L: Determination of ammonia in natural waters by the phenol hypochlorite method. Limnol Oceanogr 14:799–801, 1969.

61. Tolman J, Steele J: A ouabain-sensitive (Na$^+$-K$^+$)-activated ATPase in the rectal epithelium of the American cockroach, Periplaneta americana. Insect Biochem 6:513–517, 1976.

62. Towle DW: Role of Na$^+$ + K$^+$-ATPase in ionic regulation by marine and estuarine animals. Marine Biol Lett 2:107–122, 1981.

63. Towle DW: Transport-related ATPases as probes of tissue function in three terrestrial crabs of Palau. J Exp Zool 218:89–95, 1981.

64. Towle DW, Palmer GE, Harris JL III: Role of gill Na$^+$ + K$^+$-dependent ATPase in acclimation of blue crabs Callinectes sapidus to low salinity. J Exp Zool 196:315–321, 1976.

65. Towle DW, Gilman ME, Hempel JD: Rapid modulation of gill Na$^+$ + K$^+$-dependent ATPase activity during acclimation of the killifish Fundulus heteroclitus to salinity change. J Exp Zool 202:179–186, 1977.

66. Umbreit WW, Burris RH, Stauffer JF: "Manometric techniques." Minneapolis: Burgess Publishing, 1957.

67. Warren MK, Pierce SK: Changes in blood ions and osmotic solute in Limulus acclimated to low salinity. Paper presented, American Society of Zoologists, Division of Comparative Physiology and Biochemistry, February 14–16, 1980, Blacksburg, Virginia.

68. Weiland AL, Mangum CP: The influence of environmental salinity on hemocyanin function in the blue crab, Callinectes sapidus. J Exp Zool 193:265–274, 1975.

69. Woodring JP: Comparative morphology, functions, and homologies of the coxal glands in oribatid mites (Arachnida: Acari). J Morphol 139:407–430, 1973.

Physiology and Biology of Horseshoe Crabs: Studies on
Normal and Environmentally Stressed Animals, pages 173-188
© 1982 Alan R. Liss, Inc., 150 Fifth Avenue, New York, NY 10011

The Relationship Between the Capacity for Oxygen Transport, Size, Shape, and Aggregation State of an Extracellular Oxygen Carrier

G.K. Snyder and Charlotte P. Mangum

INTRODUCTION

The respiratory pigments that are found in a very diverse group of animals, including representatives from the invertebrates and the vertebrates, may be placed in one of three major types of proteins: the heme proteins, the hemerythrins, and the hemocyanins. In some animals the respiratory pigments are carried in cells whereas in others they exist extracellularly in the blood. For example, the hemerythrins are usually if not always intracellular, whereas the heme proteins may be either intracellular or extracellular, and the hemocyanins are always extracellular. In addition, with few exceptions, the extracellular pigments have high molecular weights ($> 3 \times 10^6$) compared with the intracellular pigments, which tend to have relatively low molecular weights ($< 1 \times 10^5$).

It is now widely accepted that these proteins do in fact augment oxygen transport. The relative effectiveness of each is still unclear, however, because of marked differences in the disposition of the pigments and their very different molecular weights. For example, it is often said that animals with high concentrations of hemoglobin have blood corpuscles, and it has been suggested that the concentrations of the respiratory pigments, when they occur in free solution, are limited by constraints other than oxygen transport, such as the fluid osmotic pressure or blood viscosity. In fact, the extracellular oxygen carriers do not always occur in lower concentrations than the intracellular carriers. Extracellular hemoglobin, for example, reaches levels of 10–14 g/100 ml in annelid lugworms of the genus Arenicola [21, 40], which is well within the range found in most of the vertebrates [31]. Hemocyanins, however, rarely occur in concentrations greater than about 10 g/100 ml, and typical values lie in the range of 4–8 g/100 ml [21].

It has been suggested that the concentration of the extracellular respiratory pigments may be limited by their colloid osmotic pressure [23]. The osmotive behavior of both extracellular hemoglobins [33] and hemocyanins [1] deviates from the ideal and becomes exponential at relatively low concentrations, well within the expected physiological range. If the balance between colloid osmotic pressure and hydrostatic pressure in the blood is perturbed by an excess of colloid osmolytes, renal function would be seriously impaired and cell volume regulation might also be impaired. The few available data suggest that the problem is most serious in animals that utilize the hemocyanins as oxygen carriers [23]. These molecules contain one oxygen binding site per 50–80 $\times$ 10^3 dalton protein, a ratio only one-third to one-half that of the extracellular heme proteins; thus a relatively high protein concentration is required to achieve the same blood oxygen carrying capacity. The problem of fluid balance might be mitigated by polymerizing the functional units of the molecule, and thus increasing the number of oxygen binding sites per colloid osmolyte. This trend, however, might aggravate the viscosity problem.

Several investigators have suggested that the concentrations of the extracellular respiratory pigments are limited by their viscosities [8, 18]. A simple model, constructed to predict the optimal concentration of a respiratory pigment, tended to support this view [36]. In the model, the capacity of the blood for oxygen transport, defined as the ratio of total oxygen concentration to the relative viscosity of the molecule, was described as a complex function of the concentration of the molecule. Indices of the viscosities of the respiratory pigments, in turn, were based on the relation of viscosity to concentration of linear polymers. When the hemocyanins of the gastropod mollusc Helix pomatia [6] or the hemoglobin of Arenicola marina [37] are treated as simple linear polymers, the predicted optimal concentrations are considerably lower than the optima obtained from actual observations on viscosity. This relationship suggests that the geometric arrangement of the subunits into more compact polygons is an important adaptation that mitigates excessive viscosities [37].

Although it is clear that both colloid osmotic pressure and viscosity could be determinants of the concentration of hemocyanin in a blood and the overall size and arrangement of subunits within the molecule, the actual relationship is poorly known. In this chapter we report the colloid osmotic pressures and viscosities of native hemocyanins and various subunits prepared from three groups, the chelicerate arthropod Limulus polyphemus (Linnaeus), the crustacean arthropod Callinectes sapidus Rathbun, and two species of the gastropod mollusc Busycon, B. canaliculatum (Linnaeus), and B. contrarium (Conrad). These species were chosen to represent different combinations of protein concentration, molecular weight and hydrostatic pressure in the blood. Callinectes sapidus has low concentrations [25] of a relatively low molecular weight (ca. 940 $\times$ 10^3 daltons) hemocyanin [14]; L. polyphemus has higher concentrations [22] of a high molecular weight (ca. 3.3 × 10^6 daltons) hemocyanin [15]; and Busycon has moderately high concentrations [24] of a very high molecular weight (ca. 9 × 10^6 daltons) hemocyanin [28]. In addition, hydrostatic pressures in the bloods of the arthropods, with their solid exoskeletons, are generally lower than in the gastropod molluscs with their fluid skeletons (see examples quoted by Mangum and Johansen [23]; also data for Limulus, this volume).

MATERIALS AND METHODS
Collection and Maintenance of Material

The animals were captured near Beaufort, North Carolina, or the coast of Virginia and maintained either in running seawater (35‰) or a recirculating system (32–33‰) at 22–25°C.

Collection and Treatment of Blood

Blood samples were usually obtained by direct needle puncture, but the pedal sinus of Busycon was slashed and drained on a few occasions when large volumes were needed. Cellular debris and clot material, when present, were removed by centrifugation, and then the hemocyanin was pelleted by centrifugation at 15–40 × 10^{3}g. The pellet was resuspended in seawater or buffer solution to obtain various hemocyanin concentrations, ranging upwards to levels of 4–8 times greater than found in vivo; these preparations are designated below as "super-blood."

Some samples were dialyzed for 1–3 days against 10 mM EDTA + 0.05 M Tris maleate buffer (pH 8.97–9.03). These conditions dissociate the molecules into their smallest functional subunits [4].

Measurement of Colloid Osmotic Pressure

The basic design of the osmometer is described in detail by Prather et al [30]. Briefly, it consists of an ultrafiltration membrane separating a sample chamber from a saline-filled chamber holding a pressure transducer so that application of the sample causes movement of the saline into the sample and a negative pressure at the transducer; dilution of the sample is assumed to be negligible. For the present experiments, an Amicon PM-10 membrane, a Statham P23Dc pressure transducer, Grass D7P1B preamplifier, Grass Polygraph 7B driver amplifier and Linear Instruments Co. 255 potentiometric recorder were used. A 20 µl sample was injected into the sample chamber from a glass capillary attached to a microsyringe fitted with a Chaney adaptor. The tip of the capillary was placed on the O-ring holding the membrane, so that the more viscous samples would have to travel less than one mm before covering the membrane. The records were calibrated as follows. First, the zero point was located on the recorder by injecting a sample of saline (32–33‰ seawater) into the sample chamber. Then a column of saline was connected to the sample chamber after filling the chamber to remove air. Using a laboratory jack, the column was raised in 8–12 steps, the increment depending on the expected range of the unknown readings. The amplification of the signal was adjusted to permit the positive pressure changes to deflect the recorder pen over more than 90% of the 10-in. chart span. The column was then disconnected, the zero point relocated, and the recorder pen moved to the opposite side of the chart to allow negative pressure readings. The calibration was repeated at the end of each set of determinations of the unknowns, and the zero point relocated and the sample chamber washed repeatedly in between each individual determination. The calibration was always linear in the range examined (0–50 cm H_2O), and it did not change in the period required to complete a set of determinations. The readings were taken at room temperature (20–22°C).

At high colloid osmotic pressures (greater than ca. 15 cm H_2O), the readings sometimes failed to stabilize within the usual period of about a minute or even very much longer periods. After moving toward the equilibration point in the usual direction of increasingly negative pressure, the pen would reverse direction and begin to return very slowly towards zero. This behavior was always followed by a mirror image response when a sample of saline was injected afterwards to relocate zero. It is believed to result from an excessive loss of fluid from the very small transducer chamber, which would distend the membrane to its limit and cause drift of the zero line in a direction opposite to that of the osmotic pressure. When this response was detected the data were discarded; however, it is possible that the response was not detected at values immediately lower, and thus the highest values reported may underestimate the actual deviation from ideal osmotic behavior.

Measurement of Viscosity

The viscosities of the hemocyanins resuspended in seawater or buffer solutions were measured in Cannon-Manning semimicro viscometers calibrated against standard oils (Cannon Instrument Co., State College, Pennsylvania). The individual viscometer used depended on the approximate viscosity of the sample fluid, but in each case the viscometer required a charge of approximately 0.35 ml and operated under an average driving pressure equivalent to 16.5 cm H_2O.

The temperature of the solution was maintained constant at ± 0.1°C by immersing the viscometers in a constant temperature water bath. Viscosities were measured at 10, 15, 20, 25, and 30°C. All of the variation in viscosity with temperature could be accounted for as variation in the solvent phase; thus relative viscosities only are reported here.

Measurement of Protein Concentration

The relationship between absorbance at the Cu band (335–345 nm, depending on species) of the native polymer (diluted 1:39 or 1:79 with seawater), the subunits (diluted with 0.05 M Tris maleate buffer, pH 8.97–9.03, + 10 mM EDTA), and protein concentration estimated by dye binding (Bio-Rad Laboratories) was described. These data indicated that absorbance of the subunits is the most repeatable index of protein concentration over the range studied. At high concentrations, light scattering by the very large molecules becomes appreciable, and the dye binding reagents induce the formation of floc, even after considerable dilution (1:999). In some instances, absorbance of the native molecule was used and the values calibrated by one of the alternative methods, but most of the values were calculated from the absorbance of the preparation diluted with Tris maleate buffer (pH 8.97–9.03) + 10 mM EDTA, a far more convenient method of eliminating the scatter than subtracting the absorbance of a deoxygenated aliquot of the sample. Absorbance was measured with various spectrophotometers (Bausch and Lomb Spectronic 20, Beckman DK-2A, and Beckman DB). The extinction coefficients reported by Nickerson and Van Holde [28] were used to calculate the hemocyanin concentrations.

RESULTS
Osmotic Pressures of the Native Polymers and Their Subunits

The observed osmotic pressures (π) are shown in Figure 1 in relation to values predicted from the Van't Hoff equation

$$\pi = \frac{CRT}{M} \qquad (1)$$

where C = protein concentration (g/l), R = the gas constant, T = temperature (K), and M = molecular weight. The predicted values assume a uniform molecular weight of 940×10^3 daltons for the native polymers and 72×10^3 daltons for the monomers of Callinectes hemocyanin [14], 3.3×10^6 daltons for the native polymers and 66×10^3 daltons for the monomers of Limulus hemocyanin [15, 38], and 8.9×10^6 daltons for the native polymers and 300×10^3 for the monomers of Busycon hemocyanin [32]. We should emphasize that this assumption is not strictly true, and that appreciable fractions of the preparations may have consisted of both larger and, in the case of the superbloods, smaller, particles.

All of the solutions of the native polymers exhibit deviations from ideal osmotic behavior of the proteins (Fig. 1), and the deviations are too great to be explained by the presence of other multiples of the size and in the concentrations noted in the sources cited. The curves describing osmotic pressure as a function of protein concentration become highly exponential in the two arthropods, in the superblood range at about 5–6 g/100 ml. The magnitude of the exponent, however, appears to be related to molecular weight, with the osmotic pressure

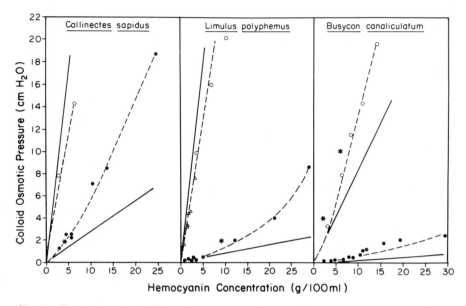

Fig. 1. The relation of colloid osmotic pressure and hemocyanin concentration. Symbols: ● = Whole molecules this study, ○ = subunits this study, △ = data from Burke [5], * = mean in vivo concentration. See text for further explanation. The discontinuous lines have been fitted by eye to the data points, and the continuous lines are based on calculated colloid osmotic pressures for molecules of the same molecular weights as the whole molecules and the subunits for each species using equation (1).

of Callinectes hemocyanin clearly rising at a greater rate. Thus the extension of the physiological range into the highly exponential phase does not occur in this species, and it is responsible for only a fraction of a cm H_2O in Limulus. In contrast, the relationship between colloid osmotic pressure and protein concentration of solutions of the much larger Busycon canaliculatum molecule (Fig. 1) is nearly linear, even at very high protein concentrations. If superimposed upon the data in Figure 1, a single value of 4.2 cm H_2O for B. contrarium superblood at 40 g/100 ml would extend the virtually straight line.

Dialyzing the preparations of superblood against a "stripping" medium that dissociates the polymers [2] into monomers causes very large increases in osmotic pressure. However, the data for the two arthropods deviate from the ideal in an anomalous fashion which, we suggest, is due largely to the presence of larger particles in the preparations. One of the five major groups of subunits of Limulus hemocyanin, for example, tends to form dimers [2]. Alternatively, or perhaps in conjunction, the anomaly may be due to the behavior of the osmometer at very high pressures, which would underestimate the actual values (see Methods).

For example, we obtained a value of 32.2 cm H$_2$O for the Limulus subunits at a concentration of 12.6 g/100 ml after replacing the membrane used to collect the data shown in Figure 1; if superimposed on the data in Figure 1, it would fall on an extension of the curve, suggesting that the point at 10.2 g/100 ml is slightly low.

We do not, however, believe that the osmometer is responsible for significant underestimation in the rest of the data. The agreement between our data and the osmotic pressures of the Limulus subunits reported by Burke [5] is remarkable (Fig. 1). And yet, his data, which yield a figure of 140–150 × 10^3 daltons for molecular weight, were obtained with a classical static type of osmometer consisting of a collodion sac connected to a glass manometer. The agreement also suggests that the osmotic activity of the Limulus subunits deviates from the ideal even at very low concentrations; hence the erroneous estimates of molecular weight.

Viscosities of the Native Polymers and Their Subunits

The relation of increase in viscosity with increasing hemocyanin concentration appears to be exponential for Busycon and for Limulus, although the absolute values for viscosity at any given concentration of hemocyanin are greater for the mollusc than for the arthropod (Fig. 2). The general pattern for the relation of viscosity to hemocyanin concentration is similar to that reported for the hemocyanin of the snail, Helix pomatia [6], and for the hemoglobins of the terrestrial annelid, Lumbricus terrestris [13] and the marine annelid, Arenicola marina [42]. For both of the species used here, dissociating the whole molecule into subunits produced an increase in the viscosity of the resulting solution (Fig. 2). The increase in viscosity with dissociation appears to be consistent with the findings for the high molecular weight pigments from a wide variety of invertebrate species (see below).

The significance of the relation of viscosity to hemocyanin concentration can be best shown by the model predicting optimal oxygen transport. First, the total amount of oxygen transported by the pigment in solution is equated to hemocyanin concentration [36]. Here, the total oxygen transported is obtained by dividing the oxygen capacity of the solution by the viscosity of the solution. For both species, initially, the amount of oxygen transported increases dramatically as the concentration increases, followed by the superblood region in which the increment in oxygen transport becomes progressively less, reaching a plateau at approximately 9 g/100 ml for Busycon and 11 g/100 ml for Limulus (Fig. 3). Further increases in hemocyanin concentration result in a reduction in the capacity for oxygen transport in both species.

The asterisks placed on the oxygen transport curves represent the mean values for concentrations found in vivo during the warmer months of the year [22, 24]. For both species, the in vivo concentrations result in an expected oxygen transport

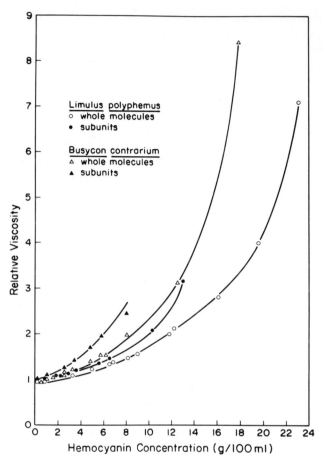

Fig. 2. The relation of viscosity and hemocyanin concentration. See text for explanations of the preparation of the whole molecules and the subunits.

capacity within 10% of the maximum. In addition, in order to reach the absolute maximum, ie, to increase the oxygen transport capacity by between 5% and 10%, the amount of respiratory pigment would have to be augmented by 30–50%, suggesting that the in vivo concentration may represent the most cost effective quantity of pigment rather than the amount necessary to produce the absolute maximum value for oxygen transport. This conclusion is consistent with the findings for hemocyanin concentration in the snail, H. pomatia [6], and for the hemoglobin concentration in the marine annelid, A. marina [37].

DISCUSSION

The Influence of Colloid Osmotic Pressure on Molecular Size and Physiological Concentration

In the two arthropod species, the advantage of assembling the functional subunits into large polymers is quite clear from the present data. At physiological concentrations of the protein, the colloid osmotic pressure of solutions of a 66–72 × 10³ dalton hemocyanin could not be balanced by a hydrostatic pressure generated largely by the heart and the movements of the appendages. In Limulus, hydrostatic pressures at the tissue sinuses average about 3–7 cm H$_2$O in a freely moving animal [23] (see also Redmond et al, this volume). Although no information is available for Callinectes, Blatchford's [3] extensive observations on the related portunid crab Carcinus maenas indicate hydrostatic pressures of only 1–2 cm H$_2$O in the sinuses of resting or walking animals.

Our data also suggest that the oxygen carrying capacity of the blood is limited by the osmotic pressure of the native polymers. Although a freely moving Limulus may maintain an ample margin of hydrostatic over colloid osmotic pressure, in resting animals hydrostatic pressure falls to levels as low as 1–2 cm H$_2$O [23], essentially the colloid osmotic pressure of the blood (Fig. 1).

If the information for Carcinus proves to be representative of Callinectes, our data indicate no excess of hydrostatic over colloid osmotic pressure at the tissues. The question of interest is no longer why the crabs have such low levels of hemocyanin, but how fluid balance is maintained with little or no margin of safety.

The question of fluid balance in the gastropod molluscs is complicated by rather bizarre features of the cardiovascular and oxygen transport systems. Deflation of the foot during "rapid" escape responses is accompanied in several species by the extrusion of blood into the medium [9, 20]. When the foot is fully inflated, the hemocyanin concentration in samples of blood taken from the foot is lower than that of samples taken from the heart, gills or nephridium of the same animal, suggesting the uptake of water from the ambient medium into the pedal sinus [20]. Thus two concentrations are marked on the abscissa of Figure 1, one representing the more concentrated blood in other organs and one the apparently dilute blood in the foot.

Regardless of which is the more meaningful of the two figures, it is clear that our conclusions on the importance of the colloid osmotic pressure of the blood in determining the structural and functional features of the gastropod oxygen carrier must be different. The results of other investigations presented in this volume (G. Bourne, Personal Communication) indicate high pressures (10–30 cm H$_2$O) throughout the range of motor activity, which would be expected in an animal with a fluid skeleton [7]. In view of the enormous size of the pedal muscles and their critical role in locomotion, it is unlikely that hydrostatic pressures are much lower in Busycon. Thus the data in Figure 1 provide no answer to the question of why the native polymer is not the smallest functional subunit, providing that it is present in concentrations less than 7–8 g/100 ml, which is no answer to the question of why the levels of the native polymer do not rise to 40 g/100 ml, and no answer to the question of why the subunits are assembled into the giant among the hemocyanin molecules.

The Influence of Viscosity on Molecular Size and Physiological Concentration

The extent to which the hemocyanins augment oxygen transport is inversely related to the contribution that the addition of the pigment makes to blood viscosity [36]. This is consistent with the results presented here for the oxygen transport curves of the hemocyanin from Limulus where the increase in viscosity which attends dissociation of the molecule (Fig. 2) is concomitant with a reduction in oxygen transport (Fig. 3). These data make it possible to determine the extent to which the shape of the high molecular weight pigments determines their viscosity characteristics [37].

Recently, Ross and Minton have developed a relatively simple model which accurately describes the hydrodynamic properties of concentrated solutions of human hemoglobin. Here we expand on the hydrodynamic model of Ross and Minton [34, 35] to describe the features of the high molecular weight extracellular pigments, which are important to oxygen transport. Their model is based on the semiempirical equation of Mooney [27]:

$$\eta = \eta_o \exp\left[\frac{v\phi}{1 - k\phi}\right] \qquad (2)$$

where η is the viscosity of the final solution, η_o is the viscosity of the suspending medium, v is the coefficient of viscosity, ϕ is the volume fraction of the suspended particles, and k is a "crowding factor."

The value of ϕ cannot be accurately evaluated as a function of pigment concentration, a problem that is circumvented by use of the intrinsic viscosity [η], since the latter term can be equated to the weight concentration of pigment in solution, c. For example, in the limit of infinite dilution, equation (2) reduces to the Einstein relation and

$$\lim_{\phi \to 0} \frac{\eta - \eta_o}{\eta_o} = v\phi \qquad (3)$$

For the same conditions of infinite dilution, the intrinsic viscosity is described by

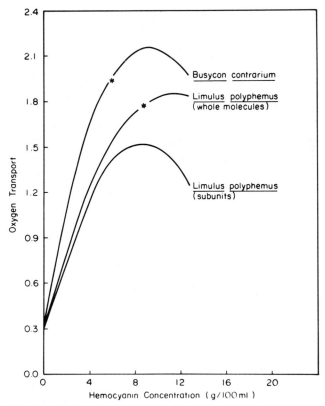

Fig. 3. The relation of oxygen transport and hemocyanin concentration. The oxygen transport term is the ratio of the oxygen capacity of the final solution and the solution viscosity. Because of overlap, the oxygen transport curve for Busycon contrarium subunits is not shown. * = mean in vivo concentration; the value for Busycon is based on values from B. canaliculatum and B. carica [20, 24].

$$[\eta] \;=\; \lim_{c \to 0} \frac{\eta - \eta_o}{\eta_o c} \tag{4}$$

Combining equations (3) and (4),

$$v\phi \;=\; [\eta]c \tag{5}$$

and by substituting equation (5) into equation (2) the viscosity of solutions containing the extracellular respiratory pigments becomes

$$\eta \, - \, \eta_o \, \exp \left[\frac{[\eta]c}{1 \, - \, (k/v) \, [\eta]c} \right] \qquad (6)$$

Although this approach holds strictly only in the limit of infinite dilution, Ross and Minton [35] have shown that equation (6) accurately describes the viscosity of hemoglobin solutions between 1 and 45 g/100 ml.

In order to apply equation (6) to the viscosity data obtained here, the value of η_o is fixed equal to 0.935 centipoise, which is the viscosity of seawater at 25°C. The values for $[\eta]$ and k/v were determined by allowing each to vary until a least-squares best fit to the data was obtained. For all cases (Fig. 2) the coefficients of determination (r^2) exceed 0.99, suggesting that equation (6) fairly accurately represents the relation between viscosity and hemocyanin concentration.

In Table I are shown the values of $[\eta]$ and k/v for the native molecules and the various subunits of Limulus and Busycon hemocyanins. It is of interest that all of the difference in the viscosity curves for both species, when comparing the whole molecule to the smaller particles can be accounted for by differences in the intrinsic viscosities of the molecules; ie, the values for k/v do not vary (Table I). Thus any advantage of subunit aggregation should be seen as differences in the values of $[\eta]$. This is consistent with the hydrodynamic model equating solution viscosity with $[\eta]$ and k/v as shown in Figure 4. Here we have plotted the relative viscosities of a series of solutions showing the effects of varying k/v versus $[\eta]$ and for conditions of varying both parameters. Basically, for concentrations of pigment below 20 g/100 ml the interaction term, k/v, independent of $[\eta]$, has little effect on viscosity. On the other hand, the intrinsic viscosity has a marked effect on viscosity when concentration reaches approximately 10 g/100 ml. When both terms vary in tandem, their combined effects become important at concentrations exceeding approximately 5 g/100 ml (Fig.

TABLE I. Values for the Intrinsic Viscosity, $[\eta]$, and Interaction Term, k/v, as Defined in Equation (5), and Determined According to the Methods Described in the Text for the Horseshoe Crab, Limulus polyphemus, and the Whelk, Busycon contrarium

Species	$[\eta]$	k/v
L. polyphemus		
Whole molecules	4.4×10^{-2}	0.49
Subunits	5.9×10^{-2}	0.49
B. contrarium		
Whole molecules	5.4×10^{-2}	0.58
Subunits	9.1×10^{-2}	0.58

4). However, within the range of pigment concentrations found in the invertebrates, a lowering of blood viscosity can be best achieved by reducing the value
of [η].

The intrinsic viscosities of the whole molecules versus the subunits from a
variety of species support the view that subunit aggregation may represent adaptations to lower [η] (Fig. 5). In each case, the intrinsic viscosity of the subunit
very closely approximates the value predicted for a linear polymer, a condition
which has been shown previously to be of limited value with respect to oxygen
transport [36]. The intrinsic viscosities of the whole molecules, on the other
hand, are considerably lower and appear to be independent of molecular size
(Fig. 5). Taken as a whole, the data suggest a possible role for subunit aggregation, that of decreasing hemolymph viscosity by lowering the intrinsic viscosity
of the carrier molecule.

In conclusion, subunit aggregation has important implications for both the
osmotic properties and the viscosity properties of the whole blood. While, at
present, the osmotic properties appear to be limiting in terms of restricting the
oxygen carrying capacity and hence the oxygen transport only in the arthropods,

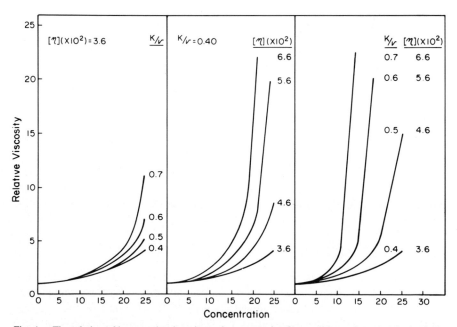

Fig. 4.   The relation of increase in viscosity and concentration for conditions of varying the intrinsic
viscosity of the molecule and the combined term, and when both terms vary in tandem. See text and
equation (6) for further explanation.

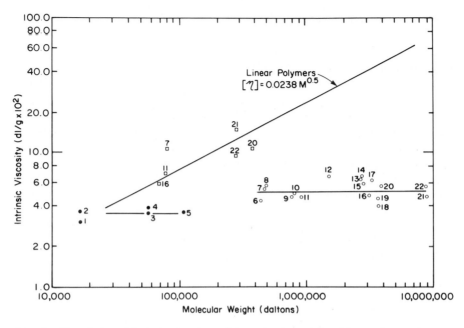

Fig. 5. The relation of intrinsic viscosity and the molecular weight of the respiratory pigment. Symbols: ● = intracellular respiratory pigments, ○ = extracellular respiratory pigments as whole molecules, □ = extracellular respiratory pigments as subunits. References: 1) [26]; 2) [29]; 3) [39]; 4) [29]; 5) [17]; 6) [29]; 7) [11]; 8) [16]; 9, 10) [29]; 11) [10]; 12, 13, 14) [29]; 15) [37]; 16) this study; 17, 18) [29]; 19) [13]; 20) [41]; 21) [29]; 22) [12, 31] and this study.

the advantages of the viscosity properties of a highly polymerized oxygen carrier are clear in both groups. In the molluscan as well as the arthropod species studies here, and also in a variety of other species for which data are available in the literature, the viscosities of the subunits are consistently higher than the values for the whole molecules. Thus, subunit aggregation in general may be an evolutionary strategy to minimize the viscosity characteristics of the oxygen carrier molecules.

ACKNOWLEDGMENTS

We are grateful to Dr. K.E. Van Holde for reading the manuscript and providing many valuable comments and suggestions. This work was supported in part by the University of Colorado Council on Research and Creative Works; BRSG grant RR07713-15 awarded by the Biomedical Research Program, Division of Research Resources NIH to G.K.S.; and NSF grant 77-20159 (Regulatory Biology) to C.P.M.

REFERENCES

1. Adair GS, Elliott FG: Measurements of very small osmotic pressures of the hemocyanin of Pila leopoldvillensis. Nature (London) 219:81–82, 1968.
2. Bijlholt MM, Van Bruggen EFJ, Bonaventura J: Dissociation and reassembly of Limulus polyphemus hemocyanin. Eur J Biochem 95:399–405, 1979.
3. Blatchford B: Haemodynamics of Carcinus maenas (L.). Comp Biochem Physiol 39A:193–202, 1971.
4. Brenowitz M, Van Holde KE, Bonaventura C, Bonaventura J: Calcium specific stabilization of the quaternary structure of Limulus polyphemus hemocyanin. Fed Proc 39:1768, 1979.
5. Burke NF: Osmotic pressure, molecular weight and dissociation of Limulus hemocyanin. J Biol Chem 133:511–520, 1948.
6. Burton RF: Possible factors limiting the concentration of haemocyanin in the blood of the snail, Helix pomatia (L.). Can J Zool 43:433–438, 1965.
7. Dale B: Blood pressure and its hydraulic function in Helix pomatia (L.). J Exp Biol 59:477–490, 1973.
8. Dawson CR, Mallette MF: The copper proteins. Adv Protein Chem 2:179–248, 1945.
9. Deyrup-Olsen I, Martin AW: Blood venting (BV) and surface exudation of fluid (SEF) in terrestrial slugs. Am Zool 20:768, 1980.
10. Ellerton HD, Carpenter DE, Van Holde KE: Physical studies of hemocyanins. V. Characterization and subunit structure of the hemocyanin of Cancer magister. Biochemistry 9:2225–2232, 1970.
11. Ellerton HD, Collins LB, Gale JS, Yung AYP: The subunit structure of the hemocyanin from the crayfish Jasus edwardsii. Biophys Chem 6:47–57, 1977.
12. Eriksson-Quensel IB, Svedberg T: The molecular weights and pH stability regions of the hemocyanins. Biol Bull 71:498–574, 1936.
13. Gros G: Concentration dependence of the self-diffusion of human and Lumbricus terrestris hemoglobin. Biophys J 22:453–468, 1978.
14. Hamlin LM, Fish WW: The subunit characterization of Callinectes hemocyanin. Biochim Biophys Acta 491:46–52, 1977.
15. Johnson ML, Yphantis DA: Subunit association and heterogeneity of Limulus polyphemus hemocyanin. Biochemistry 17:1448–1455, 1978.
16. Joubert FJ: Haemocyanin of the crawfish (Jasus lalandii). Biochim Biophys Acta 14:127–135, 1954.
17. Klotz IM, Keresztes-Nagy S: Hemerythrin: Molecular weight and dissociation into subunits. Biochemistry 2:445–452, 1963.
18. MacFarlane RG, Robb-Smith AHT: "Functions of the Blood." New York and London: Academic. Press, 1961, pp 35–113.
19. Mangum CP: The oxygenation of hemoglobin in lugworms. Physiol Zool 49:85–99, 1976.
20. Magnum CP: A note on blood and water mixing in large marine gastropods. Comp Biochem Physiol 63A:389–391, 1979.
21. Mangum CP: Respiratory function of the hemocyanins. Am Zool 20:19–38, 1980.
22. Mangum CP, Booth CE, Defur PL, Heckel N, Henry RP, Oglesby LC, Polites G: The ionic environment of hemocyanin in Limulus polyphemus. Biol Bull 150:453–467, 1976.
23. Mangum CP, Johansen K: The colloid osmotic pressures of invertebrate body fluids. J Exp Biol 63:661–671, 1975.
24. Mangum CP, Polites G: Oxygen uptake and transport in the prosobranch mollusc, Busycon canaliculatum. I. Gas exchange and the response to hypoxia. Biol Bull 158:77–90, 1980.
25. Mangum CP, Weiland AL: The function of hemocyanin in respiration of the blue crab Callinectes sapidus. J Exp Zool 193:257–264, 1975.

26. Marcy HO, Wyman J: Dielectric studies on muscle hemoglobin. J Am Chem Soc 64:638–643, 1942.

27. Mooney M: The viscosity of a concentrated suspension of spherical particles. J Colloid Sci 6:162–170, 1951.

28. Nickerson KW, Van Holde KE: A comparison of molluscan and arthropod hemocyanin. I. Circular dichroism and absorption spectra. Comp Biochem Physiol 39B:855–872, 1971.

29. Polson A: Über die berechnung der gestalt von proteinmolekülen. Kolloid Zeitschrift 88:51–61, 1939.

30. Prather JW, Brown WH, Zweifach BW: An improved osmometer for measurements of plasma colloid osmotic pressure. Microvasc Res 4:300–305, 1972.

31. Prosser CL: "Comparative Animal Physiology." Philadelphia, London, Toronto: W.B. Saunders, 1973.

32. Quitter S, Watts LA, Crosby C, Roxby R: Molecular weights of aggregation states of Busycon hemocyanin. J Biol Chem 253:525–530, 1978.

33. Roche J, Combette R.: Osmotic pressure and molecular weight of different erythrocruorins (invertebrate hemoglobins). Compt Rend 204:155–157, 1937.

34. Ross PD, Minton AP: Analysis of non-ideal behavior in concentrated hemoglobin solutions. J Mol Biol 112:437–452, 1977.

35. Ross PD, Minton AP: Hard quasipherical model for the viscosity of hemoglobin solutions. Biochem. Biophys Res Commun 76:971–976, 1977.

36. Snyder GK: Blood corpuscles and blood hemoglobins: A possible example of coevolution. Science 195:412–413, 1977.

37. Snyder GK: Blood viscosity in annelids. J Exp Zool 206:271–277, 1978.

38. Sullivan B, Bonaventura J, Bonaventura C: Functional differences in the multiple hemocyanins of the horseshoe crab, Limulus polyphemus L. Proc Natl Acad Sci USA 71:2558–2562, 1974.

39. Tanford C: "Physical Chemistry of Macromolecules." New York: Wiley and Sons, 1961.

40. Toulmond A: Tide-related changes of blood respiratory variables in the lugworm Arenicola marina. Respir Physiol 19:130–144, 1973.

41. Van Holde KE, Cohen LB: Physical studies of hemocyanins. I. Characterization and subunit structure of Loligo pealei hemocyanin. Biochemistry 3:1803–1813, 1965.

42. Wells RMG, Dales RP: Subunit organisation in the respiratory proteins of the polychaeta. Comp Biochem Physiol 54A:387–394, 1976.

Physiology and Biology of Horseshoe Crabs: Studies on
Normal and Environmentally Stressed Animals, pages 189–230
© 1982 Alan R. Liss, Inc., 150 Fifth Avenue, New York, NY 10011

The Nature of the Binuclear Copper Site in Limulus and Other Hemocyanins

E.I. Solomon, N.C. Eickman, R.S. Himmelwright, Y.T. Hwang, S.E. Plon, and D.E. Wilcox

The oxygen binding site in Limulus hemocyanin was studied and compared to that of molluscs and other arthropods. Spectroscopic analysis indicates that in each case the binuclear cupric active site binds peroxide in a μ-dioxo fashion between the equatorial planes of two tetragonal coppers. In addition to this exogenous bridge, which is formed by oxygen, there is an endogenous bridge between the two coppers. This description is based on studies of the active site after chemical modification, which results in the formation of the following active site derivatives: half apo, met apo, half met, dimer, and met. On the basis of spectroscopic studies we conclude that the arthropod forms are quantitatively different from the molluscs and that Limulus is different from the other arthropods. The arthropod site appears to be somewhat distorted, which strongly affects exogenous ligand binding to the binuclear copper site and, by extension, the peroxide regeneration of the met form to oxy. The arthropods have a much lower catalase activity than molluscs, which is likely a result of this effect. Furthermore, the arthropods are found to have a significant fraction ($\sim 35\%$) of unstable active sites that are irreversibly disrupted by exogenous ligands. This active site instability seems to be associated with a heterogeneous strain induced by the protein. The Limulus active site differs from those of molluscs and other arthropods in terms of access for peroxide displacement reactions ($k_{Limulus} \ll k_{molluscs} < k_{arthropods}$).

Finally, a spectral comparison of the active site of the five major fractions of Limulus hemocyanin is presented. These studies show that the above site disruption is found in four of the five fractions and not isolated in one. Also, all five fractions appear to have similar electronic and thus geometric structures as seen in the spectra of the oxy, half met, and met forms.

INTRODUCTION

Hemocyanin is the binuclear copper protein which binds oxygen (1 O_2:2 Cu) [18] in arthropods and molluscs. The hemocyanins are the only well defined copper molecules that bind oxygen reversibly. The deoxy form of hemocyanin contains two Cu(I)s. The oxygenated protein has been found to have dioxygen bound as peroxide at the copper site [7]. Therefore the coppers have been formally oxidized to two Cu(II)s. We would then expect oxyhemocyanin to exhibit the spectral properties of a cupric site.

Cu(II) (d^9 configuration) in a distorted tetragonal environment exhibits the energy-level splitting seen in Figure 1. The one electron in the $d_{x^2-y^2}$ ground state will produce an EPR signal with $g_\parallel > g_\perp > 2$. The copper-nuclear spin of 3/2 will further split the signal into four hyperfine components in the parallel region. The tetragonal energy level diagram in Figure 1 also predicts three weak ligand field transitions at similar energies, which produce one broad band in the red spectral region (500–800 nm). The optical absorption and EPR spectra of oxy hemocyanin are presented as solid lines in Figure 2. Oxyhemocyanin has very unusual features in comparison to inorganic cupric complexes. The absorption spectrum is dominated by two intense bands, one at about 530 nm with $\varepsilon \sim 1,000$ M^{-1} cm^{-1} and a striking absorption at about 350 nm with $\varepsilon \sim 20,000$ M^{-1} cm^{-1}. In addition, oxyhemocyanin is EPR-nondetectable.

There could be a number of explanations for the lack of an EPR signal. First, the 2-electron oxidation could occur on the protein ligand (ie, two thiols to a disulfide). Alternatively, the oxidation could be localized on the coppers with 1) strongly assymetric sites such that one copper loses both electrons, or 2) symmetric coppers interacting either through a copper-copper bond or bridging ligand. All these types of coupling would lead to a diamagnetic ground state.

The goal of this research is to increase our understanding of the function of hemocyanin by interpreting the electronic and, therefore, geometric structure of the copper site. In a series of recent papers [5, 10–15, 22, 26], we have reported the preparation and characterization of a series of active-site derivatives of Busycon hemocyanin. The structure of the active site was studied by spectroscopic evaluation of these systematic variations. This has now been used to study a variety of other mollusc and arthropod hemocyanins with emphasis on Limulus. Below are shown the effective structures of these chemical derivatives. These structures were determined from the following results.

The half apo (Cu(I) −) derivative of Busycon hemocyanin was oxidized to a met apo (Cu(II) −) form which exhibited the spectral properties of a tetragonal cupric site with one exchangeable ligand position in the equatorial plane of the copper. A comparison of met apo and half met (Cu(II)Cu(I)) derivatives showed that this exogenous ligand bound with much higher affinity in half met [11]. When the Cu(I) was reversibly coordinated with CO, the ligand in half met

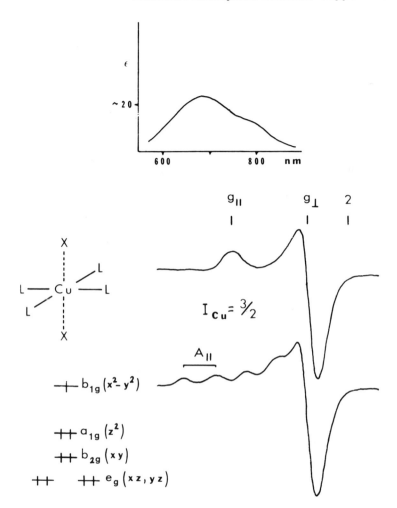

Fig. 1. Energy level diagram for Cu(II) (d^9) in a tetragonal geometry (left). EPR spectrum of tetragonal Cu(II) (middle) with hyperfine interaction (lower). Optical absorption spectrum in the region of ligand field transitions for Cu(II) (upper).

bound much less tightly [12]. Also, certain half met forms show EPR and optical features indicating electron delocalization between the copper (II) and copper (I) through the exogenous ligand L [13]. All these observations required the exogenous ligand to bridge the two coppers.

Furthermore, the exogenous ligands were found to divide into two groups [13]. Group 1 ligands (acetate, F^-, Cl^-, Br^-, I^-, NO_2^-, and aquo) bridge the two

OXYHEMOCYANIN ———
NORMAL COPPER ------

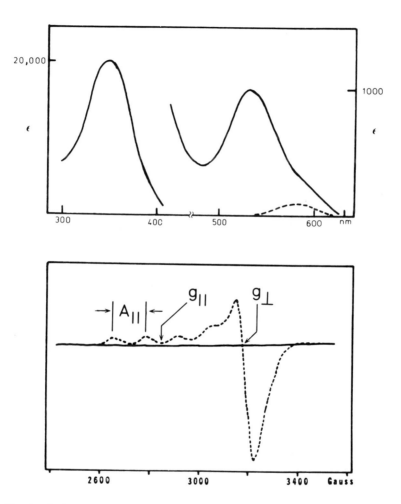

Fig. 2. Optical and EPR spectrum of oxyhemocyanin (—) and normal copper(II) (---).

coppers with a separation of less than 4Å; only one group 1 ligand coordinates at the site in the presence of excess ligand. However, group 2 ligands (N_3^-, SCN^-, CN^-) can require a Cu-Cu distance greater than 5 Å and provide a second coordination position at the copper (II) for binding of a second ligand. This indicates the presence of an endogenous ligand (R) bridging the two coppers, which is broken when group 2 ligands force the coppers apart.

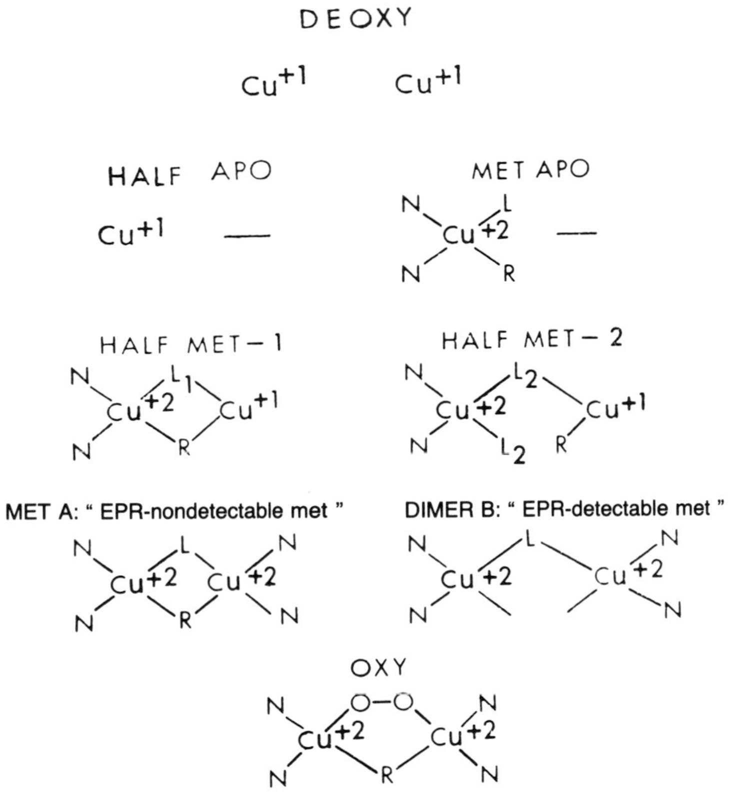

DEOXY

Cu^{+1} Cu^{+1}

HALF APO   MET APO

Cu^{+1} —

$\begin{array}{c} N \\ \diagdown \\ N \diagup \end{array} Cu^{+2} \begin{array}{c} L \\ \diagup \\ \diagdown R \end{array}$ —

HALF MET−1   HALF MET−2

MET A: " EPR-nondetectable met "   DIMER B: " EPR-detectable met "

OXY

An analogous effect was observed for the met and dimer forms [14]. Both are binuclear cupric sites (Cu(II)Cu(II)) but with different magnetic ground states. Met is EPR-nondetectable [14, 16], whereas dimer exhibits an EPR signal. They can be interconverted by exogenous ligand substitution chemistry. The EPR of the dimer form is interpreted as two Cu(II)s which are coupled through very weak dipole interaction [21]. A Cu-Cu separation of ~ 6 Å can be determined from this EPR spectrum. Dimer has a group 2 ligand which breaks the endogenous protein bridge and keeps the coppers greater than 5 Å apart [14]. Met is EPR-nondetectable owing to pairing of the spins on the two copper centers through an endogenous protein bridge [14]. This is known as a superexchange pathway.

Differences in subunit molecular weight, aggregation states, and oxygen-binding behavior (P_{50} and Bohr effects) have been studied in detail for many different hemocyanins [25]. The purpose of this paper is to extend our previous bioinorganic chemical and spectral studies of the oxygen-binding site to a series of mollusc and arthropod hemocyanins and to determine their generality and the nature of any correlations that exist between phyla. We will present evidence demonstrating that the active sites of all oxyhemocyanin are quite similar. However, important differences are observed in those chemical and spectral properties which directly relate to a) the large differences in catalase activity [9], b) protein-ligand effects on the active site, and c) factors that require Limulus to be considered separately from the other arthropods with respect to its active-site reactivity [10, 15]. Finally, we will present new spectral results for the isolated fractions of Limulus in order to understand the effects of heterogeneity on the binuclear copper active site.

EXPERIMENTAL

Hemolymph was obtained from Busycon canaliculatum, Lunatia heros, Helix pomatia, and Megathura crenulata by foot puncture; from Limulus polyphemus and Homarus americanus by heart puncture; and from Cancer borealis, Cancer irroratus, and Cancer magister by removal of several legs. The Octopus bimaculatus hemolymph was purchased from Pacific Bio-Marine Laboratories, Venice, California. The hemocyanin was isolated and purified by ultracentrifugation and extensive dialysis at 4°C in pH 6.3 phosphate or pH 8.2 Tris buffer.

The half apo form of mollusc hemocyanin was prepared by dialysis of 50 ml of 0.4 mM protein in pH = 8.2 Tris buffer (0.1 M) containing 0.1 M $CaCl_2$ and 0.05 M KCN at 4°C for 12.5 h [11]. After extensive dialysis in pH = 8.2 Tris buffer to remove excess $CaCl_2$ and KCN, the half apo was dialyzed in pH = 6.3 phosphate buffer. Incubation of half apo in 30-fold excess $NaNO_2$ at room temperature for 36 h yielded the met apo form. Ligand substitution reactions of met apo were carried out by dialyzing aliquots of protein in buffer solutions containing the appropriate excess of added ligand.

Half met hemocyanin was obtained by treatment of oxyhemocyanin with 10-fold excess $NaNO_2$ and 10-fold excess ascorbic acid for 12 hours in pH 6.3 phosphate buffer [20]. (The variations required in these conditions for preparation of the arthropod half met forms are presented in the Results section.) Ligand substitution reactions were performed by dialysis in buffer solutions containing the appropriate excess of ligand. Carbon monoxide reactions were carried out in a high pressure reaction vessel by equilibration of ~ 2.0 ml of protein solution with 30 psi CO for 30 minutes. Spectra were recorded after removal of CO and exposure to the atmosphere.

Dimer hemocyanin was prepared by treatment of deoxy with NO [20], and trace amount of O_2 [24], or by addition of 100-fold excess $NaNO_2$ to met [14] at pH < 7. The dimer forms were reacted with 50–100-fold excess N_3^- (direct addition) at room temperature to produce the dimer-N_3^- forms [14].

Met hemocyanin of the molluscs was prepared by incubation of oxy at 37°C with 100-fold excess N_3^- or F^- for 48 h [27] in pH 5.0 acetate buffer. The arthropod met forms were obtained by oxidation of deoxy with 5-fold excess H_2O_2 [6]. Direct addition of ligand solutions was used to effect ligand substitution in the met forms.

Ligand displacement reactions of peroxide by N_3^- and SCN^- from oxyhemocyanin were performed at 4°C in pH 6.3 phosphate buffer. Large enough volumes (10–15 ml) of oxyhemocyanin were used so that aliquots could be removed to record spectra at various reaction times.

EPR spectra were recorded on a Varian E-9 spectrometer operating at 9.1 GHz, 100 KHz modulation frequency, 20 Gauss modulation amplitude, and 10 mW microwave power in the $g \simeq 2$ region (100 mW microwave power in the $g = 4$ region). Spectra were obtained as frozen solutions at 77K using a liquid nitrogen dewar and at temperatures < 77K using an Air Products Helitran liquid helium flow system.

Variable temperature optical spectra were obtained using a Cary 17 spectrometer and a Spectrim II cryocooler. Low temperature spectra were recorded as 1:1 (volume) sucrose:buffer solutions which glass on cooling. Difference spectra of N_3^- forms were obtained by using a nonchromophoric derivative, such as met apo-aquo, half met-$CH_3CO_2^-$, or met-aquo, as the reference.

Fractions of Limulus hemocyanin for the half met-NO_2, met-azide, and oxy spectral studies were obtained by ion-exchange chromatography [23] (DEAE-Sephadex, NaCl gradient of 0.1–0.5 M on a 0.9 × 50 cm column) in "stripping buffer" (pH 8.9, 0.02 M Tris-glycine, 0.01 M EDTA). After collection of the five Limulus fractions, they were concentrated to approximately one millimolar and dialyzed to pH 8.9 (0.02 M Tris-glycine, 0.01 M EDTA) without NaCl. For the EPR experiment on "active site instability" of met, fractions of Limulus hemocyanin were isolated according to a modified form of the protocol of Brenowitz et al [4] using stripping buffer, a 1.8 × 50 cm column of DEAE Sephacel and elution with a 0.17–0.40 M Cl$^-$ buffered gradient, followed by a 0.5 M Cl$^-$ flush.

Half met-NO_2^- was obtained for the separated fractions of Limulus by direct addition of NO (anaerobically) to 1 mM solutions of fractions in pH 8.9 stripping buffer on an evacuated Schlenk line. CD spectra of $\sim$ 1 mM solutions of isolated fractions were obtained on a Cary 61 spectrometer at room temperature.

RESULTS

A comparison of the chemical and spectral properties of the met apo, half apo, half met, met, dimer, and oxy forms of five mollusc (Busycon caniculatum, Lunatia heros, Megathura crenulata, Octopus bimaculatus, and Helix pomatia) and five arthropod (Cancer borealis, Cancer irroratus, Cancer magister, Homarus americanus, and Limulus polyphemus) hemocyanins has been carried out. Detailed studies were performed on the derivatives of the mollusc Busycon, and these results were then extended to the other members of the phylum by performing a series of characteristic survey experiments to test the generality of the Busycon results. For the arthropods, Cancer borealis derivatives were treated in detail and found to be representative of all other arthropods except Limulus. Limulus hemocyanin was found to exhibit a number of different chemical and spectral properties; it was therefore also subjected to detailed study, independent of other arthropod hemocyanins. Complete results will be presented for Busycon, Cancer, and Limulus.

Further investigation of the properties of Limulus hemocyanin was performed by separating the five major fractions by ion-exchange chromatography. Several representative chemical derivatives of the fractions were prepared and investigated by spectral analysis. These results will be presented after comparison of the three representative species.

Met Apo Hemocyanin (Cu(II) −)

One significant difference that is observed in a comparison of mollusc and arthropod hemocyanins is based on metal binding to the protein ligand [11]. Figure 3A and B presents representative curves for metal removal from Limulus and Busycon. Here are plotted the relative concentrations of deoxy, half apo, and apo forms present after increasing dialysis times against cyanide (250-fold excess cyanide for Busycon, 25-fold for Limulus) in pH 8.2 Tris buffer, 0.1 M $CaCl_2$. The total copper content was obtained by atomic absorption spectroscopy, and the amount of deoxy hemocyanin was obtained by the difference between the oxygenated form (absorption at 345 nm) and the total amount of active site present. The solid lines were obtained from a pseudo first order kinetic analysis.

$$\text{deoxy(Cu(I)Cu(I))} \xrightarrow{k_1} \text{half apo(Cu(I)} -) \xrightarrow{k_2} \text{apo(— —)}$$

The rate for removal of the second copper (k_2) from Limulus is about an order of magnitude higher than for the first copper (k_1), whereas the reverse is true for molluscs (Limulus: $k_1 = 0.27$ h^{-1}; $k_2 = 1.8$ h^{-1}; Busycon: $k_1 = 0.48$ h^{-1}, $k_2 = 0.024$ h^{-1}). This result indicates that both coppers are needed to form the active site in Limulus and to maintain it once formed.

The half apo derivative of mollusc hemocyanin can be oxidized, generating the met apo (Cu(II) −) derivative. Met apo undergoes labile ligand substitution chemistry [13] characteristic of one equatorial coordination position at a tetragonal copper(II) site [2].

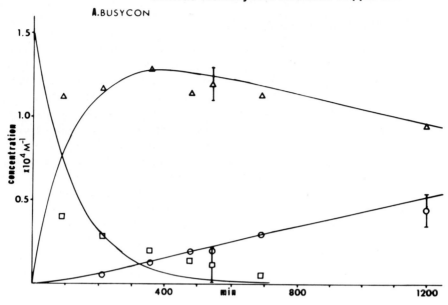

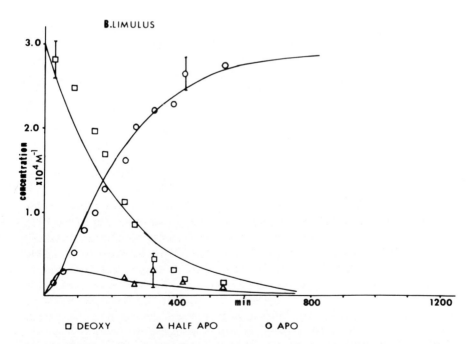

Fig. 3. Predicted (solid lines) and actual (symbols) time dependence of the concentration of A) Busycon and B) Limulus deoxy (Cu(I)Cu(I)), half apo (Cu(I) −), and apo (— —) forms observed during removal of the copper with cyanide.

Half Met Hemocyanin (Cu(II)Cu(I))

The half met derivative contains a copper(II) and a copper(I) at the active site and an intact endogenous protein bridge. The half met-NO_2^- derivative of both mollusc and Limulus hemocyanins is obtained by treatment of oxyhemocyanin in pH 6.3 phosphate buffer with a 10-fold excess of ascorbic acid and nitrite. This chemistry for the other arthropod hemocyanins, however, is more complicated. The half met-NO_2^- form was found to undergo facile conversion to dimer hemocyanin with lower excesses of NO_2^- than the respective mollusc or Limulus forms. On dialysis to remove the excess NO_2^- and ascorbic acid, the dimer sites produced were converted to EPR-nondetectable met (see below, Results—Dimer). Arthropod half met-NO_2^- could, however, be obtained in pure form by initial preparation with 10-fold excess NO_2^- and 20-fold excess ascorbic acid at pH 6.3 phosphate buffer. (Any dimer produced is reduced to half met-NO_2^- by the excess ascorbic acid.) Dialysis to remove excess nitrite and ascorbic acid was then performed in pH 8.0 phosphate buffer to prohibit further generation of NO, followed by dialysis in pH 6.3 phosphate buffer.

The series of half met-L forms where L = NO_2^-, $CH_3CO_2^-$, F^-, Cl^-, Br^-, I^-, aquo, N_3^-, SCN^-, and CN^- has been generated for the mollusc, arthropod, and Limulus hemocyanins. The ligand substitution chemistry is similar for the half met derivatives of all species investigated. However, in general, Limulus derivatives required as much as 1,000-fold excess of ligand to effect substitution compared to the 5–100-fold excesses used in the mollusc and other arthropod forms. The chemistry of the half met forms of the arthropods (excluding Limulus) is further complicated by an irreversible disruption of the site (see later this section) observed when treated with 10-fold excess of N_3^- (or any excess of SCN^-). Therefore, to obtain the half met-N_3^- form, N_3^- had to be added in less than 10-fold excess.

Representative results are now presented which indicate the general similarities of the half met derivatives among the different species studied. Figure 4A shows the half met-Br^- EPR spectra of Busycon, Limulus, and Cancer hemocyanin (representative of all other derivatives). After dialysis of these forms for 72 h in pH 6.3 phosphate buffer, very little change was observed in the EPR spectra (Fig. 4B). This is found for all exogenous ligands and indicates that these ligands remain tightly coordinated to the half met (Cu(II)Cu(I)) active site. EPR spectra of the half met-N_3^- derivatives of Busycon, Limulus, and Cancer hemocyanin are presented in Figure 5A. These spectra all undergo a reversible change upon treatment of half met-N_3^- with 30 psi of carbon monoxide for 30 min (Fig. 5B). Evacuation followed by flushing with nitrogen several times results in recovery of the original half met-N_3^- spectrum in each case.

The EPR (77K) and optical absorption ($\sim$ 15K) spectra of a series of half met-L forms where L = NO_2^-, Cl^-, Br^-, I^-, and N_3^- of Busycon, Limulus, and

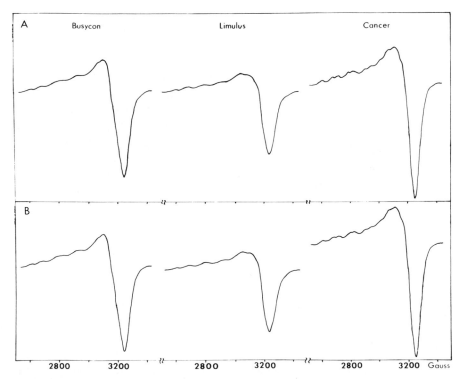

Fig. 4. EPR spectra (77K, pH 6.3 phosphate buffer) of A) half met-Br⁻ in 100-fold excess bromide and B) half met-Br⁻ after 72 h dialysis to pH 6.3 in phosphate buffer of Busycon, Limulus, and Cancer hemocyanin.

Cancer hemocyanin are presented in Figure 6A, B, and C, respectively. The half met-X (X = Cl⁻, Br⁻, and I⁻) spectra are similar for Busycon, Limulus, and Cancer.

Copper(II) d-d transitions are observed between 550 and 720 nm. The low energy transitions have been assigned as intervalence transfer (IT) transitions, which are due to optical excitation of an electron from Cu(I) to Cu(II). The energies of the d-d and IT transitions decrease in the series Cl⁻ > Br⁻ > I⁻ and the intensity of the IT transition increases with Cl⁻ < Br⁻ < I⁻. It is seen that these class II mixed-valent properties [19] correlate with the ability of the exogenous ligand to provide an effective pathway for electron delocalization between the copper(II) and copper(I).

However, significant differences do exist among these three sets of half met-X spectra. In particular, the transitions occur at higher energy for the Limulus

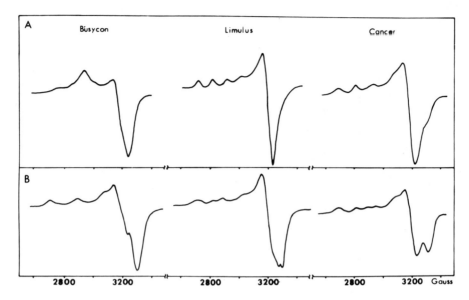

Fig. 5. EPR spectra (77K, pH 6.3 phosphate buffer) of A) half met-N_3^- and B) half met-N_3^- after treatment with carbon monoxide of Busycon, Limulus, and Cancer hemocyanin.

and Cancer derivatives as compared to Busycon, and the IT transitions are most intense in the Busycon half met derivatives. The arthropod derivatives are similar to one another, but Limulus does have more intense IT transitions. Thus exogenous ligands provide the most effective pathway for electron delocalization between the coppers in mollusc half met-X forms. Similarly, in the half met-N_3^- spectra, only Busycon shows a discontinuous change in the absorption (leading to an intense IT transition) and EPR spectra as the temperature is decreased. All molluscs exhibit this effect with some variation in the temperature dependence.

As summarized in the introduction, ligands can be placed in two groups based on their ability to induce binding of a second ligand to the half met Busycon active site [13]. Both group 1 (L_1 = NO_2^-, F^-, Cl^-, Br^-, I^-, $CH_3CO_2^-$, and aquo) and group 2 (L_2 = CN^-, N_3^-, SCN^-) ligands are found to bind tightly to the half met site of both mollusc and arthropod hemocyanins; as demonstrated in Figure 4, these ligands (excluding F^- and aquo) are not readily removed by dialysis in pH 6.3 phosphate buffer. In parallel to what has been reported in Busycon, addition of 100-fold excess of any group 1 ligand to a respective half met-L_1 derivative of all molluscs and arthropods does not result in any spectral changes, indicating that a second group 1 ligand does not bind. Furthermore, treatment of group 2 half met derivatives with excess L_2 results in large changes in the

EPR spectra. This is shown for half met-CN$^-$ in Figure 7. These changes indicate the binding of an additional group 2 ligand by all mollusc and arthropod half met forms.

However, a rather significant difference between Limulus and other arthropods in group 2 ligand binding behavior (for N_3^- and SCN$^-$) is demonstrated by the optical spectra of the half met-N_3^- forms shown in Figure 8. All three hemocyanins exhibit a low energy $N_3^- \rightarrow$ Cu(II) charge transfer transition at ~ 500 nm associated with the tightly bound bridging N_3^-. The Busycon and Limulus half met-N_3^- forms coordinate a second N_3^- (group 2 behavior) with a binding constant similar to that observed for mononuclear copper(II) complexes and for the met apo (Cu(II) $-$) form. With this is associated the appearance of a second $N_3^- \rightarrow$ Cu(II) CT transition at higher energy (~ 400 nm) (unbridged equatorial coordination) in addition to the 500 nm band that remains. For Cancer half met-N_3^-, however, the 500 nm transition is irreversibly replaced by a transition at ~ 400 nm in the presence of 100-fold excess N_3^- [10]. Loss of the 500 nm $N_3^- \rightarrow$ Cu(II) CT transition indicates that N_3^- is no longer bridging. Furthermore, upon dialysis, all the $N_3^- \rightarrow$ Cu(II) CT intensity disappears, demonstrating that the N_3^- is no longer tightly bound at the active site and that the active site has been irreversibly disrupted for arthropod (excluding Limulus) hemocyanin.

The half met derivatives of Busycon and Limulus (but not Cancer) hemocyanin can be regenerated to oxyhemocyanin by reduction with $Na_2S_2O_4$. Treatment of the half met-CH$_3$CO$_2^-$ or half met-aquo forms with 10-fold excess $Na_2S_2O_4$ in pH 6.3 phosphate buffer under nitrogen results in reduction of copper(II) to copper(I), as shown by almost complete loss of EPR intensity for each protein. After dialysis in pH 6.3 phosphate buffer, followed by exposure to oxygen, the 345 nm absorption band in the optical spectra associated with oxyhemocyanin is recovered ($> 90\%$) for Busycon and Limulus. However, although no increase in EPR intensity is observed after dialysis of the Cancer half met-aquo reduced with dithionite, no increase in absorption intensity at 340 nm is observed. This indicates that the Cancer half met forms cannot be regenerated to oxyhemocyanin by $Na_2S_2O_4$ reduction; this effect may be related to the tendency of the arthropod but not Limulus active site to be disrupted, as demonstrated above.

Met Hemocyanin (Cu(II)•••(Cu(II))

Met hemocyanin (Cu(II)•••(Cu(II)) contains two Cu(II)s exchange-coupled through an endogenous protein bridge leading to lack of an EPR signal. Met is prepared for the molluscs by ligand displacement of peroxide from oxyhemocyanin with fluoride or azide [27] and for the arthropods (including Limulus) by two-electron oxidation of deoxy with peroxide [6]. Only mollusc met can be regenerated with peroxide to oxy hemocyanin, demonstrating the catalase activity associated with this phyla. Reaction of the met derivative with group 1 (F$^-$,

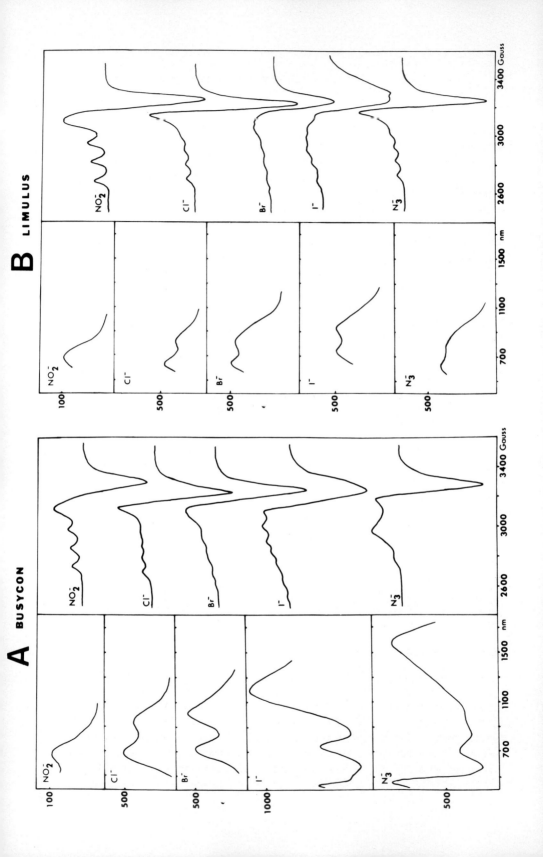

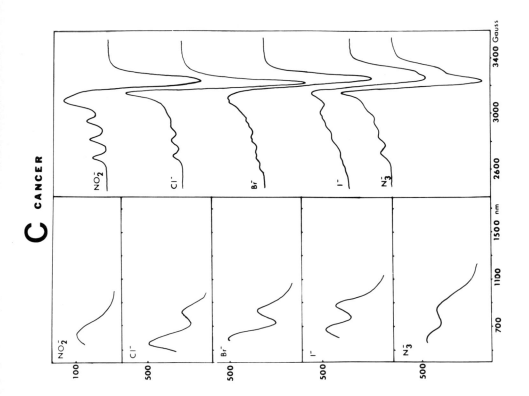

Fig. 6.   Absorption spectra (~ 15K, pH 6.3 phosphate buffer in 1:1 sucrose glass) and EPR spectra of the half met-L series of A) Busycon, B) Limulus, and C) Cancer hemocyanin derivatives. L is indicated for each spectrum.

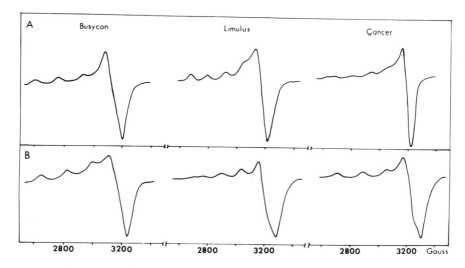

Fig. 7. EPR spectra (77K, pH 8.0 phosphate buffer) of A) half met-CN⁻ and B) half met-CN⁻ in 100-fold excess cyanide of Busycon, Limulus, and Cancer hemocyanin.

Cl⁻, Br⁻, $CH_3CO_2^-$) and group 2 (N_3^- and SCN⁻) ligands has been investigated by EPR and optical spectroscopy.

Although met is EPR-nondetectable, an instability for a small percentage of sites in each phyla (arthropod > mollusc) leads to interesting EPR signals (Wilcox et al, unpublished results). The instability of these sites is dependent upon pH and exogenous anion. For arthropods (including Limulus), ~ 35% of the sites exhibit this instability. Low pH conditions reversibly induce broad (0–5,000 Gauss), weak EPR signals characteristic of dipolar coupled Cu(II) ions, as seen in Figure 9. Exogenous ligands in low concentration reversibly increase and modify these broad signals. Simulation of these signals has shown that for group 1 anions, the Cu-Cu distance is less than 4 Å. The N_3^- uncoupled site (Cu-Cu > 5 Å) is stable only at pH > 7.

For higher anion concentration or lower pH these broad signals are irreversibly replaced by a typical mononuclear Cu(II) EPR signal [26]. The lack of Cu-Cu interaction indicates that the metals are unbridged and separated by > 7 Å in this "sprung" site [17]. The unstable Limulus active sites show somewhat different behavior than the other arthropods. Only the anion Cl⁻ at low pH (≤ 5.3) stabilizes the reversible broad EPR signals, and irreversible springing occurs only in this quite low pH region. The slow reactivity of Limulus requires longer reaction times or higher anion concentration (compared to other arthropods) for complete springing. Less than 10% of the mollusc active sites are unstable.

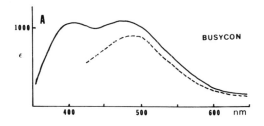

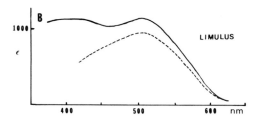

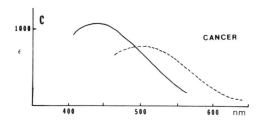

Fig. 8. Absorption spectra (room temperature, pH 6.3 phosphate buffer, presented as difference spectra) of half met-N_3^- (---) and half met-N_3^- in 100-fold excess azide (—) of A) Busycon, B) Limulus, and C) Cancer hemocyanin.

Although both group 1 and group 2 ligands show the characteristic broad EPR signals at low pH, only group 2 ligands induce the mononuclear EPR signals (springing).

The met forms of Busycon, Limulus, and Cancer are converted to the half met-NO_2^- derivative upon aerobic treatment with nitric oxide in pH 6.3 phosphate buffer. It is important to note this reaction since the arthropod (including Limulus) met derivatives cannot be regenerated to oxy hemocyanin by treatment with H_2O_2 or by any other methods which have been attempted. The half met-NO_2^- form obtained from the Limulus met hemocyanin can be further regenerated to

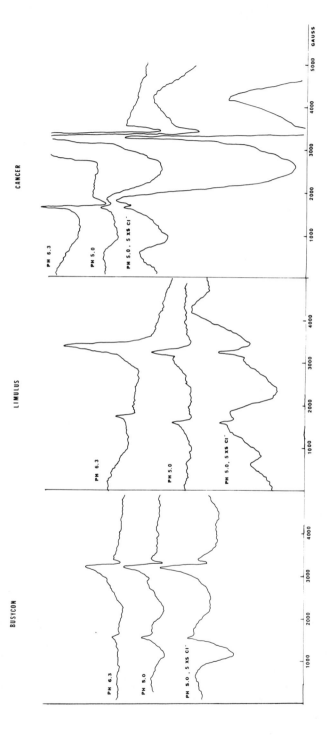

Fig. 9. EPR Spectra (7K) of met A) Busycon, B) Limulus, C) Cancer at pH 6.3, pH 5.0, and pH 5.0 + 5 xs Cl⁻.

oxy hemocyanin, as described in the half met results section, using dithionite. This indicates that at least for Limulus hemocyanin the met derivative is not an irreversibly damaged protein form.

In an effort to understand the lack of peroxide binding by the arthropod met forms (ie, regeneration to oxy), the optical spectral perturbations of ligand binding to the Busycon, Limulus, and Cancer met forms were investigated. Addition of excess group 2 ligands to arthropod mets is complicated since a mixture of forms due to $\sim 35\%$ site disruption is present. However, under normal pH conditions reasonably pure forms are present for spectroscopic study of Busycon and Limulus met derivatives.

The low temperature met-aquo absorption spectra of Busycon, Limulus, and Cancer are given in Figure 10A, B, and C. The only spectral features in the visible and near-IR region are the overlapping d-d transitions of the two unresolvable cupric ions. The spectra are, in general, similar in energy and intensity. The peak maximum shifts to higher energy over the series Busycon $<$ Limulus $<$ Cancer ($\lambda_B = 690$ nm, $\lambda_L = 650$ nm, $\lambda_C = 635$ nm), and the shoulder to lower energy appears to lose intensity.

Fluoride (group 1 ligand) binds to all three mets and greatly perturbs the d-d spectra (Fig. 10) without the added complication of mixed forms due to site disruption. In all cases, the binding constant is on the order of 10^3 M^{-1}. Titrations of met with fluoride were done by monitoring the shift in d-d spectra, and K is in the range $600 < K < 4,000$ M^{-1}. The spectra show a significant loss in intensity along with a large shift (~ 2000 cm^{-1}) to lower energy for each of the three groups.

Azide also binds to met but, unlike fluoride, appears to interact differently with the various species. The d-d transitions of Busycon met shift down in energy by ~ 400 cm^{-1} upon binding azide, whereas Limulus exhibits a larger shift of almost 1500 cm^{-1} (Fig. 10). The situation is complicated for Cancer met hemocyanin because of the site disruption. It is not obvious from the d-d spectrum that the 70% EPR-nondetectable Cancer met is binding azide. The spectrum shows an increase in absorption around 800 nm, and there is a slight shift in the peak maximum of ~ 250 cm^{-1}.

The azide to copper charge transfer spectra of the three met azides show large differences (Fig. 11). One broad band with an extinction coefficient of $\sim 1,500$ M^{-1} cm^{-1} and a peak maximum at 380 nm is found for Busycon met-N_3^-. The binding constant is calculated to be 500 M^{-1}. Limulus met-N_3^- shows a much lower binding constant. Appreciable conversion to the azide-bound form occurs only at relatively high anion concentrations (0.1 M), indicating that K is on the order of 10 M^{-1}. The charge transfer band for Limulus met-N_3^- (Fig. 11B) is also quite different from that observed for Busycon met-N_3^-. The Limulus spectrum shows a band at ~ 500 nm with an ε of 500 M^{-1}. At higher energy, another very intense band grows in, but its peak maximum is not well defined ($\lambda < 375$

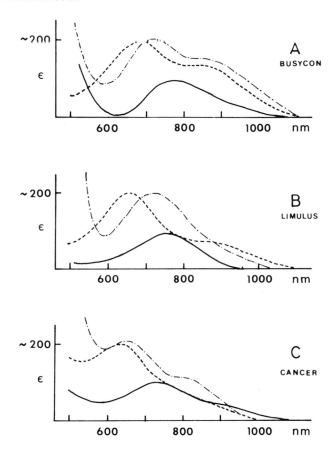

Fig. 10. Absorption spectra ($\sim$ 15K, pH 6.3 phosphate buffer in 1:1 sucrose glass) of met-aquo (---), met fluoride (—), and met-N$_3^-$ (-·-·-) of A) Busycon, B) Limulus, and C) Cancer hemocyanin.

nm; $\varepsilon > 1{,}500$ M^{-1} cm^{-1}). The charge transfer band in the Cancer met-N$_3^-$ spectrum grows in simultaneously with the EPR signal of the "sprung" site. This suggests that at these concentrations azide is binding only to the EPR-detectable copper in the protein. The binding constant for this site is then 100 M^{-1}, and the N$_3^-$ CT has an ε of $\sim$ 1200 M^{-1} cm^{-1} at 420 nm. The CD spectra of the charge transfer bands have also been included in Figure 11. For the Cancer azide-bound form, two bands are observed that can be directly correlated with absorption bands. Alternatively, the CD spectra of Busycon and Limulus met-N$_3^-$ are more complicated, with three or more transitions required to fit the observed spectra.

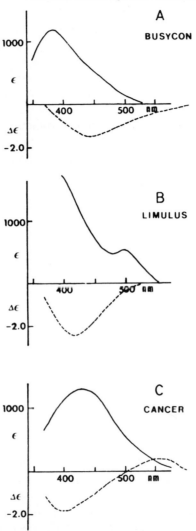

Fig. 11. Absorption (—) and circular dichroism (---) spectra (room temperature, pH 6.3 phosphate buffer) of A) Busycon, B) Limulus, and C) Cancer met-azide hemocyanin.

Dimer Hemocyanin (Cu(II)Cu(II))

The dimer hemocyanin active site (determined by spectroscopic analysis) consists of two copper(II)s with an exogenous ligand pushing the coppers > 5 Å apart and breaking the endogenous bridge. Dimer is obtained either by treatment of deoxy with nitric oxide in the presence of trace amounts of oxygen [24] or by addition of 100-fold excess $NaNO_2$ at pH < 7 to met hemocyanin [14]. However, dimer is not simply a met-NO_2^-, as this reaction does not occur at high pH. Thus, this reaction seems to proceed by generation of NO from NO_2^- in solution at low pH. NO reduces met to half met-NO_2^- and subsequent reoxidation of half met with excess NO_2^- (NO + O_2 reaction) yields dimer [14]. The dimer EPR spectra of Busycon, Limulus, and Cancer are shown in Figure 12. The EPR spectrum of Limulus is similar to that of other arthropods, and these differ significantly from the dimer spectra of molluscs. Although accurate quantitation of the NO and O_2 reaction is difficult, preparation of Busycon and Limulus dimer by addition of excess NO_2^- to met or half met-NO_2^- requires much higher concentrations of $NaNO_2$ than the other arthropods (Fig. 13).

The dimer derivatives of all three hemocyanins undergo a reaction with azide. Figure 12 shows the EPR spectra for each obtained after treatment of the NO dimer with 100-fold excess NaN_3. Figure 14 presents the change in integrated intensity of the g $\sim$ 2 EPR signal with time for this reaction. A significant reduction in intensity is associated with the formation of dimer-N_3^-. This reduction is much larger for molluscs. The dimer-N_3^- form is found to be stable for > 100 h but can be further converted to EPR-nondetectable met (as can the original dimer forms) by dialysis for $\sim$ 12 h to remove excess ligand (Fig. 14; 190 h). The residual EPR spectra (Fig. 12) observed after dialysis is due to half met necessarily present in the preparation (14% B, 19% L, 20% C). For Busycon, the met obtained after dialysis can be regenerated to oxy by addition of 5-fold excess H_2O_2.

Oxy Hemocyanin (Cu(II)-$O_2^=$-Cu(II))

Oxy hemocyanin has two copper(II)s with dioxygen bound as peroxide bridging the copper(II)s. The oxyhemocyanin of all species, excluding Limulus, was found to undergo a peroxide displacement reaction with excess N_3^- or SCN^- [10, 15]. Figure 15 presents the effects observed in the optical and EPR spectra of Busycon, Limulus, and Cancer oxyhemocyanin upon addition of excess N_3^- in pH 6.3 phosphate buffer. The absorption features at 340 and 570 nm are gradually replaced by an N_3^- (or SCN^-) $\rightarrow$ Cu(II) charge transfer transition in the 400 nm region of the spectrum. (Dialysis to remove in pH 6.3 phosphate buffer for 24 h does not result in recovery of the oxy spectral features, indicating that methemocyanin has been produced.)

The pseudo first order rate constants (k) for the N_3^- (and SCN^- in a few cases) displacement of peroxide from several species are given in Table I. In general, the arthropod hemocyanins exhibit about an order of magnitude faster reaction rate than the molluscs, with Limulus showing essentially no reaction. Whereas F^-, and to a much lesser extent Cl^-, Br^-, and I^-, have been reported to displace peroxide also from mollusc hemocyanins [27], the arthropod oxyhemocyanins showed no reaction at 4°C with any halide anions.

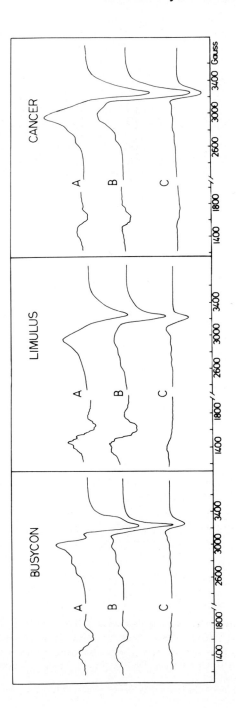

Fig. 12. EPR spectra (77K, pH 5.7 acetate buffer) of A) NO-generated dimer, B) NO-generated dimer after addition of 100-fold excess azide, and C) 24 h dialysis of the sample protein in B for Busycon, Limulus, and Cancer hemocyanin.

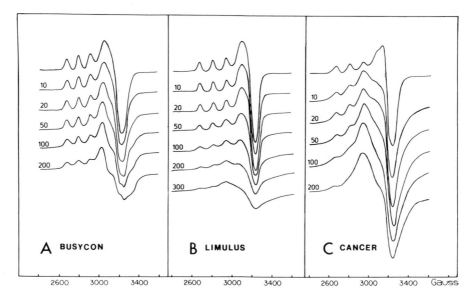

Fig. 13. EPR spectra (77K, pH 5.7 acetate buffer) of the concentration dependence of dimer formation by addition of excess nitrite to A) Busycon, B) Limulus, and C) Cancer half met-NO_2^- hemocyanins. The first spectrum represents the original half met-NO_2^-, and the addition of the appropriate excess of NO_2^- is indicated above each successive spectrum.

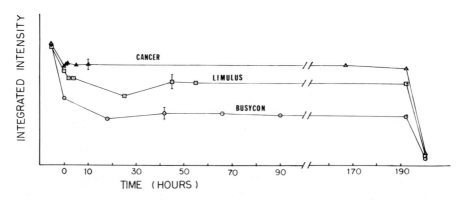

Fig. 14. Time dependence of the integrated intensity of the $g \sim 2$ signal of the dimer-N_3^- form of ○ Busycon, □ Limulus, and △ Cancer hemocyanins. The initial points represent the integrated intensities of the original dimer form, the intermediate points the integrated intensity after addition of 100-fold excess NaN_3 from zero to >190 h, and the final points the remaining integrated intensity after dialysis to remove excess azide.

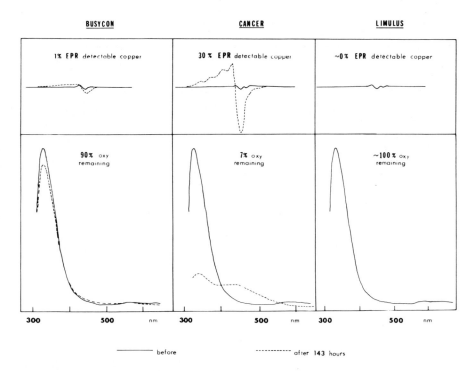

Fig. 15.   Optical (room temperature) and EPR (77K) spectra before and 143 h (at 4°C) after addition of excess N_3^- (pH = 6.3) to Busycon, Limulus, and Cancer oxy hemocyanin.

Along with loss of the oxy absorption features there is a gradual appearance of an EPR spectrum (Fig. 15) for arthropod (excluding Limulus) hemocyanins. With the conversion of 70–90% of oxy sites to met, the resulting EPR spectrum can account for only 30 ± 5% of total copper, and no reduction in intensity is observed upon dialysis to remove the excess N_3^- or SCN^-. These EPR spectra are identical (in quantitation, ~ 30% of total copper, and shape) to those obtained by direct addition of excess N_3^- or SCN^- to peroxide generated met forms. Similar but much less intense (< 10% of total copper) EPR signals are obtained with the mollusc hemocyanins.

The oxyhemocyanin absorption spectrum of Busycon has been studied in detail and assigned [5] using a transition dipole vector coupling model [8] and comparison to spectra of other hemocyanin derivatives. Two components are expected for each $O_2^=$ → Cu(II) transition (π_v^* and π_σ^* → copper $d_{x^2-y^2}$)) for a bridging peroxide due to coupling to the two coppers. The intense band at 345 nm is assigned as one component of the peroxide π_σ^* → copper $d_{x^2-y^2}$ charge

TABLE I. Pseudo First Order Rate Constants for Displacement of Peroxide from Oxyhemocyanin by Excess Ligand[a]

	N_3^-	SCN^-
Molluscs[b]		
Busycon canaliculatum	0.002[c]	0.0004[c]
Lunatia heros	0.006[d]	
Megathura crenulata	0.004[e]	
Arthropods		
Homarus americanus	>0.4[d]	
Cancer magister	0.3[d]	
Cancer irroratus	0.09[d]	
Cancer borealis	0.06[d]	0.005[f]
Limulus polyphemus	<0.0001[c]	<0.0001[c]

[a]In h^{-1}.
[b]The reactions of mollusc hemocyanins are complicated by the biphasic nature of the reactions, most noticeably for the reactions with SCN^-. The loss of oxygen as O_2 initially proceeds at a much higher rate, which is then superseded by the loss of oxygen as O_2^{2-} to form met.
[c]200-fold excess.
[d]500-fold excess.
[e]600-fold excess.
[f]100-fold excess.

transfer transition. The band at 570 nm in the absorption spectrum and the positive CD band at 480 nm are the two components of the peroxide $\pi_v^* \rightarrow Cu$ charge transfer. The weak shoulder at 425 nm is associated with a protein ligand—most likely phenolate—[1, 5] to copper charge transfer, and the shoulders on the low energy side of the 570 nm band are the ligand field transitions of the cupric ions.

All of these transitions are found in the spectra of Limulus and Cancer oxyhemocyanins, and although the room temperature absorption spectra of all the hemocyanins are similar, variations are discerned in the low temperature visible spectrum and in the room temperature CD spectrum (Fig. 16). These spectra can be resolved into gaussian bands, and it is observed that one set of gaussians fits the peroxide charge transfer spectra of all three with shifts in energy and intensity. Ligand field transitions and the 425 nm band were obtained by subtracting absorption due to the more intense peroxide charge transfer bands. The d-d transitions were simply fit to an effective band envelope. Using both absorption and circular dichroism spectra to obtain band positions and half-widths, the room temperature spectra were analyzed first. Low temperature absorption spectra were then fit, allowing the peak maxima to move to higher energy and decrease in half-width. The peak positions and intensities for both room and low temperature spectra are given in Table II, and the $\sim$ 15K spectra with gaussian components are shown in Figure 16.

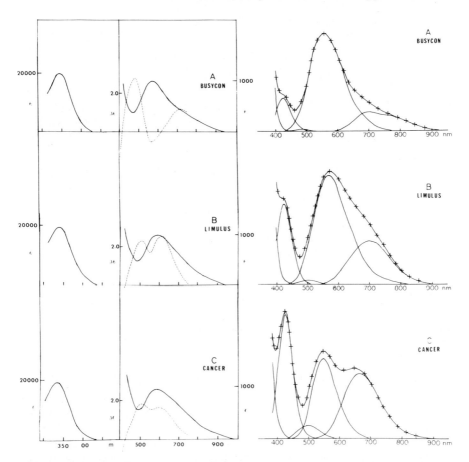

Fig. 16.   Absorption (—) and circular dichroism (---) spectra at room temperature and guassian resolution of absorption spectra at low temperature for A) Busycon, B) Limulus, and C) Cancer oxy hemocyanin.

Differences are found in peak positions and intensities, which account for the observed low temperature absorption and room temperature CD spectral differences. The observed component of the peroxide $\pi_\sigma^* \rightarrow$ copper CT (~ 340 nm) shifts to higher energy going from Busycon to Limulus to Cancer. Splitting between the two components of the peroxide $\pi_v^* \rightarrow$ copper CT transition decreases, and intensity of the higher energy component increases in the order Busycon < Limulus < Cancer. The protein ligand (most likely phenolate) $\rightarrow$ Cu(II) CT at 425 nm does not show any significant change in energy, but its intensity does increase in the series Busycon < Limulus < Cancer. Intensity of the d-d bands also increases over the series Busycon < Limulus < Cancer and

TABLE II. Gaussian Resolution of Oxyhemocyanin Spectra

	Busycon canaliculatum	Limulus polyphemus	Cancer borealis
Room temperature			
π_σ*	28 850 (~20 000)	29 520 (~20 000)	29 850 (~20 000)
Phenolate	23 000 (360)	23 000 (580)	23 000 (830)
π_v*	20 250 (50)	20 000 (35)	19 500 (310)
	17 500 (1000)	17 000 (960)	17 250 (780)
"d-d bands"[a]	13 800 (230)	13 700 (300)	14 390 (520)
Low temperature			
π_σ*	29 350 (~20 000)	30 000 (~20 000)	30 350 (~20 000)
Phenolate	23 500 (400)	23 600 (890)	23 500 (1700)
π_v*	21 000 (20)	20 250 (45)	20 000 (180)
	17 850 (1180)	17 500 (1200)	18 125 (1090)
"d-d bands"	14 280 (250)	14 280 (500)	15 000 (890)
$\Delta\pi_v$* Room temp	2,750	3,000	2,250
Low temp	3,150	2,750	1,875
Average π_v*			
Room temp	18,875	18,500	18,375
Low temp	19,425	18,875	19,062

[a]The value given for "d-d bands" is the peak maximum of the remaining absorption in the ligand field region after the absorption due to charge transfer bands is subtracted. The presence of six possible transitions (three d-d transitions for each copper) would make any gaussian analysis of this region inconclusive.

the bands shift to somewhat higher energy. The peak maximum of the Cancer band envelope is 700 cm^{-1} higher than either Busycon or Limulus and, although the peak maxima of the latter two coincide, the Limulus bands are not skewed to lower energy as is the Busycon band shape. Thus, the double peak in low temperature visible absorption spectrum of arthropod oxyhemocyanin (Fig. 16) is associated with a relative increase in energy and intensity of the ligand field transitions. This increase in energy of the d-d transitions is also accompanied by a shift to higher energy of a positive CD spectral feature. This overlaps the weak negative band associated with the low energy component of the $O_2^=$ π_v* → Cu CT transition and dominates this region of the arthropod CD spectrum.

The ligand field and 425 nm absorptions of the oxy form (with $O_2^=$ → Cu CT transitions subtracted out) can now be compared to those transitions in the analogous met-aquo derivatives. Changes in energy and bandshape seen in Figure 17 must be considered within the error of subtracting the more intense π_v*→Cu CT transitions; however, significant variations in intensity are observed. Essentially, no change in intensity of either the 425 nm or the ligand field region are found for Busycon. In contrast, for both arthropods, large decreases (a factor of 3–4) in intensity of these transitions are observed between oxy and met.

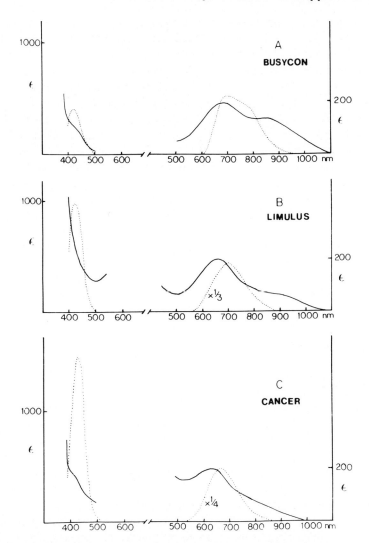

Fig. 17. Absorption spectra of oxyhemocyanin after subtraction of the 570 nm $O_2^= \rightarrow$ Cu(II) CT transition (...) and met-aquo hemocyanin (—) of A) Busycon, B) Limulus, and C) Cancer.

Limulus Subunits

As many hemocyanins including Limulus have heterogeneous fractions, it is important to determine the relation of aggregated protein spectral features to those of the individual fractions. The heterogeneous subunits of Limulus were separated by ion-exchange chromatography and subjected to a survey of spectral studies as previously performed on aggregated hemocyanins. Half met-NO_2^- derivatives of the five fractions were made by direct addition of NO to deoxy. This avoided the low pH conditions of the usual preparation (NO_2^- and ascorbate) and the associated reaggregation complications [12]. EPR spectra of these derivatives (Fig. 18) show very little difference between the individual fractions, deaggregated hemocyanin and aggregated Limulus protein. Optical spectra of oxy in the 300–750 nm region (Fig. 19) and CD spectra in the 400–600 nm region (Fig. 20) reveal only small differences in the charge transfer and ligand field transitions of these protein samples. Most noticeable are the lower energy $O_2^= \rightarrow$ Cu(II) CT transitions at ~ 590 nm for fractions II and V and the distinct ligand field shoulders of fractions III and IV. The $N_3^- \rightarrow$ Cu(II) CT transitions of met-N_3^- are important spectral probes of the active site. Again, very little difference among the fractions was found for the low energy CT peak (Fig. 21). The binding constants and $\Delta\varepsilon$ values for N_3^- on met are tabulated (Table III); all show values in the same order of magnitude. The very low (unmeasurable) binding constant for fraction I is anomalous. Oxygen-binding affinities are also correlated in this table. Individual heterogeneous fractions of Limulus have provided information about the nature of the small amount of met active site instability. As Table III shows, this low pH springing is not isolated in any of the five major heterogeneous fractions but occurs to varying degrees in the Limulus components.

DISCUSSION

The most general results to come from our parallel studies of five mollusc and five arthropod hemocyanins are a strong similarity in the chemistry and spectroscopy of these different species. All these results are consistent with the active site pictured in Figure 22. In this active site the two copper(II)s are considered close to equivalent based on all present spectral data.* In all cases, a half met form is accessible through similar chemical pathways. This half met form binds ligands very tightly at the active site, reversibly coordinates carbon monoxide, and exhibits class II mixed-valent properties that correlate with the nature of the exogenous ligand. This is all consistent with exogenous ligand bridging of the binuclear copper site. Furthermore, all arthropod and mollusc hemocyanin half met forms exhibit group 1–group 2 ligand binding behavior, in which a second coordination position is present at the copper(II) only in group 2 forms (half met-L_2 where $L_2 = N_3^-$, SCN^-, CN^-). These ligands force the coppers > 5 Å apart and rupture an endogenous protein bridge. For all species

---

*It has been proposed that the coppers are not equivalent based on a misassignment of the $O_2^= \rightarrow$ Cu(II) CT transition as d-d transitions: Mori W, et al: Biochem Biophys Res Commun 66:725, 1975.

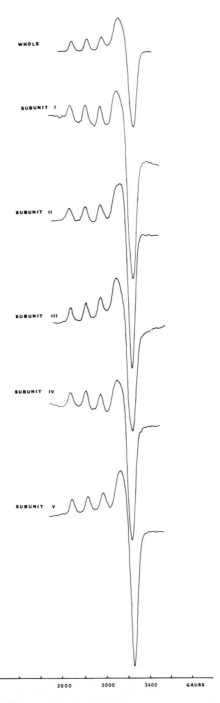

Fig. 18. EPR spectra (77K, pH 8.9, Tris-glycine buffer) of the half met-NO_2^- derivatives of aggregated (whole) Limulus and separated fractions (I–V).

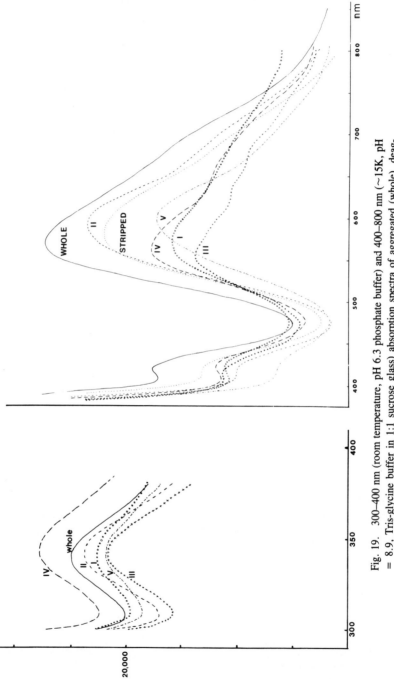

Fig. 19. 300–400 nm (room temperature, pH 6.3 phosphate buffer) and 400–800 nm (~15K, pH = 8.9, Tris-glycine buffer in 1:1 sucrose glass) absorption spectra of aggregated (whole), deaggregated (stripped), and five fractions (I–V) of Limulus oxy hemocyanin.

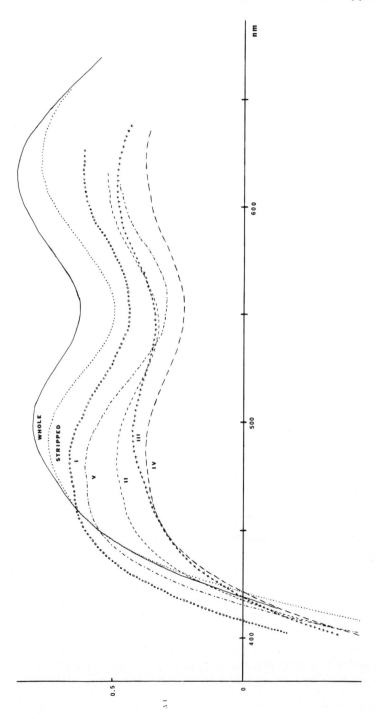

Fig. 20. CD spectra (room temperature, pH 8.9, stripping buffer) of five separated fractions (I–V), deaggregated (stripped) and aggregated (whole; pH = 6.3 phosphate buffer) oxy hemocyanin of Limulus.

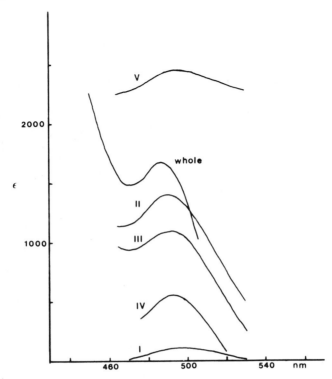

Fig. 21. Lowest energy $N_3^- \rightarrow$ Cu(II) CT transition of met-N_3^- Limulus separated fractions (I–V) (difference spectra) and aggregated (whole) protein.

it is possible to prepare an EPR-nondetectable met and dipolar coupled dimer that can be interconverted (addition of excess NO_2^- at low pH to met, which proceeds with initial reduction by NO to half met-NO_2^-, followed by oxidation with NO + O_2 yielding dimer, and dialysis of dimer, which yields met). Little difference is observed in the ligand field transitions of these forms. Again, this is consistent with breaking an endogeneous protein bridge in the dimer form and eliminating the antiferromagnetic coupling. The dimer form of all hemocyanins undergoes a reaction with N_3^- producing a new EPR-detectable binuclear cupric dimer-N_3^- derivative that also converts to met upon dialysis. Finally, CD and absorption spectral differences of the oxy forms simply reflect increases in energy and intensity of ligand field transitions in the series $\nu_{Busycon} < \nu_{Limulus} < \nu_{Cancer}$.

There are, however, some very specific quantitative differences between arthropods and molluscs in terms of reactivity and spectral properties. Furthermore, we find that Limulus behaves differently from the other arthropods and thus must

TABLE III. Properties of Limulus Hemocyanin: Aggregated Protein and the Five Major Heterogeneous Fractions

	Aggregated		1	2	3	4	5
% of whole protein[a]	—		13	25	37	16	9
O_2 affinity $\quad$ pH 7.5[a]	3.5	(pH = 7.0)	2.1	1.4	1.4	1.0	5.9
(P_{50}:mm Hg) $\;$ pH 9.0[a]	14.1		2.2	1.62	1.5	1.0	5.7
N_3^- binding to met							
$\quad$ K (sec^{-1})	11.5		very small	5.0	5.5	25	1.0
$\quad$ $\Delta\varepsilon$ (M^{-1} cm^{-1})	1,674		small	1,400	1,100	550	2,450
springing (%)	35[b]		40	40	25	60	10

[a]From Ref [23].
[b]weighted average of subunit springing ~35%.

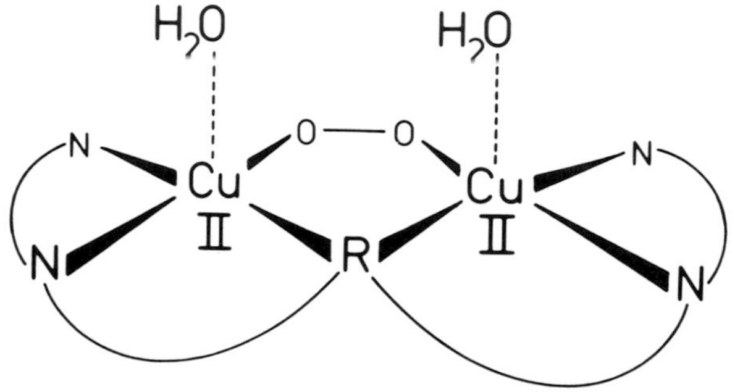

Fig. 22.   Structural representation of the oxyhemocyanin active site.

be considered separately in a comparison of active sites [10, 15].** This is apparent in the ligand displacement reactions of peroxide from the oxyhemocyanin site. Although the oxy spectra and therefore active sites are quite similar, Limulus is observed to be the least reactive: $k_{Limulus} \ll 10^{-4}$ h^{-1}, $k_{mollusc} \sim 10^{-3}$ h^{-1} and $k_{arthropod} \sim 10^{-1}$ h^{-1} for N_3^- reactions. This is most reasonably explained by lack of access to an axial coordination position of the copper(II) in Limulus. Axial access is required for associative ligand substitution chemistry in tetragonal cupric systems. It thus appears from the average energies of the ligand field transitions and ligand substitution reactivity of oxy sites that the tetragonal nature of the cupric sites is best considered 5 coordinate square pyramidal (C_{4v}) with the axial position exchangeable (H$_2$O) for Cancer, less exchangeable for Busycon, and blocked by a weakly coordinating protein ligand in Limulus. It should be noted that this trend in axial accessibility is also observed in ligand substitution reactivity of the half met forms: Limulus requires higher excesses than Busycon, and Cancer exhibits the most substitution lability.

For all binuclear copper active site derivatives of hemocyanin, we have found a very strong correlation in spectral properties among the arthropods, including Limulus, that differ quantitatively from those of the molluscs. As spectral properties probe active site geometric structure, these differences demonstrate that arthropod sites are distorted compared to those of molluscs. First, in all derivatives, the ligand field transitions are at higher energy in the arthropods. In the half met forms, the intervalent transfer transitions are weaker for arthropods with

---

**The energies of tetragonal copper(II) d-d transitions are predominantly dependent upon the effective ligand field strength of the four equatorial ligands, but can be perturbed to a lesser extent by approach of a fifth and/or sixth ligand (in the axial positions) or by a low symmetry distortion of the equatorial ligands. The positions of hemocyanin peak maxima confirm the tetragonal nature of the sites since they are similar to that observed for well defined inorganic complexes. Cu(imid)$_2^{2+}$ in aqueous solution has $\lambda_{max} = 690$ m, ($\bar{\nu} = 14,500$ cm^{-1}), which compares favorably to the hemocyanin values: $\bar{\nu}_{Busycon} = 13,800$ cm^{-1}, $\bar{\nu}_{Limulus} = 13,700$ cm^{-1}, $\bar{\nu}_{Cancer} = 14,400$ cm^{-1}.

no low temperature half met-N_3^- form. This demonstrates that there is less electron delocalization between the coppers and thus a poorer bridging mode for exogenous ligands. For dimer and dimer-N_3^- the EPR spectra of the arthropods are similar and differ from those of the molluscs; differences in the $g{\sim}2$ region of dimer EPR spectra reflect different Cu-Cu separation. These spectral differences between mollusc and arthropod dimer and dimer-N_3^- derivatives are also associated with a distortion which affects the exogenous ligand bridge; in this case the distortion keeps the coppers closer together in arthropods. Furthermore, for the oxy form of arthropods the $O_2^= \pi_v^* \rightarrow Cu(d_{x^2-y^2})$ splitting is smaller, and intensity is mixed into the higher energy component of π_v^*. The decrease in π_v^* splitting suggests that the copper planes may be tilted with respect to each other, again affecting exogenous ligand ($O_2^=$) bridging between the coppers.

The mechanism of catalase activity (high for the molluscs, very low for the arthropods) presented in equations 1–4 below involves the coordination of $O_2^=$ to the

$$\text{deoxy(Cu(I)Cu(I))} + H_2O_2 \xrightarrow{+2H^+} \text{met(Cu(II)Cu(II))} + 2H_2O \qquad (1)$$

$$\text{met(Cu(II)Cu(II))} + H_2O_2 \longrightarrow \text{oxy(Cu(II)Cu(II))}O_2^= + 2H^+ \qquad (2)$$

$$\text{oxy(Cu(II)Cu(II))}O_2^= \rightleftarrows \text{deoxy(Cu(I)Cu(I))} + O_2 \qquad (3)$$

$$\text{Net reaction:} \quad 2H_2O_2 \longrightarrow O_2 + 2H_2O \qquad (4)$$

met site generating oxy. Those structural changes which interfere with exogenous ligand bridging in the arthropod active site are likely to be associated with the lack of catalase activity. Our chemical and spectroscopic studies of met support the idea that a structural distortion is the dominant factor affecting peroxide binding at this active site. First, for Limulus we have shown that an arthropod met can be regenerated to oxy by stepwise reduction to deoxy and exposure to oxygen, as in equation 5. Thus, the protein ligand has

$$\text{met} \xrightarrow{NO} \text{half met-NO}_2^- \xrightarrow{N_3^-} \text{half met-N}_3^- \long'\!\!\bigg\downarrow CH_3CO_2^- \qquad (5)$$

$$\text{oxy} \xleftarrow{O_2} \text{deoxy} \xleftarrow{Na_2S_2O_4} \text{half met-CH}_3CO_2^-$$

not been destroyed in the met preparation (by generation of OH, etc). Next, studies involving fluoride show that it binds with high affinity at all sites, including those of arthropods, producing significant spectral changes. Fluoride is not expected to bind based on aqueous cupric chemistry, and this high binding constant suggests that the active site of all met (and oxy) hemocyanins stabilizes a highly electronegative anion. Specific residue variation in the active site pocket, however, cannot be excluded.

Although the arthropods are generally complicated by springing, data obtained upon binding N_3^- to the Limulus met site also demonstrate that a significant structural change is present in the met form. If we first consider met Busycon, addition of N_3^- leads to a small decrease in the d-d transition energies and a reasonably intense ($\varepsilon \sim 1000$) $N_3^- \rightarrow Cu(II)$ charge transfer transition at 380 nm. These spectral features and the observed binding constant (k = 500 M^{-1}) are consistent with results found for equatorial coordination of N_3^- to a Cu(dien) model complex [15] and the met apo site. This is also consistent with simple N_3^- replacement of the equatorial $O_2^=$ at the oxy site. Specifics of the charge transfer absorption and CD spectra further suggest that azide bridges the two coppers.

At least three transitions are required to fit the combined CD and absorption N^{3-} CT region. Therefore N_3^- must coordinate to both coppers. For N_3^- bound to a single copper, only two transitions are possible ($N_3^- \pi_v \rightarrow Cu\, d_{x^2-y^2}^2$ and $N_3^- \pi_\sigma \rightarrow Cu\, d_{x^2-y^2}^2$). This is observed for met apo and sprung met-N_3^-; both have N_3^- bound to a single copper. In contrast, for Limulus and other arthropods, a site distortion seems strongly to affect the binding of exogenous ligands. The N_3^- binding constant is greatly reduced (k < 10 m^{-1}), and a large distortion is required at the site for N_3^- bridging. The latter is demonstrated by the significant change in ligand field absorption energies in met-N_3^- versus met-aquo (Δv = 1,484 cm^{-1}). Furthermore, the resulting Limulus met-N_3^- CT spectrum is significantly different from that of Busycon. There are still three observed transitions supporting a bridging mode for the N_3^-. However, a weak absorption band is present at 500 nm and there is a larger separation between the major peaks in absorption and CD. These spectral changes are difficult to interpret but indicate a somewhat different bridging mode when azide is forced to coordinate to the distorted Limulus met site. This may relate to some protein-induced tenseness in Limulus which distorts the coppers relative to those in the mollusc site. Although the nature of this distortion requires further spectroscopic study, it is clearly related to the lack of catalase activity in arthropods.

Comparison of the reactivity and spectroscopy of the different hemocyanin derivatives leads to some significant correlations concerning instability of the active site in arthropods. First, a half apo form cannot be prepared for the arthropods, as the rate of removal of the second copper in excess cyanide is more rapid than the first. Furthermore, it is observed for the arthropods (but not Limulus) that a group 2 ligand will irreversibly disrupt the active site of the half met form. We find this disruption mechanism proceeds initially through a reversible group 2 ligand-bridged intermediate. This is followed by irreversible disruption of the site as shown below:

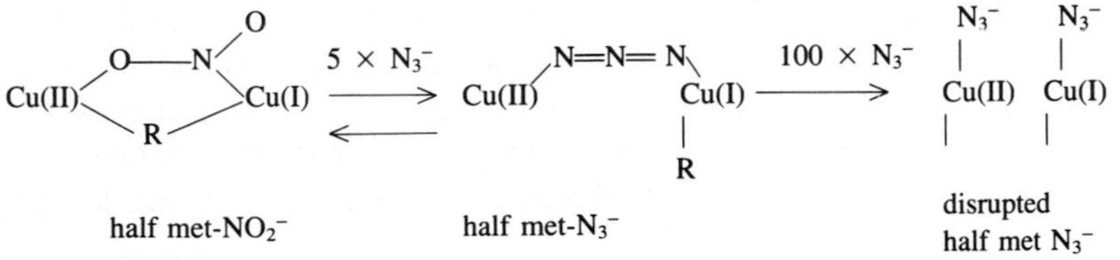

$$\text{(6)}$$

An analogous propensity for larger Cu-Cu separation in the arthropods (but less so for Limulus) can also be found in the dimer chemistry. Arthropod dimer is more easily formed and is more stable toward conversion to dimer-N_3^- or to met than Limulus or molluscs.

An instability with similar characteristics is also manifested in the met form. Although all sites are accessible, this is a limited instability (molluscs < 10%, arthropods ~ 35%), which shows a pH effect as well as exogenous ligand concentration characteristics shown below:

$$\text{(7)}$$

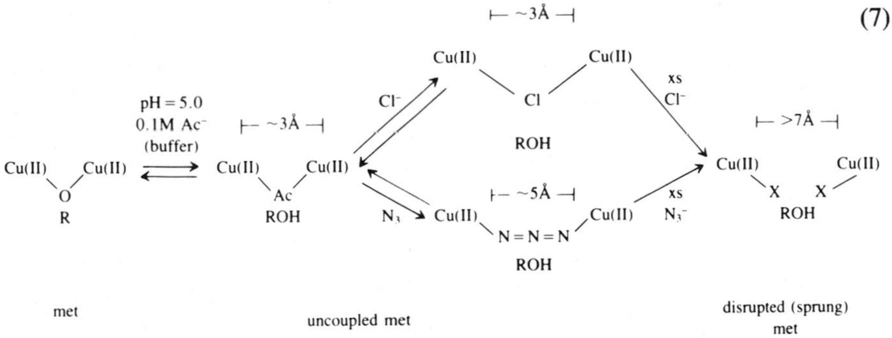

The reversibly uncoupled site shows dipolar metal-metal interaction modified by bridging exogenous ligands. Subsequent irreversible springing allows determination of the extent of this instability. The differences between other arthropods and Limulus (sharp pH effect and somewhat less tendency toward springing) indicate different protein influences at the site. The limited instability of met has been studied in the heterogeneous fractions of Limulus and shown not to be localized in any of the five major components of aggregated protein.

These active-site instability characteristics are in contrast to the quantitative spectral (and thus, detailed geometric structure) comparison of the hemocyanins. All arthropods including Limulus seem to be spectroscopically similar and somewhat different from the molluscs. These spectral correlations indicate that the arthropods, including Limulus, have very similar active site structures, yet Limulus shows less tendency toward disruption of the site. This tenseness at the active site must then be associated with more distant protein effects, tertiary or quaternary in nature.

The chemical and spectral comparisons of aggregated, deaggregated, and individual heterogeneous subunits of Limulus hemocyanin have answered several important questions about the protein as well as the approach used to interpret spectral data probing the active site. First, results show that there are only very small spectral differences between aggregated and deaggregated (stripped) Limulus hemocyanin. This indicates that interaction among the subunits in the aggregate does not affect spectral features of the oxy, met, and half met $-NO_2^-$ sites (probably all in a relaxed quaternary structure). Second, the individual fractions have spectral features that are very similar and that are similar to the native protein. The heterogeneity evident in ion-exchange chromatography [23], isoelectric focusing immunoelectrophoresis [4], and reaggregation [3] has limited effect on the spectral features of the active sites. Spectroscopic correlation is not found for the few anomalous difference in reactivity with exogenous ligands (in particular, the O_2 affinity of fraction V) [23]. Finally, these results validate the assumptions of the "single site model" used to interpret the spectroscopy of aggregated hemocyanin. No unusual spectral characteristics of active sites in any heterogeneous fraction have been found. Also, none of the aggregated spectral features are localized in special heterogeneous sites. Therefore, at least for Limulus, spectroscopic data of the aggregated protein reflect that of the individual active sites.

Although there are strong similarities among oxyhemocyanin sites, the differences have become better understood. All the arthropods (including Limulus) exhibit similar spectral properties quantitatively different from the molluscs. These differences are associated with a distortion of the active site, which seems to relate to lack of catalase activity. Protein tenseness at the active site varies between Limulus, other arthropods, and molluscs as evidenced by different irreversible site disruption behavior. Active-site instabilities may be associated with tertiary or quaternary characteristics of the protein. Finally, ligand substitution reactions of the oxy form indicate large difference in access to an axial coordination position necessary for associative ligand substitution. Among the different hemocyanins, Limulus is least reactive and therefore most stable in the presence of exogenous ligands.

ACKNOWLEDGMENTS

We are grateful to the National Institute of Arthritis, Metabolism, and Digestive Diseases of the U.S. Public Health Service (AM 20406).

REFERENCES

1. Amundsen AR, Whelan J, Bosnich B: Biological analogues. On the nature of the binding sites of copper-containing proteins. J Am Chem Soc 99:6730, 1977.
2. Basolo F, Pearson RG: Substitution reactions of square-planar complexes. In: "Mechanisms of Inorganic Reactions," Ed 2. New York: John Wiley & Sons, 1967, pp 421–423.
3. Bijlholt MMC, van Bruggen EFJ, Bonaventura J: Dissociation and reassembly of Limulus polyphemus hemocyanin. Eur J Biochem 95:399, 1979.
4. Brenowitz M, Bonaventura C, Bonaventura J, Gianazza E: Subunit composition of a high molecular weight oligomer Limulus polyphemus hemocyanin. Arch Biochem Biophys 210:748–761, 1981.
5. Eickman NC, Himmelwright RS, Solomon EI: Geometric and electronic structure of oxyhemocyanin: Spectral and chemical correlations to met apo, half met, met and dimer active sites. Proc Natl Acad Sci USA 76:2094, 1979.
6. Felsenfeld G, Printz MP: Specific reactions of hydrogen peroxide with the active site of hemocyanin. The formation of "methemocyanin". J Am Chem Soc 81:6259, 1959.
7. Freedman TB, Loehr JS, Loehr TM: A resonance Raman study of the copper protein, hemocyanin. New evidence for the structure of the oxygen binding site. J Am Chem Soc 98:2809, 1976.
8. Gay RR, Solomon EI: Polarized single-crystal spectroscopic studies of oxyhemerythrin. J Am Chem Soc 100:1972, 1978.
9. Ghiretti F: The decomposition of hydrogen peroxide by the hemocyanin and by its dissociation products. Arch Biochem Biophys 63:165, 1956.
10. Hepp AF, Himmelwright RS, Eickman NC, Solomon EI: Ligand displacement reactions of oxyhemocyanin: Comparison of reactivities of arthropods and molluscs. Biochem Biophys Res Commun 89:1050, 1979.
11. Himmelwright RS, Eickman NC, Solomon EI: Spectroscopic studies of ligand perturbation effects on the half oxidized active site of Busycon canaliculatum hemocyanin. Biochem Biophys Res Commun 81:237, 1978.
12. Himmelwright RS, Eickman NC, Solomon EI: Chemical and spectroscopic conformation of an .exogenous ligand bridge in half met hemocyanin. Biochem Biophys Res Commun 84:300, 1978.
13. Himmelwright RS, Eickman NC, Solomon EI: Comparison of half-met and met apo hemocyanin. Ligand bridging at the binuclear copper active site. J Am Chem Soc 101:1576, 1979.
14. Himmelwright RS, Eickman NC, Solomon EI: Reactions and interconversion of met and dimer hemocyanin. Biochem Biophys Res Commun 86:628, 1979.
15. Himmelwright RS, Eickman NC, LuBien CD, Solomon EI: Chemical and spectroscopic comparison of the binuclear copper active site of mollusc and arthropod hemocyanins. J Am Chem Soc 102:5378, 1980.
16. Makino N, ven der Deen H, McMahill P, Gould DC, Moss TH, Simo C, Mason HS: The binuclear cupric site cluster of Cancer magister methemocyanin. Biochim Biophys Acta 532:315, 1978.

17. McMahill P, Mason HS: Structural states of the binuclear copper cluster of Cancer magister methemocyanin. Biochem Biophys Res Commun 84:749, 1978.
18. Redfield AG, Coolidge T, Montgomery H: The respiratory products of the blood. II: The combining ratio of oxygen and copper in some bloods containing hemocyanin. J Biol Chem 76:197, 1928.
19. Robin MB, Day P: Mixed valence chemistry—A survey and classification. Adv Inorg Chem Radiochem 10:247, 1967.
20. Schoot Uiterkamp AJM: Monomer and magnetic dipole-coupled Cu^{2+} EPR signals in nitrosylhemocyanin. FEBS Lett 20:93, 1972.
21. Schoot Uiterkamp AJM, van der Deen H, Berendsen HCJ, Boas JF: Computer simulation of the EPR spectra of mononuclear and dipolar coupled (Cu(II) ions in nitric oxide and nitrite-treated hemocyanins and tyrosinase. Biochim Biophys Acta 372:407, 1974.
22. Solomon EI: Binuclear copper active site. In Spiro TG (ed): "Copper Proteins," Chapter 2. New York: Wiley Interscience, 1980.
23. Sullivan B, Bonaventura J, Bonaventura C: Functional difference in the multiple hemocyanins of the horseshoe crab, Limulus polyphemus L. Proc Natl Acad Sci USA 71:2558, 1974.
24. Van der Deen H, Hoving H: Nitrate- and nitric oxide-treatment of Helix pomatia hemocyanin: single and double oxidation of the active site. Biochemistry 16:3519, 1977.
25. Van Holde KE, van Bruggen EF: The hemocyanins. In Timasheff SN, Fashman GD (eds): "Subunits in Biological Systems," part A. New York: Marcel Dekker, 1971, pp 1–53.
26. Wilcox DE, Long JR, Solomon EI: Unpublished results.
27. Witters R, Lontie R: The formation of Helix pomatia methaemocyanin accelerated by azide and fluoride. FEBS Lett 60:400, 1975.

Physiology and Biology of Horseshoe Crabs: Studies on
Normal and Environmentally Stressed Animals, pages 231–256
© 1982 Alan R. Liss, Inc., 150 Fifth Avenue, New York, NY 10011

Chloride and pH Dependence of Cooperative Interactions in Limulus polyphemus Hemocyanin

Marius Brouwer, Celia Bonaventura, and Joseph Bonaventura

Hemocyanin of the horseshoe crab, Limulus polyphemus, is a large oligomeric protein containing 48 polypeptide subunits. Structurally, the oligomer appears to be based on a system of eight hexameric units. In this chapter we present a detailed analysis of the effects of pH and chloride on oxygen binding by this high molecular weight respiratory protein. Its oxygen-binding behavior can be satisfactorily described by a modified form of the two state model for allosteric transitions of J. Monod et al [26]. In an earlier study [9] it was found that the oxygen dissociation constant of the T-state, K_T, is subject to modulation by chloride ions. In this study we show that protons also alter the T-state, whereas the oxygen dissociation constant of the R-state, K_R, does not appear to be affected either by chloride ions or protons. The insensitivity of the R-state is apparent in rapid mixing experiments where the apparent rate constant for oxygen dissociation is 8 s^{-1}, irrespective of the pH or chloride concentration. Analysis of the oxygen equilibrium data strongly suggests that the number of subunits involved in cooperative interactions is pH dependent. The allosteric unit appears to be the hexamer (n = 6) in the pH range from 7 to 8 and the dodecamer (n = 12) at pH 8.9. The stage of oxygenation at which the allosteric transition occurs and the six sequential Adair constants describing the oxygen binding by the Limulus hexamer were calculated from the parameters of the two-state model. The analysis indicates that binding of either protons or chloride results in a stabilization of partially liganded forms of the hexamer during the oxygenation process. It was estimated that there are a maximum of four oxygen-linked protons and two oxygen-linked chloride ions per hexamer at pH 7.5. The stage at which chloride ions are released during the successive oxygen binding steps was found to depend on the chloride concentration, whereas the total number of chloride ions released during the process was constant over the range of chloride concentrations studied.

INTRODUCTION

Limulus polyphemus, one of the four living species of horseshoe crabs, occupies a unique phylogenetic position. The morphology and ventilatory mechanisms of its gills are exceptional among water-breathing animals. In addition its hemocyanin-containing blood shows the rare quality of a reverse Bohr effect, resulting in increased oxygen affinity at lowered pH (increased pCO_2). Limulus polyphemus is therefore of special interest to respiratory physiologists involved in the study of environmental adaptations. It has been demonstrated that the reverse Bohr effect is an adaptation to low in vivo oxygen tensions, which result from hypoventilation during several normal activities, such as subtidal feeding, intertidal exposure, sand burrowing and prolonged air exposure during copulation and egg laying. Low oxygen pressure in the blood may occur for longer periods in animals inhabiting the hypoxic bottom layers of stratified estuaries. The drop in blood oxygen tension and the retention of CO_2 as a result of hypoventilation induce an increase in hemocyanin function to a value unequaled by other invertebrate oxygen carrying proteins [18, 22].

When L. polyphemus enters dilute waters, as during the spring migration into estuaries, blood NaCl is reduced by almost half, even though active hyperosmotic regulation occurs. This reduction will increase the oxygen affinity of L. polyphemus hemocyanin [9], and may therefore lead to impaired oxygen delivery to the tissues. However, blood oxygen tension decreases in low salinity as a result of bradycardia. Although the oxygenation of hemocyanin at the gill does not change appreciably, deoxygenation at the tissues is enhanced and, thus in dilute water the pigment becomes more important in oxygen transport. The adaptation to low salinity consists of concomitant changes which have opposite but counterbalancing effects on oxygen consumption in an unstable ionic environment [23].

To clarify the mechanism by which physiologically important effectors modulate Limulus hemocyanin function, we analyzed the oxygen-binding properties of this hemocyanin over a wide range of pH values and chloride concentrations. Limulus polyphemus hemocyanin contains 48 subunits and has a molecular weight of 3.3×10^6 [19, 28]. The oligomer contains a number of distinct subunits, each of which appears to be structurally and functionally different [5-8, 29]. Limulus hemocyanin shows cooperativity in oxygen binding. In view of the large number of oxygen-binding sites in the undissociated molecule, it is of considerable interest to know whether the interactions responsible for cooperativity are confined to functionally independent allosteric units, or whether these interactions radiate out over the entire subunit ensemble. We addressed this question in an earlier study in which we studied the effect of chloride ions on the oxygen binding properties of Limulus hemocyanin. We showed that the effect of chloride on oxygen binding by Limulus hemocyanin could be satisfactorily described by the two-state model for allosteric transitions [26], with the modification that chloride binding alters not only the allosteric equilibrium constant but also the oxygen affinity of the unliganded state [9]. A number of relevant studies with other hemocyanins have been reported. It was found in Helix pomatia β-hemocyanin that the affinity of the T-state of the molecule and the number of sites involved in cooperative interactions were dependent on the pH at which the experiments were carried out [34]. Arisaka [4] and Brouwer et al [10] have shown that oxygen binding by hemocyanins of the shrimp Callianassa californiensis and the shrimp Penaeus setiferus could be described by the two-state model for allosteric transitions, with the introduction of one symmetrical hybrid state. Oxygen-binding data for hemocyanins of the lobster Panulirus interruptus and α-hemocyanin of the snail Helix pomatia appear to be described satisfactorily by the unmodified two-state model [13, 20], although this conclusion may be drawn with more assurance when a more comprehensive data set is analyzed. In all cases thus far analyzed, it appears appropriate to consider the oxygen affinity of the hemocyanins as a function of their quaternary conformations and allosteric effectors as acting largely on the equilibrium between conformers of differing oxygen affinity. The results of this study allow us to describe quantitatively the number of effector molecules bound or released upon oxygenation of Limulus hemocyanin and the release of the free energy of quaternary restraint over successive steps in the oxygen-binding sequence. The analysis suggests that in Limulus hemocyanin, as in hemocyanin of the mollusc Helix pomatia, the number of interacting sites in the oligomer is a function of pH.

MATERIALS AND METHODS

Preparation of Limulus hemocyanin, measurement of oxygen-binding curves, stopped-flow spectrophotometry, and analytical ultracentrifugation were carried out as described previously [9].

Data Analysis

Hill plots were calculated according to the two-state model with

$$\frac{\overline{Y}}{1 - \overline{Y}} = \frac{\alpha(1 + \alpha)^{n-1} + L c\alpha (1 + c\alpha)^{n-1}}{(1 + \alpha)^{n-1} + L (1 + c\alpha)^{n-1}} \tag{1}$$

where $\alpha = pO_2/p_{50,R}$. $p_{50,R}$ is the intrinsic dissociation constant of the R-state, L is the allosteric equilibrium constant, and c is the nonexclusive binding coefficient, ie, the ratio of the intrinsic dissociation constant of the R-state and the T-state, $p_{50,R}/p_{50,T}$ [26]. The number of interacting sites involved in cooperative interactions is represented by n. L was evaluated from the p_{50} value according to:

$$L = \frac{(\alpha_{1/2} - 1)}{(1 - c\alpha_{1/2})} \left(\frac{1 + \alpha_{1/2}}{1 + c\alpha_{1/2}}\right)^{n-1} \qquad (2)$$

where $\alpha_{1/2} = p_{50}/p_{50,R}$ and $n = 6$ as previously established [9]. The six Adair constants describing the oxygen-binding function of the hemocyanin hexamer were estimated from their mathematical equivalence to the parameters of the two-state model. According to Adair's successive oxygenation theory, the fractional saturation, $\overline{Y}$, of a hexameric hemocyanin with oxygen is given by:

$$\overline{Y} = \frac{a_1p + 5a_2p^2 + 10a_3p^3 + 10a_4p^4 + 5a_5p^5 + a_6p^6}{1 + 6a_1p + 15a_2p^2 + 20a_3p^3 + 15a_5p^4 + 6a_5p^5 + a_6p^6} \qquad (3)$$

in which p is the partial pressure of oxygen given in mm of Hg, and

$$a_1 = k_1$$

$$a_2 = k_1k_2$$

$$a_3 = k_1k_2k_3$$

$$a_4 = k_1k_2k_3k_4$$

$$a_5 = k_1k_2k_3k_4k_5$$

$$a_6 = k_1k_2k_3k_4k_5k_6$$

in these equations, k_i is the intrinsic association constant for the reversible reaction:

$$Hc(O_2)_{i-1} + O_2 \xrightarrow{k_i} Hc(O_2)_i, \text{ for } i = 1\text{--}6$$

According to the two-state model the oxygen saturation function for a hexamer is given by:

$$\overline{Y} = \frac{\alpha(1 + \alpha)^5 + Lc\alpha(1 + c\alpha)^5}{(1 + \alpha)^6 + L(1 + c\alpha)^6} \qquad (4)$$

By multiplying out the polynomials in equation 4 and rearranging terms, we find by comparison with equation 3 the following relationship between the parameters of the two-state model and the association constants in Adair's theory:

$$k_i = \frac{Lc^i + 1}{(Lc^{i-1} + 1) \, p_{50,R}} \tag{5}$$

This equation permits us to assign values to the Adair constants for curves that can be described by the parameters of the two-state model.

The difference between the free energy of interaction associated with the binding of the first and last ligands [27] was evaluated from:

$$\Delta F_I = -RT \ln k_6/k_1 = -RT \ln \frac{(Lc^6 + 1)(L + 1)}{(Lc^5 + 1)(Lc + 1)} \tag{6}$$

The distribution of the individual fractions of $Hc(O_2)_i$, for $i = O - 6$, during the course of ligation was calculated according to:

$$Hc = 1/D; \quad Hc(O_2) = 6a_1 p/D; \quad Hc(O_2)_2 = 15a_2 p^2/D;$$

$$Hc(O_2)_3 = 20a_3 p^3/D, \text{ etc} \tag{7}$$

where D is given by the denominator in equation 3. The median oxygen pressure p_m is given by the equation:

$$p_m = 1/\sqrt[6]{a_6} \text{ (see appendix for derivation)} \tag{8}$$

The total number of oxygen-linked Bohr protons per hexamer that are bound on full oxygenation of the hemocyanin was obtained from

$$\Delta H^+ t = 6 \frac{\log(1/p_m)}{dpH} \tag{9}$$

at constant chloride concentration [17, 33]. From the pH dependence of the logarithm of the individual Adair constants the number of oxygen-linked Bohr protons bound per oxygen binding step was obtained according to:

$$H^+_t = \frac{d \log k_i}{dpH} \tag{10}$$

where H^+_i ($i = 1 - 6$) is the number of oxygen-linked Bohr protons bound at the ith stage of ligation. In a similar way the total number of oxygen-linked chloride ions released upon full oxygenation of hemocyanin was obtained from:

$$Cl_t = -6 \frac{\text{dlog } (1/p_m)}{\text{dlog(Cl)}} \tag{11}$$

The number of oxygen-linked chloride ions released per binding step was calculated with

$$Cl_i = - \frac{\text{dlog} k_i}{\text{dlog(Cl)}} \tag{12}$$

(A more detailed analysis of the linkage between oxygen, chloride, and pH, is presented in the Discussion.)

In terms of the two-state model, T_i and R_i denote concentrations of T and R states that have combined with i molecules of oxygen. The ratio of T_i over R_i is given by:

$$T_i/R_i = Lc^i \tag{13}$$

where $i = 0 - 6$. The switchover point in the allosteric transition i_s, ie, i at $T_i = R_i$ is obtained from equation 13 [15].

$$i_s = -(\log L)/(\log c) \tag{14}$$

The fraction of T_i in $T_i + R_i$ is given by:

$$T_i = \frac{Lc^i}{Lc^i + 1} \tag{15}$$

RESULTS

The large oligomeric hemocyanin found in the hemolymph of the horseshoe crab Limulus polyphemus is subject to allosteric control of its oxygen binding properties. The homotropic interactions between oxygen-binding sites and the heterotropic effects of pH and chloride ions are discussed separately in the following.

Effect of Chloride on Oxygen Binding

Curves 3, 4, and 5 of Figure 1 were obtained at pH 8 with varied concentrations of chloride. Increasing chloride concentrations shift the deoxy asymptotes of the

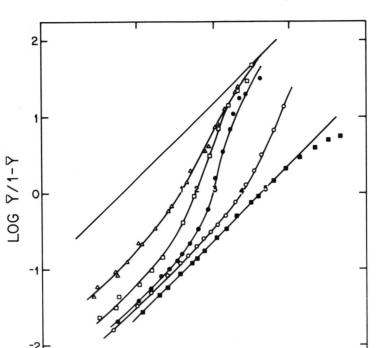

Fig. 1. Hill plots for oxygen binding at 20°C in a 50 mM Tris buffer, ionic strength 0.1, containing 10 mM $CaCl_2$. Protein concentration was about 4 mg/mL. 1) pH 7.0; 2) pH 7.5; 3) pH 8.0; 4) pH 8.0 + 1.0 M NaCl; 5) pH 8.0 + 3.77 M NaCl. This figure shows only part of the measured binding data. Symbols represent experimental data. Lines are calculated with equation 1 and the L and c values listed in Table I and the number of interacting sites as n = 6. The straight line with slope unity represents the hypothetical binding curve of the R-state.

Hill plots and reduce the oxygen affinity of Limulus hemocyanin. At high chloride concentration the protein is completely frozen in a low oxygen-affinity state. The analysis of the chloride effect within the framework of a modified two-state model has been presented elsewhere in greater detail [9].

Effect of pH on Oxygen Binding

The oxygen Bohr effect, ie, the shift of the oxygen equilibrium curve brought about by changes in pH, is one of the characteristic allosteric features of hemoglobins and hemocyanins. Curves 1, 2, and 3 of Figure 1 show the effect of pH on oxygen binding by Limulus hemocyanin. Increasing values of pH increase the maximum slope of the Hill plots and lower the oxygen affinity. The reverse Bohr effect is expressed by an increase in the partial pressure of oxygen needed for half saturation of hemocyanin as the pH is increased. The most dramatic effect of pH is observed in the low saturation part of the Hill plot, where an increase from pH 7 to pH 8 is accompanied by a decrease of the affinity of the apparent T-state from 5.6 to 24.5 mm of Hg (curves 1 and 3). This implies that protons do not behave as allosteric effectors as defined within the framework of the two state model for allosteric transitions, since in the original model an allosteric effector is supposed to change only the ratio of the quaternary states [26]. In the case of Limulus hemocyanin protons not only change the ratio of the quaternary states, but also change their binding constants, thereby changing the nonexclusive binding coefficient. Taking this into account the allosteric parameters of the two state model and the free energies of interaction were calculated from the Hill plots in Figure 1. The values are listed in Table I. The free energy of interaction increases with pH (at constant chloride concentration), and decreases with the chloride concentration (at constant pH). Theoretical Hill plots, based on the two-state model modified in such a way that the allosteric effector also changes the allosteric parameter c, were calculated by taking n = 6 and substituting the values for L and c listed in Table I into equation 1. The fit between the experimental data and theoretical curves is good (Fig. 1). However, at pH values above 8 the experimental Hill plots cannot be described adequately with the modified two-state model, taking the hexamer as the allosteric unit. At pH 8.5, the experimental Hill plot lies between the theoretical binding functions of the hexamer (n = 6) and the dodecamer (n = 12). As shown by the theoretical curves and data points of Figure 2, the dodecamer appears to be allosteric unit at pH 8.9.

Oxygen Dissociation Kinetics

The kinetics of oxygen dissociation from Limulus hemocyanin was studied as a function of pH. The time course is autocatalytic, in the sense that the apparent dissociation rate constant increases as the reaction proceeds. The in-

TABLE I. Effect of Chloride and pH on the Allosteric Parameters of Limulus polyphemus Hemocyanin

pH	Cl (M)	$\alpha_{1/2}$[a]	$L \times 10^{-5}$[b]	$c \times 10^{2}$[a]	i_s[c]	ΔF_I[d]
7.0	0.1	5.51	0.1245	11.2	4.31	1,173
7.5	0.1	8.97	2,178	4.53	3.97	1,778
8.0	0.1	14.79	37.40	3.16	4.38	2,019
8.0	1.0	32.37	3,281	2.40	5.26	1,460
8.0	3.77	53.02	∞	1.89		0

[a]$\alpha_{1/2}$ and c were calculated from Figure 1.
[b]L was calculated with equation 2.
[c]Switchover point in the allosteric transition was calculated with equation 14.
[d]Free energy of interaction (cal/mol of O_2) was calculated from equation 6.

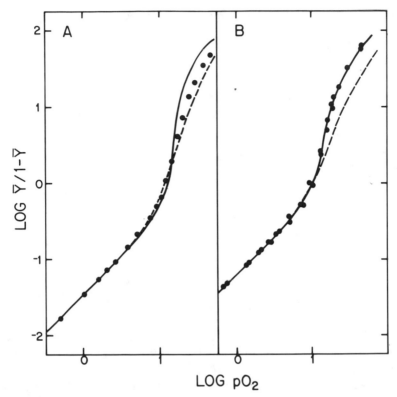

Fig. 2.   Hill plots for oxygen binding at 20°C in a 50 mM Tris buffer, ionic strength 0.1, containing 10 mM $CaCl_2$. Protein concentration about 4mg/mL. A) pH 8.5; B) pH 8.9. Symbols represent experimental data. Lines are calculated with equation 1. A) Broken line calculated with c = 0.0238; L = 1.088×10^7 and n = 6. Continuous line: c = 0.0238; L = 5.459×10^{13} and n = 12. B) Broken line calculated with c = 0.0397; L = 5.428×10^6 and n = 6. Continuous line: c = 0.0397; L = 7.199×10^{12} and n = 12.

crease in the apparent first order rate constants with the extent of the reaction is shown in Figure 3. From this figure it can be seen that the curves for the different pH values extrapolate back to an initial oxygen dissociation rate constant of 8 s^{-1}.

Principal Oxygenation Pathway as Obtained From the Allosteric Parameters

Figure 4A shows the dependence of the fraction T_i in $T_i + R_i$, upon the degree of ligation. T_i was obtained from equation 15 using the values of L and c in Table I. Oxygen binding to Limulus hemocyanin is considered to proceed predominantly via the T-state if the fraction of T_i in $R_i + T_i$ at a ligation step is above 0.95. Conversely, if the fraction of T_i is below 0.05 at a certain ligation

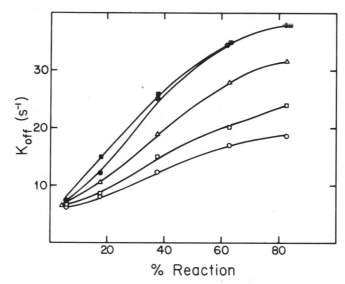

Fig. 3.   Apparent oxygen dissociation rate constants plotted as a function of the percentage reaction. Buffer conditions as in Figure 1 (○:pH 7.0, □:pH 7.5, △:pH 8.0, ●:pH 8.5, and ■:pH 9.0).

step, the binding of oxygen will be considered to proceed via the R-state pathway. For intermediate values we consider that T_i and R_i coexist. With these criteria we can deduce the principal course of oxygenation from the curves in Figure 4A. The courses obtained in this manner are presented in Figure 4B. The switchover points of allosteric transition are indicated in Figure 4A by the open circles. The values of i corresponding to these points can also be obtained from equation 14 and are listed in Table I. At pH 7.5 (Fig. 4B, 1) the allosteric transition takes place after the fourth oxygen molecule is bound and proceeds then via the R-state. In other words, the $T \rightarrow R$ transition takes place at a single ligation step, consistent with a value of 3.97 for the value of i at the switchover point of allosteric transition (Table I). At pH 8, ionic strength 0.1 (Fig. 4B, 2), the $T \rightarrow R$ transition also takes place after the 4th oxygen molecule has been bound. The main pathway proceeds them along the R-state. In this case, a minor pathway still proceeds via the T-state and switches over to the R-state only after the fifth oxygen molecule has been bound. In 1.02 M chloride (Fig. 4B, 3) most of the allosteric transition takes place after the binding of the fifth oxygen.

Evaluation of the Free Energies at the Successive Oxygen-Binding Steps

The six Adair constants, describing the oxygen binding function of the Limulus hemocyanin hexamer at pH 7.5 ionic strength 0.1, at pH 8.0 ionic strength 0.1, and at pH 8.0 ionic strength 1.0, were calculated with equation 5 using the

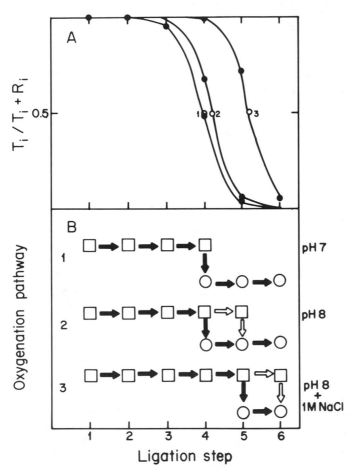

Fig. 4. A) Dependence of the fraction T_i in $T_i + R_i$ upon the degree of ligation. Buffer conditions as in Figure 1. 1) pH 7.5; 2) pH 8.0; 3) pH 8.0 + 1.0 M NaCl. B) Principal oxygenation courses. Solid arrows represent the main pathway of oxygen binding. Open arrows represent minor pathways.

L and c values in Table I and with $P_{50,R} = 0.63$ mm of Hg. They are listed in Table II. The sequential Adair constants were converted to equilibrium constants and the median oxygen pressures to median oxygen concentrations through the use of Henry's law constant: 1 mm of Hg $= 1.82 \times 10^{-6}$ mol of O_2/L. The corresponding free energies of binding, ΔG_i, are listed in Table II. The successive energy changes experienced by the molecule relative to the R-state as the reference or unconstrained state are calculated from: $\Delta G_R - \Delta G_i$ and listed in the same table. The total free energy change for fully saturating the hemocyanin hexamer was calculated from the median oxygen concentration according to: $- 6 RT \ln (O_2)_m/6$ mol of O_2, in which $(O_2)_m$ is the median O_2 concentration.

TABLE II. Oxygen-Linked Free Energies of Limulus polyphemus Hemocyanin

	Stage of oxygenation	Sequential Adair constant[a]	Median oxygen pressure[b]	Total binding free energy[c]	Binding free energy per step[d] ΔG_i	Change in free energy of quaternary constraint[e]	Free energy for T → R transition[f]
A	1	0.0677	5.19	−40.41	−6.127	−1.836	
	2	0.0677			−6.127	−1.836	
	3	0.0707			−6.152	−1.811	
	4	0.135			−6.528	−1.435	
	5	0.810			−7.571	−0.392	
	6	1.436			−7.905	−0.058	
					sum = −40.41	sum = −7.368	−7.155
B	1	0.0407	8.22	−38.80	−5.830	−2.133	
	2	0.0407			−5.830	−2.133	
	3	0.0412			−5.837	−2.126	
	4	0.0591			−6.047	−1.915	
	5	0.533			−7.328	−0.635	
	6	1.507			−7.933	−0.030	
					sum = −38.80	sum = −8.972	−8.811
C	1	0.0338	18.46	−35.98	−5.722	−2.180	
	2	0.0338			−5.722	−2.180	
	3	0.0338			−5.722	−2.180	
	4	0.0341			−5.727	−2.175	
	5	0.0463			−5.905	−1.997	
	6	0.415			−7.182	−0.720	
					sum = −35.98	sum = −11.432	−11.415

A) pH 7.5, ionic strength 0.1, 10 mM $CaCl_2$.
B) pH 8.0, ionic strength 0.1, 10 mM $CaCl_2$.
C) pH 8.0, ionic strength 1.0, 10 mM $CaCl_2$.

[a]In mm^{-1} of Hg.
[b]Calculated from the Adair constants with equation 8.
[c]Calculated from the median oxygen activity and expressed in kcal/6 mol of O_2.
[d]Expressed in kcal/mol of O_2.
[e]Successive energy changes experienced by the molecule relative to the R-state as the reference state: $\Delta G_R - \Delta G_i$. Expressed in kcal/mol of O_2.
[f]From $-RT \ln L$.

In these calculations, it is assumed that activity coefficients are near unity, so that $[O_2]_m$ does not differ appreciably from the median ligand activity.

Uptake of Protons During the Oxygenation Process

Protons decrease the allosteric equilibrium constant of Limulus hemocyanin (Table I) in the pH range from pH 7 through pH 8. They do so by preferentially binding to the R-state and stabilizing this state. During the process of oxygenation protons are therefore taken up by the protein. It is possible to calculate the total number of oxygen-linked Bohr protons and the distribution of proton binding over the successive oxygen binding steps as described in Materials and Methods. For this purpose the Adair constants and median oxygen pressures were estimated for 16 oxygen equilibrium curves obtained at pH values between pH 7 and pH 8, ionic strength 0.1, in the presence of 10 mM $CaCl_2$. From the pH dependence of plots of $\log (1/p_m)$ and $\log k_i$ (Fig. 5A and B) the number of oxygen-linked Bohr protons bound upon complete oxygenation were calculated using equations 9 and 10. The result is shown in Figure 6. The distribution of the number of Bohr protons bound over the successive oxygenation steps is not uniform. At pH 7.5, for example, contributions of the first, second, third, fourth, and fifth oxygen-binding steps to proton binding are, approximately, 26, 26, 26, 18, and 3% respectively. This situation changes at other pH values. Over the pH range covered by the experiments, the contribution of the sixth binding step is negligible. This implies that all the oxygen-linked Bohr protons are bound before the sixth stage of oxygenation.

Release of Chloride Ions During the Process of Oxygenation

The effect of chloride ions on oxygen binding by Limulus hemocyanin is opposite to that of protons. Chloride ions increase the allosteric equilibrium constant (Table I) and bind preferentially to the T-state. Oxygenation is therefore accompanied by a release of oxygen-linked chloride ions. Adair constants and median oxygen pressures were calculated from the allosteric parameters as given in Table I of a previous paper [9]. The plot of $\log(1/p_m)$ vs $- \log(Cl)$ is linear, as shown in Figure 7. This implies that the number of oxygen-linked chloride ions released is independent of the chloride concentration. The calculated value is 2.05 ± 0.05 chloride ions per mole of hexamer. The number of oxygen-linked chloride ions released at the successive oxygen binding steps was calculated from the slope of $\log k_i$ vs $- \log(Cl)$ (Fig. 7), according to equation 12. The results obtained are plotted in Figure 8. There is a small release of oxygen-linked chloride ions at the first three oxygenation steps, which is constant over the chloride concentration range studied. The partitioning of the release of the remaining chloride ions over the oxygen binding steps is strongly dependent on the chloride concentration. The number of chloride ions released at the fourth

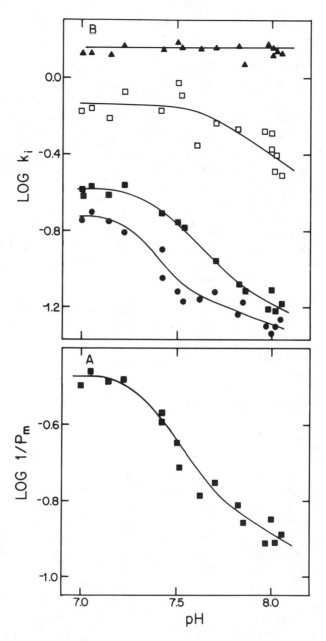

Fig. 5. A) pH dependence of the logarithm of the reciprocal value of the median oxygen pressure P_m (in mm Hg). B) pH dependence of the logarithm of the Adair constants k_i ($i = 1, 2, 3, 4, 5,$ and 6). ● k_1, k_2, k_3. ■ k_4. □ k_5. ▲ k_6.

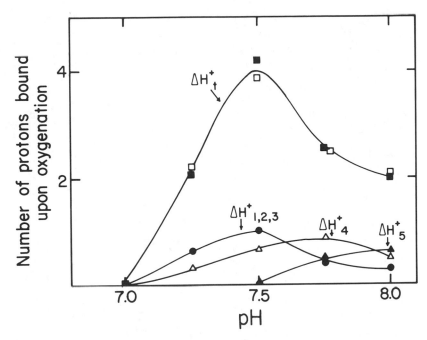

Fig. 6. Number of oxygen-linked Bohr protons bound on the first, second, third ($\triangle H^+_{1, 2, 3}$), fourth $\triangle H^+_4$), and fifth ($\triangle H^+_5$) oxygen binding steps. $\triangle H^+_t$ is the total number of oxygen-linked Bohr protons that are bound on full oxygenation of the hemocyanin hexamer. ■——■, calculated using equation 9. □——□, represents $\triangle H^+_{1, 2, 3} + \triangle H^+_4 + \triangle H^+_5$.

and fifth oxygen binding steps decreases with increasing chloride concentration, whereas the number released at the sixth binding step is increased with increasing chloride concentrations.

Fractional Population of Deoxy, Oxy, and Intermediate Molecular Species of Limulus Hemocyanin as a Function of Oxygen Saturation

Figure 9 shows the derived distribution of the successively liganded species of hexamer at pH 7, ionic strength 0.1; at pH 8, ionic strength 0.1; at pH 8 with 1 M NaCl; and at pH 8 with 3.77 M NaCl (see Fig. 1 for oxygen-binding curves). The maximum fraction of $Hc(O_2)$, $Hc(O_2)_2$ $Hc(O_2)_3$, $Hc(O_2)_4$, and $Hc(O_2)_5$ occurs at $\overline{Y} = 1/6$, $1/3$, $1/2$, $2/3$, and $5/6$, respectively. If there is no homotropic interaction, then equation 3, which expresses the saturation function for an Adair scheme, collapses into $\overline{Y} = ap/(1 + ap)$. From this it can be easily calculated that the maximum values of the various fractions are 0.402, 0.329, 0.312, 0.329, and 0.402, respectively, regardless of the value of a. This particular distribution, which is symmetrical around $\overline{Y} = 1/2$, occurs in 3.77 M NaCl (Fig.

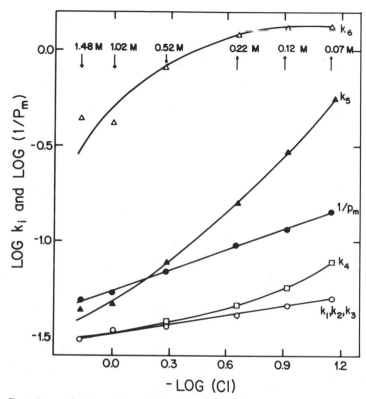

Fig. 7. Dependence of the logarithm of the reciprocal value of the median oxygen pressure (in mm Hg) and the logarithm of the six Adair constants (in mm^{-1} Hg) on the negative logarithm of the chloride concentration. Data collected with proteins at 4 mg/ml at 20°C in I = 0.05 Tris buffer with 10 mM CaCl$_2$, pH 8.0.

9D), where homotropic interactions are not apparent. In cooperative oxygen binding, homotropic interactions result in a stabilization of the fractions of unliganded hemocyanin, singly liganded Hc(O$_2$), and fully liganded Hc(O$_2$)$_6$, over fractions in intermediate stages of ligation, as is most clearly seen by comparing Figure 9B and D. The hexamer distribution at low chloride concentration (Fig. 9B) includes only small amounts of triply and quadruply liganded hemocyanin, consistent with the high degree of cooperativity under these conditions (Fig. 1). The binding of an allosteric effector, chloride, results in an increase of the amount of these intermediates in oxygen binding, which ultimately results at high chloride concentration in the theoretically expected distribution for non-cooperative oxygen binding (Fig. 9B–D). The fraction of quadruply liganded hexamer has values of 0.069, 0.188, and 0.329 in 0.1, 1.02, and 3.77 M NaCl. Increasing proton concentrations also slightly increases the fraction of intermediates in oxygen binding, as can be seen by comparing Figure 9A and B.

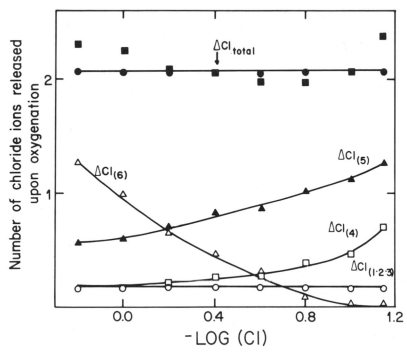

Fig. 8. Number of oxygen-linked chloride ions released on binding of the first, second, third ($\triangle$ $Cl_{1,2,3}$), fourth ($\triangle$ Cl_4), fifth ($\triangle$ Cl_5), and sixth ($\triangle$ Cl_6) oxygen molecule. $\triangle$ Cl total is the total number of chloride ions released on full oxygenation of the hexamer. ●——●, Calculated with equation 11. ■——■, Represents $\triangle$ $Cl_{1,2,3}$ + $\triangle$ Cl_4 + $\triangle$ Cl_5 + $\triangle$ Cl_6.

DISCUSSION

Homotropic and heterotropic allosteric interactions arise from conformational equilibria in which the conformers have different reactivities toward both active and nonactive site ligands. The attempts to describe experimental data within the constraints of a model are a means of quantifying the homotropic and heterotropic effects occurring under a given experimental condition. The fit between theoretical and experimental binding curves allows one to evaluate the appropriateness of the model. Additionally, if the agreement is satisfactory, the analysis can provide insight into the molecular basis and mechanism involved. Many enzymes are allosteric, in the sense that homotropic and heterotropic interactions influence their reactivity toward substrates. The respiratory proteins, having active sites on each of their interacting subunits, provide convenient model systems for analysis of allosteric mechanisms. The most extensive and detailed application of theoretical models to experimental data has been done with hemoglobin as a model protein. It has been established that oxygen binding by human

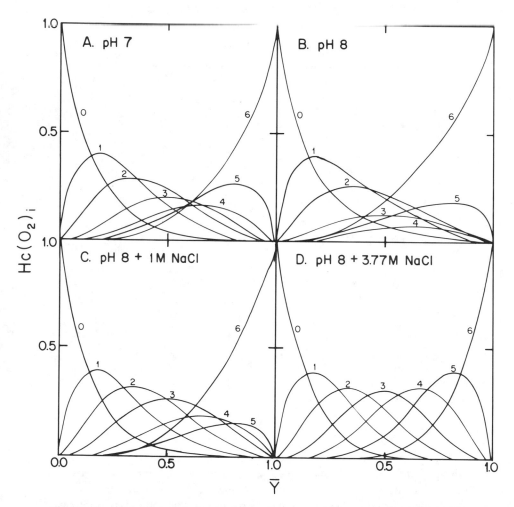

Fig. 9. The relative abundance of hexameric Limulus hemocyanin in various liganded states as a function of the fractional oxygen saturation $\overline{Y}$. $\overline{Y}$ was calculated with equation 3 and the k values listed in Table II. $Hc(O_2)_i$ was calculated using equation 7. A) pH 7. B) pH 8.0. C) pH 8.0 + 1.0 M NaCl. D) pH 8.0 + 3.77 M NaCl.

hemoglobin can be described by specifically modified forms of the two-state allosteric model [14, 25] or alternatively, by equations based on Adair's theory of stepwise oxygenation [3, 16, 17, 30]. The stepwise oxygenation theory and the two-state model of oxygen binding present distinctive advantages in terms of conceptualization of the events that occur within allosteric units as oxygen is bound.

The same kind of considerations that have been previously applied to tetra-meric hemoglobins are applied within the scope of this paper to oxygen binding by undissociated Limulus hemocyanin, a 48-mer. Recent studies have shown that analysis of hemoglobin function within an Adair scheme or within the two-state model has to take into account the oxygen-dependent dissociation of hemo-globin tetramers into dimers [1, 2, 24]. This has not been necessary in modeling the behavior of Limulus hemocyanin since under the experimental conditions of the investigation the structure was stable as a 48-mer. Cooperative oxygen bind-ing by hemoglobin is accompanied by a change in binding free energy and a change in free energy of quaternary constraint. The same considerations apply to Limulus hemocyanin. Stabilizing interactions, present in the "constrained" deoxy quaternary structure of this hemocyanin, are abolished upon oxygenation. This was determined by measuring the rates of dissociation of 60S oxy and deoxy Limulus hemocyanin into its subunits by means of stopped-flow light-scattering experiments [12].

Calculation of Adair constants is important since they permit us to evaluate the oxygenation-linked changes in free energy of binding and quaternary con-straint accompanying successive oxygenation steps (Table II). The Adair con-stants allow us to calculate the median oxygen pressure, from which the total uptake of oxygen-linked Bohr protons and release of oxygen-linked chloride ions upon oxygenation can be determined. The distribution of this uptake and release over the sequential binding steps can be obtained from the individual Adair constants (Figs. 5, 6, 7, and 8). Finally, knowledge of the Adair constants makes it possible to study the effect of allosteric effectors on the distribution of the successively liganded species of hexamer during the oxygenation course (Fig. 9).

Since in most cases only the first Adair constant could be determined from the initial slopes of the Hill plots (Fig. 1), we would have to rely on curve fitting to find the remaining five constants. There will hardly be a unique solution for this problem. Therefore the six Adair constants were calculated with the values of L and c listed in Table I according to equation 5. It has been shown by the elegant studies of Imai that for human hemoglobin, the agreement between the experimentally derived Adair constants and those calculated with the two state allosteric parameters is generally good [16].

Hill plots of oxygen equilibrium data of hemoglobins and hemocyanins ob-tained in the presence of allosteric effectors seem to have one important feature in common: the upper asymptotes converge, whereas the lower asymptotes di-verge [9, 16, 17, 30, 34] (see also this study). This is a general indication that the binding of the first oxygen molecule is more dependent on the allosteric effector than the binding of the last oxygen molecule. In terms of the two-state allosteric transition model, this implies that the oxygen affinity of the T-state is altered by the presence of allosteric effectors, whereas the affinity of the R-state is not. The existence of a single R-state in Limulus hemocyanin is supported by oxygen dissociation experiments [9], and is further confirmed by the kinetic experiments described in this chapter. The initial oxygen-dissociation rate constant, which can be taken as the dissociation rate constant of the R-state, is 8 s^{-1} and is independent of pH (Fig. 3). Similar dissociation rate constants have been found for the R-states of the hemocyanins of Helix pomatia, 10 s^{-1} [31], Penaeus setiferus, 10 s^{-1} [10], and Murex fulvescens, 10 s^{-1} [11]. The dissociation rate constants of the R-states of the hemocyanins of Buccinum undatum, 30–70 s^{-1} [32], and Panulirus interruptus, 60 s^{-1} [20], are somewhat higher.

As shown in Figure 1, the oxygen binding data of Limulus hemocyanin in the pH range from 7 to 8 can be described satisfactorily with a modified two-state model with six interacting binding sites, taking the hexamer as the allosteric unit. At pH values above 8 the experimental binding curves are steeper than the binding functions of a hexamer (Fig. 2). At pH 8.5, pH 8.75 (data not shown), and pH 8.9 the experimental binding curves can be described with 8, 10, and 12 interacting sites respectively. The estimated number of interacting sites above pH 8 and below pH 8.9 have no relation to the molecular architecture of the 48-subunit hemocyanin molecule. The molecule contains 48 O_2 binding sites and is composed of two 24-mers, each of which consists of two dodecamers, each of which, in turn, is composed of two hexamers [5, 19, 28]. It therefore seems probable that between pH 8 and pH 8.9 we are dealing with two molecular species, one having the hexamer and the other having the dodecamer as the allosteric unit. The distribution of these species is pH-dependent. The binding curves between pH 8 and 8.9 can be described on the basis of this assumption. A pH dependence of the number of interacting sites has been previously described for Helix pomatia β-hemocyanin, where the number of interacting sites is approximately doubled between pH 8 and pH 7.4 [34].

The oxygenation pathways shown in Figure 4B are consistent with the oxygenation-linked free energies listed in Table II. Under the experimental conditions examined, the binding of the first three oxygen molecules to the Limulus hemocyanin hexamer proceeds noncooperatively, irrespective of pH or chloride concentration. This implies that the free energies of oxygen binding and release of quaternary constraint do not change when the first three oxygen molecules are bound. At pH 7.5, ionic strength 0.1, most of the change in free energy of binding and quaternary constraint takes place after the fourth oxygen molecule has bound. Thus most of the conformational constraint, which provides for low oxygen affinity, is released after the fourth oxygen molecule is bound, in accordance with the pathway shown in Figure 4B, 1. At pH 8.0, ionic strength 0.1, the largest changes in free energy occur after binding of the fourth and fifth oxygen molecule. In the presence of 1 M NaCl (Fig. 4B, 3), this change in free energies is shifted to the fifth and sixth oxygen binding step. The picture developed above is a reflection from the fact that successive steps in the ligand-binding process are accompanied by changes in ligand-binding energy and by changes in energy of quaternary constraint that are equal in magnitude but opposite in sign (Table II). This principle of complementarity shows that Limulus hemocyanin, within the context of the modified two-state model, operates at a constant energy with respect to these two classes of interactions. The same principle has been shown to apply, independent of any model, to oxygen binding by hemoglobin [24]. The total oxygenation-linked release of quaternary constraint equals -7.37, -8.97, and -11.4 kcal for cases A, B, and C in Table II. These values are in good agreement with the energy values associated with the T $\rightarrow$ R transition as calculated from $-RT\ln L$, using the L values reported in Table I. The values obtained are -7.15, -8.81, and -11.41 kcal respectively (Table II). Finally, we wish to point out that the total change in free energy for fully saturating hemocyanin at pH 7.5, ionic strength 0.1, is -6.73 kcal/mol of O_2 (Table IIA). It is interesting to note the similarity of the corresponding value for stripped human hemoglobin at pH 7.4 with 0.1 M NaCl, which is -6.79 kcal/mol of O_2 [24].

In studying the pH and chloride dependence of the allosteric properties of Limulus hemocyanin in Tris-HCl/NaCl buffers, we are concerned with a system containing three linked components: oxygen, chloride, and protons. The linkage relations are analyzed according to the theory of linked functions [33]. Since other anions also act as allosteric effectors [9], the use of other buffers will not reduce the number of linked components to two. The present situation is basically described by the following three linkage equations:

$$\left(\frac{\delta H^+}{\delta \overline{Y}}\right)_{pH, Cl} = \left(\frac{\delta \ln p}{\delta \ln H^+}\right)_{p, Cl} \tag{16}$$

in which p is the partial pressure of oxygen and $\overline{Y}$ the fractional saturation of hemocyanin with oxygen. From equation 16, equation 9 is obtained. The second linkage equation is

$$\left(\frac{\delta Cl}{\delta \overline{Y}}\right)_{Cl, pH} = -\left(\frac{\delta \ln p}{\delta \ln(Cl)}\right)_{p, pH} \tag{17}$$

from which equation 11 is obtained, and the third linkage equation is:

$$\left(\frac{\delta H^+}{\delta \overline{Cl}}\right)_{p, pH} = -\left(\frac{\delta \ln(Cl)}{\delta \ln H^+}\right)_{Cl, p} \tag{18}$$

in which $\overline{Cl}$ is the fractional saturation of hemocyanin with chloride. The number of chloride-linked protons can be obtained from:

$$\frac{d\ln Cl_m}{dpH} - \left({}^{H^+}HcCl - {}^{H^+}Ho \right) - \Delta H^+ \tag{19}$$

in which Cl_m stands for the median chloride activity. HcCl has a lower oxygen affinity that Hc without chloride bound. Since H^+ binds preferentially to high affinity hemocyanin, the quantity $\left({}^{H^+}HcCl - {}^{H^+}Hc \right)$ will be negative: ΔH^+ is the number of Bohr protons released upon saturating hemocyanin with chloride. The proton-linked chloride ions can be obtained from:

$$\frac{dpH_m}{d\ln(Cl)} = \left({}^{Cl}HcH^+ - {}^{Cl}Hc \right) = \Delta Cl \tag{20}$$

in which pH_m is the negative logarithm of the median proton activity and Cl is the number of chloride ions released upon fully saturating hemocyanin with protons. Therefore in our linked three-component system the following situation exists: Upon oxygenation of hemocyanin there will be an oxygen-linked uptake of protons (equation 9), together with a chloride-linked uptake of Bohr protons (equation 19). There will be an oxygen-linked release of chloride ions (equation 11) together with a proton-linked release of chloride ions (equation 20). Equations 9 and 10 can be solved experimentally since oxygen binding curves can be determined spectroscopically as a function of pH and chloride. Since the binding of either chloride or protons to hemocyanin is spectrally silent, there is no such way for determining ΔH^+ or ΔCl in equations 19 and 20. Therefore we could only calculate the oxygen-linked proton uptake and oxygen-linked chloride release using equations 9 and 11. The numbers obtained in this way do not take into account the chloride-linked Bohr protons and proton-linked chloride ions. With this limitation in mind let us have a closer look at Figures 5, 6, 7, and 8. At pH 7 there is no oxygen-linked uptake or release of Bohr protons. At pH 7.5 the Bohr proton uptake reaches a maximum value of about 4 oxygen-linked Bohr protons per hexamer (Fig. 6). The number of Bohr protons bound during the first, second, and third oxygen-binding step is the same, namely, one oxygen-linked Bohr proton per hexamer. As can be seen in Fig. 4B, 1, the oxygenation proceeds under these conditions along the T-state pathway. Therefore this oxygen-linked uptake of Bohr protons is not associated with a change in quaternary structure, but is a reflection of the proton-induced increase of the oxygen affinity of the T-state (Fig. 1). The fourth binding step is associated with the uptake of Bohr protons and with the T $\rightarrow$ R transition (Fig. 4B, 1). The oxygenation proceeds then via the R-state pathway and no additional oxygen-linked protons are taken up. At pH 8, ionic strength 0.1, there are about two oxygen-linked Bohr protons associated with oxygenation of the Limulus hemocyanin hexamer. Approximately one proton is associated with completion of the first three oxygen binding steps, $\Delta H^+_1 = \Delta H^+_2 = \Delta H^+_3$, which proceed along the T-state pathway (Fig. 4B, 2). The allosteric transition takes place after the fourth and fifth oxygen molecule is bound. This transition is accompanied by an uptake of the additional Bohr proton (Fig. 6). After this, the oxygenation proceeds along the R-state pathway, and no additional protons are taken up.

Increasing chloride concentrations reduce the values of all six Adair constants (Table II, cases B and C). This seems contradictory to the statement made earlier, that there is a single R-state of Limulus hemocyanin since in this case one would expect k_6 to be independent of the chloride concentration. However, the decrease of k_6 with increasing chloride concentrations (Fig. 7) is a simple reflection of the fact that fully oxygenated hemocyanin is not completely in the R-state at high chloride concentrations. This can be seen by using the $\overline{Y}$-function (equation 4) and R-state function:

$$\overline{R} = \frac{(1 + \alpha)^6}{(1 + \alpha)^6 + L(1 + c\alpha)^6} \tag{21}$$

and the values of L and c in Table I. It can be calculated that at pH 8 at a high oxygen pressure, where $\overline{Y} = 1$ ($\alpha = 10,000$), the $\overline{R}$ values with 0.1 M NaCl and 1.02 M NaCl will be 0.996 and 0.94 respectively. The chloride effect described here is similar to the pronounced effect of inositol hexaphosphate on human hemoglobin. Inositol hexaphosphate, a highly charged polyanion, reduces the values of all four oxygen-binding constants for human hemoglobin [30], whereas 2,3-diphosphoglycerate [16] and 0.1 M NaCl [30] are less effective and reduce only the first three oxygen-binding constants.

The foregoing analysis indicates that in Limulus hemocyanin the total number of oxygen-linked chloride ions is independent of the chloride concentration (Fig. 8). This is in marked contrast with the pH-dependent uptake of oxygen-linked Bohr protons (Fig. 6). This might be explained by the fact that the chloride dependent shift of the deoxy asymptotes is much smaller than the pH-dependent shift (Fig. 1). Second, we see that at high chloride concentrations, where the deoxy asymptotes are greatly shifted, the T → R transition is incomplete. The distribution of the release of oxygen-linked chloride ions with respect to the successive oxygen-binding steps is consistent with the oxygenation pathways as given in Figure 4B, 2 and 3. The small release of chloride ions at the first three oxygen-binding steps is again a reflection of the chloride-induced decrease of the oxygen affinity of the apparent T-states. In 0.1 M NaCl, oxygen-linked chloride ions are released at the fourth and fifth oxygenation step (Fig. 8), where the allosteric transition takes place (Fig. 4B, 2). At 1.02 M NaCl chloride ions are released at the fifth and sixth oxygen-binding steps (Fig. 8), again in accordance with the oxygenation pathway (Fig. 4B, 3).

The analysis presented in this chapter is an extension of the detailed and elegant modeling that has been successful in describing tetrameric hemoglobin's functional behavior. We have addressed the question of whether the allosteric transitions in a molecule containing 48 oxygen-binding sites are localized, or spread throughout the molecule. Our results suggest that hexamers within the 48-mer are the allosteric units below pH 8 and that at pH 9 the quaternary conformational changes are expressed at the dodecamer level. Hexamers and dodecamers (which are thought to be bridged hexamers) appear to be structural elements in Limulus hemocyanin [5, 21]. The allosteric analysis presented here is thus interpretable in terms of our present knowledge of the molecular architecture of this giant molecule.

ACKNOWLEDGMENTS

The work reported in this chapter was funded by grants HL 15460 and ESO 1908 from the National Institutes of Health, and grant PCM 7906462 from the National Science Foundation. The Netherlands Organization for the Advancement of Science provided support for M.B. J.B. is an established investigator of the American Heart Association.

REFERENCES

1. Ackers GK, Halvorson HR: The linkage between oxygenation and subunit dissociation in human hemoglobin. Proc Natl Acad Sci USA 71:4312–4316, 1974.
2. Ackers GK, Johnson ML, Mills FC, Halvorson HR, and Shapiro S: The linkage between oxygenation and subunit dissociation in human hemoglobin: Consequences for the analysis of oxygenation curves.
3. Adair GS: The hemoglobin system, VI: The oxygen dissociation curve of hemoglobin. 63:529–545, 1925.
4. Arisaka F, Van Holde KE: Allosteric properties and the association equilibria of hemocyanin from callianassa californiensis. J Mol Biol 134:41–73, 1979.
5. Bijlholt M, Van Bruggen EFJ, Bonaventura J: Dissociation and reassembly of Limulus polyphemus hemocyanin. Eur J Biochem 95:399–405, 1979.
6. Bonventura J, Bonaventura C: Hemocyanins: Relationships in their structure, function and assembly. Amer Zool 20:7–17, 1980.
7. Bonaventura J, Bonaventura C, Sullivan B: Hemoglobins and hemocyanins: Comparative aspects of structure and function. J Exp Zool 194:155–174, 1975.
8. Bonaventura J, Bonaventura C, Sullivan B: Non-heme oxygen transport proteins. In Jobsis F (ed): "Oxygen and Physiological Functions." Dallas, Texas, Texas: Professional Information Library, 1977, pp 177–220.
9. Brouwer M, Bonaventura C, Bonaventura J: Oxygen binding by Limulus polyphemus hemocyanin: Allosteric modulation by chloride ions. Biochemistry 16:3897–3902, 1977.
10. Brouwer M, Bonaventura C, Bonaventura J: Analysis of the effect of three different allosteric ligands on oxygen binding by hemocyanin of the shrimp, Penaeus setiferus. Biochemistry 17:2148–2154, 1978.
11. Brouwer M, Ryan MC, Bonaventura J, Bonaventura C: Functional and structural properties of Murex fulvescens hemocyanin: Isolation of two different subunits required for reassociation of a Molluscan hemocyanin.

12. Brouwer M, Bonaventura C, Bonaventura J: Effect of oxygen and allosteric effectors on structural stability of oligomeric hemocyanins of the arthropod, limulus polyphemus, and the mollusc, Helix pomatia.

13. Colosimo A, Brunori M, Wyman J: Oxygen binding to haemocyanin: A tentative analysis in the framework of a concerted model. "Structure and Function of Haemocyanin." Berlin: Springer-Verlag, 1977, pp 189–192.

14. Edelstein SJ: Cooperative interactions of hemoglobin. Ann Rev Biochem 44:209–232, 1975.

15. Hopfield JJ, Shulman RG, Ogawa S: An allosteric model of hemoglobin: I. Kinetics. J Mol Biol 61:425–443, 1971.

16. Imai K: Analysis of oxygen equilibria of native and chemically modified human adult hemoglobins on the basis of Adair's stepwise oxygenation theory and the allosteric model of Monod, Wyman, Changeux. Biochemistry 12:798–808, 1973.

17. Imai K, Yonetani T: pH dependence of the Adair constants of human hemoglobin. J Biol Chem 250:2227–2231, 1975.

18. Johansen K, Petersen JA: Respiratory adaptations in Limulus polyphemus (L). In Vernberg JF (ed): "Physiological Ecology of Estuarine Organisms." Columbia, S.C.: University of South Carolina Press, 1975, pp 129–145.

19. Johnson ML, Yphantis DA: Subunit association and heterogeneity of Limulus polyphemus hemocyanin. J Mol Biol 116:569–576, 1977.

20. Kuiper HA, Brunori M, Antonini E: Kinetic control of co-operativity in the oxygen binding of Panulirus interruptus hemocyanin. J Mol Biol 116:569–576, 1977.

21. Lamy J, Lamy J, Weill J, Bonaventura C, Bonaventura J, Brenowitz M: Immunological correlates between the multiple subunits of Limulus polyphemus and Tachypleus tridentatus. Arch Biochem Biophys 196:324–339, 1979.

22. Mangum CP, Freadman MA, Johansen K: The quantitative role of hemocyanin in aerobic respiration of Limulus polyphemus. J Exp Zool 191:279–285, 1975.

23. Mangum CP, Booth CE, DeFur PL, Heckel NA, Henry RP, Oglesby LC, Polites G: The ionic environment of hemocyanin in Limulus polyphemus. Biol Bull 150:453–467, 1976.

24. Mills FC, Johnson ML, Ackers GK: Oxygenation-linked subunit interactions in human hemoglobin: Experimental studies on the concentration dependence of oxygenation curves. Biochemistry 15:5350–5362, 1976.

25. Minton AP, Imai K: The three-state model: A minimal allosteric description of homotropic and heterotropic effects in the binding of ligands to hemoglobin. Proc Natl Acad Sci USA 71:1418–1421, 1974.

26. Monod J, Wyman J, Changeux JP: On the nature of allosteric transitions: A plausible model. J Mol Biol 12:88–118, 1965.

27. Saroff HA, Minton AP: The Hill plot and the energy of interaction in hemoglobin. Science 175:1253–1255, 1972.

28. Schutter WG, van Bruggen EFJ, Bonaventura C, Bonaventura J, Sullivan B: Structure, dissociation, reassembly of Limulus polyphemus hemocyanin. In Bannister JV (ed): "Structure and Function of Haemocyanin." New York: Springer-Verlag, 1977, pp 13–21.

29. Sullivan B, Bonaventura J, Bonaventura C: Functional differences in the multiple hemocyanins of the horseshoe crab, Limulus polyphemus L. Proc Natl Acad Sci USA 71:2558–2562, 1974.

30. Tyuma I, Imai K, Shimizu K: Analysis of oxygen equilibrium of hemoglobin and control mechanism of organic phosphates. Biochemistry 12:1491–1498, 1973.

31. Van Driel R, Brunori M, Antonini E: Kinetics of the co-operative and non-cooperative reaction of Helix pomatia haemocyanin with oxygen. J Mol Biol 89:103–112, 1974.

32. Wood EJ, Cayley GR, Pearson JS: Oxygen binding by the haemocyanin from Buccinum undatum. J Mol Biol 190:1–11, 1977.

33. Wyman J: Linked functions and reciprocal effects in hemoglobin: A second look. Adv Prot Chem 19:223–286, 1964.
34. Zolla L, Kuiper HA, Vecchini P, Antonini E, Brunori M: Dissociation and oxygen-binding behavior of β-hemocyanin from Helix pomatia. Eur J Biochem 87:467–473, 1978.

APPENDIX

The median ligand activity, p_m, is that value of p for which

$$\int_{p=0}^{p=p_m} \overline{Y} \, d\ln p = \int_{p_m}^{p=\infty} (1 - \overline{Y}) \, d\ln p \tag{A1}$$

[33]. The denominator of equation 3 in the text is the so-called binding polynomial or generating function and can be written as:

$$B = 1 + \sum_{i=1}^{6} a_i p^i \tag{A2}$$

The fractional saturation of the hexamer with ligand is given by [10, 33]:

$$\overline{Y} = \frac{1}{n} \frac{d\ln B}{d\ln p} = \frac{1}{n} \frac{p}{B} \frac{dB}{dp} \tag{A3}$$

Substitution of A3 in A1 gives

$$\int_{p=0}^{p=p_m} \frac{1}{nB} \, dB = \int_{p=p_m}^{p=\infty} \frac{1}{p} \, dp - \int_{p=p_m}^{p=\infty} \frac{1}{nB} \, dB \tag{A4}$$

Solving A4 gives

$$\left(\frac{p}{p_m}\right)^6 = 1 + a_1 p + a_2 p^2 \ldots\ldots + a_6 p^6 \tag{A5}$$

For $p \to \infty$ A5 becomes

$$\left(\frac{1}{p_m}\right) = \sqrt[6]{a_6} \tag{A6}$$

which is equation 8 of the text.

Physiology and Biology of Horseshoe Crabs: Studies on
Normal and Environmentally Stressed Animals, pages 257–267
© 1982 Alan R. Liss, Inc., 150 Fifth Avenue, New York, NY 10011

The Subunit Structure of Limulus Hemocyanin

Michael Brenowitz and Margaret Moore

INTRODUCTION

The high molecular weight and multisubunit structure of hemocyanins make these proteins useful tools for investigating the principles of subunit interaction and assembly. The functional properties of a multisubunit protein are greater than the simple sum of the properties of the subunits. Cooperativity and allosteric modulation of hemocyanin function provide finer control over oxygen transport than is possible with single, independent subunits. These processes are dependent on the interactions between the subunits in the native molecule. A precise understanding of the subunit composition and the particular structural and functional characteristics of these subunits is a prerequisite for understanding the interactions within the oligomer.

Detailed study of the structure and function of Limulus hemocyanin will perhaps also suggest answers to questions concerning the role of hemocyanin in the respiratory physiology of Limulus. In this chapter we bring together some of our recent biochemical investigations on the structure, function, and assembly of Limulus hemocyanin. In particular, we will address two questions: Under what conditions is the quaternary structure of the native molecule stable; and how extensive is the structural and functional heterogeneity of the constituent subunits?

OLIGOMER STRUCTURE

Sedimentation equilibrium analysis of purified Limulus hemocyanin preparations show it to be a 3,140,000-dalton oligomer composed of 48 ca. 70,000-dalton monomers [6]. The protein has a sedimentation coefficient of around 60S. The same sedimentation coefficient is measured upon centrifugation of unpurified hemolymph diluted with either seawater or with the supernatant obtained when the hemocyanin is pelleted from the hemolymph by ultracentrifugation (unpublished data). Centrifugation of the native hemocyanin collected from individual specimens has never shown any component other than the 60S molecule. However, Limulus will encounter fluctuations in salinity and oxygen availability during its life cycle which alter the ionic conditions in the hemolymph. The conditions under which the native molecule may aggregate or dissociate could be physiologically relevant. Therefore the stability of Limulus hemocyanin as a function of pH, ionic strength, and divalent cation concentration was studied to investigate the interactions stabilizing the quaternary structure [4]. The 60S, 48-subunit aggregate is the largest aggregate that formed under the buffer conditions used. A somewhat surprising result is that different levels of aggregation are stabilized by different ionic and pH conditions. For example, the stability of the 60S molecule is specifically calcium-dependent (Table I) [2]. At ionic strength 0.1, with 10 mM $CaCl_2$, the 60S native molecule remains intact between pH 7 and 9. As the calcium concentration decreases, the native molecule dissociates at progressively lower pH values (Fig. 1). At pH 7.8 in zero calcium

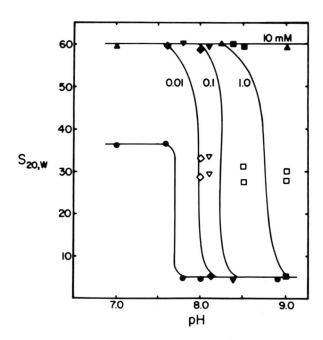

Fig. 1.   Sedimentation velocity analysis of the aggregation state of Limulus hemocyanin as a function of pH and $CaCl_2$ concentration. Buffer is Tris/HCl, I = 0.1 with (▲) 10 mM $CaCl_2$ (■) 1 mM $CaCl_2$, (▼) 0.1 mM $CaCl_2$, (◆) 0.01 mM $CaCl_2$, (●) 10 mM EDTA. Solid symbols indicate the S value of the major component, and open symbols indicate minor peaks [from 2].

(10 mM EDTA), dissociation into monomers is complete. At neutral pH chelating divalent cations with EDTA dissociates the 60S molecule to a homogeneous population of 24-subunit molecules with a sedimentation coefficient of 37S (Fig. 1). Neither high concentrations of monovalent cations nor magnesium will stabilize the 60S molecule in the absence of calcium (Table I). However, increasing the ionic strength will prevent dissociation of 24-mers to monomers. It is apparent that under physiological conditions of ionic strength and calcium concentration, the native 60S molecule is stable throughout the pH range it might encounter in vivo. Without calcium stabilization of the 48-subunit structure dissociation–association phenomenon could occur in vivo with fluctuating pH and ionic strength. The stability of the aggregated molecule is thus primarily dependent on calcium ion concentration.

The 48-subunit molecule is unique to the hemocyanin of horseshoe crabs. Other Chelicerates only aggregate to 24 subunits [8,12]. We thus investigated whether the aggregation from 24 to 48 subunits conferred different oxygen binding properties to Limulus hemocyanin. These results show that dissociation to 24-subunit molecules has a minor effect on both the cooperativity and affinity of the protein at neutral pH when compared to the 48-subunit molecule at the same pH (Table II). That calcium is not required for cooperativity is typical for arthropod hemocyanins [7].

TABLE I. Specificity of Calcium Stabilization of the 60S Oligomer*

Added salt	$S_{20,w}$
10 mM CaCl$_2$	60.0
10 mM CaSO$_4$	59.5
10 mM EDTA	36.0
10 mM EGTA plus 100 mM MgCl$_2$	38.1
10 mM EDTA plus 500 mM NaCl	38.8

*Buffer is Tris/HCl, $I = 0.1$, at pH 7.0.

TABLE II. Oxygen Binding Characteristics of Limulus Hemocyanin

Sample	P_{50}	n_{50}
60S, 10 mM CaCl$_2$[a]	2.8	1.8
37S, 10 mM EDTA[a]	1.8	1.6
Trilobite[b]	5.0	1.8
Adult[b]	7.2	1.8

[a]In Tris/HCl, $I = 0.1$, pH 7.0.
[b]In Tris/HCl, $I = 0.1$, pH 8.0, 10 mM CaCl$_2$.

The Tris buffers and low protein concentration (5 mg/ml) used in these studies do not simulate in vivo conditions. However, as the higher ionic strength and protein concentrations found in vivo would favor large aggregates, our data probably underestimate the stability of the native protein. Thus, although there is no advantage to the animal, with respect to cooperativity or modulation of its oxygen binding, from forming a 48-subunit over a 24-subunit oligomer, the calcium-stabilized native hemocyanin is highly resistant to dissociation.

ELECTROPHORETIC STUDY OF CHAIN HETEROGENEITY

The heterogeneity of the constituent polypeptide chains of Limulus hemocyanin has been extensively documented [3, 5, 9, 14, 18, 19]. Studies of the hemocyanin of individual animals by both polyacrylamide and immunoelectrophoresis fail to detect differences in the subunit composition of animals of different ages (prosomal widths from 2 to 30 cm), sex, place of collection (either Beaufort, North Carolina or Woods Hole, Massachusetts), and season of capture (unpublished data). The hemocyanin purified from pooled samples of trilobite and first tailed stage Limulus larvae had electrophoresis banding patterns identical to those of adults. Preliminary oxygen-binding experiments on the larval hemocyanin show similar affinity to that of the adult (Table II). It is apparent that the subunit composition and functional properties of Limulus hemocyanin are constant through its life cycle.

Using anion exchange chromatography it has been possible to purify the constituent subunits (Fig. 2). A summary of the electrophoretic and immunological properties of the constituent subunits is shown in Figure 3. Polyacrylamide electrophoresis resolves all but two of the charge isomers detected by the higher resolution technique of isoelectric focusing. Though 15 bands can be identified on polyacrylamide gels, only eight proteins can be distinguished immunoelectrophoretically.

An extensive series of control experiments has demonstrated that the bands observed on polyacrylamide gels are not artifacts, but are indicators of minor differences that are not distinguishable immunoelectrophoretically. Of these eight proteins two pairs show cross-reactivity (subunits IIa and IIIa, and subunits V and VI [9]). In evaluating the extent of subunit complexity it is important to consider the characteristics detected by each technique. Polyacrylamide electrophoresis and isoelectric focusing are primarily sensitive to net charge (although other factors, such as conformation or the location of an amino acid substitution, can influence electrophoretic mobility on gels [17]). The determinants that distinguish the subunits immunologically represent unique structures on the surface of the subunit. As subunit interactions occur on these surfaces, a close relationship would be expected between immunological and assembly properties of the subunits. On the other hand, substitutions that do not alter the interaction surfaces

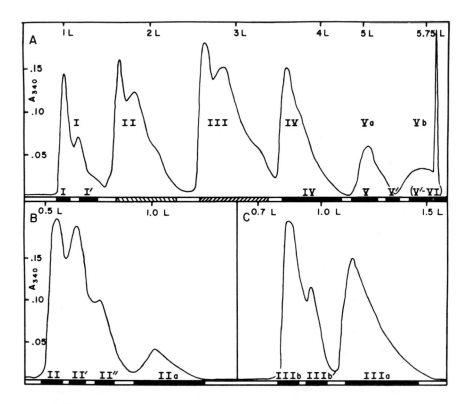

Fig. 2. Elution profiles of Limulus hemocyanin subunits from DEAE chromatographic columns. Graph A represents a typical elution of whole stripped hemocyanin eluted with a salt gradient from a pH 8.9 column. Graphs B and C show the rechromatography of zones II and III respectively for the purification of subunits II, II′, II″, IIa, IIIa, and IIIb. The solid bars under the peaks indicate which fractions were pooled to obtain pure subunits. The striped area under zones II and III of A are the fractions used for rechromatography [from 3].

(such as the electrophoretically distinct yet immunologically identical subunits) would not be expected to differ in their properties in assembly. As will be shown below, this is in fact the case.

STRUCTURAL STUDY OF CHAIN HETEROGENEITY

It is evident from the immunological and electrophoretic studies that there are two levels of heterogeneity in subunits of Limulus hemocyanin. The lack of cross-reacting determinants in the subunits that are distinguished immunoelectrophoretically suggests that these proteins have quite different primary struc-

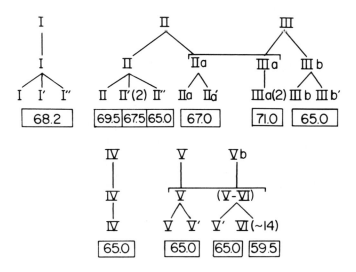

Fig. 3. Relationship of chromatographic isolation (row 1), immunoelectrophoretic identification (row 2), alkaline gel electrophoresis (row 3), and SDS electrophoresis band identification (row 4). The brackets over IIa and IIIa, and V and (V′–VI) in row 2 indicate immunological cross-reactivity [from 3].

tures. Amino acid compositions (Table III) and preliminary peptide mapping studies appear to bear this out. These differences are visible in terms of amino acid composition, cyanogen bromide fragment sizes, and partial preolytic digestion patterns [18]. However, an analysis of the degree of homology between the components will require the determination of their sequences. Such work is now in progress.

Electrophoretically detectable subunits, which are not immunologically distinguishable are found in all of the fractions except IV. These different charge forms are of some concern to those studying the structure and x-ray diffraction patterns of these fractions [13,15]. Fraction II was selected because it forms the best crystals for study of the x-ray diffraction patterns. This property makes it the most interesting one for sequence study, even though it is also the most complex of the five column fractions. Zone II obtained from DEAE Sephadex chromatography at pH 8.9 consists of subunits II, II′, II″, IIa, and IIa′. Rechromatography by DEAE Sephadex at pH 8.0 separates II, II′, and II″ from IIa and IIa′. If II, II′, and II″ were very different in sequence, it would be very difficult to determine the structures of any of them from a mixture. To answer this question II, II′, and II″ were each isolated (Fig. 2). Amino acid analysis was performed on all three [16]. No significant differences were found in the

TABLE III. Amino Acid Compositions of the Components of Limulus polyphemus Hemocyanin[a]

Amino acid	I	II	IIa	IIIa	IIIb	IV	Va	Vb
Lysine	43	42	36	36	30	30	59	56
Histidine	41	40	39	44	46	47	83	83
Arginine	29	29	31	32	26	35	62	60
Tryptophan[b]	4	6	7	6	4	4	ND	ND
CM cysteine[c]	9	10	6	7	7	7	11	12
Aspartic acid	68	78	64	76	64	58	129	126
Threonine[d]	31	26	28	37	30	27	55	59
Serine[d]	33	46	45	33	32	31	58	52
Glutamic acid	55	56	59	64	63	68	124	123
Proline	29	34	30	28	24	24	59	62
Glycine	38	42	39	40	32	34	73	72
Alanine	35	36	36	28	29	32	57	54
Valine	38	37	41	44	33	35	73	75
Methionine	16	15	16	17	16	14	33	32
Isoleucine[e]	34	32	27	23	27	31	54	44
Leucine[e]	49	51	53	57	54	52	109	99
Tyrosine	19	26	22	22	22	20	47	46
Phenylalanine	31	31	24	28	29	29	55	53

[a]Values are the molar averages obtained after 24- and 72-hour hydrolysis.
[b]Tryptophan was determined after 24-hour hydrolysis in methane sulfonic acid.
[c]Half cystine was measured as CM cysteine.
[d]Threonine and Serine values were extrapolated to zero time.
[e]Only the 72-hour value was used.

compositions. However, amino acid analysis is not sensitive enough to pick up the difference of only a few residues. Tryptic mapping was performed as well, and again no significant differences were found. The fraction II has been found to be blocked at the amino terminus and so is not accessable to sequence analysis directly. It is apparent that the basis of the heterogeneity lies in a very few sites on the peptide chain.

There are several possible sources of this heterogeneity. The presence of carbohydrate on the different forms might account for a charge difference. The anthrone reaction was found to be negative for the five fractions from DEAE-Sephadex chromatography. The quantity of sugar present thus cannot exceed two moles per mole protein. Methanolysis of the fractions obtained from DEAE-Sephadex followed by gas chromatography was performed by C. H. W. Hirs. The only evidence for sugar was two or three moles of sialic acid per mole of subunit II and a mixture of subunits IIIa and IIIb. This was followed in our laboratory with the thiobarbituric acid assay using neuraminidase to cleave the sialic acid from the protein [20]. No sialic acid was found in rechromatographed

II, II', and II'' mixture. It is possible that there is a glycoprotein contaminant in the original column fractions that is not found in rechromatographed material. Thus although it is still possible that there is sugar on some Limulus hemocyanin chains, it is likely to be a very small amount. It has been noted that II, II', and II'' run with different mobilities on SDS gel electrophoresis (Fig. 3). This may indicate differences in some posttranslational processing of the hemocyanin chains, possibly size or a modification that alters SDS binding to the protein. Another possibility is that there have been gene duplications for each subunit type, which are constrained by role in assembly as to remain nearly identical in surface contacts, yet vary in charge. This would imply that subunit IV is the most highly conserved of the subunits, as it has no charge variants that we have been able to find. The basis of the electrophoretic heterogeneity is still unknown, but appears likely to be a matter of a very few sites on the subunits. It is very possible that the different bands may be accounted for by differences in the number of amides on the polypeptide chains. This will be seen in the course of the sequence determination.

SUBUNIT REASSEMBLY

The dissociation of the native hemocyanin into its constituent subunits occurs at pH 8.9, with 10 mM EDTA present. Bijlholt et al [1] found that dissociated Limulus hemocyanin subunits are capable of reassembling to a 48-subunit aggregate when the pH is brought back to neutrality and then calcium is restored to the buffer. This study was performed with partially purified preparations [18]. It was also found that these fractions could self-assemble. The maximum aggregate formed by reassociation of an individual subunit is a hexamer. In experiments where one fraction was omitted from the reassembly mixture, the size of the aggregate formed depended on which fraction was omitted. These studies have been elaborated with the use of electrophoretically and immunologically pure subunits. The subunits can be differentiated by their varying abilities to assemble when brought to neutral pH in the presence or absence of calcium. Subunits I, I' and IIIb, IIIb' do not associate. Subunits IIa, IIIa and IV form hexamers in the absence of calcium whereas subunits II, II', and II'' will form hexamers only in the presence of calcium. This result suggests that subunits II, II', and II'' are responsible for the calcium sensitivity of the 24–48-subunit aggregation. Subunits V and V', VI aggregate to form dimers (V–V) and (V'–VI). These results show that only the properties of the immunologically distinct subunits differ with regard to subunit assembly while immunologically identical subunits behave identically.

Experiments in which only a single electrophoretically distinct subunit was omitted from the mixture of the subunits used for reassembly show that immunoelectrophoretically identical subunits, which are electrophoretically distinct, can substitute for each other in the formation of an oligomer. For example, if subunits II, II', and II'' are omitted from the reassembly mixture, only a hexamer can be formed [1]. Addition of either II, II' or II'' singly to the reassembly mixture resulted in formation of the 60S, 48-subunit molecule (unpublished data).

Markl et al [14] have proposed that there is a relationship between the number of subunits and the aggregation state of the native molecule for arthropod hemocyanins. Their work is based on subunit compositions determined by polyacrylamide electrophoresis. However, our data with Limulus hemocyanin suggest that immunoelectrophoretic identity is a superior indicator of subunit differences that cause different subunit reassembly and functional properties. Hemocyanin from the related chelicerates Androctanus australis and Eurypelma californicum, which aggregate to the 24-subunit level, have 8 and 7 immunoelectrophoretically distinct subunits, respectively [10, 11]. Limulus also has eight immunologically distinct subunits. Thus it appears that, using the criteria of immunoelectrophoretic identity, the aggregation from 24 to 48 subunits seen in Limulus hemocyanin does not require greater subunit complexity compared to the other chelicerates.

SUMMARY AND CONCLUSIONS

The picture of the Limulus hemocyanin molecule that is now emerging is one of intricate interactions between eight quite diverse subunits. The 48-subunit oligomer found in the animal is formed by the calcium-dependent association of two 24-subunit aggregates. This calcium-mediated association increases the stability of the aggregate to dissociation by pH and low ionic strength. The properties of the isolated subunits in terms of function and assembly are indicators of the roles played by the subunits in assembly of the native molecule and in the modulation of oxygen binding. However, it is important to consider the properties of the subunits in association with other subunits in assessing their importance to the overall properties of the native molecule.

The complex pattern of subunit heterogeneity does not appear to be the result of polymorphism or any function of degradation due to sample handling. There are 15 electrophoretically distinguishable subunits but only eight immunoelectrophoretically distinguishable types. The immunological differences are reflected in oxygen binding, role in assembly, and by a number of structural criteria. The immunologically identical subunits II, II', and II'' have been found to be identical not only in terms of oxygen affinity and role in assembly, but also by tryptic-peptide mapping and amino acid composition. The differences between these subunits have yet to be found. The precise disposition of 15 types of subunits into the native molecule and the contribution of each to the function and assembly of the whole are questions central to the understanding of this complex molecule. The continued study of the biochemistry of Limulus hemocyanin will no doubt continue to elucidate principles of subunit assembly and intersubunit interactions as well as suggest answers to hemocyanin's role in the physiology of Limulus.

ACKNOWLEDGMENTS

We thank Dr. Austen Riggs for advice and encouragement. M.M. would like to thank Florence Waddill, Marie Erwin, and Dr. Eisuke Yokota for their assistance and encouragement in the sequence work. The sequence work has been supported by grants PCM79-04053 from the National Science Foundation, GM21314 and GM28410 from the National Institute of Health, and F-213 from the Robert A. Welch Foundation. The other studies were supported by grants HL 15460 and ESO 1908 from the National Institutes of Health, and PCM 7906462 from the National Science Foundation.

REFERENCES

1. Bijlholt M, Van Bruggen EFJ, Bonaventura J: Eur J Biochem 251:399–405, 1979.
2. Brenowitz M, Van Holde KE, Bonaventura C, Bonaventura J: Calcium specific stabilization of the quarternary structure of Limulus polyphemus hemocyanin. Fed Proc 39:1968, 1980.
3. Brenowitz M, Bonaventura C, Bonaventura J, Gianazza E: Subunit compostion of a high molecular weight oligomer: Limulus polyphemus hemocyanin. Arch Biochem Biophys 210:748–761, 1981.
4. Brenowitz M, Bonaventura C, Bonaventura J: Subunit interactions in limulus polyphemus hemocyanin stability and oxygen binding of the 48-, 24-, and 12-subunit aggregrates (in preparation).
5. Hoylaerts M, Preaux G, Witters R, Lontie R: Immunological heterogeneity of the subunits of Limulus polyphemus hemocyanin. Arch Int Physiol Biochem 87:417–418, 1979.
6. Johnson M, Yphantis D: Subunit association and heterogeneity of Limulus polpyphemus hemocyanin. Biochemisty 17:1448–1455, 1976.
7. Klarman A, Daniel E: Built in cooperativity of oxygen binding by arthropod hemocyanins. J Mol Biol 115:257–261, 1977.
8. Lamy J, Lamy L, Baglin MC, Weill J: Scorpion hemocyanin subunits: Properties, dissociation, association. In Bannister JV (ed): "Structure and Function of Hemocyanin." Berlin, New York: Springer Verlag, 1977.
9. Lamy J, Lamy J, Weill J, Bonaventura J, Bonaventura C, Brenowitz M: Immunological correlates between the multiple hemocyanin subunits of Limulus polyphemus and Tachypleus tridentatus. Arch Biochem Biophys 196:324–339, 1979.
10. Lamy J, Lamy J, Weill J: Arthropod hemocyanin structure: Isolation of eight subunits in the scorpion. 193:140–149, 1979.
11. Lamy J, Lamy J, Weill J, Markl J, Schneider HJ, Linzen B: Hemocyanins in spiders, VII. Immunological comparison of the subunits of eurypelma californicum hemocyanin. Hoppe-Seyler's Z Physiol Chem 360, S: 889–895, 1979.
12. Loewe R, Linzen B: Subunits and stability region of dugesiella californica haemocyanin. Hoppe-Seyler's Z Physiol Chem 354, S:182–188, 1973.

13. Magnus K, Love W: Three dimensional structure of Limulus II hemocyanin subunit at 5.5A resolution. Fed Proc 39:1968, 1980.

14. Markl J, Markl A, Schartau W, Linzen B: Subunit heterogeneity in arthropod hemocyanins: I. Chelicerata. J Comp Physiol B 130:283–292, 1979.

15. Moore M, Riggs A: Structural studies of cyanogen bromide fragments from component II of Limulus polyphemus hemocyanin. Fed Proc 39:1969, 1980.

16. Moore M, Riggs A: Structural studies of component II of the hemocyanin of Limulus polyphemus. In Lamy J, Lamy J (eds): "Invertebrate Oxygen Binding Proteins: Structure, Active Site, and Function." New York: Marcel Dekker, 1981.

17. Ramshaw JA, Coyne JA, Lewontin RC: Genetics 93:1019–1038, 1979.

18. Sullivan B, Bonaventura J, Bonaventura C: Functional differences in the multiple hemocyanins of the horseshoe crab Limulus polyphemus. Proc Natl Acad Sci USA 711:2558–2562, 1974.

19. Sullivan B, Bonaventura J, Bonaventura C, Godette G: Hemocyanin of the horseshoe crab Limulus polyphemus. Structural differentiation of the isolated components. J Biol Chem 251:7644–7648, 1976.

20. Warren L: The thiobarbituric acid assay of sialic acids. J Biol Chem 254:1971–1975, 1959.

Physiology and Biology of Horseshoe Crabs: Studies on
Normal and Environmentally Stressed Animals, pages 269–282
© 1982 Alan R. Liss, Inc., 150 Fifth Avenue, New York, NY 10011

Electron Microscopy of Limulus Hemocyanin

Martha M. C. Bijlholt, Wilma G. Schutter, Trijntje Wichertjes, and
Ernst F. J. van Bruggen

INTRODUCTION

In studying the structure of hemocyanins the electron microscope has played
an important role [22]. The aim of this chapter is to show what results have
been obtained in the electron microscopical study of Limulus hemocyanin. In
the first section we will discuss the structure of the single hemocyanin molecules
and of their dissociation and reassembly products. Then we turn our attention
to the study of crystalline structures, and finally to some new techniques for the
study of the quaternary structure of Limulus hemocyanin.

ELECTRON MICROSCOPY OF SINGLE MOLECULES

Hemocyanin from Limulus polyphemus has a $M_r \approx 3.3 \times 10^6$ and a sedimentation coefficient of 60S. It is built from 48 subunits, which are arranged
in eight hexameric "building blocks" with a sedimentation coefficient of 16S
each.

The first electron micrograph of Limulus hemocyanin was published by Stanley and Anderson in 1942 [17]. They used unstained specimens and concluded
that the molecules were spherical with a diameter of about 20 nm. However,
they could not see any substructure in the molecules.

The development of the negative staining technique [5] brought new perspectives to the study of proteins in the electron microscope. By embedding the
protein molecules in a thin layer of heavy metal salt not only was contrast
improved, but also substructure could be seen in the molecules.

Several investigators started studies on the structure of Limulus hemocyanin
using the technique of negative staining [13, 19, 24]. Although they described
the same EM views of Limulus hemocyanin prepared at neutral pH, their interpretations of these profiles differed somewhat.

Three characteristic views of Limulus hemocyanin can be seen on electron micrographs (Fig. 1a): a circular or pentagonal view with a diameter of about 24 nm; a rectangular view of 21×24 nm^2 consisting of two parallel bars of 24×9 nm^2 each, and a square view built from four smaller squares of 9×9 nm^2, attached to each other at the corners.

The first two views mentioned were interpreted as octamers of the 16S "building block", thus representing the whole 60S Limulus molecule [19, 24]. The third view, however, was subject to different interpretations. Levin [13] and Van Bruggen [19] thought it represented a tetramer of the 16S unit. Wibo [24] on

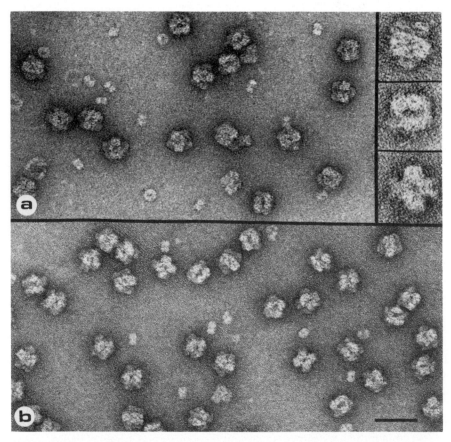

Fig. 1. a) Hemolymph from Limulus polyphemus negatively stained with uranyl acetate. The large molecules are hemocyanin; three characteristic views are shown in the inset. The small molecules are hemagglutinin. b) Hemolymph from Tachypleus tridentatus. The bar is 50 nm.

the other hand, concluded on the basis of the staining pattern and of the structure of the tetramers occurring in other arthropods like scorpions and spiders that this view also represented the octamer. This last interpretation is still valid today.

Figure 1b shows the hemocyanin from Tachypleus tridentatus, another member of the class of Merostomata. This hemocyanin is very similar to that of Limulus, showing the same characteristic profiles.

In addition to hemocyanin, another protein is found in the hemolymph of Limulus, hemagglutinin. This is a cylindrical molecule with $M_r \approx 400,000$. In electron micrographs of the hemolymph it is seen as circles of 11.5 nm diameter or as rectangles of 11.5×6 nm^2 (Fig. 1a) [10, 15].

Changing the pH can cause stepwise dissociation of Limulus hemocyanin from 60S to 34S, 24S, and perhaps 16S intermediates (Fig. 2a) into 5S monomers (Fig. 2b). This dissociation is facilitated by the presence of EDTA, while mono- and divalent cations have a stabilizing effect [8, 16]. In the case of NaCl this stabilizing effect may also be due to the chloride ions. These have been found to influence the functional properties of Limulus hemocyanin [6, 18], but until now no effect of chloride ions on the aggregation state of the hemocyanin molecules has been reported.

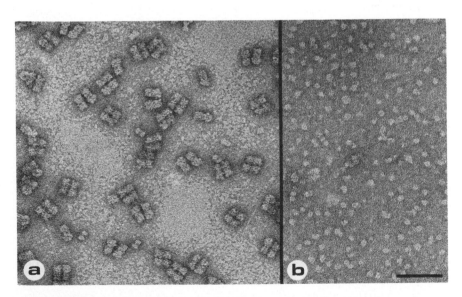

Fig. 2. a) Dissociation intermediates of Limulus hemocyanin. b) 5S monomers of Limulus hemocyanin. The bar is 50 nm.

The 5S monomers which have a $M_r \approx 70,000$ can be seen in the electron microscope as rounded or rectangular profiles with a diameter of about 6 nm (Fig. 2b).

Most data on the 16S structure have been obtained from studies on the 16S hemocyanin from the spiny lobster Panulirus interruptus, which is morphologically indistinguishable from 16S structures of Limulus hemocyanin. The 16S dissociation intermediates from Limulus are rarely found and have never been isolated. The 16S structure is built from six kidney-shaped 5S monomers in a trigonal antiprismatic arrangement with point group symmetry 32 as determined by x-ray diffraction of Panulirus hemocyanin [23]. Electron micrographs show hexagonal and rectangular profiles of about 11.5 nm across (Fig. 3a). The hexagonal profile is viewed along the threefold axis. The rectangular profile, which shows two sharp and two "fuzzy" edges, represents a sideview of the hexagon. The threefold axis is now parallel to the "fuzzy" edges.

The 24S structure is a dimer of the 16S structure. In the electron microscope this structure is often observed as a combination of a hexagon and a rectangle attached side by side (Fig. 3b). The rectangle has its sharp edges parallel to the length direction of the molecule.

The 34S structure in its turn is a dimer of the 24S structure. Electron micrographs show two views of this molecule. The first is a rectangle of 23.5 × 23 nm^2 consisting of two parallel bars of 23.5 × 10 nm^2 separated by a 2 nm wide cleft. The two halves of the molecule are connected by two "bridges" over this cleft (Fig. 3c). The second view consists of two small squares of about 9 × 9 nm^2 connected at the corner (Fig. 3d). This sideview of the 34S structure is easily recognizable in negatively stained specimens because of its dark halo of stain. The 34S dissociation intermediates of Limulus are morphologically identical to the 34S hemocyanin of scorpions and spiders.

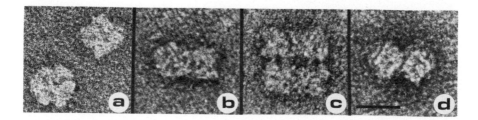

Fig. 3. a) 16S hexamers from Panulirus interruptus hemocyanin. b–d) dissociation intermediates of Limulus hemocyanin: b) 24S two-hexamer; c) top view of 34S four-hexamer; d) side view of 34S four-hexamer. The bar is 15 nm.

The whole 60S Limulus hemocyanin molecule is built from two 34S structures on top of each other. The exact orientation of these two four-hexamers is not yet known, but it is supposed that they are in a staggered position [16].

Dissociation of Limulus hemocyanin is a reversible process. By using a two-step procedure it is possible to reassemble 60S eight-hexamers from 5S monomers in a high yield [3, 16]. The first step is a dialysis vs 0.02 M Tris-HCl + 0.01 M EDTA, pH 7.0. The reassembly reaches the stage of 34S four-hexamers (Fig. 4a). In the second step (dialysis vs 0.02 M Tris-HCl + 0.01 M CaCl$_2$, pH 7.0) the eight-hexamers are formed (Fig. 4b).

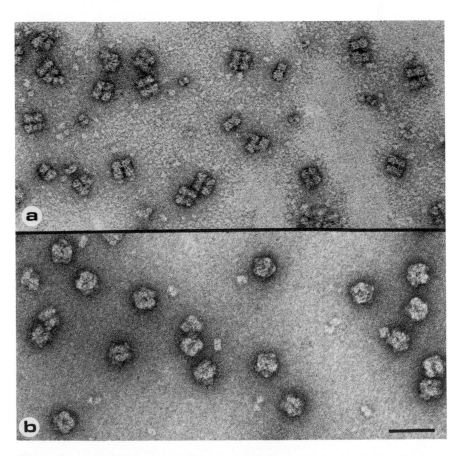

Fig. 4. Two-step reassembly of Limulus hemocyanin from an unfractionated mixture of monomers negatively stained with uranyl acetate: a) 34S four-hexamers formed after dialysis versus Tris-HCl buffer pH 7.0 + EDTA; b) 60S eight-hexamers formed after sequential dialysis versus Tris-HCl buffer pH 7.5 + CaCl$_2$. The bar is 50 nm.

The 5S monomers of Limulus hemocyanin are not homogeneous but can be separated into five zones by DEAE-Sephadex chromatography [18]. This subunit heterogeneity has led to the question of whether these five zones play specific roles in the assembly of the whole molecule. To answer this question reassembly experiments have been carried out with separate zones and with various mixtures of the zones. The reassembly products have been analyzed by electron microscopy and by sedimentation analysis [3, 16].

None of the five zones can form 60S structures on its own. Zones II, III, and IV are only capable of forming 16S hexamers (Fig. 5a), whereas zone V forms dimers with a sedimentation coefficient of 7S (Fig. 5b). From reassembly experiments with mixtures with one zone missing, it appears that all zones except zone I are essential for the formation of 60S molecules. When zone II or zone V is missing, the reassembly stops at the hexamer stage (Fig. 6a), whereas the omission of zone IV leads to the formation of 34S four-hexamers as the largest structures (Fig. 6b). Irregular reassembly products are formed when zone III is missing (Fig. 6c).

We can now draw some conclusions on the specific roles of these five zones in the reassembly of Limulus hemocyanin. In doing so however, we must keep in mind that the five zones do not represent pure polypeptide chains [4] so that only a rather crude picture can be obtained. Zone II and zone V are needed to form structures larger than 16S. They appear to play a role in the linking together of 16S hexamers. We therefore call them "linkers". Zone III plays a role in the correct assembly of the molecules. Its absence leads to irregular aggregation.

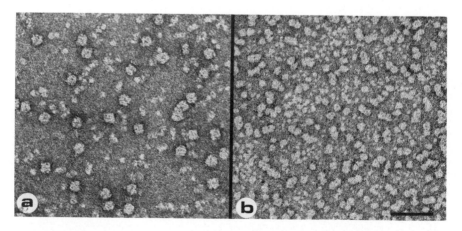

Fig. 5.   a) 16S hexamers formed by reassembly of zone II. b) 7S dimers formed by reassembly of zone V. The bar is 50 nm.

Zone IV and perhaps also zone II is needed to form eight-hexamers from four-hexamers. It is supposed that zone IV is located at the interface of the two four-hexamers that form the eight-hexamer. In this way a "closed" structure can be formed, thus explaining why structures larger than 60S have never been found.

From mixed reassembly experiments in which subunits from Limulus, the scorpion Androctonus australis, and the spider Eurypelma californicum were used, it appeared that there exists a relationship between the subunits of these three species. It has been possible to make hybrid hemocyanin molecules by

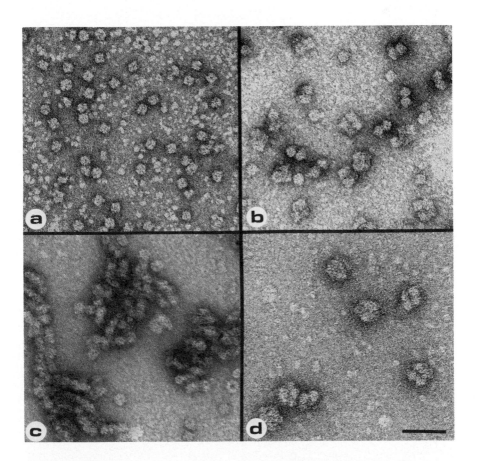

Fig. 6.   Reassembly products of incomplete mixtures of subunits: a) 16S hexamers formed from a mixture containing all zones except zone V; b) 34S four-hexamers formed from a mixture containing all zones except zone IV; c) irregular aggregates formed from a mixture containing all zones except zone III; d) hybrid 60S eight-hexamers formed from a mixture containing Limulus zones II + III + IV and the "linker" subunit of Androctonus australis hemocyanin. The bar is 50 nm.

reassembling a mixture of hexamer-forming subunits from one species and a linker from another species. Even hybrid eight-hexamers have been obtained from the combination of Limulus zones II + III + IV with the linker subunit of Androctonus (Fig. 6d) [20].

In this section much information has been presented on the electron microscopy of single molecules and their dissociation and reassembly products. From this information, however, only a crude idea of the quaternary structure of Limulus hemocyanin emerges. In the last section of this chapter we will discuss some new techniques which we hope will help in getting a more detailed picture of this structure.

ELECTRON MICROSCOPY OF CRYSTALLINE STRUCTURES

Also from the electron microscope studies of Limulus hemocyanin we can distinguish two kinds of crystalline structures. The first is hemocyanin crystallized in vivo. Fahrenbach [9] describes hemocyanin crystals occurring in special cells (cyanoblasts) in the compound eye of Limulus. The crystals are composed of hexagonally packed hollow-appearing cylinders of 19 nm diameter and with a center-to-center spacing of 26 nm (Fig. 7a). The molecules are longitudinally

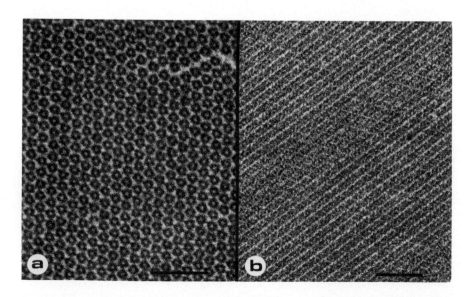

Fig. 7. Sections of cyanoblasts containing hemocyanin crystals: a) hexagonally packed cylinders; b) longitudinal view of the cylinders showing columns of stacked molecules. The bar is 100 nm.

stacked in these cylinders and show a faint periodicity of 10 nm (Fig. 7b). Optical diffraction of these stacked cylinders revealed that the periodicity is 20 nm with each period consisting of two layers [22, p 29].

When the cyanoblast is maximally filled with crystalline hemocyanin (at this stage the cell is called cyanocyte), the cell ruptures, and the hemocyanin crystals are liberated in the hemocoel whence they gradually dissolve into the hemolymph [9].

The second kind of crystalline hemocyanin of Limulus is formed in vitro by adding polyethyleneglycol (PEG) 6000 to a solution of hemocyanin [14]. After standing at room temperature for some hours, small needle-like crystals are formed. These crystals can be used to study the quaternary structure of Limulus hemocyanin in the electron microscope.

After freeze-etching and shadowing of the crystals with platinum/carbon, very nice, shadowed replicas of the surface of the crystal planes are obtained (Fig. 8) [25]. However, interpretation of these images is not easy. Many different views are obtained which necessarily must belong to only a limited number of crystal planes (compare, eg, Fig. 8a and 8b). The allocation of a view to a crystal plane is hampered by the fact that the crystals are randomly oriented in the specimen. Therefore both the shadowing angle relative to the crystal plane and the shadowing direction can vary. This can cause one plane to have several different appearances.

Fig. 8.   Surface of Limulus hemocyanin crystals after freeze-etching showing two different views. The bar is 100 nm.

One possible solution to this problem, which will be tried in the near future, is to rotate the specimen during shadowing. In this way uncertainties due to different shadowing directions will be eliminated so that interpretation of the replicas will be simpler. It may then be possible to determine the position of the molecules in the crystals as well as the orientation of the two 34S halves of the molecule relative to each other.

NEW TECHNIQUES FOR SOLVING THE MOLECULAR ARCHITECTURE OF LIMULUS HEMOCYANIN

Recently two new techniques have been used in the study of hemocyanin structure with very promising results. We want to describe these techniques and to try to point out what their use can be in studying the quaternary structure of Limulus hemocyanin.

The first method is *correspondence analysis*. This mathematical method [2], which has been applied to biological macromolecules by Van Heel and Frank [21], can distinguish between different sets of particles. In electron micrographs often different views of molecules or even different kinds of molecules can be found (see, eg, Fig. 1a). This is a problem when one wants to use image averaging techniques for getting structural information about the molecules. Averaging is only allowed when a homogeneous set of molecular images is used. This is where correspondence analysis comes in. With this technique it is possible to divide a population of computer-aligned images into several subsets, each of which can subsequently be used in image averaging.

As a test object for this method Van Heel and Frank [21] used the 34S dissociation intermediate of Limulus hemocyanin. By visual inspection of electron micrographs they found that the 34S structure is slightly rhombic. They could distinguish between two types of these molecules, which were mirror-related. These have been called FLIP and FLOP, respectively, and possibly arise from a different orientation on the specimen support film of the molecules: face-up or face-down. By applying the correspondence analysis to the whole population of molecules, they expected to find two groups of molecules: the FLIPs and the FLOPs. But to their surprise they found four groups of molecules. Averaging of the molecules in each group showed that two groups consisted of FLIPs and two groups were FLOPs (Fig. 9).

The difference between the two groups belonging to either the FLIPs or the FLOPs is explained by assuming that the four hexamers in the 34S molecule are not coplanar so that the molecule can rock around one diagonal. If we look for instance at the average FLIP molecules (Fig. 9c, d), we see three hexamers with a high contrast and one with a lower contrast. This last hexamer is situated some distance above the specimen support film and is therefore less well stained, causing the lower contrast [21].

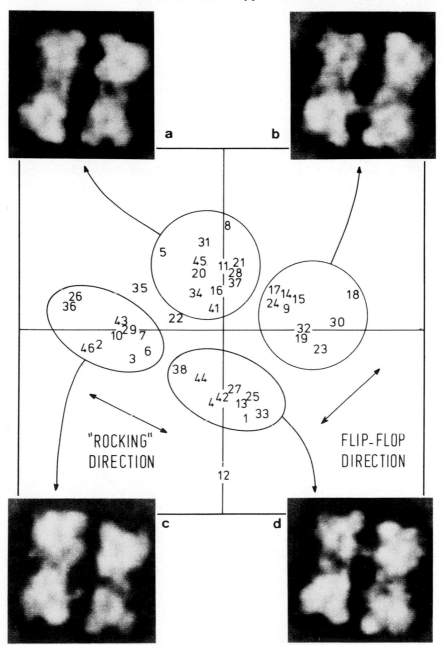

Fig. 9. Correspondence analysis map of 34S dissociation intermediates of Limulus hemocyanin. The numbers indicate individual molecules. Four clusters of molecules are shown with their average images: a and b) FLOP projections with different rocking directions; c and d) FLIP projections with different rocking directions. (Reproduced with kind permission of North Holland Publishing Comp.)

These results are not only important as a proof that correspondence analysis is a powerful method for selecting subpopulations of molecules that can subsequently be averaged, but they also give information on the structure of the 34S molecule. Combination of these results with data on the structure of the 5S monomers, the 16S hexamers, and the 24S two-hexamers has led to a model of the 34S hemocyanin shown in Figure 10 [12]. We hope the application of correspondence analysis to the whole 60S Limulus hemocyanin will lead to a determination of the position of the two halves of the molecule relative to each other.

The second technique that we want to discuss is of a more biochemical nature. We have seen above that the different subunits of Limulus hemocyanin play specific roles in the reassembly of the hemocyanin molecule. On knowing this we can also ask whether they take specific positions in the molecule. To answer this question the *antibody-labeling technique* has proved to be very useful. The idea of this technique, which was used by Lake [11, and references cited therein] for the study of ribosomes, is to label a molecule with antibodies specific for one subunit. The immunocomplexes thus formed can be studied in the electron microscope to locate the attachment site of the antibody on the molecule. The application of this technique to the hemocyanin of Androctonus australis has led to the localization of all eight subunits of this hemocyanin [12]. One difference with the method as used by Lake [11] is that Lamy et al [12] used specific Fab-fragments instead of IgG [1, 7]. This is needed to prevent the formation of large precipitating complexes, because of the greater number of antigenic attachment

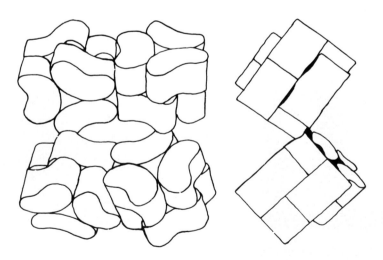

Fig. 10.   Model of 34S hemocyanin showing both the top view and the side view.

sites of hemocyanin as compared to ribosomes. We hope that this method of antibody labeling will also prove useful in the localization of the different subunits of Limulus hemocyanin.

In this chapter we have seen that much is already known on the structure of Limulus hemocyanin because of electron microscope studies and that we are coming nearer to the solution of this problem every day.

ACKNOWLEDGMENTS

We want to thank Dr. W. H. Fahrenbach for kindly sending us the pictures for Figure 7 and K. Gilissen for the printing and mounting of the photographs. This work was supported in part by the Netherlands Foundation for Chemical Research (S.O.N.) with financial aid from the Netherlands Organization for the Advancement of Pure Research (Z.W.O.).

REFERENCES

1. Aebi U, Ten Heggeler B, Onorato L, Kistler J, Showe MK: Proc Natl Acad Sci USA 74:5514–5518, 1977.
2. Benzécri JP: In Watanabe S (ed): "Methodologies of Pattern Recognition." New York: Academic Press, 1969, pp 35–74.
3. Bijlholt MMC, Van Bruggen EFJ, Bonaventura J: Eur J Biochem 95:399–405, 1979.
4. Bonaventura J, Bonaventura C, Sullivan B: J Exp Zool 194:155–174, 1975.
5. Brenner S, Horne RW: Biochim Biophys Acta 34:103–110, 1959.
6. Brouwer M, Bonaventura C, Bonaventura J: Biochemistry 16:3897–3902, 1977.
7. Craig R, Offer G: J Mol Biol 102:325–332, 1976.
8. Eriksson-Quensel I, Svedberg T: Biol Bull 71:498–546, 1936.
9. Fahrenbach WH: J Cell Biol 44:445–453, 1970.
10. Fernández-Morán H, Marchalonis JJ, Edelman GM: J Mol Biol 32:467–469, 1968.
11. Lake JA: In Koehler JK (ed): "Advanced Techniques in Biological Electron Microscopy," Vol 2. Berlin, Heidelberg, New York: Springer-Verlag, 1978, pp 173–211.
12. Lamy J, Bijlholt MMC, Sizaret P-Y, Lamy J, Van Bruggen EFJ: Biochemistry 20:1849–1856, 1981.
13. Levin O: Arkiv Kemi 21:29–35, 1963.
14. Magnus KA, Love WE: In Bannister JV (ed): "Structure and Function of Haemocyanin." Berlin, Heidelberg, New York: Springer-Verlag, 1977, pp 71–76.
15. Marchalonis JJ, Edelman GM: J Mol Biol 32:453–465, 1968.
16. Schutter WG, Van Bruggen EFJ, Bonaventura J, Bonaventura C, Sullivan B: In Bannister JV (ed): "Structure and Function of Haemocyanin." Berlin, Heidelberg, New York: Springer-Verlag, 1977, pp 13–21.
17. Stanley WM, Anderson TF: J Biol Chem 146:25–30, 1942.
18. Sullivan B, Bonaventura J, Bonaventura C: Proc Natl Acad Sci USA 71:2558–2562, 1974.
19. Van Bruggen EFJ: In: Proc 3rd Eur Reg Conf Electr Micr, Vol II, 1964, Prague: Publishing House Czechoslovak Academy of Sciences, pp 57–58.
20. Van Bruggen EFJ, Bijlholt MMC, Schutter WG, Wichertjes T, Bonaventura J, Bonaventura C, Lamy J, Lamy J, Leclerc M, Schneider H-J, Markl J, Linzen B: FEBS Lett 116:207–210, 1980.

21. Van Heel M, Frank J: In Gelsema ES, Kanal LN (eds): "Pattern Recognition in Practice." Amsterdam: North Holland, 1980, pp 235 243.
22. Van Holde KE, Van Bruggen EFJ: In Timasheff SN, Fasman GD (eds): "Subunits in Biological Systems," Vol 5. New York: Marcel Dekker, 1971, pp 1–53.
23. Van Schaick EJM, Schutter WG, Gaykema WPJ, Van Bruggen EFJ, Hol WGJ: In Lamy J, Lamy J (eds): "Invertebrate Oxygen Binding Proteins. Structure, Active Site and Function." New York: Marcel Dekker, 1981, pp 353–361.
24. Wibo M: Doctors thesis, Louvain, 1966.
25. Wichertjes T, Kwak EJ, Van Bruggen EFJ: In: Proc 9th Int Congr Electr Micr Toronto, Vol II, 1978, pp 176–177.

Physiology and Biology of Horseshoe Crabs: Studies on
Normal and Environmentally Stressed Animals, pages 283–288
© 1982 Alan R. Liss, Inc., 150 Fifth Avenue, New York, NY 10011

Limulus Lectins: Analogues of Vertebrate Immunoglobulins

Thomas G. Pistole

INTRODUCTION

The heart of the immunological defense system of higher vertebrates is two separate but interacting systems: humoral immunity and cellular immunity. The basic components of the humoral system are immunoglobulins whose structures have been extensively studied. In such vertebrates, immunoglobulins function as antibodies: recognition molecules identifying, among other things, potential pathogens, which are subsequently destroyed by other components of the immune system, eg, complement and phagocytic cells.

Molecules with structures resembling immunoglobulins have not been found in invertebrate species. Such animals do resist invasion and infection by microorganisms, and there is growing evidence to suggest that the mechanisms involved are similar to those found in higher vertebrates [see 6,14,18]. Many invertebrates possess lectins in their body fluids. Lectins are proteins or glycoproteins which react with specific sugars [12]. Although these lectins have been used extensively as tools, their natural role remains unclear. One possibility is that these molecules function in ways analogous to vertebrate immunoglobulin. The possibility that lectins from Limulus polyphemus function in this capacity is explored here.

EXPERIMENTAL DATA
General Structure of Limulin

The hemagglutinin found in Limulus serum, now known as limulin [29], was first characterized by Marchalonis and Edelman [19]. The basic model developed by these workers is a relatively large protein (molecular weight 400,000) composed of 18 identical or nearly identical subunits, each with a molecular weight of about 22,500. The subunits are held together by noncovalent bonds. Subsequent studies by others [7,8,21,29] have confirmed the general structural features of this molecule. As shown in Table I, the structure of limulin is quite unlike that of vertebrate immunoglobulin.

Additional studies on limulin have reinforced this distinction. Using circular dichroic analysis, Finstad et al [7] found that limulin differed markedly from similar analyses on vertebrate immunoglobulins. Amino acid sequence analysis of limulin revealed no obvious homology with vertebrate immunoglobulin [15]. Clearly the evidence is compelling to consider these two types of molecules structurally distinct.

Biological Activity of Limulin

Limulin agglutinates erythrocytes and other vertebrate cells by virtue of its specific binding to sialic acid residues [30]. This lectin also precipitates sialic acid-containing polysaccharides obtained from bacteria (E. McSweegan and T. Pistole, unpublished data), and it reacts with bacterial lipopolysaccharide (LPS) [27,31]. The specific site on the LPS molecule responsible for this interaction is 2-keto-3-deoxyoctonate (KDO) [32]. KDO is a key component of LPS molecules found in a wide variety of gram-negative bacteria. It provides the direct linkage between the polysaccharide side chain and the glucosamine backbone of lipid A [17]. Recent studies by Bhattacharjee et al [4] have indicated a number of structural similarities between the sialic acid N-acetyl neuraminic acid (NANA) and KDO.

A critical point that follows from these studies is that limulin reacting with NANA residues on vertebrate erythrocytes may be a valuable tool for studying these cells. Limulin reacting with bacterial LPS has the added attractive feature of being a potential part of the host defense system of L. polyphemus.

TABLE I. Some Structural Differences Between Limulin and Human Immunoglobulin G

Property	Limulin*	Human immunoglobulin G**
Molecular weight	400,000 (335,000–460,000)	150,000
Number and type of subunits	18 identical or near-identical units	4 subunits: 2 heavy (H) and 2 light (L)
Subunit molecular weight	22,500 (22,000–27,000)	H: 50,000 L: 25,000
Chemical bonds between subunits	noncovalent	covalent (disulfide)

*From Marchalonis and Edelman [19], Finstad et al [8], Nowak and Barondes [21], Roche and Monsigny [29], and Kaplan et al [15].
**From Benacerraf and Unanue [3].

Biological Activity of Limulus Serum

In addition to those activities directly attributable to limulin, serum from the horseshoe crab mediates a number of reactions with microorganisms. Studies in our laboratory have shown that Limulus serum agglutinates a wide variety of heat-killed bacterial species [23]. Agglutination of gram-negative bacteria can be attributed to the presence of KDO on their cell surface [23,27,31]; the reactivity of many gram-positive bacteria, however, cannot be readily accounted for [20]. (It should be noted that although certain bacteria, both gram-positive and gram-negative, have NANA as a constituent of their extracellular capsule, this material is typically released from the organisms during heat treatment.) Further studies, using cross-adsorption, supported our contention that at least two separate agglutinins are present in Limulus serum [23,24]. This second lectin, which has been recovered and partially characterized, appears indeed to be distinct from limulin [10] (E.R. Brandin and T.G. Pistole, unpublished data).

Whole serum also exhibits bactericidal activity for selected microorganisms [9,26]. The greatest activity was found against those gram-negative bacilli found naturally in the marine environment, eg, Pseudomonas putida and Flavobacterium sp., whereas lower values were recorded for microbial species typically associated with warm-blooded animals and present in marine sites as transient contaminants, e.g., Escherichia coli, Salmonella spp., and Micrococcus sp. Of particular interest was the observation that in paired serum and plasma samples, only the former exhibited any cidal activity. This suggests a role for the circulating amebocytes since these cells lyse during clotting, releasing their intracellular contents [see 16].

Amebocytes alone have not been shown to exert a bactericidal effect, although activation of amebocyte clotting by gram-negative bacteria is well recognized [2,16]. Limulus amebocytes are capable of phagocytosing inanimate particles, eg, carbonyl iron [2]; no evidence of microbial uptake, however, has been reported. There appears to be a synergistic effect on certain bacteria by amebocytes plus serum or plasma [25]. These data suggest an opsonizing component in Limulus serum which mediates amebocyte-killing of these bacteria. Serum opsonins have been reported in a number of invertebrates, and lectins are the leading choice for the active component [see 34].

COMMENTARY

The observation that extracts from certain leguminous plants will agglutinate human erythrocytes was noted independently by two groups over 30 years ago [5,28]. We now acknowledge the fact that lectins are widely distributed throughout the biosphere including nonleguminous plants, invertebrates, vertebrates including humans, and microorganisms [12]. Much progress has been made in elucidating the physical and chemical characteristics of these molecules, and, for a growing number, we have knowledge of the molecular basis for their specific binding properties [11]. Despite this, the function of these lectins in situ remains uncertain.

The most intensive effort to date to determine the natural role of lectins has been in leguminous plants. Although the consensus is not universal, there is growing evidence to indicate that lectins are responsible for the specific association of legume plants and their corresponding symbiotic Rhizobium species [33]. This mutualistic association of plant and bacterium results in the fixation of nitrogen in a form usable by the plant and by other life forms.

There are scattered reports in both plant and animal systems of lectins functioning in a protective capacity. In invertebrates, the bulk of the evidence supporting this idea comes from in vitro studies on the opsonizing effect of serum [see 1]. Unfortunately, the experimental design for many of these studies requires one to use caution in ascribing such a role to lectins in situ. First of all, many of these studies have used mammalian erythrocytes to detect enhanced phagocytosis. Obviously the ability to opsonize and phagocytose such cells cannot be directly related to an animal's defense mechanism. Second, a number of these studies have used whole serum or serum fractions to assess opsonic activity. Although such studies may provide evidence for the presence of such activity, they do not determine whether the lectins themselves are involved.

In the case of Limulus our evidence for a role of serum lectins in host defense is suggestive but not conclusive. Lectins reactive with microorganisms are definitely present in this animal. Furthermore, antibacterial activity with some degree of specificity is present in Limulus serum. Given these results, we can develop a model for describing the role of lectins in host defense. The model is consistent with the data currently available; further data are needed to substantiate (or refute) it.

In our proposed model Limulus possesses in its serum a small number of distinct lectins. The number is at least two and may be higher, but is certainly considerably lower than that seen with antibody populations in mammals. Again in contrast to vertebrate antibody, each lectin is reactive with a reasonably large group of microorganisms. For limulin, this is accomplished by binding to KDO, a moiety found in many gram-negative bacteria. Binding specificity at the molecular level is maintained; the key is that the ligand involved is common to many microorganisms. The specific ligands for other lectins present in Limulus serum are not known at present, but presumably a similar mechanism would hold.

In this proposed model the lectin-microbe complex is now selectively acted upon by circulating amebocytes. One mechanism for this is to postulate a site on the lectin, distinct from that involved in its interaction with the microbe, through which it binds to amebocytes. Parish [22] has developed a model to account for self-nonself discrimination in invertebrates which incorporates this proviso. This dual binding is similar to that seen with certain mammalian immunoglobulins that bind to specific antigens via antigen-specific sites in the Fab region of the molecule and to phagocytic cells via immunoglobulin-specific sites in the Fc region.

Alternatively, the lectin may be present as an integral part of the amebocyte cell membrane. In this case binding to serum lectins may be an in vitro artifact, the in vivo event being direct binding of potential pathogen to the membrane-bound lectin. Subsequent events leading to actual destruction of the particular microorganism are also speculative, and since they are not directly involved in elaborating the role of lectins, I will not discuss them.

The potential remains that lectins are not involved in host defenses at all. Their ability to bind sugars has led to the suggestion that lectins are involved in sugar transport within the host organism. Recent evidence that certain lectins may possess enzymatic activity [13] may indicate their possible role in biosynthesis. At present neither of these ideas has been verified in Limulus.

In conclusion, the horseshoe crab has been shown to contain at least two lectins in its serum. With regard to the well-characterized limulin, although it differs from mammalian immunoglobulin in several important ways, eg, physical/chemical structure and inducibility, evidence is available to suggest a functional similarity with immunoglobulin. Additional studies are needed to verify this hypothesis.

REFERENCES

1. Acton RT, Weinheimer PF: Hemagglutinins: Primitive receptor molecules operative in invertebrate defense mechanisms. In Cooper EL (ed): "Contemporary Topics in Immunobiology," Vol 4. Invertebrate Immunology. New York: Plenum Press, 1974, pp 271–282.
2. Armstrong PB, Levin J: In vitro phagocytosis by Limulus blood cells. J Invert Pathol 34:145–151, 1979.
3. Benacerraf B, Unanue ER: "Textbook of Immunology." Baltimore: Williams and Wilkins, 1979.
4. Bhattacharjee AK, Jennings HJ, Kenny CP: Structural elucidation of the 3-deoxy-D-manno-octulosonic acid containing meningococcal 29-e capsular polysaccharide antigen using carbon-13 nuclear magnetic resonance. Biochemistry 17:645–651, 1978.
5. Boyd WC, Reguera RM: Hemagglutinating substances in various plants. J Immunol 62:333–339, 1949.
6. Cooper EL (ed): "Contemporary Topics in Immunobiology, Vol 4 (Invertebrate Immunology)." New York: Plenum Press, 1974.
7. Finstad CL, Litman GW, Finstad J, Good RA: The evolution of the immune response. XIII. The characterization of purified erythrocyte agglutinins from two invertebrate species. J Immunol 108:1704–1711, 1972.
8. Finstad CL, Good RA, Litman GW: The erythrocyte agglutinin from Limulus polyphemus hemolymph: Molecular structure and biological function. Ann NY Acad Sci 234:170–182, 1974.
9. Furman RM, Pistole TG: Bactericidal activity of hemolymph from the horseshoe crab, Limulus polyphemus. J Invert Pathol 28:239–244, 1976.
10. Gilbride KJ, Pistole TG: Isolation and characterization of a bacterial agglutinin in the serum of Limulus polyphemus. Progr Clin Biol Res 29:525–535, 1979.
11. Goldstein IJ, Hayes CE: The lectins: Carbohydrate binding proteins of plants and animals. Adv Carbohydrate Chem Biochem 35:127–340, 1978.

12. Goldstein IJ, Hughes RC, Monsigny M, Osawa T, Sharon N: What should be called a lectin? Nature 285:66, 1980.

13. Hankins CN, Shannon LM: The physical and enzymatic properties of a phytohemagglutinin from mung beans. J Biol Chem 253:7791–7797, 1978.

14. Hildemann WH, Benedict AA (eds): "Advances in Experimental Medical Biology, Vol 64 (Immunologic Phylogeny)." New York: Plenum Press, 1975.

15. Kaplan R, Li SS-L, Kehoe JM: Molecular characterization of limulin, a sialic acid binding lectin from the hemolymph of the horseshoe crab, Limulus polyphemus. Biochemistry 16:4297–4303, 1977.

16. Levin J: The reaction between bacterial endotoxin and amebocyte lysate. Progr Clin Biol Res 29:131–146, 1979.

17. Lüderitz O, Galanos C, Lehmann V, Nurminen M, Rietschel ET, Rosenfelder G, Simon M, Westphal O: Lipid A: Chemical structure and biological activity. In Kass EH, Wolff SM (eds): "Bacterial Lipopolysaccharides. The Chemistry, Biology, and Clinical Significance of Endotoxins." Chicago: University of Chicago Press, 1973, pp 9–21.

18. Maramorosch K, Shope RE (eds): "Invertebrate Immunity. Mechanisms of Invertebrate Vector–Parasite Relations." New York: Academic Press, 1975.

19. Marchalonis JJ, Edelman GM: Isolation and characterization of a hemagglutinin from Limulus polyphemus. J Mol Biol 32:453–465, 1968.

20. Ng S-S, Dain JA: The natural occurrence of sialic acids. In Rosenberg A, Schengrund C-L (eds): "Biological Roles of Sialic Acid." New York: Plenum Press, 1976, pp 59–102.

21. Nowak TP, Barondes SH: Agglutinin from Limulus polyphemus. Purification with formalinized horse erythrocytes as the affinity adsorbent. Biochim Biophys Acta 393:115–123, 1975.

22. Parish CR: Simple model for self-non-self-discrimination in invertebrates. Nature 267:711–713, 1977.

23. Pistole TG: Broad-spectrum bacterial agglutinating activity in the serum of the horseshoe crab, Limulus polyphemus. Dev Comp Immunol 2:65–76, 1978.

24. Pistole TG: Bacterial agglutinins from Limulus polyphemus—An overview. Progr Clin Biol Res 29:525–535, 1979.

25. Pistole TG, Britko JL: Bactericidal activity of amebocytes from the horseshoe crab, Limulus polyphemus. J Invert Pathol 31:376–382, 1978.

26. Pistole TG, Furman RM: Serum bactericidal activity in the horseshoe crab, Limulus polyphemus. Infec Immun 14:888–893, 1976,

27. Pistole TG, Rostam-Abadi H: Lectins from the horseshoe crab, Limulus polyphemus, reactive with bacterial lipopolysaccharide. In Peeters H (ed): "Protides of Biological Fluids," 27th Colloquium. Oxford & New York: Pergamon Press, 1980, pp 423–426.

28. Renkonen KO: Studies on hemagglutinins present in seeds of some representatives of leguminosae. Ann Med Exp Fenn (Helsinke) 26:66–72, 1948.

29. Roche A-C, Monsigny M: Purification and properties of limulin: A lectin (agglutinin) from hemolymph of Limulus polyphemus. Biochim Biophys Acta 371:242–254, 1974.

30. Roelcke D, Uhlenbruck, G Metaxas MN: Untersuchungen über die serologische Spezität neuraminsäurehaltiger Rezeptoren auf Humanerythrozyten. Z Immun-Forsch 141:141–151, 1971.

31. Rostam-Abadi H, Pistole TG: Sites on the lipopolysaccharide molecule reactive with Limulus agglutinins. Progr Clin Biol Res 29:525–535, 1979.

32. Rostam-Abadi H, Pistole TG: Lipopolysaccharide-binding lectin from the horseshoe crab, Limulus polyphemus, with specificity for 2-keto-3-deoxyoctonate (KDO). Dev Comp Immunol 1982, in press.

33. Schmidt EL: Initiation of plant root-microbe interactions. Ann Rev Microbiol 33:355–376, 1979.

34. Weir DM: Surface carbohydrates and lectins in cellular recognition. Immunol Today 1:45–51, 1980.

Physiology and Biology of Horseshoe Crabs: Studies on
Normal and Environmentally Stressed Animals, pages 289–296
© 1982 Alan R. Liss, Inc., 150 Fifth Avenue, New York, NY 10011

Pathologic Principles Revealed By Study of Natural Diseases of Invertebrates

Frederik B. Bang and Betsy G. Bang

INTRODUCTION

Everything that is known about infectious diseases of vertebrates has grown out of experimental analysis of natural diseases. The little that is known about invertebrate diseases is described in terms borrowed from the vertebrate vocabulary. This view through the wrong end of the evolutionary telescope could seriously retard the growth of new concepts. A giant step toward a unified vocabulary is the growing field of association biology, which looks at host–parasite and symbiotic associations together across phylogenetic lines [23]. Clearly, each host and each disease agent are involved in a continuing experimental adjustment between host tissues and the nutrient drives of the agent.

The purpose of this essay is to point out the enormous wealth of imperfect associations (diseases) that are waiting to be explored in marine invertebrates. The cellular and humoral responses of marine invertebrates are rapidly effective against invasive agents despite the lack of antibodies or a complex clotting system. They have survived millions of years of infections and contusions by efficient homeostasis and wound-healing. We will discuss responses of two very different ancient invertebrates to natural diseases: the horseshoe crab, Limulus polyphemus, and the soft, worm-shaped coelomate, Sipunculus nudus. In both cases, curiosity about what was going on in spontaneous diseases has uncovered principles of general application to the study of disease in other hosts.

LIMULUS

Limulus and its close relatives are apparently ancient animals whose origin seems to have been among the trilobites; the first instars of extant Limulus embryos have beautiful trilobitic larvae. The rise of predators [16] produced the need for a hard exoskeleton, which in turn required complicated circulation. Blood loss became a danger, a closed vascular system was developed, and bacteria had to be kept out of the circulating blood. Thus, in retrospect, one might well have expected that wound-sealing, blood-clotting, and reaction to bacteria might all be part of a basic reaction to injury. Among fossil trilobites, there are clear examples of recovery from acute injury and of repair of excised eyes or damaged spines. These are apparent in the fossilized moults which took place after the injury. Both Limulus and contemporary spiders [9] develop similarly elevated, hard external clots during wound repair, and in both cases the scars are replaced when the injured exoskeleton is moulted.

Ecology

From the time of early molts and throughout the life of the Limulus, its external surface is covered with gram-negative organisms. The gills of some animals may be so covered with bacteria that the mat of organisms could conceivably prevent oxygenation of the hemocyanin, causing an "external pneumonia." The estuarine waters in which the adults live are areas of great concentration of gram-negative bacteria and contain huge amounts of endotoxin, a breakdown product of the cell wall of these organisms. The ecology of this ancient animal is well described elsewhere in this volume.

Diseases of Limulus

There has been no systematic study of diseases of Limuli, but investigation of an infection induced by a Vibrio led to the finding that there is a three-stage reaction of Limulus blood to gram-negative endotoxin. First, the normally circulating amoebocytes stick to the inside of the vascular channels in the gill leaflets; next, these amoebocytes degranulate; finally, a gel is initiated by the reaction of endotoxin with an enzyme released from the amoebocytes [6,18]. Despite the extensive use of the Limulus test for detecting endotoxin in a wide variety of pharmaceutical materials and human body fluids, including urine, blood, and spinal fluid from cases of meningitis, little work has been done on intact, living Limulus. Even less has been done in terms of looking for other diseases of an animal that in some parts of the world has become an endangered species.

Limuli were injected with bacteria in 1950–51 in an attempt to produce some reaction. Noguchi [21] had, years before, found that there is an agglutinin, now one of the best characterized of the animal lectins [20], of horse red cells present in the serum, and so it was thought that some changes in Limulus agglutinin titer might be produced. We did not find any valid evidence showing a change in titer of any protective substance in the blood, following stimulation or natural disease. Instead the animals developed an infection with another bacteria, a Vibrio, one of the most common of marine pathogens. This pathogen grew readily in young animals, but did not invariably kill; when given in large doses, it killed adult Limuli. The presence of intravascular clotting, the capacity of gram-negative endotoxin to substitute for bacteria, the failure of gram-positive organisms to produce changes, and the gelation of a product of the cells in vitro were all the results of that first series of summer studies [5]. The subsequent realization of the extreme sensitivity of the Limulus amoebocyte lysate (LAL) to endotoxin led to its medical and commercial application [12].

The three-stage reaction of Limulus to endotoxin (cellular adhesion, degranulation, and gel formation) within the vascular system of the infected animal, which is often fatal, would, at first glance, seem to be disadvantageous to the animal, although it occurs in other marine arthropods such as Carcinus, the shore crab, and Callinectes, the blue crab. But let us go back to the trauma produced by some predators on the trilobites. Assuming a similar cell function within the Devonian or Cambrian trilobites, immediately after the trauma, the trilobite amoebocytes would pour out to meet the gram-negative bacterial ooze surrounding them. (The most ancient of bacteria, the cyanobacteria, are also gram-negative.) After this initial contact, the cells would stick fast to the edge of the chitin, send out processes, pile on top of each other, and release granules containing the coagulogen, and this, in turn, would form a firm gel untouched by the continued presence of bacteria. Thus protection against further bacterial entrance would occur, and the first stages of healing would follow.

Of course we cannot know if the trilobites' internal vascular system was similar to that of the modern, but ancient, Limulus, for Limulus has many polymorphisms of its enzymes as do a number of other, more recent, invertebrates. In addition, new findings on echinoderm fossils show that the internal organ variation may be much greater than external morphology would suggest. Despite this, the trilobites must have had a circulatory system and the gram-negative bacteria were surely there.

One important heritage of contemporary Limulus may be the coat of mucus that covers the external carapace, a secretion evidently continually produced by gland cells beneath the shell and excreted onto the surface through minute pores. Whether the carapace itself, when viewed by scanning electron microscopy, will reveal a veritable ecosystem like that on the surface of the deep-sea mussels [17] remains to be seen.

SIPUNCULUS

The soft-bodied, thin-skinned, worm-shaped Sipunculus nudus has few characteristics in common with Limulus: It lacks gills, vascular channels, and clottable serum proteins. But both have habitats in offshore sands that swarm with bacteria, both have integuments covered with thin films of mucus, and both have exceptional internal defenses against gram-negative organisms. S. nudus probably originated in Indo-Malay waters, and its pelagic larvae have carried it to coastal waters throughout the temperate zone.

Ecology

S. nudus live in eutrophic offshore sands which, when animals are dug from their burrows, are redolent of the sulfur dioxide associated with sulfite-producing bacteria. The animals burrow in, and eat, these sands; they also filter-feed by extending their mucociliated tentacles into the seawater. The outer epidermis (cuticle) and the gut wall are thin, semipermeable membranes which fine and sharp, quartz sand crystals readily penetrate, carrying with them whatever microorganisms may be attached. The cells in the normally sterile coelomic fluid must then deal with the foreign particles and bacteria. Certain coelomic fluid cells combine to do this.

Coelomic Fluid Cells

Erythrocytes, amoebocytes, the urn cells, and enigmatic vesicles, peculiar to sipunculids, intermingle freely in the undivided coelom. Cell clotting, which occurs only in time of trouble, involves all but the erythrocytes. As in most invertebrates, amoebocytes phagocytose foreign particles. Such activated amoebocytes tend to form veils when their greatly extended pseudopodia adhere tip to tip; these clumps of amebocytes are then collected by motile urn cells.

Urn cells.* These mucociliated cell complexes originate in the coelomic epithelial lining, break away, and become free-swimming. They selectively remove from the fluid foreign particulates that adhere to brief tails of mucus they secrete. In response to bacteria, a second secretory apparatus is activated, and the urn cells produce streams of mucus in which bacteria are trapped. They also collect activated amoebocytes. At this point in clot formation, the enigmatic vesicles are activated.

Enigmatic vesicles. These vesicles function in both cell clotting and wound repair. Single forms of these nucleated, platelet-like cells break away from huge (up to 500 μm), biconcave, discoid, multicellular, and multinucleated clones, which enclose a fluid matrix. Normally all sizes of vesicles float freely in the fluid. Long, needle-like crystals form in the internal matrix of the mature vesicles. During infection, the surfaces of the mature vesicles become changed so that the urn cell-amoebocyte clumps adhere to them; the vesicles collapse, releasing the internal fluid and its contents. These packets of collapsed vesicles, urn cells,

---

*Properly called "urn cell complexes" (see page 293). The shorter term "urn cell" will be used throughout.

and actively phagocytosing amoebocytes form soft, capsule-shaped "brown bodies," which may reach 5 mm in length. We have observed that "brown bodies" are then eliminated from the coelom by way of a terminal pore. These procedures continue until the fluid (blood) is again sterile, recovery taking about 2 weeks. Meanwhile the animal is markedly depleted of the cell types involved in the cleanup [11].

Enigmatic vesicles are also the primary repair cells for puncture wounds in the coelomic cavity wall; they rapidly congregate at the wound site, fuse, elongate, and form a tough waterproof patch, which is further sealed in place by amoebocytes [14]. S. nudus seems to have developed a specialized "megakaryocyte"-platelet system, while in Limulus, as Dekhuysen [13] and Loeb [19] pointed out, the amoebocyte acts also as a platelet.

Cantacuzène's Studies (1922–1928)

The Roumanian bacteriologist-immunologist Ian Cantacuzino [10,11], writing under his adoptive French name Jean Cantacuzène, published a remarkable series of studies on the general subject of invertebrate immunity, which he carried out at the Station Biologique, Roscoff. He summarized the work on Sipunculus in 1928 shortly before his sudden death [11]. We will abstract one experiment. Cantacuzène injected healthy S. nudus with a "considerable dose" of a suspension of gram-negative bacteria. These were cleared from the coelomic fluid in 4 days, after which the fluid was sterile. He then gave four successive doses of increasing concentrations at intervals, examining samples of the coelomic fluid from 4 hours to 8 days after the last injections. He found that 1) the number of urn cells in the blood showed transient responses to the injections, and 2) the secretory responses of urn cells were greatly augmented in response to the injections, producing thick, glairy mucus in which bacteria were embedded; amoebocytes invaded these "paquets." Within the viscous secretion produced by the "immunized" urns, he observed a rapid transformation of the bacteria into ghosts, "a veritable Pfeiffer phenomenon." Successive injections of sheep erythrocytes or anemone nematocysts into S. nudus elicited similar responses in urn cells.

Recent Studies

Between 1961 and 1979, we have spent eight summers at Roscoff following Cantacuzène's tradition of combined in vivo and in vitro studies of S. nudus coelomic fluid and its constituent cells. We will touch on the responses of S. nudus serum and cells to two natural diseases, and the response of urn cells to mucus-stimulating substances in foreign biological fluids.

We now know that the "urn cell" is a complex of three cell types: a thinly stretched vesicle that is attached to a mucociliated cell (the two enclosing a fluid matrix) and a cluster of small, secretory "R" cells attached to the central non-ciliated area of the mucociliated cell [3,22]. The normal function of R cells seems to be slow secretion of the sticky substance to which foreign particles and autologous cell debris adhere and by which they are removed from the fluid. They also have an apparent regulatory effect on the hypersecretory response of the mucociliated cell.

Spontaneous disease of skin. A pox-like skin disease appears spontaneously and sporadically in laboratory-maintained S. nudus. The etiological agent has not been identified, nor has the question of virus infection been tested. The disease can be transmitted experimentally by direct exposure of skin-scarified, healthy animals to infected animals in open bowls of running seawater. From 4 to 6 days after exposure, a lysin against the ciliate Anophrys appears in the blood of the exposed animals; the lysin persists until death by 16 to 20 days [8].

The effect of the lysin on urn cells has not been followed systematically, but occasional light microscopy of urn cells from animals with high titers of lysin showed greatly swollen R cells that were secreting enhanced amounts of clear, granular mucus.

Bacterial disease. Laboratory-maintained S. nudus, when recently collected, develop a spontaneous bacterial infection, probably owing to the trauma involved in forking them from the sand. In one such case, filtered serum from an acutely infected animal induced modest hypersecretion in an in vitro suspension of urn cells from a healthy S. nudus. To see whether this factor was related to the highly heat-labile lysin induced by the pox disease [7], filtered serum from the infected animal was heated to 63°C, 84°C, and 98°C for 5 minutes. As temperature was increased, there was progressive enhancement of rapid hypersecretion by normal urn cells in vitro. Heated serum from healthy S. nudus induced no hypersecretion in urn-cell suspensions [1].

This reproducible response to serum of actively infected animals led to a study of responses of urn cells to seawater dilutions of human serum. Normal human serum (or plasma) diluted 1:10 in boiled, filtered seawater had no effect on urn cells, but when such dilutions were heated to 85°C for 5 minutes, the urn cells quickly produced tails of mucus, which could be seen to grow in length as the observer watched by light microscopy. A succession of body fluids from human and other vertebrate and invertebrate sources was subsequently tested. Urn cells responded positively without heating to mucus-stimulating substances in some of these fluids: human tears, saliva, serous nasal fluid, homogenates of chick nasal mucous membranes resuspended in normal saline, and human and invertebrate (including autologous S. nudus) sperm [2].

The next concept to be tested was whether the urn cells would respond differently to fluids from healthy vertebrate subjects and fluids from those in diseased states. This seems true in several cases: Mucus-stimulating substances were greatly increased in isotonic dilutions of unheated sera of rabbits with acute mucoid enteritis, whereas sera of healthy rabbits lacked mucus-stimulating substances. Isotonic dilutions of serum of healthy human beings, when heated to 85°C for 4 minutes, contained mucus-stimulating substances, but similarly treated serum from immunosuppressed patients was depleted of mucus-stimulating substances. Tears from patients with dry-eye conditions had greatly decreased amounts of mucus-stimulating substances [15], and filtered stools of patients with acute cholera had periodic, extraordinary increases in mucus-stimulating substances [7].

Finally, living urn cells may have the unique property of metabolically reducing the oxidized form of Janus green B, then of reexcreting the dye in either the reduced form or the blue-green oxidized form, depending on the stimulus. This is the first recognized model in which a supravital dye seems to be metabolically bound to, and incorporated in, the synthetic apparatus of a living secretory cell and subsequently reoxidized (or remain reduced) during exocytosis in vitro [4].

Exploitation of the urn cell complex of S. nudus as a model for study of mucus secretion is in its infancy, awaiting biochemical understanding of the secretory events and ultrastructural analysis of the synthetic apparatus itself. At Woods Hole last summer, we found that the urn cells of Phascolosoma agassizii also responded to the stimulus of heated, human serum. Although these curious cell complexes do not produce measurable tails of secretion, the response is voluminous. The ultrastructure of the secretory apparatus may be of equal interest.

CONCLUSION

Two examples in which the study of invertebrate disease phenomena have led to theoretical and practical insights concerning vertebrate disease have been given. The tremendous variety of invertebrate animals, their imperfect and non-static associations with other organisms, and their unique diseases offer many new opportunities for future studies of host–parasite interactions.

REFERENCES

1. Bang BG, Bang FB: Hypersecretion of mucus in isolated non-innervated cells. Cahiers Biol Marine 12:1–10, 1971.
2. Bang BG, Bang FB: The mucous secretory apparatus of the free urn cell of Sipunculus nudus. Cahiers Biol Marine 17:423–432, 1976.
3. Bang BG, Bang FB: The urn cell complex of Sipunculus nudus: A model for study of mucus-stimulating substances. Biol Bull 159:571–581, 1980.
4. Bang BG, Cooperstein SJ: Janus green B: A vital stain during the process of mucus secretion. Biol Bull 159:447–448, 1980.
5. Bang FB: The toxic effect of a marine bacterium on Limulus and the formation of blood clots. Biol Bull 105:361–362, 1953.
6. Bang FB: A bacterial disease of Limulus polyphemus. Bull Johns Hopkins Hosp 98:325–351, 1956.

7. Bang FB: Serologic response in a marine worm, Sipunculus nudus. J Immunol 96:960–972, 1966.
8. Bang FB, Shin HS; A lytic molecule active against a ciliate during a transmissible disease of Sipunculus nudus. Biol Bull 161:98–103, 1981.
9. Bursey CR: Histological response to injury in the horseshoe crab, Limulus polyphemus. Can J Zool 55:1158–1165, 1977.
10. Cantacuzène J: Réactions d'immunité chez Sipunculus nudus vacciné contre une bactérie. CR Soc Biol 87:264–266, 1922.
11. Cantacuzène J: Recherches sur les réactions d'immunité chez les invertébrés. Arch Roum Pathol Exp Microbiol 1:7–80, 1928.
12. Cohen E, Bang FB, Levin J, Marchalonis JJ, Pistole TG, Prendergast RA, Shuster C Jr, Watson SW (eds): "Biomedical Applications of the Horseshoe Crab (Limulidae)." New York: Alan R. Liss, 1979, 688 pp.
13. Dekhuysen MC: Ueber die Thrombocyten (Blutplätchen). Anat Anzeiger 19:529–540, 1901.
14. Dogiel VA: Sur la fonction des "vésicules énigmatiques" du sang de Sipunculus nudus. Rev Zool Russe 1:6–8, 1916.
15. Franklin RM, Bang BG: Mucus-stimulating factor in tears. Invest Ophthalmol Visual Sci 19:430–432, 1980.
16. Hutchinson GE: "The Ecological Theater and the Evolutionary Play." New Haven: Yale University Press, 1965, 139 pp.
17. Jannasch HW, Wirsen CO: Morphological survey of microbial mats near deep-sea thermal vents. Appl Environ Microbiol 41:528–538, 1981.
18. Levin J, Bang FB: Clottable protein in Limulus: Its localization and kinetics of its coagulation by endotoxin. Thromb Diathes Haemorrh (Stuttg) 19:186–197, 1968.
19. Loeb L: The blood lymph cells and inflammatory processes of Limulus. J Med Res 2:145–158, 1902.
20. Marchalonis JJ, Waxdal MJ: Limulus agglutinins: Past, present and future. In Cohen E et al (eds): "Biomedical Applications of the Horseshoe Crab (Limulidae)." New York: Alan R. Liss, 1979, pp 665–675.
21. Noguchi H: On the multiplicity of serum haemagglutinins of cold blooded animals. Zentral Bact Abt 1 Orig 34:286–288, 1903.
22. Reissig M, Bang BG, Bang FB: Mucus secretion in the urn complex of Sipunculus nudus. J Cell Biol 83:SP2512 (abstr), 1979.
23. Whitfield PJ: "The Biology of Parasitism: An Introduction to the Study of Associating Organisms." Baltimore: University Park Press, 1979, 277 pp.

Physiology and Biology of Horseshoe Crabs: Studies on
Normal and Environmentally Stressed Animals, pages 297–300
© 1982 Alan R. Liss, Inc., 150 Fifth Avenue, New York, NY 10011

Man's Influence as an Environmental Threat to Limulus

Anne Rudloe

Today we find ourselves faced with an appalling fact. Species after species that has long been biologically successful is suddenly at the brink of extinction owing to human activities. It has recently been estimated that by the year 2,000 over a half million species will become extinct, some 15% of all species of plants and animals [2].

In recent years attention has focused on the more spectacular symbols of the problem—the endangered eagles, tigers, crocodilians. Even the humble frobish lousewort has been brought to our attention.

Terrestrial and freshwater species are, however, relatively easier to catalog and monitor than those of the ocean. Aside from the whales, the other marine mammals, and the sea turtles, little attention has been given to marine species of fish and invertebrates. Commercially important species of fish and shellfish have repeatedly been fished to depletion, with only their large natural fecundities to protect them from biological extinction. Modern fishing technology, industrialization of coastal areas, and exploding human populations have depleted coastal resources throughout the world.

Despite their ancient lineage [7,10] and their successful passage through several mass extinctions of the geologic past, horseshoe crabs are not exempt from this new threat.

In Japan, Tachypleus tridentatus has been depleted through habitat loss and collection to the point that it has been declared a national monument, and an Association for the Conservation of Horseshoe Crabs has been established [6] to protect it from total extinction. Although the eggs of Tachypleus gigas and Carcinoscorpus rotundicauda are eaten in Thailand, little information is available concerning the status of the populations involved or of these species in other parts of their range.

The fourth species, Limulus polyphemus, continues to be subjected to a variety of human impacts throughout its range in the United States. As early as the 1850s, literally millions of animals were harvested annually from the breeding beaches of Delaware Bay to be ground up for fertilizer and livestock food. This fishery reduced the formerly huge population to tens of thousands by the 1950s [8]. In New England, fisherman have long regarded the crabs as pests to be destroyed whenever possible owing to their impact on bottom communities and their predation on juvenile clams [9,11], and bounties have been paid for Limulus. In addition, large numbers of animals are wantonly destroyed on breeding beaches every year by local residents [5].

Within the last several years, horseshoe crabs have become a preferred bait for newly developed fisheries for live American eels and whelks. The crabs are collected, frozen and then chopped up for bait. United States landings of eels for 1975 were 3.5 million pounds according to National Marine Fisheries Service statistics. Information on the quantities of horseshoe crabs used is not available, but three fishermen interviewed estimated that they each used some 2,000 crabs per year. As of 1980 several Gulf of Mexico shrimp trawlers began fishing for horseshoe crabs rather than shrimp in the Tampa, Florida, area for the first time (J. Rudloe, personal communication). Clearly, this is a rapidly developing use of horseshoe crabs, the magnitude of which should be determined.

Another fishery for horseshoe crabs has developed in recent years to support the production from horseshoe crab blood of Limulus amebocyte lysate by the pharmaceutical industry [1,3]. It is estimated by industry sources that approximately 30,000 crabs are collected annually and bled of varying amounts of blood, often 200–300 ml. What percentage of the total blood volume this represents is not clear, although some workers estimate it to be approximately one-third of the total [6]. Animals collected by licensed producers are returned to the water after bleeding, and our studies relate to postbleeding survival of horseshoe crabs under field conditions.

Animals are also collected by several biological supply companies for use in neurophysiological and other basic research. Our analysis leads us to estimate that this involves some 3,000–5,000 animals per year.

Habitat destruction is often the critical factor in depletion of a species, although overcollecting can also be important. The situation concerning habitat protection for Limulus is not at all clear at this time. Although large populations of horseshoe crabs continue to occur through the U.S. range, it must be remembered that Limulus is an estuarine species, and that significant amounts of our coastal wetlands have been seriously altered or destroyed within the last few decades. Many estuaries are also heavily stressed as a result of sewerage and industrial waste. The impact of these factors on Limulus's future is unknown.

Populations of crabs have again reached relatively high levels in Delaware Bay [8] following the termination of the fertilizer fishery, yet massive kills of crabs occur every summer in Delaware Bay. On one beach alone some 10,000 dead crabs were observed in one day during June 1979. It is not known whether this annual die-off is due in some way to natural causes or to some human alteration, but such kills are not known to occur routinely elsewhere.

In the Gulf of Mexico, undocumented reports of severe declines in Limulus populations in the last 30 years have been received from Escambia Bay (Pensacola, Florida) and from Mobile Bay, Alabama. The lack of baseline data for years past makes it difficult to evaluate such reports. However, both of these estuaries have significant concentrations of heavy industry located along their shores. Whether or not Limulus populations are affected by this is unknown.

Clearly, it is not possible at this time to make any definitive statement concerning human impacts on horseshoe crabs and whether or not they will continue their long crawl through geological time much beyond today. We do not have sufficient data concerning the status of existing populations, whether and where and how much they have declined or recovered from earlier exploitation, or how much pressure they are likely to be subjected to in the future. Most of our data on Limulus populations is based on breeding beaches [4,8]. Information on offshore nonbreeding populations is especially lacking.

Although the participants at the recent conference [1] on biomedical uses of horseshoe crabs expressed commendable concern for the impact of pharmaceutical uses, it may well prove that estuarine pollution and/or commercial fishermen will have more serious impacts.

What is clear is that better information must be developed if horseshoe crabs are to be managed as a renewable resource rather than left to uncontrolled exploitation. The mechanism for developing such information is available through the Fisheries Management Act of 1977. Even as efforts are underway to ensure the future of T. tridentatus in Japan, so should a fisheries management plan for Limulus polyphemus be developed and implemented in the United States.

With all of our detailed knowledge of ecological mechanisms, many of us have forgotten what primitive human societies knew well—that the earth is our life-giving mother, to be revered and protected, and that its other species have an equally valid claim to her bounty. One of the most valuable contributions of the space program may eventually prove to be the concept of Spaceship Earth, a modern restatement of that ancient wisdom.

REFERENCES

1. Cohen E (ed): "Biomedical Applications of the Horseshoe Crab (Limulidae)." Progress in Clinical and Biological Research, Vol 29. New York: Alan R. Liss, 1979.
2. Council on Environment Quality: "The Global 2000 Report to the President. Washington, DC: U.S. Government Printing Office, 1980.
3. Pearson FC, Weary M: The Limulus amebocyte lysate test for endotoxin. Bio Sci 30:461–464, 1980.
4. Rudloe A: The breeding behavior and patterns of movement of horseshoe crabs, Limulus polyphemus, in the vicinity of breeding beaches in Apalachee Bay, Florida. Estuaries 3:177–183, 1980.

5. Rudloe A, Rudloe J: The changeless horseshoe crab. Natl Geogr 159:562–572, 1981.
6. Sekiguchi K, Nakamura K: Ecology of extant horseshoe crabs. In Cohen E (ed): "Biomedical Applications of the Horseshoe Crab (Limulidae)." Progress in Clinical and Biological Research, Vol 29. New York: Alan R. Liss, 1979.
7. Selander RK, Yang SY, Lewontin RC: Genetic variation in the horseshoe crab (Limulus polyphemus), a phylogenetic relic. Evolution 24:402–414, 1970.
8. Shuster C: An estimate of the 1977 spawning population of the horseshoe crab, Limulus polyphemus, in Delaware Bay. Unpublished ms, 1977.
9. Smith OR: Notes on the ability of the horseshoe crab Limulus polyphemus to locate soft shell clams Mya arenaria. Ecology 34:636–637, 1953.
10. Stormer L: Phylogeny and taxonomy of fossil horseshoe crabs. J Paleontol 26:630–639, 1952.
11. Woodin SA: Refuges, disturbance, and community structure: A marine soft bottom example. Ecology 59:274–284, 1978.

Physiology and Biology of Horseshoe Crabs: Studies on
Normal and Environmentally Stressed Animals, pages 301–306
© 1982 Alan R. Liss, Inc., 150 Fifth Avenue, New York, NY 10011

Today Limulus, Tomorrow the World: The Roles and Responsibilities of Practicing Biologists in Contemporary American Society

Sidney R. Galler and Bernard J. Zahuranec

Except for the title, this paper has nothing to do with Limulus; it has, however, to do with practicing biologists who study Limulus. We take this opportunity to explore with practicing biologists some specific concerns about biology and biologists that affect society, first presented during the Limulus Expedition held in the summer of 1980 at Duke University Marine Laboratory, Beaufort, North Carolina, and expanded here.

We should like to emphasize the phrase "practicing biologists," because in addition to authoritative knowledge, there should be a large reservoir of discipline, communications, and ethical principles about biology. Practicing biologists are those who make their living by acquiring knowledge about organisms which has to be communicated in traditional ways, subject to peer review, through publication in appropriate journals.

One of the most opaque paradoxes of our time is that, while so many contemporary problems are biological in character, the role of practicing biologists in the formulation of national policy for either preventing or solving those problems is largely overlooked, not only by the general public, the leaders of scientific thought, and those responsible for setting science policy, but also by most practicing biologists themselves.

On the national level, the list of science advisors to the President has been most impressive. Their ranks have included physicists, engineers, chemists, and a geophysicist. Biologists are only noticeable by their absence!

The Council of Environmental Quality (CEQ), which is concerned with the formulation and implementation of our national environmental policies, also has a list of distinguished members who are competent and recognized professionals in their fields: lawyers, jurists, politicians, journalists, engineers, chemists, and an ecologist, Dr. Beatrice E. Willard. Under Title II of the National Environmental Policy Act (NEPA), the CEQ is the principal advisor to the President on environmental policy issues; and yet, over an eleven-year period, only one member, Dr. Willard, has been a practicing biologist. This is in spite of the fact that the NEPA, Public Law 91-190, is basically a law that is biological in scope. For example, under Section 101 of that law it states that Congress will use all practical measures, including technical and financial aid and assistance from state and local governments, industry and other private organizations, to facilitate man's existence in productive harmony toward fulfilling the social, economic, and other requirements of present and future generations of Americans. Section 102.2c of the Act requires responsible federal officials to prepare environmental impact statements for all major federal actions which may have a significant effect on the quality of the human environment. The Act refers to a "significant effect" on the quality of the human environment, not an adverse effect or an adverse impact. It was designed not to pass judgment per se but to develop an institution and to initiate a series of processes that would require everyone to examine the potential effects of his proposed actions, beneficial as well as adverse. In the process, we would begin to refine the procedures and improve the quality of those institutions to the point where an environmental assessment would be a very useful instrument for decision-makers to project the effects of any particular action. This is marvelous! Humanity has never been able to do that before; it has had only the benefit of hindsight, and even that, not always with 20/20 vision. However, largely because of the misconceptions about NEPA and the lack of leadership by biologists in the policy formulation process, the environmental assessment process is still very primitive and ineffectual.

Because of the "lawyerish" approach to the implementation of the environmental–impact–statement requirement, NEPA has been long on procedure and short on substance. Indeed, the lack of a coherent research program specifically designed to improve the reliability of our environmental projections remains a major lacuna in our national research and development policy. This lack has led to unnecessary and unwarranted debate, argument, purple prose, and litigation. A prime example, familiar to most scientists, is the environmental assessment program administered by the Bureau of Land Management (BLM), Department of the Interior, for proposed mineral exploration lease-sites on the Outer Continental Shelves. In the view of most thoughtful, practicing, marine biologists who have had involvement with the program, the policies set by BLM have been a legalistic response to Congress's mandate that an assessment, valid or not, of the environment be produced before drilling for mineral exploration can proceed. Undoubtedly, the involvement of these practicing biologists at the time of policy implementation could have mitigated some of the problems and resulted in a scientifically stronger product. The BLM story typifies the approach to environmental assessments followed by most federal agencies, to wit: custom tailoring of environmental impact statements to support the agency's original proposal. So much for NEPA and the CEQ.

In 1971, Congress created the Environmental Protection Agency, which brought together pieces from the old Federal Water Pollution Control Administration of the Interior Department, the Department of Health, Education, and Welfare, and several other agencies. The intent was very useful: to implement government policy for protecting human health and the environment from pollutants and the adverse effects of development. There are now more than 58 major environmental protection acts, among them the Clean Air Act and its several amendments, the Federal Water Pollution Control Act, the Safe Drinking Water Act, and more recently, the Resource Conservation Recovery Act, for the management of solid and hazardous wastes, and the Toxic Substances Control Act. The objectives and goals of these acts are substantively biological. Yet who has been responsible for this agency over the years? Primarily, they have been lawyers, presumably competent and accomplished in their profession; but unless they are able to acquire a knowledge of biology through some intellectual osmosis, they are neither trained to diagnose complex biological problems or offer reliable prescriptions for their environmental solutions.

As a result of the pattern of leadership that we have had at the federal level— a pattern which, incidentally and unfortunately, has been largely followed by state and local agencies—we have adopted the legalistic adversarial approach in dealing with complex environmental problems.

Finally, let us look at the leadership appointments to the federal agency that employs more practicing marine biologists than any other public agency in the United States today: the National Oceanic and Atmospheric Administration (NOAA). The first administrator of NOAA was Robert H. White, a distinguished geophysicist. The second head of NOAA was not even a scientist, but an environmentalist lawyer. The number-two and number-three officials were also lawyers; the principal science advisor was a widely respected geophysicist. The point is: the National Oceanic and Atmospheric Administration has never had a biologist as administrator: nor has there been a biologist as administrator of EPA. In fact, the only federal agency headed by a biological scientist has been the National Institutes of Health.

What can be done to remedy the situation? For biologists, it is going to take some honest introspection.

To aid in this process of introspection, we offer the following comments and questions. Traditionally some professions have been perceived as public-service professions that interface directly with the public, such as medicine, pharmacy, law, and accountancy. Has the practicing biologist been perceived as belonging to a profession (except insofar as biology can be considered part of the teaching profession)? Indeed, has the practicing biologist perceived his role as a professional? In the traditional professions, it has been recognized over the years that there is a need for self-policing or codes of ethics because the members are dealing with human beings. Have practicing biologists recognized that they are members of a profession that can and should deal with human beings or, at least, have an indirect and profound impact on human beings and their problems? The Code of Ethics recently promulgated by the Ecological Society of America, published in 1980 in Ecological Monographs, indicates that there is some awareness. In practicing their profession, biologists are participating in the collection and analysis of data that can have just as profound an impact on the problems of humanity as do the efforts of the more traditional professions. That there are numbers of practicing biologists who do not appreciate the significance of that role does not mean that the reality of the role is diminished.

Practicing biologists who refuse to take an active part in the public service aspect of their profession not only do a disservice to society in general but to science, and, ultimately, to themselves as well. In this context, we wish to distinguish between the practicing biologist, i.e., the scientist-teacher, and the "leader" biologist, i.e., the practicing biologist who recognizes his or her responsibility in formulating policies for dealing with social problems that are essentially biological.

Indeed, those practicing biologists who are teachers have a responsibility to encourage their students to recognize their role in meeting societal needs. They should counter the traditional attitude that the applications of basic research are somehow inferior and undesirable pursuits. Such attitudes must be modified for both the betterment of society and the advancement of science.

In his most recent "incarnation" as the Deputy Assistant Secretary for Environmental Affairs in the Department of Commerce, the senior author was in close touch with business leaders. If the need to bring more biologists into problem solving was mentioned, there would be an almost classical reflex response from the business people: their lips would purse, and they would issue a few, almost silent, expletives and a grimace of pain. They view practicing biologists as "eco-freaks" who have little or no scientific training but are perfectly willing to issue pious pronouncements.

It is very important, therefore, for practicing biologists to do a better job of communicating with the public. This responsibility has been largely overlooked in the training of most practicing biologists. Given the recent trends away from a broad, liberal-arts education in college, there are probably fewer biologists than ever who, in the course of their education, are exposed to public communications. Yet this is enormously important today because biologists must be able to explain to society who they are, what they do, and where they and their research fit into the larger societal context; that they are not indulging in esoterica, though it may seem extremely esoteric at first glance; that the research being conducted by practicing biologists is fundamental and has, by implication, long-term benefits for society.

This difficult job would be much easier, especially on the national level, if there were a national, professional, representational organization for biologists. Such an organization could sponsor seminars or workshops involving members of all three major communities—academic, business and industry, and government, including local, state, and federal—to deal with specific, real-world problems. To increase their understanding, it is important to draw leaders from the business community closer to the scientific arena through seminars, special groups, retreats and symposia, at both the scientific or technical level and the management or policy-making level.

As an essential prerequisite for assuming national leadership responsibilities, the professional biologist desperately needs an institutionalized code of ethics. The code should be explicit, without muzzling or censuring the biologist who has strong views on a public issue or a social problem. It should be made clear that the biologist either is appearing before the public as a bona fide expert, authorized as such by his or her peers, or is speaking as a citizen, not as an authority. For the biologist to usurp, misuse or abuse the profession in order to give an impression to the public that he speaks with greater authority and knowledge than that actually possessed, is a great disservice to society as well as to himself and his profession.

Finally, there are certain kinds of problems that are so complex that, unless there is an institutionalized mechanism exhibiting and explaining all their dimensions, society will continue being enormously handicapped. A single example, one not requiring any great explanation, follows:

Subject: Energy
Subheading: Increasing Energy Supply through Biomass Conversion - Gasohol

One problem in producing alcohol from grain that has always received considerable attention, and is still unresolved, is whether the energy required to produce the alcohol would be greater than the product. It is a valid concern, but whether the answer can be a simple yes or no is something else again. It is not just the energy requirement; it is how the energy is transduced into the form that is needed.

There is another major problem of biomass energy that is barely being addressed. Enormous energy is required today in a high-technology agribusiness to meet the demands for food, shelter, and the amenities, both by our society and the world at large; and because of the push for alcohol from biomass for the production of methane, etc., the pressures are increasing. At the same time that these pressures on agriculture are increasing, there are explicit policies at all levels of government which encourage the removal of productive land from agriculture to other kinds of use. As time goes on and productive acres become scarce, the need for more energy-intensive technology, including machinery, fertilizers, biocides, and the whole panoply of what it takes to produce a unit of harvest, will increase in order to meet the ongoing demands. Thus, we are going to have to invest more energy than before because of the number of acres that are being removed. Added to that are the complexities and the effects of these methods on both the agricultural ecosystem and the natural ecosystem involved in increasing yields through the use of traditional methods (fertilizers, insecticides, etc.) and new methods (broadscale use of plant hormones, and advances in genetics through recombinant-DNA techniques).

It is painfully obvious that practicing biologists have an enormous responsibility to help display the complexity of these issues in a way that everyone can understand and that they participate in making intelligent decisions. It is clear that practicing biologists have a role, an increasingly vital role, in helping solve the problems of society. Biologists must be leaders in the search for an improved human environment for our nation and world. So, let us look back to the title of this paper and paraphrase it to read: "Today the Practicing Biologist, Tomorrow the Policy Maker."

Index

Adair constants, 231, 234, 235, 240, 241, 243, 249, 253
Adair's successive oxygenation theory, 234
Agglutinins in Limulus serum, 285
Alanine, 126, 128
Aldolase, kinetic properties, 125
Allosteric control, 236
Allosteric mechanisms, 247
Allosteric transitions, 231, 238, 240, 253
Amlyomma hebraeum
    $Na^+ + K^+$-ATPases in, 168
Anaerobiosis in Limulus, 125–131
Androctonus australis Hcy
    quaternary structure, 280
    subunits, 265, 275, 276
Anophrys
    Sipunculus nudus lysin against, 294
Anoxia, 126, 129
Antennal gland, 148, 149, 163, 165, 169
Antibodies, 283, 286
Arenicola marina hemoglobin, 174, 179, 180
Argas, urine of, 165
Arginine kinase
    kinetic properties, 125
    molecular weight of, 126
Arrhenius plot, 158, 161
Artemia salina
    $Na^+ + K^+$-ATPases in, 168
Aspartate, radioactive labelling of, 128
Autotomy, 97, 98
Avogadro's number, 186

B-1 protein, 76, 77, 79, 80, 81
B-2-like protein, 76
Ballooning of book gills, 41, 163
Binuclear copper site, 189–229
Blastoderm, 56, 59
Blastopore, 61, 64
Blattella germanica
    autotomy and limb regeneration in, 97
Blood of Limulus
    composition, 151
    endotoxins and, 290
Blood pressure, 133, 138, 144
Bohr effect, 34, 193, 232, 237
Bohr proteins, 235, 236, 243, 252, 253
Bradycardia, response to hypoxia, 138, 141, 144, 232
Buccinum undatum, dissociation rate constant, 250
Bureau of Land Management, 302
Busycon canaliculatum hemocyanin, 174, 175, 177, 178, 179, 183, 187, 189–229
Busycon carica hemocyanin, 183
Busycon contrarium hemocyanin, 174, 175, 177, 178, 179, 183, 184, 185

Callinanassa californiensis Hcy, 233
Callinectes blood
    reaction to endotoxin, 291
Callinectes sapidus
    ecdysteroids in, 96
    hemocyanin, 174, 177–181

Na$^+$ + K$^+$-ATPases in, 167, 168
urine production of, 148
Calliphora stygia
ecdysteroids in, 96
molt hormones, 95
Cancer antennarius
blood and urine of, 164
Cancer borealis hemocyanin, 189–229
Cancer irroratus hemocyanin, 193, 195
Cancer magister
blood and urine of, 164
hemocyanin of, 193, 195
Na$^+$ + K$^+$-ATPases activity in, 169
Carcinoscorpius rotundicauda, 1, 3, 5,
9, 13, 297
Carcinus blood
reaction to endotoxin, 291
Carcinus maenas
ecdysteroids in, 94
hydrostatic pressure in sinuses of,
181
Na$^+$ + K$^+$-ATPases in, 168
Cardiac cycle and output, 139, 144
Cardisoma guanhumi
Na$^+$ + K$^+$-ATPases in, 168
Catalase activity, 189, 193, 225, 228
Cecropia moth, molting control, 86, 92,
96
Chironomus thummi
Na$^+$ + K$^+$-ATPases in, 168
Circular dichroic analysis, 214, 284
Circulatory physiology, 133–146
Circulatory system, 133–146
Clean Air Act, 303
Conservation of horseshoe crab, 297
Council of Environmental Quality,
301, 303
Coxal gland
role of in L. polyphemus, 147–172
Crangon vulgaris
blood and urine of, 164
Cumulus posterior, 71

Defense system
immunological of vertebrates, 283
of Limulis polyphemus, 42, 284

Deutovum, 64
2,3-diphosphoglycerate
effect on human hemoglobin, 253
Diseases, 41, 283–296
DNA synthesis, 87

Ecdysone, 83, 86, 87, 89, 91, 96
Ecdysteroid compounds, 83, 84, 85, 89,
91–95
Echinoderm fossils, 291
Eggs
collection and maintenance, 85
hypoxia and, 115–124
normal development of, 53–73
Electron microscopy of hemocyanin,
269–282
Electron transport system (ETS), 116,
118, 121
Embryo extracts
protein compounds of, 76
Embryos, 115–124
development of, 24, 53–73, 105, 108
physiological adaptation, 75
salinity and, 103–113
temperature and, 103–113
Environment
and Limulus, 232, 297
Environmental impact statements, 302
Environmental stress, 115
Environmental Protection Agency, 303
Enzyme assays, 117
Escherichia coli
Limulus serum and, 285
Euproops danae, extinct species, 17
Eurypelma californicum Hcy
subunits, 265, 275
Extinction of species, 297

Federal Water Pollution Control Act,
303
Flavobacterium
Limulus serum and, 285
Gasohol, 305
Gaussian bands, 214
Gecarcinus
epidermal cells of, 89

Gecarcinus lateralis
  autotomy and limb regeneration in,
    97
Germ band, 61, 71
Germ disk, 61, 64, 70, 71
Gill, 147, 148, 150, 151, 157, 158, 162,
    163, 165
Glucose, use by Limulis, 125, 127, 129
Gram-negative bacteria, 284, 285, 286,
    290
Gram-negative endotoxins, 43, 290

Heart
  of Limulus, 34, 133–146
Helix pomatia hemocyanin, 172, 177,
    178, 185, 193, 195, 233, 250
Hemagglutinin, 271, 283
Heme proteins, 173, 174
Hemerythrin, 173
Hemigrapsus nudus
  blood and urine of, 163, 164
Hemigrapsus oregonensis
  blood and urine of, 164, 167
Hemocyanin, 173–177, 180, 182
  active site derivatives, 189–229
  catalase activity in, 189, 193, 225,
    228
  dimer form of, 189, 193, 194, 198,
    209, 222, 225, 227
  electronic structure of, 190
  geometric structure of, 190
  half apo form of, 189, 190, 193,
    196, 226
  half met form of, 189, 194, 195,
    198–201, 205, 210, 218, 222,
    224–227
  hybrid, 275
  identification of, 76
  larval, 76, 260
Hemocyanin
  Limulus polyphemus
    allosteric unit, 231
    amino acid compositions, 260,
      262, 263, 265
    anthrone reaction, 263

assembly properties, 261
chain heterogeneity, 260, 261,
    263
chromatographic zones, 274
cooperative interactions, 231–
    256, 259
crossreactivity of subunits, 260
crystalline structures, 269, 276,
    277
dissociation, 269, 271, 273
electrophoretic mobility, 260
gene duplication, 264
homology, 262
molecular weight, 232, 269
NaCl, stabilizing effect of, 271
oxygen-binding properties, 34,
    232, 237, 259, 260, 265
oxygen-binding sites, 250
oxygen dissociation constant, 231
primary structure, 261
R-state, 231, 234, 239, 240, 241,
    249, 252, 253
reassembly linkers, 274, 276
reassembly products, 269, 273,
    274
sedimentation coefficient, 257,
    269
sequence determination, 262
subunits, 218, 227, 231, 257–267
  association, calcium
    dependence, 265
  purification of, 260
  self assembly, 264
T-state, 231, 234, 239, 240, 243,
    249, 252, 253
two-state model, 231, 233
whole molecule, 273
x-ray diffraction, 262
met apo form of, 189, 190, 193, 195,
    196, 201, 226
met form of, 189, 193, 195, 198,
    201, 204, 205, 207, 210,
    213, 217, 218, 222, 225, 226
    227
oxy form of, 210, 213, 225, 227
oxygen affinity

allosteric effectors and, 233, 238, 249, 251
quaternary conformations and, 233, 238, 252
oxygen binding of, 190, 218
chloride effect on, 231–256
pH effect on, 231–256
preolytic digestion, 262
quaternary structure, 249, 250, 257
new study techniques, 269, 278, 280
stability of, 258–260
Hemoglobin, 173, 179
Henderson-Hasselbalch equation, 162
Henry's law constant, 241
Hexokinase, activity in Limulus muscle, 125
High pressure liquid chromatography (HPLC), 94
Hill plots, 233, 237, 249
Homarus americanus, 85, 164, 193, 195
Horseshoe crab
human impact on, 299
Horseshoe crab meal, 45
Human immunoglobulin G, 284
Humoral immunity, 283
Hypoxia, 34, 115–124, 126, 136, 144, 149, 158

Immature Limulus, diet of, 35
Immunoelectrophoresis of hemocyanin, 260
Immunoglobulins, 283–288
Inositol hexaphosphate, 253
Invertebrate antibodies, 289
Invertebrate clotting system, 289
Invertebrate diseases, 289–296
cellular responses, 289
humoral responses, 289
Ion-exchange chromatography, 195, 228, 260
Isoelectric focusing of hemocyanin, 228, 260

Jasus lalandei, ecdysteroids in, 96
Juvenile hormones, 83, 85, 96

Lactate dehydrogenase (LDH), 116, 119, 121, 125, 127
Lactate, production of, 126, 128, 129, 150, 158
Lactic acid, production of, 126, 127
Larvae
hemocyanin, 76, 262
hypoxia and, 115–124
salinity and, 103–113
swimming activity of, 33
temperature and, 103–113
Laser-beam irradiation, 85, 87
Lectin, 283–288
Lectin-microbe complex, 286
Limb regeneration, 84, 97, 98
Limulidae
behavior and orientation, 1, 32–34
commercial uses, 1, 42, 45, 297, 298, 299
evolutionary significance, 6
extant species, 1
external appearance, 1, 9–21
food and feeding, 1, 34, 35, 105
fossils of, 6
hybridization, 4
interrelationships, 1–9
life cycle, 1, 22–31
natural history, 1–51
scientific uses, 1
spermatozoa, 4
symbiotic relationships, 1, 35–41
taxonomic affinities, 6
taxonomic classification, 5
Limulin, 283, 284, 287
molecular weight, 283
Limulus amoebocyte lysate (LAL) 291
Limulus bioassay, 94
Limulus polyphemus
adult size, 26, 31
salinity and, 110
temperature and, 111
aerobic metabolism of, 33
age at maturity of, 22
blood of, 34, 151, 232, 283–296
compound eye of, 22, 43, 278
diseases, 41, 283–296

ectocommensals of, 35, 29
endangered species, 290, 297
evolution of, 290
exoskeleton, 1–51
habitat destruction, 298
hemocyanin of, 282
hyperosmotic regulation, 232
hypoventilation, 232
medical uses, 298
nests of, 22, 24, 25, 33, 43
parasites of, 43
predators of, 43–45
range, 2, 8
response to injury, 290
salinity and, 33, 75–82, 103–113
spawning, 22, 24, 25, 26
temperature and, 33, 75–82, 103–113
tissue content, 125
trilobite larva, 83–101, 116, 117, 165
Lineweaver-Burke inversion and
    regression analysis, 157
Lipoplysaccharide (LPS)
    and limulin, 284
Locusta migratoria, 94, 168
Loligo respiratory pigment, 187
Lumbricus terrestris hemoglobin, 179,
    187
Lunatia heros hemocyanin, 193, 195

Malate, radioactive labelling of, 128
Mandibulate arthropod, 83
Manduca molt hormones, 95
Manduca sexta
    $Na^+ + K^+$-ATPases in, 168
    Marine larvae, 85
    Megathura crenulata hemocyanin,
        193, 195
    Metabolism, evolution of, 125
    Methanolysis of hemocyanin, 263
    Michaelis constants, 126, 157
    Micrococcus
        Limulus serum and, 285
Molt cycle, 27–30, 83–101, 117
Molting
    crustacean, 86
    hormones, 83, 93, 95

insects, 86
    neuroendocrine control of, 83
    physiology, 83–101
Mooney's equation, 182
Murex fluvescens dissociation rate
    constant, 250

National Environmental Policy Act,
    302, 303
National Institutes of Health, 303
National Oceanic and Atmospheric
    Administration, 303
Negative staining technique of
    hemocyanin, 269
Neuroendocrine system, 93, 94
Neurohormone
    in regulation of molting, 86
Neurosecretory cells
    guanine pigment in, 86
Normoxia, 122, 133

Octopus respiratory pigment, 185,
    193, 195
Oka's vital stain, 53
Opsonin, 285, 286
Ornithodoros
    juvenile hormones, 96
    urine of, 165
Oxygen
    binding site, 174, 189, 193
    consumption, 33, 117, 118, 121, 122
    dissociation kinetics, 238
    transport, 173–187

Palaemonid shrimp
    blood and urine of, 164
Paleolimulus, 110
Palinurus respiratory pigment, 185
Panulirus interruptus hemocyanin, 233,
    250, 272
Pathogens, 283, 287
Penaeus setiferus hemocyanin
    dissociation rate constant, 250
    oxygen binding, 233
Peptide mapping, 262, 265
Periplanata americana

Na$^+$ + K$^+$-ATPases in, 168
Perivitelline fluid, 75, 76, 77, 82
Phagocytic cells, 283
Phagocytosis, 286
Phascolosoma agassizii
  urn cells, 295
Phosphoenolpyruvate carboxykinase
    (PEPCK), 125, 126, 129
Pisaura mirabilis
  molt cycle of, 87
Polyacrylamide gel electrophoresis, 76,
    260
Potamon, 163, 164
Procambarus
  Na$^+$ + K$^+$-ATPase activity, 168, 169
Pseudomonas putida
  Limulus serum and, 285
Pyruvate kinase, 125, 129

R-state 231, 234, 239, 240, 241, 249,
    252, 253
Radioimmunoassay (RIA), 94
Resource Conservation Recovery Act,
    303
Respiratory proteins, viscosity of, 179
Rhithropanopeus harrisii
  salinity and temperature effects on,
    110, 111
Rhizobium
  lectins in legumes and, 286
Rhodnius epidermal cells, 89
Rossia respiratory pigment, 185

Safe Drinking Water Act, 303
Salinity, effect of on L. polyphemus,
    147, 148, 152, 157, 163
Salinity, horseshoe crab eggs and, 80,
    82
Salmonella
  Limulus serum and, 285
Sarcophaga peregrina
  molt hormones and, 96
Sedimentation equilibrim analysis, 257
Self-nonself discrimination, 286
Sesarma reticulatum
  limb regeneration in, 93

Sialic acid, limulin and, 284
Sipunculus nudus, 291–295
  "brown bodies", 293
  coelomic fluid cells, 292
  diseases of, 289, 294
  enigmatic vesicles, 292
  Jean Cantacuzène's studies of, 293
  lysin, 294
  origins and ecology, 292
  "R" cells, 293
  urn cells, 292, 294, 295
Sodium chloride
  effect on human hemoglobin, 253
Sodium-potassium-dependent ATPase,
    147, 148, 150, 151, 157, 161, 168,
    169
Stopped-flow light-scattering
    experiments, 249
Stopped-flow spectrophotometry, 233
Student's t test, 149
Succinate, 126, 128, 129
Succinate dehydrogenase, 126, 127
Succinic acid
  production of, 126

T-state, 234, 239, 240, 243, 249, 252,
    253
Tachypleus gigas, 1, 3, 9, 297
Tachypleus hoveni, 1
Tachypleus tridentatus, 1, 3, 9, 11, 12,
    53, 271, 297, 299
  embryonic development, 53, 54
  hemocyanin, 75, 273
  perivitelline fluid, 75, 76, 79
  range, 5
Tenebrio
  juvenile hormones and, 96
Thin layer chromatography (TLC), 94,
    127
Thiobarbituric acid assay, 263
Toxic Substances Control Act, 303
Transepithelial potentials, 148, 150,
    151, 152, 153, 165
Transporting epithelium, 147, 165, 167
"triol"
  molt stimulator, 95

Tryptic mapping of Hcy, 263
Two-state model, 231, 233, 238, 248

Uca pugilator
    autotomy and limb regencration in,
        93, 97
Ultracentrifugation, analytical, 233
Urine of L. polyphemus

osmotic and ionic composition of,
    151

Van't Hoff equation, 177
Venous system, 136
Vibrio, marine pathogen, 290, 291
Viscosity, respiratory proteins, 180–185

PROGRESS IN CLINICAL AND BIOLOGICAL RESEARCH

Series Editors

Nathan Back
George J. Brewer

Vincent P. Eijsvoogel
Robert Grover
Kurt Hirschhorn

Seymour S. Kety
Sidney Udenfriend
Jonathan W. Uhr

Vol 1: **Erythrocyte Structure and Function,** George J. Brewer, *Editor*

Vol 2: **Preventability of Perinatal Injury,** Karlis Adamsons and Howard A. Fox, *Editors*

Vol 3: **Infections of the Fetus and the Newborn Infant,** Saul Krugman and Anne A. Gershon, *Editors*

Vol 4: **Conflicts in Childhood Cancer: An Evaluation of Current Management,** Lucius F. Sinks and John O. Godden, *Editors*

Vol 5: **Trace Components of Plasma: Isolation and Clinical Significance,** G.A. Jamieson and T.J. Greenwalt, *Editors*

Vol 6: **Prostatic Disease,** H. Marberger, H. Haschek, H.K.A. Schirmer, J.A.C. Colston, and E. Witkin, *Editors*

Vol 7: **Blood Pressure, Edema and Proteinuria in Pregnancy,** Emanuel A. Friedman, *Editor*

Vol 8: **Cell Surface Receptors,** Garth L. Nicolson, Michael A. Raftery, Martin Rodbell, and C. Fred Fox, *Editors*

Vol 9: **Membranes and Neoplasia: New Approaches and Strategies,** Vincent T. Marchesi, *Editor*

Vol 10: **Diabetes and Other Endocrine Disorders During Pregnancy and in the Newborn,** Maria I. New and Robert H. Fiser, *Editors*

Vol 11: **Clinical Uses of Frozen-Thawed Red Blood Cells,** John A. Griep, *Editor*

Vol 12: **Breast Cancer,** Albert C.W. Montague, Geary L. Stonesifer, Jr., and Edward F. Lewison, *Editors*

Vol 13: **The Granulocyte: Function and Clinical Utilization,** Tibor J. Greenwalt and G.A. Jamieson, *Editors*

Vol 14: **Zinc Metabolism: Current Aspects in Health and Disease,** George J. Brewer and Ananda S. Prasad, *Editors*

Vol 15: **Cellular Neurobiology,** Zach Hall, Regis Kelly, and C. Fred Fox, *Editors*

Vol 16: **HLA and Malignancy,** Gerald P. Murphy, *Editor*

Vol 17: **Cell Shape and Surface Architecture,** Jean Paul Revel, Ulf Henning, and C. Fred Fox, *Editors*

Vol 18: **Tay-Sachs Disease: Screening and Prevention,** Michael M. Kaback, *Editor*

Vol 19: **Blood Substitutes and Plasma Expanders,** G.A. Jamieson and T.J. Greenwalt, *Editors*

Vol 20: **Erythrocyte Membranes: Recent Clinical and Experimental Advances,** Walter C. Kruckeberg, John W. Eaton, and George J. Brewer, *Editors*

Vol 21: **The Red Cell,** George J. Brewer, *Editor*

Vol 22: **Molecular Aspects of Membrane Transport,** Dale Oxender and C. Fred Fox, *Editors*

Vol 23: **Cell Surface Carbohydrates and Biological Recognition,** Vincent T. Marchesi, Victor Ginsburg, Phillips W. Robbins, and C. Fred Fox, *Editors*

Vol 24: **Twin Research, Proceedings of the Second International Congress on Twin Studies,** Walter E. Nance, *Editor*
Published in 3 Volumes:
    Part A: **Psychology and Methodology**
    Part B: **Biology and Epidemiology**
    Part C: **Clinical Studies**

Vol 25: **Recent Advances in Clinical Oncology,** Tapan A. Hazra and Michael C. Beachley, *Editors*

Vol 26: **Origin and Natural History of Cell Lines,** Claudio Barigozzi, *Editor*

Vol 27: **Membrane Mechanisms of Drugs of Abuse,** Charles W. Sharp and Leo G. Abood, *Editors*

Vol 28: **The Blood Platelet in Transfusion Therapy,** G.A. Jamieson and Tibor J. Greenwalt, *Editors*

Vol 29: **Biomedical Applications of the Horseshoe Crab (Limulidae),** Elias Cohen, *Editor-in-Chief*

Vol 30: **Normal and Abnormal Red Cell Membranes,** Samuel E. Lux, Vincent T. Marchesi, and C. Fred Fox, *Editors*

Vol 31: **Transmembrane Signaling,** Mark Bitensky, R. John Collier, Donald F. Steiner, and C. Fred Fox, *Editors*

Vol 32: **Genetic Analysis of Common Diseases: Applications to Predictive Factors in Coronary Disease,** Charles F. Sing and Mark Skolnick, *Editors*

Vol 33: **Prostate Cancer and Hormone Receptors,** Gerald P. Murphy and Avery A. Sandberg, *Editors*

Vol 34: **The Management of Genetic Disorders,** Constantine J. Papadatos and Christos S. Bartsocas, *Editors*

Vol 35: **Antibiotics and Hospitals,** Carlo Grassi and Giuseppe Ostino, *Editors*

Vol 36: **Drug and Chemical Risks to the Fetus and Newborn,** Richard H. Schwarz and Sumner J. Yaffe, *Editors*

Vol 37: **Models for Prostate Cancer,** Gerald P. Murphy, *Editor*

Vol 38: **Ethics, Humanism, and Medicine,** Marc D. Basson, *Editor*

Vol 39: **Neurochemistry and Clinical Neurology,** Leontino Battistin, George Hashim, and Abel Lajtha, *Editors*

Vol 40: **Biological Recognition and Assembly,** David S. Eisenberg, James A. Lake, and C. Fred Fox, *Editors*

Vol 41: **Tumor Cell Surfaces and Malignancy,** Richard O. Hynes and C. Fred Fox, *Editors*

Vol 42: **Membranes, Receptors, and the Immune Response: 80 Years After Ehrlich's Side Chain Theory,** Edward P. Cohen and Heinz Köhler, *Editors*

Vol 43: **Immunobiology of the Erythrocyte,** S. Gerald Sandler, Jacob Nusbacher, and Moses S. Schanfield, *Editors*

Vol 44: **Perinatal Medicine Today,** Bruce K. Young, *Editor*

Vol 45: **Mammalian Genetics and Cancer: The Jackson Laboratory Fiftieth Anniversary Symposium,** Elizabeth S. Russell, *Editor*

Vol 46: **Etiology of Cleft Lip and Cleft Palate,** Michael Melnick, David Bixler, and Edward D. Shields, *Editors*

Vol 47: **New Developments With Human and Veterinary Vaccines,** A. Mizrahi, I. Hertman, M.A. Klingberg, and A. Kohn, *Editors*